Class, Race, and Gender
in American Education

SUNY Series

FRONTIERS IN EDUCATION
Philip G. Altbach, Editor

The Frontiers in Education Series features and draws
upon a range of disciplines and approaches in the
analysis of educational issues and concerns, helping to
reinterpret established fields of scholarship in education by encouraging the latest synthesis and research.

Other books in the series include:

Class, Race, and Gender

in American Education

Edited by

Lois Weis

State University of New York Press

Published by
State University of New York Press, Albany

©1988 State University of New York

For information, address State Univeristy of New York
Press, State University Plaza, Albany, N.Y., 12246

Library of Congress Cataloging in Publication Data

Class, race, and gender in American education / edited by Lois Weis.
    p.   cm. -- (SUNY Series, Frontiers in education)
    Includes index.
    ISBN 0-88706-715-8.   ISBN 0-88706-716-6 (pbk.)
    1. Educational equalization--United States.   2. Social classes-
-United States.   3. Labor and laboring classes--Education--United
States.   4. Women--Education--United States.   5. Minorities-
-Education--United States.   6. Equality--United States.   I. Weis.
Lois.   II. Series.
LC213.2.C52 1988
370.19'34--dc19   87-21929
                                                                              CIP

10   9   8   7   6   5   4   3

Contents

PART II
CULTURAL FORMS IN SCHOOL

Acknowledgments

Many people have helped to shape this book in one way or another. Special thanks are due to Caroline Gaynor and Mariajose Romero who copyedited a number of the manuscripts, and Jeanne Ferry, Pat Glinski, Carol Norris, and Sally Claydon who provided much-needed secretarial help.

Thanks are also due to Lois Patton of SUNY Press, who supported the project from the beginning, and all the contributing authors. They all apparently survived my continual harassment over deadlines.

My sincere thanks to all who made this book possible.

Introduction

LOIS WEIS

Education plays a crucial role in both offering opportunities for individual mobility, and at the same time legitimating large-scale structural inequalities. The ideology of schooling in the United States is that it offers opportunity to scale the class structure, and the notion of an "open" class structure means that people have to accept their position as at least partially "deserved," as not simply ascribed or "passed on." Not every group or individual has believed this, of course, and the struggle over the racial state in the 1950s and 1960s, and the resurgence of the women's movement in the 1960s, are recent and obvious testimonies to this. Nevertheless, there are no longer any *formal* barriers to the "top." The way in which individuals and groups are prepared for, and prepare themselves for, their own future positions, thus leaving the class structure largely intact, needs to be carefully assessed.

Within the past ten years there has been a great deal of work on the way in which social inequalities are maintained through schools. There has been work on schooling and student social class, race, and gender. There is a tension in this work, although not generally stated, which I wish to capture in this volume. There are those who focus on the differential distribution of messages through school based on student class, race, or gender. Such scholars emphasize that schools actively prepare students for unequal futures. Others focus more on the way in which students construct cultures in educational institutions, and argue that such cultures themselves encourage large-scale inequalities. At least part of this debate has been characterized as that between the "structuralists" and "culturalists." This book elaborates and fleshes out empirically these positions, with an eye toward enriching both and encouraging dialogue. These positions have been elaborated within both mainstream and critical traditions, and authors represent a range of perspectives.

This volume pulls together the work of others in order to advance discussion about schooling and race, class, and gender inequality. The book is divided into two parts. The first part emphasizes the ways in which

1

schools may perpetuate inequalities directly, in that messages distributed through schools are linked to student background characteristics. In other works, authors focus largely on the way in which knowledge, messages transmitted through the "hidden curriculum" and so forth, differ by student race, class, and gender. The second part focuses more on the response of students to school—on the way in which cultural forms or collective identities as created and lived out in schools may encourage the structural bases of society, which give rise, paradoxically to unequal educational experiences to begin with. I will briefly discuss each of these perspectives below. This is not meant to be exhaustive, but rather to highlight the ways in which these perspectives lend shape and form to the work in this volume.

UNEQUAL STRUCTURES, UNEQUAL OUTCOMES

marxist

Ten years ago Samuel Bowles and Herbert Gintis touched off a lively debate regarding the role of schools in the reproduction of the class structure.[1] They attempted to show that education is a crucial element in the reproduction of a division of labor favorable to the maintenance of capitalism. Schools, they argued, reproduce the social relationships necessary to the security of capitalist profits, and the stability of the capitalist division of labor. This includes "patterns of dominance and subordination in the production process, the distribution of ownership of productive resources, and the degree of social distance and solidarity among various fragments of the working population—men and women, blacks and whites, and white-collar and blue-collar workers."[2]

What is particularly important here, and what has helped to frame the debate sustained in this volume regarding class, race, and gender, is the notion that educational messages are differentially distributed. For Bowles and Gintis, not only does education integrate youth into the economic system "through a structural correspondence between its social relations and those of production,"[3] but students learn attitudes and modes of behavior suited to that level in the production process that they will ultimately occupy. Thus, blacks are concentrated in schools "whose repressive, arbitrary, generally chaotic internal order, coercive authority structure, and minimal possibilities for advancement mirror the characteristics of inferior job situations."[4] Working-class students attend schools that emphasize rule following, and close attention to the specification of others. In contrast, schools in affluent neighborhoods have "relatively open systems that favor greater student participation, less direct supervision, more student electives, and in general, a value system stressing internalized standards of control."[5]

Bowles and Gintis did not actually go into schools to see whether this is the case; their argument is deduced largely from their theoretical stance and has been subject to much critical analysis during the last decade.[6] Despite these criticisms (and there have been many cogent ones), they offer a guiding framework for those who examine the way in which schools act to differentially distribute messages to students of varying backgrounds. The well-known work of Jean Anyon, who examined the distribution of knowledge and messages regarding the nature of "work" through the "hidden curriculum" to children of varying social class backgrounds, is only one such example.[7]

Certainly not all, and perhaps not even most of the authors in this volume share Bowles and Gintis's basic perspectives. Bowles and Gintis touched off a lively debate within a Marxist problematic and not all the authors here align themselves with this problematic. What the authors in PART I do share, however, is that all focus on one or more aspects of the way in which the schools themselves may prepare students for unequal futures based on class, race, or gender. Thus, Sally Lubeck talks about differential early childhood experiences for black and white students. Linda Valli discusses messages embedded in a cooperative educational program which prepares clerical workers; Jeannie Oakes talks about tracking and student social class and race; Amaury Nora and Laura Rendon discuss the role of the community college for Hispanic Americans; and Carl Grant and Christine Sleeter talk about the way in which college knowledge denies the perspectives of minorities and females even when authors pay attention to social class. All the authors in this section address one or more aspects of differential schooling for students of varying backgrounds.

Cultural Forms in Schools

Students respond to school in ways that often contribute to their own, less-valued, position in society, thus contributing to the maintenance of structured inequalities. They create their own norms and valued styles within the school setting—valuations which may or may not match those of the school. Paul Willis's research offers an excellent example of this. *Learning to Labour* is an ethnographic account of a group of working class boys at an all male comprehensive school in an industrial area of England.[8] Rather than internalize messages distributed through the school (regarding the value of mental labor, for example), the "lads" self-consciously reject school-based meanings and spend their time "working the system": they use school time to "have a laff," for instance, in order to gain some control over obligatorily spent time. In contrast, the "ear'oles" (so named by the lads because they simply sit and listen), comply with educational authority and the notions of qualifications and credentials. Willis suggests that the lads, at the level of their own culture, helped to reproduce existing social structures. By rejecting the world of the school, the lads cross-valorised patriarchy and the distinction between mental and manual labor. Manual labor became associated with the social superiority of masculinity, and mental labor with the social inferiority of femininity. Since, as Harry Braverman, Michael Buroway and others have argued, hierarchical capitalist social relations demand the progressive divorce of mental from manual labor, and certainly profit from (if not demand) gender based distinctions, the lads' rejection of the world of the school and the way in which this rejection is linked to masculinity, reproduced at an even deeper level the social relations of production necessary for the maintenance of a capitalist economy.[9]

Angela McRobbie has argued similarly with respect to females,[10] and John Ogbu and I have focused on the ways in which located cultural forms of racial minorities may contribute to their own less-valued positions within society.[11] The point here is that scholars have begun to explore the ways in which located cultural forms may encourage the structural bases of an unequal society: females, working class students, and minority students may contribute to their own future condition in some rather powerful ways. This is not to deny that skills, norms, and values are differentially distributed through school (and indeed, this is partially what cultural forms are a response to), nor that schools serving varying clientele articulate with the economy at different points.[12] *Both* these issues must be considered when assessing the linkages between schooling and the social structure. There has been some work done on the ways in which located cultural forms may challenge social structures in the long run. Much more work needs to be done in this area, however.

I have organized this volume in such a way as to capture both the differential experiences of students, as well as the way in which located cultural forms and collective identities are created. John Ogbu, James Stanlaw and Alan Peshkin, and Patrick Solomon discuss minority culture in schools. Kathryn Borman, Margaret Eisenhart and Dorothy Holland, and I discuss the identity formation process of females of varying social class and racial backgrounds. Philip Wexler discusses the limitations of the ways in which the cultural production process has been conceived thus far, and offers new perspectives based on data gathered as part of his recent ethnographic study. Most importantly, Wexler argues that we need to conceptualize youth culture as the production of symbolic identity systems and analyze the ways in which these identity systems are created by youth of differing backgrounds in different types of institutions. This will enable us to move away from current "snapshots" of culture and encourage us to explore the ways in which youth fashion actual meaning systems within institutional boundaries.

There have been a number of volumes on race and class which have focused on England.[13] Comparable volumes on gender and education in the United States also exist. Rarely, however, have the three foci been combined in one volume, and most work on class and race has a distinctly male bias. I have intentionally included analyses in this volume of the condition of females of varying race and class backgrounds.

Volumes on girls and women in the United States do not often focus on education per se, but rather, have a chapter or two devoted to schooling. They also exhibit a distinctly middle-class bias with little if any attention being paid to the experiences of working class and/or minority girls. Again, I have specifically targeted authors who focus on the experiences of girls and women of varying class and race backgrounds.

Obviously, in any volume, whether edited or otherwise, there are perspectives that are "left out." It is not my intention here to cover the spectrum of work on class, race, and gender in schools in the United States, nor to include every conceivable group in this volume. That would be impossible. I have, however, attempted to gain representative pieces in order to illustrate the "state of the art" regarding the differential distribution of messages through schools, as well as the production of cultural form. This inevitably leaves out work done in the stratification tradition, but, as Michael Apple and Cameron McCarthy point out in their theoretical overview, such work has influenced the study of class, race, and gender through schooling. Most of the data pieces in this volume are based on ethnographic studies. This is simply a frank admission that the vast majority of studies which illuminate both the differential distribution of knowledge and messages, as well as the study of cultural forms in school have used this approach. As Amaury Nora and Laura Rendon point out, however, there are many potentially useful statistical studies as well.

My intent here is to lay the groundwork for future study by providing a set of readings based on current thinking and research. There is no shared perspective in this volume, although the ethnographic method dominates. My intent is to promote controversy by including authors who work from varying perspectives. While all focus on schooling, they do not do so in the same way. We do not offer the last word here. The authors lay the groundwork for future discussion, research, and debate.

NOTES

1. Samuel Bowles and Herbert Gintis, *Schooling in Capitalist America* (New York: Basic Books, 1976).

2. Ibid., p. 126.

3. Ibid., p. 131.

4. Ibid., p. 132.

5. Ibid.

6. See, for example, Michael Apple, *Education and Power* (Boston: Routledge and Kegan Paul, 1982); Michael Apple and Lois Weis, "Ideology and Practice in Schooling: A Political and Conceptual Introduction," in Michael Apple and Lois Weis, *Ideology and Practice in Schooling* (Philadelphia: Temple University Press, 1983); Henry Giroux, "Theories of Reproduction and Resistance in the New Schooling of Education: A Critical Analysis," *Harvard Educational Review* 53 (1983b), pp. 257–293; and Henry Giroux, "Hegemony, Resistance, and the Paradox of Educational Reform," *Interchange* 12 (1981), pp. 3–26.

7. Jean Anyon, "Social Class and the Hidden Curriculum of Work," *Journal of Education* 162 (1984), pp. 67–92; and Jean Anyon, "Social Class and School Knowledge," *Curriculum Inquiry* II (1981), pp. 3–42.

8. Paul Willis, *Learning to Labour: How Working Class Kids Get Working Class Jobs* (Westmead, England: Saxon House Press, 1977).

9. Harry Braverman, *Labor and Monopoly Capital* (New York: Monthly Review Press, 1974); and Michael Buroway, "Toward a Marxist Theory of the Labour Process: Braverman and Beyond," *Politics and Society* 8 (1978), pp. 247–312. For further analyses of working-class cultural forms, see Robert Everhart, *Reading, Writing and Resistance* (Boston: Routledge and Kegan Paul, 1983); Lois Weis, "Excellence and Student Class, Race and Gender Cultures," in Philip Altbach, Gail Kelly and Lois Weis, eds., *Excellence in Education: Perspectives on Policy and Practice* (Buffalo: Prometheus Press, 1985); Mike Brake, *The Sociology of Youth Culture and Youth Sub-Cultures* (London: Routledge and Kegan Paul, 1980); and Howard London, *The Culture of a Community College* (New York: Praeger, 1978).

10. Angela McRobbie, "Working Class Girls and the Culture of Femininity," in Women's Studies Group, ed. *Women Take Issue* (London: Hutchinson, 1978). See also Linda Valli, *Becoming Clerical Workers* (Boston: Routledge and Kegan Paul, 1986), and Lois Weis, "Excellence and Student Class, Race and Gender Cultures."

11. John Ogbu, *The Next Generation: An Ethnogrophy of Education in an Urban Neighborhood* (New York: Academic Press, 1974); and John Ogbu, "Equalization of Educational Opportunity and Racial/

Ethnic Inequality," in Philip Altbach, Robert Arnove, and Gail Kelly *Comparative Education* (New York: Macmillan, 1982), pp. 269–289.

12. For an example of type of schooling and differential articulation with the economy see Jerome Karabel, "Community Colleges and Social Stratification: Submerged Class Conflict in American Higher Education," in J. Karabel and A. H. Halsey, eds., *Power and Ideology in Education* (New York: Oxford University Press, 1977), pp. 232–254.

13. See, for example, Len Barton and Stephen Walker, eds., *Race, Class and Education* (London: Croon Helm, 1983).

Race, Class and Gender in American Educational Research: Toward a Nonsynchronous Parallelist Position

CAMERON MCCARTHY AND
MICHAEL W. APPLE

[handwritten annotation: - mainstream - Radical - non-synchronous Parallelism]

I. INTRODUCTION

While we are beginning to get a clearer understanding of the ways in which the internal workings of American schools reproduce and mediate social and economic inequality and cultural difference present in American society in respect to white working class males,[1] less conceptual energy has been spent on understanding the relationship between schools and the presistence and reproduction of social and economic disadvantages that systematically affect minority youth and women. As black sociologists and feminist theorists have pointed out, both mainstream and radical educational researchers have tended to undertheorize and marginalize or "commatize" phenomena associated with race and gender.[2] We therefore know less than we should about the specific content of racial or sexual oppression in schooling.[3]

But the matter goes further; there is a tension in contemporary research in respect of the treatment of the realtionship of issues of class, race, and gender to schooling that amounts to something of a stand-off between mainstream (with its conservative and liberal "branches") and radical researchers. On the one hand, mainstream conservative and liberal reserachers approach questions of class, race, and gender through

9

the prism of particular, limited sociological and psychometric frameworks. They conceptualize prejudicial attitudes, values and differential academic achievement as having the specific effect of constraining or obstructing the careers and occupational futures of, say, girls and minority youth. On the other hand, radical sociologists of education follow a dramatically different path. They attempt to link the fortunes of racially and sexually subordinating groups within educational institutions to the structural demands and requirements of the economy. Racial and sexual oppression have, therefore, been understood in radical accounts as effects or appendages to the more "dynamic" economic forces summarized in class categories. While offering an advance, such radical positions are themselves limited, as we shall see.

In this chapter, we wish to offer a critical overview of the status of the conceptualization of racial, class, and sexual categories within current mainstream and radical research frameworks in the sociology of education. In addition, we will present a radical alternative which emphasizes the processes of structuration and formation of racial, sexual, and class identities and interests. By so doing, we will attempt to dissolve the current bifurcation in the literature between "structuralist" and "culturalist" perspectives by employing a more interactive framework in our examination of the intersection of the dynamics of race, class, and gender in schooling. For instance, while we will seek to specify the autonomy of racial and gendered relations from class, we will be arguing that they are interrelated. We see the social formation as an integrated, though contested, totality. Thus, though relations of race, gender, and class exist on autonomous and independent axes to capital, they intersect and are dependent upon each other for their reproduction and persistence.[4]

In a chapter of this size, we can not review all of the research on class, race, and gender in education. Indeed, we are both more than a little aware that many important studies will not be represented here. Instead, we shall detail the differing conceptual and political approaches taken by specific categories of analysis, illuminate their general strengths and weaknesses, and suggest a more appropriate synthetic approach to the study of class, gender, and race relations in schooling. As two authors who are themselves classed, gendered, and raced actors (one black, the other white), we realize that an attempt to synthesize race, gender, and class, to give an overview of these dynamics, may partly negate the importance of taking each one as seriously as it deserves to be treated. However, while patriarchal, racial and class relations *are* of immense import individually and must be fought against, we continue to believe that it is the interactions among all three that are little understood.

II. Mainstream Accounts of Race, Class, and Gender in Schooling

First, let us look at the discussion of race, class and gender in mainstream educational literature. Modern educational theories (radical and mainstream) share with classical social science theories general genealogical origins and connections and certain Anglo-Eurocentrism. This was most powerfully expressed in the form of a moral panic within established intellectual circles in the late nineteenth century as new social movements of women and immigrants and the lower classes came more directly into the institutional and political life of western capitalist societies. Indeed, the evolution of modern social theory is implicated in discourses and practices of social regulation.[5] However, though we intend to expand on this theme of social regulation within mainstream research in education, it is important to note the contradictory nature and progressive moments within such research.

As Wexler has pointed out, mainstream social research in education is not a unitary text.[6] It embodies, along with its conservative tradition, a "progressive possibilitarian" movement which has emphasized human agency, reform, and change. Thus, for example, the present inclusion in the social studies curriculum of a number of school districts in this country of themes of social justice, sex equity, and multicultural education has been in part the triumph of liberal interpretations of the more radical demands of subordinated minority and women's groups for radical transformations in the content of the school curriculum. We wish to maintain that these nuances and subtle differences within research and practice are not only consequential in terms of theory, but also for the politics and pedagogical practices in education. It is within the cracks and crevices of mainstream thought, as Nkomo and Sarup have argued, that a more radical discourse can be articulated.[7]

These observations aside, mainstream theories of race, class, and gender domination in education rest squarely on particular conceptualizations of the nature and effect of schooling in general. Thus, these researchers have generally attempted to grasp the inner workings of American schools and their relationship to society in terms of psychometric and individualistic frames of reference.[8] This has involved a powerful consolidation and naturalization of methods of quantification and measurement, the predominance of positivistic empiricist approaches to the analysis of educational and social phenomena, and the steady incorporation of mainstream research into establishment policies and agendas. Mainstream research has too often chosen a recourse to a genetic epistemology, grounding its hypotheses and findings ultimately y and "science."[9] Its theories have usually cast the individual ...er as the object of scientific/psychological inquiry.[10]

Against this background of "the normative gaze" of mainstream educational discourse, minority and working class youth and girls have been construed as "deviant" entities in educational and social arrangements.[11] Conventional mainstream educational research has stabilized a discourse around the "deviance" of disadvantaged groups in terms of a variety of measures of differences such as I.Q. tests, originally calibrated on the normative "performance" of middle-class white males. Having arrived at these measures of individual differences, mainstream researchers then turned around and typecast whole social groups.[12] Early race and sex relations theorists Galton, Gobineau, and Hall argued that genetic differences constituted indelible markers of the relative capacities of different groups of human beings. These genetic differences were conceptualized as determining the hierarchy of classes and races and men's superiority over women.[13] On the terrain of education, proponents of mental testing, social efficiency, and scientific management, such as Goddard, Ross, Thorndike, Bobbit, and Charters went somewhat further and argued that minorities and immigrant men and women were a threat to the social order.[14]

Though there are certain totalizing tendencies in the way in which conservative mainstream theorists (both past and present) have specified the relationships of educability to biology, there are contradictions within these frameworks. That is to say that though these conservative educators reference racial, class, and gender phenomena within a common ground of biology and science, this floor of biological common sense is manipulated in uneven, discontinuous, and contradictory ways. Not all groups are treated the same. Biology is often mobilized very differently with respect to the specification of racial or gendered or class phenomena. For example, the theme of "minority failure in schooling" has been construed in conservative mainstream frameworks in terms of a particular narrative that organizes biological scientific data to flesh out a story of "original loss." Racial minorities were construed to have a different location within the evolutionary process of human kind.[15] Thus, early twentieth century curriculum planners proposed a separate curriculum that would prepare minority youth for their secondary location in society and in the job market.[16]

The differential educability of girls and young women has often been lodged more directly in a biological/sexual narrative that distinguished women's biological and hence social functions, capacities, and orientations from those of men.[17] It was their sex/gender inscription as "feminine," as prospective procreators, "mothers," that constituted young women's chief liability educationally and determined the need for a separate curriculum.[18] Psychological and sociological theories from as early as Hall to the more contemporary formulations of Parsons and Dreeben have assembled a powerful common-sense rhetoric of "maternal instinct" to explain the differential careers and choices in education of girls and young women.[18] Indeed, the biologization of education in conservative mainstream discourse, whether it is invoked to explain racial, class, or gender differences, tacitly but ultimately attempts to place much of the blame for educational failure on women as mothers, who are seen as principally responsible for the rearing of the young.[20] A special place has been reserved in this literature for minority and working class women, with attempts to show that these women are "defective" or "inadequate" in terms of their methods of child rearing, linguistic competence, mental ability, and so on.

But conservative formulations of these and other matters do not tell the full story of mainstream accounts of education. Obviously, not all mainstream theories are so biologically reductive. There are more liberal, somewhat more socially rooted, positions. Liberal educational theories represent something of an inflection on mainstream formulations taken as a whole. They affirm the heterogeneous origins of the American populace and emphasize the plural character of modern American society.[22] American schools in these accounts comprise one set of institutions in a plurality of consensus-making social institutions through which various competing social groups seek to articulate their needs and interests, yet these social groups are conceptualized in terms of aggregates of individuals. Unlike their more conservative colleagues, liberal scholars have sought to avoid "innateness" and biological characteristics pure and simple as the bases for making causal inferences about socially disadvantaged groups, and point instead toward patterns in the social environment and culture to explain social and economic inequalities and differences.

Just before and just after the Second World War, the social psychological writings of Thomas, Myrdal, Adorno, and Allport set the liberal tone for the theorization and empirical investigation of factors underlying social inequality in American society. These writers drew attention to the attitudes, values, and beliefs of the dominant white society which served to delegitimate and undermine the social psychological status and life chances of members of working class and minority groups.[23] Henriques identifies two premises common to these social psychological approaches to racism and social prejudice. These are: (a) "the belief in rationality as an ideal for democratic society," and (b) "the emphasis on the individual as the site of the breakdown of this rationality and therefore as the object of research."[24] Liberal research did not stop with social psychology, of course. It was profoundly influenced by the sociological traditions of status attainment and social stratification research. Most of liberal analysis at the outset addressed the fortunes of the white working class and the specific question of the relationship of education to social mobility. In the 1960s, argues Hurn, sociologists of education sought to "test the meritocratic hypothesis."[25] The work of researchers such as Duncan, Sexton, Sewell, Hauser, and Jencks sought to connect the issue of unequal school performance with unequal social context.[26]

These works tended to follow one of two paths: (a) highly quantitative studies which focused on outside-school explanations (S.E.S., ethnicity, etc.) for school failure;[27] (b) qualitative studies which focused on within-school explanations of differential school performance.[28] Using data mostly on *male* students, liberal scholars revisited, assessed, and ultimately rejected the connections between I.Q. and school outcomes made by past and contemporary conservative critics such as Jensen and Shockly.[29] Hurn, for example, summarized their conclusions by stating that they maintained that "we must reject the hypothesis of distinctive patterns of performance among the black population."[30]

Liberal researchers, though rejecting the conservative emphasis on the defective innate capacities of children from minority and low socioeconomic groups (or the biologization of women) sought to explain minority failure by means of an equally damning thesis. Hurn and others have maintained that many of these liberal writers often blamed minority and working class subcultures and "deviant" family structures for the underachievement of children from these disadvantaged groups. Here again, the model of "cultural deficits" used by liberal researchers to summarize presumed normative characteristics of these groups was deduced from measurements and norms calibrated on the basis of perceived white Anglo-Saxon middle-class values, nuclear family structures, etc. Against these middle-class characteristics, minority and working class family structures were still tacitly seen as pathologically deficient.

On the other side of liberal research, qualitative researchers such as Rist, Rosenthal, and Jacobsen, and Cicourel and Kituse offered within-school explanations of school failure and high drop-out rates among low S.E.S. and minority youth. These works drew attention to the pedagogical practices of teachers and their interpretations of and expectations for the socially disadvantaged.[31]

On the whole, the liberal ethnographies and teacher expectation studies of Rist, Rosenthal, and Jacobsen and the others who expanded their focus to examine how, say, gender and race were treated in school,[32] blamed teachers for the failure of girls and minority and working-class students. They maintained that teachers' interpretations of the dress, demeanor, and speech of minority and working-class youth profoundly influenced the disproportionate assignment of these disadvantaged youth to the lower ability groups and tracks. This kind of research provided the leverage to ask a different kind of question. Even though the more qualitative approach was not structural enough, it did begin to focus on how schools themselves might be producing class, gender, and race inequalities. The research agenda, however, still remained within a limited, ameliorative perspective, though it should be noted that a good deal of effort was expended on in-school strategies to develop less sexist and more multicultural experiences based on some of this research.

Liberal Discourses and Educational Policy

Probably the most compelling feature of this liberal research on race, class, and gender, as Berlowitz, Walkerdine, and Rizvi have pointed out, has been its impact on the shaping of educational policy discourse in the United States.[33] The power of liberal positions on education and social inequality, argues Berlowitz, resides in their hegemonic connections to establishment discourses.[34] As "policy intellectuals," liberal theorists can exploit the strategic interface of their work with agendas of the state. It is, however, somewhat simplistic to maintain, as some writers have, that liberal research is unproblematically incorporated into establishment frameworks.[35] There are, for instance, radical and fragmentary moments, tensions, and breaks which systematically characterize the relationship between liberal scholarship and establishment agendas. These tensions exist even when liberal formulations retain a linguistic and instrumental affinity to establishment discourses. It is also important to realize, though, that liberal theory interacts, benefits from, redirects, and mediates the ideas of more radical social theories and the demands of protest movements, as well as the hegemonic demands of the state and conservative groups.[37] It is, thus, fundamentally contradictory.

But even with these partly positive moments and contradictions, there are some significant theoretical and political limitations to such mainstream liberal approaches to education taken as a whole. Mainstream theorists tend to see the institutional life of American society in atomistic and restrictive terms. Education is, therefore, largely conceptualized as separate and detached from the political and economic life of society.[38] When connections are proposed, as, for example, between education and the economy, the focus is not on systematic relations but on the more restrictive concern with empirical correlations between education and income differentials, and on changing attitudes, not structures. There is also very little effort expended in mainstream accounts of schooling on theorizing the relationship between the spheres of politics, culture, and the economy. In a similar manner, most liberal theorists neglect the interconnections between the variables of race, class, and gender in American society. Race, class, and gender are understood as separate phenomena which stratify the society along very different lines and create social cleavages in schooling and in the classroom.[39] Once again, if attitudes and knowledge about "difference" can be changed in schools, it is assumed that slowly but surely the problems will ultimately go away.

More broadly, within mainstream frameworks education is seen in the narrow and more restrictive sense of consumption—the acquisition of skills and competencies for adult responsibilities in working life. Education is not seen as a site of production itself, with a distinctively racial, class, and gendered labor process. This is not just the case in mainstream discussions of students but of other people involved in education as well, particularly teachers. Indeed, very little attention is paid to teaching as women's work.[40] Most liberal studies of teaching as work focus primarily on professional and occupational socialization. Accounts of women teachers in mainstream frameworks tend to be partial, descriptive and a-theoretical. There is no analysis of patriarchy.[40] The fact that most teachers *are* women remains a simple statistical fact, not an indication of a major instance in which class and gender interact and are partly produced, in crucial ways in schools.[42] Finally, liberal accounts of education are overwhelmingly psychologistic and focus on individual differences. Such an emphasis has tended to vitiate the power of liberal analysis in respect to the nature and effectivity of racial, class, and gendered collectivities. It is this very emphasis on the "unattached individual," and its inability to take seriously the truly structural relationship between schooling and patriarchal, racial, and class dynamics that ultimately weakens the progressive potential of liberal mainstram approaches.[43]

III. RADICAL THEORIES OF RACE, CLASS, AND GENDER

Radical educators begin with a critique of the basis of the questions and conclusions generated within such liberal frameworks for understanding the realtionship between education and social difference and inequality. Such criticism has tended to characterize mainstream theory and practice as "idealist."[44] Radical theorists have maintained that attempts to cast the problem of racial, class, and sexual oppression in American schooling in terms of attitudes, values, and psychological differences are grossly inadequate. They argue further that the liberal emphasis on the domain of values and individual achievement serves to divert our attention from the relationship of schooling to political economy and political power. These arguments have become more complicated over the past decade; but, basically, radical writers have asserted, in turn, that the problems of social difference and inequality are more firmly rooted in the socio-economic relations and structures generated within capitalist societies such as the United States. In so doing, they have underscored the fact that, in their view, sites within the economy, not the school, are the critical arenas of capitalism and "the fulcrums of change."[45]

Not all radical educators have taken this approach. Within the last fifteen years or so, growing dissatisfaction with Marxist dogmatism and economistic accounts of education have in part stimulated the rise of a sustained cultural analysis of American schooling and society.[46] Like mainstream theories, radical approaches to the discussion of the relationship of race, class, and gender to education are not monolithic by any means. These different approaches within radical educational research have been described as "structuralist" or "culturalist" theories of education.[47] Though this classification does not quite capture the range of nuance within current radical critiques of American schooling, it nevertheless draws attention to dominant tensions within radical theories of education. It would be useful at this stage of our essay to retrace some of the ground covered by radical theorists over the last two decades or so.

Early Structuralist Theories of American Schooling and Society

Early radical critiques of schooling narrowed the concerns over American education unproblematically to the contradiction between capital and labor and the role of schooling in the maintenance and reproduction of the economy. Here, too, women and people of color were defined largely by their absence as independent forces. Thus, these writings overwhelmingly emphasized the role of schooling in the maintenance and the reproduction of the capitalist division of labor. Perhaps Bowles and Gintis's *Schooling in Capitalist America* represented the capstone on these structuralist accounts of schooling.[48] Their analysis of American education was essentially functionalist.

For these writers, schools existed in a closed relationship with the economy. Bowles and Gintis conceptualized the ideological and cultural features of the school as being responsible for a narrow range of socially relevant effects and determinations, those stimulated by the economy. As they put it, "Major aspects of educational organization replicate the relationship of dominance and subordinance in the economic sphere."[49] Thus, in the Bowles and Gintis account, schools functionally reproduced or mirrored the class and the segmented labor market. Racial and sexual oppression in schooling was conceptualized within these structuralist formulations as effects of economic divisions in society and as by-products of a more fundamental conflict between the working class and their capitalist employers. The specific content of racial and sexual oppression was seen as consisting of divisive ideologies orchestrated and deployed by capitalists and their agents in the labor market and the firm.[50] The particular effect of such capitalist strategies, it was claimed, was that of disorganizing the working class. A current variant of this "divide and conquer" explanation of racial and sexual antagonism has been offered recently by Edari. As Edari states:

> Ethnicity, racism and sexism must be understood in the proper perspective as forms of ideological mystification designed to facilitate exploitation and weaken the collective power of the laboring class.[51]

In many ways, then, early structuralist accounts of schooling and society theorized racial and sexual phenomena in consistently negative terms, as forms of precapitalist particularism that served to divert or interrupt the major drama between the bourgeoisie and the working class.[52] In this sense, racism and sexism were conceptualized as more or less interchangeable phenomena located in the following: the evolution and trajectory of western capitalist development to a world system; "super-exploitation" (men's oppression of women in the home and slavery were two of the earliest sources of surplus value); specific capitalist strategies of "divide and conquer" of an essentially passive working class; a split or dual labor market (the entrance of minorities and women in the labor market depresses the wage scale and undermines existing privileges which a predominantly white male labor aristocracy currently enjoys).[53] Schooling was only a "pale reflection" of these structures.

In a general sense, then, early structuralist accounts of racial and sexual oppression marginalized schooling and privileged both the economy and class relations. In so far as these race and gender based antagonisms existed in schooling, they were the results of causes located exogenously in the paid workplace and in economic production. While having a clearer picture than most mainstream theorists of how inequality was produced, by basing their entire evaluation of schooling on a base-superstructure model of society in which all significant activity flowed from the economic base, these writers lost sight of the specific and autonomous contribution of schooling to the nature of social life and social relations in general. Because of this, they were unable to adequately deal with the question of the relatively autonomous workings of patriarchal and racial structures. In the process, they also had the negative effect of ignoring what some of the liberal researchers *had* contributed: a

greater sense of the importance of looking inside the schools to examine
what educational institutions really do culturally, politically, and
economically.

Radical Theories of Cultural Reproduction

American radical educators took a decisively more culturalist approach
to schooling in the mid-seventies, partly out of a dissatisfaction with
structural economic explanations of schooling and society. These critics
complained of the tendency of orthodox Marxist educational critics to:
(a) reduce all the activities of schooling and society to the singular operations and requirements of the economy; (b) define class in narrow and
restrictive economic terms; (c) marginalize the significance and effects of
the school curriculum.[54] They insisted that structural economic accounts
of education ignored the internal order, autonomous organization, and
social relations which specifically characterized schooling. These school
critics such as Apple, Anyon, and Giroux described themselves as theorists of cultural reproduction.[55] Often drawing on the work of European
sociologists of education such as Bernstein and Bourdieu and
Passeron,[56] while at the same time building on many genuinely radical
American impulses, these American cultural critics tried to distance
themselves from the economic reductionism of earlier structuralist
formulation which had so clearly subordinated school life to the
economy.

Writers such as Apple, Giroux, Anyon, and Wexler insisted that the
ideological and cultural processes of schooling were relatively
autonomous from the society's economic infrastructure.[57] Yet, even with
this "relative autonomy," the inner workings of school pedagogy and
school knowledge still constituted a "hidden curriculum" which operated
to the advantage of white middle-class youth. Anyon and Apple argued
that schools legitimated the dominant Anglo-American culture.[58] The
critical question to be asked about the school curriculum, one of these
radical critics argued, was "Whose knowledge was in the school and
whose interests did such knowledge serve?"[59] This ideological analysis of
the strategic implications of school knowledge, its silences, and its dele-
tions of the self-affirming history of the oppressed was of fundamental
importance. The attempt to explicitly link knowledge to power also partially opened up a fecund ground of possibilities for the investigation and
exploration of school life around issues of the formation and constitution of racial and sexual identities and representations.

Unfortunately, however, these "non-economic" themes were theoretically underdeveloped in cultural reproduction theory and were regret-
tably not followed through by radical researchers at the time. Instead, in

their early work, culturalist school critics chose to follow the well-tried but less knotty path of reading off ideological and cultural homologies between the formal school curriculum and *class* divisions outside the school. There *were* major gains here, however. As Apple, Bernstein and others documented, a bi-polar theory of classes was insufficient in understanding schooling. The role of the "new middle class" and of conflict within classes became much clearer.[60] Furthermore, the ability to specify what was actually happening to the work of teachers as their own labor was being transformed and "deskilled" and how they were responding to these pressures was a significant advance over structural theories that saw teachers as merely puppets.[61] Unfortunately, even with these gains, the more culturalist researchers usually retained a research practice of venerating class-motivated questions in the evaluation of the school curriculum. And all too often a determinist version of class was employed as well. The complex feature embodied in social and economic difference in a polygot, genuinely "plural" social formation such as the United States were not addressed. In this respect, a rigorous examination of the non-class features of American school life was deferred.

In the past few years, a new school of radical education theorists has begun to take up the challenge of formulating a more highly textured account of schooling that has allowed for a more systematic exploration of the non-economic, non-class features of school life without at the same time ignoring economic and class dynamics. It is to this work and its implications for the conceptualization of race, class, and gender that we now turn.

Post-Structural School Critics

In the late seventies and early eighties, challenges to some of the still too reductive neo-Marxist interpretations of schooling and society came from two broad sources: one, theory; the other, political life. With respect to theory, feminist and race relations theorists in Europe and North America[62] and post-structuralist writers in the fields of linguistics, literary theory, and psychoanalysis[63] drew attention to the inadequacy of class reductionist accounts of human society, the marginalization of women and minorities in radical research, and to the underdeveloped status of radical conceptualizations of human agency, human subjectivity, and systems of meaning. In the area of politics, there were significant new developments as reflected in the emergence of a plurality of social movements among subordinated groups. As women, gays, minorities, and others mobilized around distinctly non-class agendas, neoconservative groups soon offered a countervailing agenda expressed in terms of a highly vocal authoritarian populism. Orthodox class categories simply could not cope with these non-class movements and the right wing populist backlash in the government and the larger society. Somehow radical theories of school and society of the late seventies and early eighties seemed overtaken by events.[64] These advances were stimulated not only by political movements but by some significant new understandings of how the "state" works. Earlier formulations assumed that all aspects of governmental functions (including education) seemed to reproduce what was economically "necessary." Yet the emerging literature on the state indicated a much more complicating process in which the state often has its own needs, needs that are contradictory and do not always support capital and dominant classes. This focus on government, on the political sphere, lent support to the emerging tendencies in this research tradition to raise serious questions about economic and class reductionism as well.[65]

These developments had sobering effects on radical school critics and engendered reappraisals, self-criticism, and the emergence of yet another inflection on previous radical accounts of schooling, in the form of critical educational theory. Perhaps it was Wexler in his germinal piece "Structure, Text and Subject: A Critical Sociology of School Knowledge" who most poignantly announced the growing dissatisfaction with what he called "reproduction" and "reflection" models of schooling and society. Wexler maintained that in the discourse of cultural and economic reproduction, "conscious rational human activity is dissolved between the poles of manipulative human relations and iron-like system laws." He emphasized further that "the system reproductive perspective leads to forgetting that social structures are the result of human activity."[66] These post-structural scholars sought to emphasize even more the relative autonomy of schooling, its mediational rather than "reflective" role with respect to the economy, and especially the contradictory and contested nature of social relations within the school setting. Of great importance, class — and later race and gender — was seen not only as a structure but as *experience*, as embodied in live actors and cultures. It did not simply "happen" to people. It was a *project*.

Many of these new directions were indicated in a collected volume *Ideology and Practice in Schooling* which embarked on an ambitious theoretical and empirical project of critically evaluating both the "commodified" as well as the "lived" culture of school.[67] The authors offered an interactive view of the social formation. They went beyond a focus only on class and emphasized the *interrelations* between racial, classed, and gendered dynamics. In so doing, they also explicitly attempted to resolve the tensions in radical research between structuralism and culturalism. Combining textual and ethnographic techniques, these educators directed their attention to the lives of students and teachers in schools

and demonstrated empirically the connections between educational practice and the gender, race, and class relations being built within the
school.

Besides these cogent examples of textual and qualitative research
which got inside the school and helped substantiate a more subtle set of
radical claims about schooling and society, at approximately the same
time these and other critical scholars made several important conceptual
advances in specifying the nature of the linkages between schools, the
state, and the capitalist social formation, and, as well, the interplay of
the dynamics of race, class, and gender in American education. By showing even more how the binary logic of base-superstructure formulations
was fundamentally flawed, these educators allowed greater flexibility in
the examination of the relationship of schooling to ideology, culture,
politics, and the economy.[68] David Hogan's historical research provides
an excellent example here.[69] Hogan shows how struggles over schooling
did not just reflect, but helped form class dynamics in the United States.
In this way he demonstrates that schools were not simply passive mirrors
of class forces outside themselves.[70] He draws attention to the class experience and class development of the American working classes which
because of historical patterns of immigrant labor are profoundly ethnic
in character.

Hogan, in his account of the "proletarianization" of the American
labor force, draws attention to a multiplicity of sites of class struggle and
class formation, including ethnic community mobilization, factory work
cultures, educational policy, and the school curriculum. Struggles in each
of these sites helped form class and ethnic relations as we see them today.
In so doing, Hogan opens up a discussion on the dynamic nature of
human societies at a "conjunctural level" of analysis, at the level of the
specific and concrete issues of organization, mobilization, class capacity,
and strategy. That is, by showing the *specific* relations between class and
ethnicity, and between schooling, the economy, and state policy, in a
particular historical moment, Hogan is able to document how culture,
politics, and economy actually interact. He also helps to suggest how we
might go beyond class reductionism to include the relatively autonomous
workings of ethnicity in our theories.

Hogan's work exhibited considerable progress. It documented how
important it was to include more than a simplistic theory of class relations in understanding schooling. It indicated that we had to consider
even more sophisticated material on how political and cultural practices
functioned, not look only at the economy. And, it reminded us to focus
on what groups of people actually do, not on supposedly unyielding
structures of domination.

By directing our attention to the issue of how class development actually went on, Hogan and others helped shift the dominant focus in radical analysis of education from static issues of class composition and functional reproduction of the institutional arrangements of schooling in capitalist society to an emphasis on cultural and political formation, resistance, consciousness, the specifics of actual social contexts and, just as interestingly, helped illuminate the problem of building alliances across the mine fields of race, class, and gender. This clearly complemented the textual and qualitative research being carried on inside schools and led to the development of a more integrated conceptual framework.

This framework—one that directs our attention to the interrelationships between a number of dynamics and one that attempts to illuminate complexity, not wish it away—is what is known as the *parallelist* position. Though subject to debate, it has become one of the more generally accepted positions in the critical community. It holds that at least *three* dynamics are essential in understanding schools and other institutions. These dynamics are race, gender, and class. None are reducible to the others. Class is not necessarily primary. The parallelist position has also led to a reevaluation of economically reductive explanations as well. The economy *is* exceptionally powerful; this *is* capitalism after all. But, rather than economy explaining all, critically oriented researchers have argued that there are three spheres of social life—economic, political, and cultural. These too are in continual interaction. These are, in essence, arenas in which class, race, and gender dynamics operate. Unlike base-superstructure models, it is also assumed that action in one can sometimes have an effect on actions in another.[71] The result is a theory of *overdetermination*, in which the processes and outcomes of teaching and learning and of schooling in general are produced by the constant interactions among three dynamics in three spheres (Figure 1).

In a time when class and economic reductionism still play an important role in our explanations, this movement toward a more parallelist position is to be welcomed. Increasingly, socialist feminist work in education which argues that gender, race, and class are irreducible dynamics and that each must be taken equally seriously in analyzing what happens in schools is looked upon favorably.[72] Research which puts race at the center has also become increasingly valued.[73] Even somewhat more economistic work has now recognized how important it is to deal more adequately with cultural and political power and conflict within the state.[74] There has been greater recognition, as well, of the efficacy of non-class social movements, and movements that cut across class, gender, and race lines, in the formation of social and educational

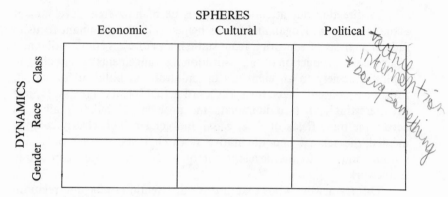

Figure 1 *The Parallelist Position* (Taken from Michael W. Apple and Lois Weis, eds. *Ideology and Practice in Schooling* (Philadelphia: Temple University Press, 1983).

policy.[75] Thus, the parallelist theoretical framework has proven to be a much more synthetic appraisal of how power operates than earlier accounts. This does not mean it is not without its own problems, however.

While we still wish to support the validity of this model of interactions as expressing the character of the U.S. social formation at a very abstract level of generalization, there are limitations of this "symmetrical" model at somewhat "lower" levels of abstraction (i.e. when applied to concrete institutional settings) that have been noted by writers such as Burawoy, Hicks, and Sarup.[76] We wish to specify some of the problems with this earlier formulation and correct it in important ways.

First, it has become clear that at a conjunctural level of analysis this model has not been totally adequate. It is often too general and loses cogency and specificity when applied to the actual operation of race, class, and gender in institutional settings such as schools and classrooms. While it does serve to have us stop and think about a broader range of dynamics and spheres than before, it is difficult to account for the various twists and turns of social and political life at the micro level if our application of theory is inappropriately "pitched" at too high a level of abstraction.[77]

Secondly, this model unfortunately has often been construed in a static and simplistically additive way. Attempts to specify the dynamics of raced, classed, and gendered phenomena in education often got formulated in terms of a system of linear "additions" or gradations of oppression.[78] Thus, for example, much of the recent argument advanced by liberal feminists with respect to the feminization of poverty has rested on the claim that women as gendered and classed subjects are doubly oppressed. Similar claims have been made in relation to women teachers. Spencer, in her insightful case study of women school teachers, draws attention to their double oppression. Simply put, these women performed onerous tasks with respect first to their domestic and emotional labor in the home and secondly with respect to their instructional labor in the classroom. The oppression of these women in the home is "added" to their oppression as teachers working in the classroom.[80] In an essentially additive or incremental model of oppression, patriarchal and class forms of domination unproblematically reproduce each other. Accounts of the intersection of race, class, and gender such as these overlook instances of tension, contradiction, and discontinuity in the institutional life of the school setting.[81] Dynamics of race, class, and gender were thus conceptualized as having individual and uninterrupted effects.

This is partly accurate, of course. However, we need to see these relations as far more complex, problematic, and contradictory. One of the most useful attempts to conceptualize these contradictions at an institutional level has been formulated by Emily Hicks. Hicks offers the thesis that the operation of race, class, and gender relations at the level of daily practices in schools, work places, etc. is *systematically contradictory or "nonsynchronous."* By invoking the concept of nonsynchrony, Hicks advances the position that "individuals or (groups) in their relation to their economic and political systems do not share similar consciousness or similar needs at the same point in time".[82]

The concept of nonsynchrony begins to get at the complexity of causal motion and effects "on the ground," as it were. It also raises questions about the nature, exercise, and multiple determination of power within that middle ground of everyday practices in schooling.[83] The fact is, as Hicks suggests, that dynamic relations of race, class, and gender do not unproblematically reproduce each other. The intersection of these relations can indeed lead to interruptions, discontinuities, attentuations, or augmentations of the original effects of race, class, or gender in a given social context or institutional setting. Gilroy, Omi and Winant, and Sarup have emphasized, in education and elsewhere, the fact that racial and sexual antagonisms can often cut at right angles to class solidarity.[84] Both Sarup and Omi and Winant point to examples of the diminution of working class solidarity outside of education, in the context of racial antagonism within British and American white-dominated trade unions. These unions have had a long history of hostility to minorities and minority causes.[85] Michael Burawoy has drawn attention to examples of the opposite effect of the intersection of race and class in the South African context. In this case, the operation of class contradictions as expressed in the differing material interests and aspirations of middle-class black teachers, nurses, state bureaucrats, etc., and their racial counterparts — the black proletariat in the Bantustans — undermines racial solidarity between these radically opposed social economic groups.[86] Similar examples of these contradictions exist in the case of the intersections of race, class, and gender in the feminist movement. Hicks and Murphy and Livingstone have drawn attention to the alienation of minority working-class women from the white middle-class dominated feminist movement.[87] It is to the literature both inside and outside education on the tensions and contradictions between race, class, and gender that critical scholarship in education should now turn. The key concepts of nonsynchrony and contradiction need to be fully integrated into the parallelist framework.

At the same time, though, we need to be careful not to fall back into a totally "structural" reading of these issues. That is, we need to emphasize the symbolic, signifying, languaging dimensions of social interactions and their integral relationship to both systems of control and strategies for emancipation.

The emphasis on symbol, signs, and representations enables us to think through other dynamics than class, since it has been *particularly* important for advancing our theoretical understanding of the ways in which racial and sexual antagonism operate within the cultural sphere. Indeed, it is to be remembered that for a long time minority and women writers had argued (much against the tide of dominant research) that racial antagonism and sexual oppression are mediated through ideology, culture, politics, and social theories themselves.[86] While orthodox Marxist and neo-Marxist research maintained that it was economic exploitation, capitalist need for surplus value, etc., that explained the oppression of the socially disadvantaged, minority and women writers drew attention to modes of devaluation of self-image, culture, and identity. For writers such as Baldwin and Shange, American schools are principal sites for the production and naturalization of myths, half truths, silences, and obfuscations about the socially disadvantaged. It is with full acknowledgement of the persuasiveness of these claims that critical theorists such as Omi and Winant and West have argued that it is precisely in these "noneconomic" arenas of self-production and identity formation such as the school and the church that Afro-Americans have sought to struggle against white oppression.[89] Only by taking these issues seriously within a parallelist framework can we overcome the past and present tendencies in radical scholarship which cultural critics such as Jameson and Said argue obliterate the specific histories and struggles of the oppressed.[90] This, of course, must be done with a full realization that culture and identity are produced in a context and with a thorough understanding of this material context.

CONCLUSION

The ongoing re-evaluation of the orthodox pillars of neo-Marxist sociology of education, particularly with respect to its pivotal organizing themes such as "mode of production," "base-superstructure," and "class," does explicitly pose to us as radical educators the challenge of rethinking some of the basic planks in our explanation of the reproduction and persistence of social differences and inequalities in American education. We believe that the growing volume of mainstream and radical educational literature on race, class, and gender which we have reviewed in this essay has already begun to point us in some very important directions. We for instance now know where some of the most significant tensions, stresses, and gaps in our current research on social difference and inequality are. We believe that it is precisely these "gaps," "stresses," "tensions," and discontinuities that must be explored if we are to begin to develop a more adequate account of the intersections of race, class, and gender in education. In this final section of our paper, we would like to address briefly three areas which we consider crucial points of difference and tension between and within mainstream and critical approaches to race, class, and gender in the educational literature. These three areas can be summarized as follows: (a) the structure-culture distinction, (b) macro-versus micro-theoretical and methodological approaches to race, class, and gender, (c) theory versus practice.

A. Structure and Culture

To begin with, we believe that the liberal emphasis on values as the site of the social motivation for the maintenance and persistence of racial, classed, and sexual inequalities can not be dismissed out of hand. The primary theoretical and practical merit of this liberal position rests in the fact that it seeks to restore human agency into the project of evaluating the relationship between social differences and education. Thus, for liberal school critics in their examination of racial, gender, and class antagonism in schooling, it is the active agency and subjectivities of students and teachers that really matter and that can, pardon the pun, make a difference. The problem here, as we have shown, is that such an emphasis on individual agency often results in the undertheorization of the effectivity of social and economic structures. In this regard, too, liberal education theorists often forfeit social collectivity as a vantage point for exploring the causes and effects of these antagonisms.

This tension between structure and agency is also powerfully expressed within radical discourses as well. Culturalist critics have in effect sought to restore subjectivity, culture, language, and agency into the debates over social difference and inequality in American education. This theoretical development has taken place partly in response to the early work of radical structuralist school critics which tended to subordinate agency, meaning, and subjectivity to economic structures (such as the work place) exogenous to the school. We believe, however, that future theoretical efforts of radical educators to understand the operation of social difference must attempt to reconcile these apparently separate modes (structural versus cultural) of appropriating the central contradictions of schooling and society. This has been, in part, the project of the latest work of critical educators. But much of the effort to develop an interactive model has still focused primarily on class and not sufficiently on the intersection of race, class, and gender. Thus, a first step towards and interim theorization of the intersection of race, class, and gender in education must involve a challenge to traditionally held class-forged arenas such as the paid labor process, the state, the sphere of production, etc. This would mean, in part, elaborating the particular racial and patriarchal dimensions of the state, the paid and unpaid labor process, and so on. How do patriarchy and racial formation work throughout society? Where and how do they reproduce and contradict each other? How do all three dynamics — race, gender, and class — interact constantly? Do they operate the same way in the economic, cultural, and political spheres? These are the questions that need to be asked at the same time that we continue to examine how each dynamic acts with its own individual power. It is our theoretical responsibility as radical educators to show where and how these racial and sexual antagonisms relate to class dynamics which have been at the center of our attention for so long.

B. Macro- versus Microperspectives

As we have indicated earlier in this chapter, previous efforts to conceptualize the relationship of race and gender to class have been formulated at a very abstract level. Furthermore, such approaches have posited simple linear additive models of gender and class domination as in the "double oppression" formulations that we reviewed. As Sarup has quite persuasively argued, these additive models have simply failed to capture the degree of nuance, variability, discontinuity, and multiplicity of histories and "realities" that exist in the school setting.[91] In a similar manner, both Omi and Winant and Burawoy have also pointed to the fact that the intersection of race and class can lead, for example, to augmentation or diminution of racial solidarity depending on the contingencies and the variables in the local setting. All of this points toward the urgent need for theoretical and practical work articulated at the middle range.[92] We need to be able to specify more directly the ways in which raced, classed, and gendered variables in all their contradictory ways operate in the educational setting.

Let us be clear about what is at issue here. We believe that the radical intuition that racial, sexual, and classed forms of domination are implicated and must be understood in the context of the development of capitalist and patriarchal macrostructures is basically correct if it takes seriously the relatively autonomous workings of the state.

This bird's eye view, however, only supplies us with a general map of relations. It does not tell us how we can get from one point to a next "on the ground." On the other hand, liberal unqualified emphasis on individual motivation and rational action as the terms of reference for "normal" behavior locates racism, classism, and sexism in idiosyncratic, arbitrary, and abnormal attitudes and actions. This forces us to abandon materialist explanations of these social antagonisms and seek recourse in differential psychology and so on. The burden and responsibility for the oppression of women and racial minorities are squarely placed on the shoulders of these irrational or authoritarian individual personalities.[93] Even more problematic is the fact that change and transformation of these oppressive relations are made conditional upon the reformation of these individuals and their return to the observance of the rational norms that supposedly guide the society and its social institutions. Needless to say, historical evidence and the very persistence of racial, sexual, and class oppression go against the grain of this thesis and the programmatic responses it has precipitated.

By contrast to this microperspective of liberal school critics, the macrostructural emphasis of radical educators draws our attention to the fact that racial, sexual, and classed forms of domination are deeply implicated in the fundamental organization of specific human societies as well as the development of capitalism as a world system and the elaboration of an international division of labor. In this way, we are able to understand race, class, and gender as profoundly social and historical categories. Racial and sexual domination, like class domination, are thus specified at the level of social collectivities and their differential relationship to the ownership, distribution, and exchange of goods and services in the society. But this level of abstraction does not allow us to get much of a handle on the way in which these dynamics operate in the conjunctural settings of social institutions such as schools. What we therefore need is some interim theory of social difference which allows for a more conjunctural emphasis. We need middle range theoretical and practical research which can combine macro- and microanalysis in a manner that will allow us to make vital links between our accounts of broader structural forces operating within a capitalist, racist, and patriarchal society and the more contextual and nuanced social relations in our schools. In this sense too, it will be necessary to specify these dynamics of race, class, and gender in such a manner that we allow for what Hicks calls "the multivocal, multiaccented nature of human subjectivity and human struggles" in the educational setting.[94]

C. Theory and Practice

Radical and neo-Marxist approaches to social differences and inequalities in education are notoriously unprogrammatic.[95] Conversely, liberal educators have been criticized for paying little attention to theory and conceptual rigor in their formulations on schooling.[96] In part, this bifurcation is misleading. Both liberal and radical school critics incorporate and address aspects of theory and practice in their writings on schooling. The tension between theory and practice in contemporary research does, however, bring into focus a far more consequential matter — that is, that the production of education theory and research is itself a site of ideological and political struggle. We can sometimes forget that within the corridors of the academy, oblique but often very direct struggles over credibility and ascendancy are constantly being waged within and between "communities" of discourses on curriculum and education.

In this regard, mainstream conservative and liberal theories have sought to appropriate the language of "practice," "practical," "pragmatic," etc. to describe only what they do. Practice in mainstream discourses has often meant the stipulations of "workable" programs, policies designed for operation within the rules and terms of reference of existing institutional structures. Practice in this mainstream sense at best merely allows for incremental modifications necessary for the maintenance of existing institutional frameworks and power relations. Hence, the variety of special programs for "at risk" youth, multicultural curriculum, etc. are in this vein products of liberal attempts to incorporate and redirect the demands of minorities and women for fundamental educational changes. These radical demands are then turned into "functional," "practical," and ultimately hegemonic educational policy. Some of these programs do show potential, but they almost always remain unpoliticized, not thoroughly enough linked to larger movements.

By contrast, radical theoretical work in education has sought to critically expose and demonstrate the limitations and the oppressiveness of many existing educational arrangements, school curricula, and differential resources on socially disadvantaged groups. Radical school critics have sought either directly or indirectly to champion strategies for fundamental changes in curricular content, pedagogical practices, and social structures.[97] This, then, in a general sense is part of the ideological vision that informs the practice of radical scholarship. As educators committed to the expansion of democracy in all its forms, we must never abandon the notion that committed theoretical work is itself a worth-while and necessary *practice* (if, and *only* if, it is also linked to the concrete attempts by real people in real institutions to create democratic cultural, political, and economic relations).

Having said this, however, it is important to recognize that radical theories of education must address actual formulation of policy and decision making, i.e., precisely those areas of educational inquiry which liberal school critics have labeled as "practical." As Troyna and Williams have pointed out, the formulation of policy and decision making within the state and the educational system constitutes a political process in which women, minorities, and socially and economically disadvantaged youth are disenfranchised and their interests and demands are delegitimated.[98] It is precisely this arena of decision making, policy formation, and the formulation of the instrumental rules that define the formal dimensions of schooling in which radical educators are too often outnumbered, out-organized and out-maneuvered.[99] Unless we focus directly on the question of what can be done at this level, given our critically informed analysis, we shall be left on the sidelines watching as the conservative restoration reconstructs education around its own principles of race, gender, and class domination.

The question of critical practice is essential then. As Aronowitz and Giroux perceptively argue, we have become more sophisticated in the "language of critique," a critique which, as we have shown in this chapter, has made considerable progress. Yet, we have not sufficiently built a "language of possibility." We have few descriptions of exemplary practices in which models of educational action — informed by the critiques of the relationship between education and differential power — actually make a difference. What we need are exemplars of what one of us has called non-reformist reforms, programs that work on the day-to-day problems of curricular and pedagogical policy and practice *and* also lead beyond themselves to further possibilities of organized cultural, political, and economic action.[100] There are already resources available for such a language of possibility in the literature on feminist pedagogy and anti-racist education. Bringing these exemplars to the forefront of our activities would be a major step in the right direction. By taking race and gender more seriously at all levels, we may make considerable movement beyond the limitations posed by existing theories and practices. Only in this way will we go beyond the biological explanations of the conservatives, the individualistic and naively possibilitarian hopes of the liberals, and the almost cynical economistic positions of the orthodox marxists.

Theories of how race, class, and gender interact, and of how economic, political, and cultural power act, in education do need to become increasingly subtle, with a recognition of the parallel status of

each. A nonsynchronous parallelist framework remains to be fully articulated. But we also need to remember what all of these theoretical labors
are about. The political, economic, and cultural lives of real people — of
real children, of real women and men, of real people of color in schools
and elsewhere — are subject not to theoretic but to lived relations of differential power. These relations are not abstract, but are experienced in
ways that now help or hurt identifiable groups of people in all too visible
ways. For this we do need conceptual advances. But one learns to see
more clearly through political action as well.

NOTES

1. For a review of this, see Michael W. Apple, *Education and Power*
(Boston: Routledge and Kegan Paul, 1982). See also Paul Willis, *Learn-
ing to Labor* (New York: Columbia University Press, 1981) and Robert
Everhart, *Reading, Writing and Resistance* (Boston: Routledge and
Kegan Paul, 1983).

2. Mary O'Brien, "The Commatization of Women: Patriarchal
Fetishism in the Sociology of Education," *Interchange* 15 (No. 2 1984),
pp. 43–60.

3. See Michael W. Apple, *Teachers and Texts: A Political Economy
of Class and Gender Relations in Education* (New York: Routledge and
Kegan Paul, 1986), Madan Sarup, *The Politics of Multiracial Education*
(New York: Routledge and Kegan Paul, 1986), Barry Troyna and Jenny
Williams, *Racism, Education and the State* (London: Croom Helm,
1986), Geoff Whitty, *Sociology and School Knowledge* (New York:
Methuen, 1985); and Len Barton and Stephen Walker, eds. *Race, Class
and Education* (London: Croom Helm, 1983).

4. Apple, *Teachers and Texts*; and Michael Omi and Howard Winant,
Racial Formation in the United States (New York: Routledge and Kegan
Paul, 1986).

5. Michael Foucault, *Discipline and Punish* (New York: Pantheon,
1977).

6. Philip Wexler, *The Sociology of Education: Beyond Equality*
(Indianapolis: Bobbs-Merril, 1976).

7. Mokubung Nkomo, *Student Culture and Activism in Black
South African Universities* (Westport: Greenwood Press, 1984); and
Sarup, *The Politics of Multicultural Education.*

8. See the essays in Julian Henriques, et al. *Changing the Subject: Psychology, Social Regulation and Subjectivity* (New York: Methuen, 1984).

9. Ibid.

10. Ibid.

11. Hazel Carby, "Schooling in Babylon," in Centre for Contemporary Cultural Studies, eds. *The Empire Strikes Back* (London: Hutchinson, 1982), pp. 183–211.   '

12. Ibid.

13. Stephen Jay Gould, *The Mismeasure of Man (New York: Norton, 1981).*

14. *Michael W. Apple, Ideology and Curriculum* (Boston: Routledge and Kegan Paul, 1979); and Steven Selden, "Educational Policy and Biological Science," *Teachers College Record* 87 (Fall 1985), pp. 35–51.

15. Herbert Spencer, *Essay: Scientific, Political and Speculative* (New York: D. Appleton, 1892); and Hans Eysenk, *The Intelligence Controversy* (New York: Wiley, 1981).

16. See Philip Altbach and Gail Kelly, eds. *Education and Colonialism* (New York: Longman, 1978); and Apple, *Ideology and Curriculum*.

17. Luce Irigaray, *This Sex Which Is Not One* (New York: Cornell, 1985); and Jean B. Elstain, "The New Feminist Scholarship," *Salmagundi* 70–71 (Spring/Summer 1986), pp. 3–26.

18. W. W. Charters, *Curriculum Construction* (New York: Arno Press, 1971).

19. Talcott Parsons, "The School Class as a Social System," *Harvard Educational Review* 29 (Fall 1959), pp. 297–318; and Robert Dreeben, *On What Is Learned in School* (Reading: Addison-Wesley, 1968).

20. Carby, "Schooling in Babylon."

21. Ibid.

22. The literature on this is vast. See, for example, Patrick Moynihan and Nathan Glazer, *Beyond the Melting Pot* (Cambridge: MIT Press and Harvard, 1963); David Easton, *A Framework for Political Analysis* (Englewood Cliffs: Prentice Hall, 1965); and

Christopher Hurn, *The Limits and Possibilities of Schooling* (Boston: Allyn and Bacon, 1979).

23. W. J. Thomas, *The Child in America* (New York: Knopf, 1928); Gunner Myrdal, *An American Dilemma* (New York: Harper, 1944); Theodor Adorno, et al., *The Authoritarian Personality* (New York: Harper, 1950); and Gordon Allport, *The Nature of Prejudice* (New York: Anchor, 1958).

24. Henriques, et al., *Changing the Subject*, p. 66.

25. Hurn, *The Limits and Possibilities of Schooling*.

26. See, e.g., Patricia Sexton, *Education and Income* (New York: Viking, 1961); James Coleman, et al., *Equality of Educational Opportunity* (Washington: U.S. Government Printing Office, 1966); Christopher Jencks, et al., *Inequality* (New York: Basic Books, 1972); and William Sewell and Robert Hauser, *Education, Occupation and Earnings* (New York: Academic Press, 1975).

27. For a brief review of this work, see Whitty, *Sociology and School Knowledge*.

28. For example, Ray Rist, "Social Class and Teacher Expectations," *Harvard Educational Review* 40 (August 1970), pp. 411–451; and Aaron Cicourel and John Kitsuse, *The Educational Decision Makers* (Indianapolis: Bobbs-Merril, 1963).

29. Selden, "Educational Policy and Biological Science."

30. Hurn, *The Limits and Possibilities of Schooling*, p. 132.

31. Rist, "Social Class and Teacher Expectations"; Cicourel and Kitsuse, *The Educational Decision Makers*; and Richard Rosenthal and Lenore Jacobsen, *Pygmalion in the Classroom* (New York: Holt, Rinehart and Winston, 1968).

32. For a review of this research, see Carl Grant and Christine Sleeter, "Race, Class and Gender in Education," *Review of Educational Research* 56 (Summer 1986), pp. 195–211.

33. Marvin Berlowitz, "Multicultural Education: Fallacies and Alternatives," in Marvin Berlowitz and Ronald Edari, eds., *Racism and the Denial of Human Rights: Beyond Ethnicity* (Minneapolis: Marxist Educational Press, 1984), pp. 129–136; Valarie Walkerdine, "Developmental Psychology and the Child-Centered Pedagogy," in Henriques, et al., *Changing the Subject*; and Fazal Rizvi, ed., *Multiculturalism as an Educational Policy* (Geelong: Deakin University Press, 1985).

34. Berlowitz, "Multicultural Education".

35. Ibid; and A. Jakubowicz, "State and Ethnicity: Multiculturalism as Ideology," in Rizvi, ed., *Multiculturalism as an Educational Policy*, pp. 43–63.

36. See Apple, *Education and Power*; and Herbert Gintis, "Communication and Politics," *Socialist Review* 10 (March-June 1980), pp. 189–232.

37. Michael Gurevitch, et al., *Culture, Society and the Media* (London: Methuen, 1982).

38. Apple, *Ideology and Curriculum*.

39. See Gwendolyn Baker, "Multicultural Imperatives for Curriculum Development in Teacher Education," *Journal of Research and Development in Education* 2 (Fall 1977), pp. 70–83.

40. Apple, *Teachers and Texts*.

41. See, for instance, Dan Lortie, *School Teacher* (Chicago: University of Chicago Press, 1975); and Robert Dreeben, *The Nature of Teaching* (Glenview: Scott Foresman, 1970).

42. Apple, *Teachers and Texts*.

43. Apple, *Ideology and Curriculum*.

44. Sarup, *The Politics of Multiracial Education*. See also, Ernesto Laclau and Chantal Mouffe, *Hegemony and Socialist Strategy* (London: Verso, 1985).

45. Jan Carew, "Fulcrums of Change," *Race and Class* 2 (Autumn 1984), pp. 1–14.

46. See, Apple, *Ideology and Curriculum*; Apple, *Teachers and Texts*; Michael W. Apple, ed., *Cultural and Economic Reproduction in Education* (Boston: Routledge and Kegan Paul, 1982); and Henry Giroux, *Theory and Resistance in Education* (South Hadley: Bergin and Garvey, 1983).

47. Ibid.

48. Samuel Bowles and Herbert Gintis, *Schooling in Capitalist America* (New York: Basic Books, 1976).

49. Ibid., p. 125.

50. John Roemer, "Divide and Conquer: Microfoundations of a Marxian Theory of Wage Discrimination," *Bell Journal of Economics* 10 (Autumn 1979), pp. 695–705.

51. Ronald Edari, "Racial Minorities and Forms of Ideological Mystification," in Berlowitz and Edari, *Racism and the Denial of Human Rights*, p. 8.

52. C. L. R. James, *Spheres of Existence: Selected Writings* (Westport: Hill, 1980).

53. Edna Bonacich, "Capitalism and Race Relations in South Africa: A Split Labor Market Analysis," in Maurice Zeitlin, ed., *Political Power and Social Theory, Volume 2* (Greenwich: JAI Press, 1981), pp. 239–277; and Michael Reich, *Racial Inequality* (Princeton: Princeton University Press, 1981).

54. Apple, *Ideology and Curriculum*.

55. Apple, *Ideology and Curriculum*; Apple, *Education and Power*; Jean Anyon, "Ideology and U.S. History Textbooks," *Harvard Educational Review* 49 (August 1979), pp. 361–386; and Henry Giroux, *Ideology, Culture and the Process of Schooling* (Philadelphia: Temple University Press, 1981).

56. Basil Bernstein, *Class, Codes and Control Volume 3* (Boston: Routledge and Kegan Paul, 1977); and Pierre Bourdieu and Jean-Claude Passeron, *Reproduction in Education, Society, and Culture* (Beverly Hills: Sage, 1977).

57. Ibid. See also Philip Wexler, "Structure, Text and Subject," in Apple, ed., *Culture and Economic Reproduction in Education*.

58. Ibid. See also Randall Collins, *The Credential Society* (New York: Academic Press, 1979).

59. Apple, *Ideology and Curricculum*.

60. Apple, *Education and Power*; and Bernstein; *Class, Codes and Control Volume 3*.

61. Apple, *Education and Power*.

62. See Angela McRobbie, "Working Class Girls and the Culture of Femininity," in Women's Studies Group, ed., *Women Take Issue* (London: Hutchinson, 1978), pp. 96–108. O'Brien, "The Commatization of Women"; Omi and Winant, *Racial Formation in the United States*; Sarup, *The Politics of Multiracial Education*; and Lois Weis, *Between Two Worlds* (Boston: Routledge and Kegan Paul, 1985). In England, the work of Madeleine Arnot and Miriam David was especially important and did have a considerable impact as well on North American work. Also important here was the work of Jane Gaskell in Canada. Both

Anyon and Apple, as well, increasingly turned their attention to the interaction between gender and class.

63. See Irigaray, *This Sex Which Is Not One*; Annette Kuhn, *Women's Pictures* (Boston: Routledge and Kegan Paul, 1982); Emily Hicks, "Cultural Marxism: Nonsychrony and Feminist Practice," in Lydia Sargent, ed., *Women and Revolution* (Boston: South End Press, 1981); Terry Eagleton, *The Function of Criticism* (London: Verso, 1984); and Edward Said, *The World, the Text and the Critic* (Cambridge: Harvard University Press, 1983).

64. Philip Wexler, *Social Analysis and Education: Beyond the New Sociology of Education* (New York: Routledge and Kegan Paul, in press).

65. See Apple, *Education and Power*; the chapters by Carnoy and Dale in Apple, ed., *Cultural and Economic Reproduction in Education*; and Martin Carnoy, *The State and Political Theory* (Princeton: Princeton University Press, 1984).

66. Wexler, "Structure, Text and Subject," p. 276. See also the excellent volume by R. W. Connell, et al., *Making the Difference* (Boston: George Allen and Unwin, 1982).

67. Michael W. Apple and Lois Weis, eds., *Ideology and Practice in Schooling* (Philadelphia: Temple University Press, 1983).

68. Apple, *Education and Power*; *Cultural and Economic Reproduction in Education*; and Giroux, *Theory and Resistance in Education*.

69. David Hogan, "Education and Class Formation," in Apple, ed. *Cultural and Economic Reproduction in Education*, pp. 32–78.

70. Ibid. See also William Reese, *Power and the Promise of School Reform* (New York: Routledge and Kegan Paul, 1986).

71. Apple, *Education and Power*; Apple, *Teachers and Texts*; and Samuel Bowles and Herbert Gintis, *Capitalism and Democracy* (New York: Basic Books, 1986).

72. Apple, *Teachers and Texts*.

73. Troyna and Williams, *Racism, Education and the State*.

74. Martin Carnoy and Henry Levin, *Schooling and Work in the Democratic State* (Stanford: Stanford University Press, 1985).

75. Ibid. and Omi and Winant, *Racial Formation in the United States*; and Allen Hunter, "Children in the Service of Conservatism,"

(unpublished paper, Department of History, University of Wisconsin, Madison, 1986).

76. Michael Burawoy, "The Capitalist State in South Africa," in Zeitlin, ed., *Political Power and Social Theory*, pp. 279–335; Hicks, "Cultural Marxism: Nonsynchrony and Feminist Practice"; and Sarup, *The Politics of Multiracial Education*.

77. See Stuart Hall, "Gramsci's Relevance to the Analysis of Racism and Ethnicity," *Communication Inquiry* 10 (Summer 1986), pp. 5–27 and the interview with Hall in the same issue.

78. Sarup, *The Politics of Multicultural Education*.

79. Lindsay Murphy and Jonathan Livingstone, "Racism and the Limits of Radical Feminism," *Race and Class* 26 (Spring 1985).

80. Dee Spencer, "The Home and School Lives of Women Teachers," *The Elementary School Journal* 84 (January 1984), pp. 283–298.,

81. Apple, *Teachers and Texts*.

82. Hicks, "Cultural Marxism: Nonsynchrony and Feminist Practice, p. 221.

83. James Scott and Tia Kerkvliet, *Everyday Forms of Peasant Resistance in South-east Asis* (London: Frank Case, 1986).

84. Paul Gilroy, "Steppin' Out of Babylon: Race, Class and Autonomy," in Centre for Contemporary Cultural Studies, ed., *The Empire Strikes Back*, p. 278–314; Omi and Winant, *Racial Formation in the United States*; and Sarup, *The Politics of Multiracial Education*.

85. Omi and Winant, *Racial Formation in the United States*; and Sarup, *The Politics of Multiracial Education*.

86. Borawoy, "The Capitalist State in South Africa."

87. Hicks, "Cultural Marxism: Nonsynchrony and Feminist Practice,"; and Murphy and Livingstone, "Racism and the Limits of Radical Feminism."

88. Thomas Pettigrew, *The Sociology of Race Relations: Reflections and Reform* (New York: Free Press, 1980); and Harold Cruse, *The Crisis of the Negro Intellectual (New York: Morrow, 1967)*.

89. *Omi and Winant, Racial Formation in the United States*; and Cornell West, *Prophecy and Deliverance* (Philadelphia: Westminster, 1982).

90. Fredric Jameson, "Post Modernism, or the Cultural Logic of Late Capitalism," *New Left Review* 146 (July-August 1984), pp. 53–111; and Edward Said, "Intellectuals in the Post-Colonial World," *Salmagundi* 70–71 (Spring/Summer 1986), pp. 44–64.

91. Sarup, *The Politics of Multiracial Education.*

92. Omi and Winant, *Racial Formation in the United States*; and Burawoy, "The Capitalist State in South Africa." On the issue of "middle range" theories, see Hall, "Gramsci's Relevance to the Analysis of Racism and Ethnity"; and Scott and Kerkvliet, *Everyday Forms of Peasant Resistance in South-east Asia.*

93. Henriques, et al., *Changing the Subject.*

94. Hicks, "Cultural Marxism: Nonsynchrony and Feminist Practice."

95. Chris Mullard, "Racism and School: History, Policy and Practice," in Rizvi, ed., *Multiculturalism as an Educational Policy*, pp. 64–81.

96. Hurn, *The Limits and Possibilities of Schooling.*

97. See, for example, Paulo Freire, *Pedagogy of the Oppressed* (New York: Seabury Press, 1968); Ira Shor, *Critical Teaching and Everyday Life* (Boston: South End Press, 1980); and the works of Apple and Giroux noted previously.

98. Troyna and Williams, *Racism, Education and the State.*

99. Said, "Intellectuals in the Post-Colonial World".

100. Apple, *Education and Power.*

Part I

DIFFERENT KNOWLEDGE, UNEQUAL STRUCTURES, UNEQUAL OUTCOMES

1

Nested Contexts

> Just as the interpretivist tries to transcend the
> categorical distinctions implicit in positivism by
> appealing to the wider context provided by a
> shared culture and form of life, so the critical
> theorist attempts to transcend the dichotomies im-
> plicit in an interpretive approach by appealing to
> an even broader context.
>
> Bredo and Feinberg, 1982

In a short film entitled "Zoom" the viewer is swept from the microsphere
of subcellular structures to the world of appearances, sucked through a
membrane of air into space, and plummeted away from a blue-green ball
quivering in blackness, past planets and galaxies, to the outer reaches of
the universe. In a physical sense, we easily accept the realization that
there are things going beyond our awareness of them. Yet in a psychological or social sense, this is somehow harder. Each of us has carefully
constructed a world view, what Shutz has called "the-world-taken-for-
granted," that helps us to make sense of our experience and our experience of others. Our working knowledge of interactions and events
continuously affirms that we can go into a situation familiar or strange
and size it up, make judgments about the people involved, and, in a
word, know it. Thus, though the physical world may be complex and ex-

---

*The author wishes to thank Patricia Garrett and Lois Weis for their comments
on an earlier version of this paper. I also wish to acknowledge support from the
National Academy of Education's Spencer Fellowship Program and the Bush Institute for Child and Family Policy.

pansive, the immediate social world appears knowable because our experience tells us every day that it is knowable.

In this paper I would like to explore different ways of constructing social knowledge and suggest that our understanding of meaning might be enhanced by using a metaphor not altogether dissimilar from the one above. I use the phrase "nested contexts" to begin to represent what is going on at different levels of inquiry, through the lenses of different disciplines. But, to begin, I will describe one example of how I see meanings to be in a sense "nested" one within the other.

Several years ago, while teaching a course in creative writing, I assigned my students the task of describing an incident from three different points of view. The purpose of the exercise was to illustrate how one's perspective or view of activities can vary. One student described a setting with particular comprehension and vividness. The first essay depicted a bleak gray plain that was occasionally and without warning illuminated by a searing white light. Corpses were strewn everywhere. The reader sees and experiences this world through the eyes of one survivor, whose thoughts, with a summoned rationality bordering on panic, race against time in a world both hostile and unpredictable. The second essay describes a small boy sitting on the sidewalk. He plays with a magnifying glass, catching the sun now and again, laughing softly to himself. In the third essay, a woman steps outside a frame house. The wooden screen door squeaks uneasily, then rattles on its hinges as it slams behind her. She yells at a boy to "stop that" and, in words halting and ineffectual, urges him into the house.

Interestingly, each of these depictions stands alone but is strangely incomplete without the others. Only when the different contexts have become nested, one within the other, does a somewhat more comprehensive picture emerge. This suggests that there is value in looking reflexively at different levels of action, for each offers a perspective that informs the others.

This suggestion attends in opposition to much of the work currently undertaken by contemporary social scientists. As the world becomes increasingly complex and differentiated, so the argument goes, fields of inquiry of necessity become more specialized. The particular way in which disciplines have evolved within American universities thus has had the effect of fracturing the world into discrete fields that deal alternatively with the individual (psychology), the cultural (anthropology), the societal (sociology), and the historical (history). Yet social scientists across fields have come to wonder if such containment not only limits but also seriously distorts.[1]

In this chapter I address the problem in interpreting—rather than conducting—field research. I try to illustrate how the notion of "nested contexts" can help to integrate different perspectives on child rearing, in this case on child rearing practices observed in an early education program for black American children. The analytic framework derives from Habermas. After a discussion of the research study on which this paper is based, I briefly look at ways in which methods and assumptions drawn from psychology, anthropology, and critical theory explicitly or implicitly offer differing perspectives on African-American child rearing and therefore different solutions to the highly specific problems which black caregivers face. I use the phrase "nested contexts" to suggest that one way of construing the relationship among them is to view them as fitting one within the other. More precisely, however, they can be seen as being recursively implicated. Through these different contexts I trace my own construction of social knowledge.

THE RESEARCH STUDY

The examples that I use are taken from a comparative study of a preschool for children of middle-income families and a Head Start center for children of low-income families.[2] The two settings are located in the same inner suburb of a large American city and are less than one mile apart. At the preschool teachers and children are white; at the Head Start center teachers and children are black.[3] Since early education teachers typically come from the same communities as their students, the classrooms are school settings that tend to be continuous with family life.

The Harmomy Preschool is housed in an Episcopal church building (though the program is non-denominational), and the Irving Head Start Center is located in a large basement room in a public elementary school.[4] The size of the classrooms and the teacher-student ratio are roughly the same in the two locations.

The study is based on fieldwork conducted throughout the course of the 1980–81 school year. For most of the year I worked as a volunteer teacher in the Head Start center. During the first two-and-one-half months I visited the preschool and center on alternating days. In each setting I made room diagrams, daily time charts, flow charts of the movements of each of the children, detailed verbatims, and ongoing fieldnotes. After mid-November, I worked in the Head Start center and only occasionally visited the preschool classroom.

The ethnographer's task is to apprehend and then to render the meaning system of an interacting group.[5] The interpretation of the collective context is one of three possible constructions of social knowledge that will be explored here. They are: the context of the individual, the collective context, and the social evolutionary context.

The Context of the Individual

Theory and Assumptions

In a modern multicultural society adults and children display group characteristics (according to class, race, ethnicity, and also gender), as well as within-group (individual) characteristics. In psychological research group characteristics frequently have been depicted as positive or negative personal traits. White middle-class mothers have been seen as indulgent and permissive, whereas poor and black mothers have been characterized as authoritarian-autocratic.[6] Since most research has concentrated on the effects of parental behavior upon children, racial, ethnic, and social class characteristics have been analyzed in terms of class differences, without reference to the fact that parents themselves live in different environments.[7] In a recent review, Maccoby and Martin summarize how class differences typically are viewed by developmental psychologists:

> We have presented evidence that children's optimal functioning is associated with fairly high levels of mutual involvement between parent and child, with mutual responsiveness and compliance, accompanied by a negotiating (rather than power assertive) style of conflict resolution when conflicts arise. Among American middle-class families, and perhaps among middle-class families in other industrialized societies as well, this appears to be the pattern that carries a relatively low risk of deviance in the children.[8]

By extension, poor and minority parents have been blamed for not rearing children according to middle-class norms. The locus of society's ills is seen to reside within individuals and families, rather than in the social and economic conditions of people's lives.[9]

Just as a causal model is used to account for the effects on children, so a causal model is posited to remedy the situation. Within American society in the last twenty years, child rearing practices not in accord with mainstream values have generally been seen, not as adaptive strategies that help people to cope with external constraints, but rather as unfortunate personal practices that indicate a lack of information or training. Black families, in particular, have been labeled "pathological," black mothers deficient, and black children deprived.[10]

Since the problem is seen to rest with individuals, it is assumed that it is individuals who need to change. Millions of dollars have been expended both to provide poor, frequently minority, children with educational experiences that their own homes "lack" or to provide poor and minority parents with training that would enable them to raise children "properly."[11] Educational programs for parents and children thus become independent variables that are expected to affect the dependent variables of children's motivation and achievement.

Research Experience and Findings

Such work both reflects and scientifically validates the consensus reality, so that "differences" stand out against the normative backdrop of the broader society.[12] As a white researcher and former preschool teacher working in a classroom with black teachers and children (an individual observing other individuals), these issues came to life for me in concrete and practical ways that were disquieting. In my early formulations of life in a Head Start classroom, I found I was limited in the words and constructs I had available to define what I was experiencing. My own values went unquestioned, therefore, when the teachers failed to do things the (my) "right" way, I felt that they were doing things wrong.

Day after day I chronicled examples of the child-rearing strategies of the (white) middle-class preschool teachers and those of the (black) working-class center teachers. Where the preschool teachers fostered individualism and self-expression, the center teachers expected obedience to authority and relative conformity. Where the preschool teachers valued the differentiation of experience, the center teachers valued convergent response. And where the preschool teachers provided children with frequent choices and were generally indulgent, the center teachers were highly directive in their interactions with children.

At the center adult authority was underscored in several ways. The teachers physically sat above the children during group time or stood above them if the children were seated for a project. The focus during group time was on social knowledge that was transmitted verbally from adult to children. Day after day, group time focused on having children recognize their names, on teaching children their addresses and phone numbers, or, later, on having them recite the month, date, and year. While the preschool children typically spent two hours fifteen minutes each day "doing their own thing," the Head Start children spent the same amount of time in group-centered activities under the teacher's control. Children were told where to be, how to behave, and what to do for much of their time at school. To my dismay, the contrast between the "permissive-indulgent" style and the "authoritarian-autocratic" style became a living reality. It was only later, through the process of becoming a participant in the setting, that I began to widen the lenses through which I experienced the social world.

The Collective Context

Theory and Assumptions

Anthropologists criticize the fact that the great majority of social science research on children and on child rearing has been done by white American and European researchers, typically with white middle-class subjects. This monocultural research has been presented as representative of the human race so that people who fail to conform to expectations have been perceived as deficient or deviant.[13] For African-Americans especially, "Traditional educational research has considered neither the collective historical experience of blacks nor the structural barriers of the wider society."[14]

Contemporary anthropologists instead have assumed the importance of the collective nature of culture, assumed, that is, "that they are dealing with shared supraindividual phenomena, that culture represents a consensus on a wide variety of meanings among members of an interacting community."[15]

Unlike the causal chains or antecedent-consequent depictions of behaviors that are driven by external factors, anthropological descriptions show meanings (internal factors) to drive behavior. Meanings "represent the world, create cultural entities, direct one to do certain things and invoke certain feelings."[16] From this perspective, the process of cultural transmission-acquisition is neither a mindless nor a static one. People act rather than react, and though adaptations are made to situations, people also draw on strategies that have worked in the past or invent new strategies in order to maintain old ways.

Efforts have been made to define African-American culture, yet controversy continues to exist over whether African institutions were obliterated by slavery or if prior experience continued to influence the values and practices of African slaves in America.[17] Some have claimed that African-Americans have maintained the interdependency and sense of collective responsibility of their African heritage, while at the same time adopting aspects of white American society.[18] Outnumbered in a dominant white society, poor black Americans particularly tend to be more group-oriented than white, middle-income Americans. "Kinship" is the word used to describe the intergenerational system of family, neighbors, and friends in which children are reared, with "parakinship" ties evident in the use of terms such as "brother," "sister," and "blood-brother" when no ties of blood exist.[19] Based on three years of fieldwork in a ghetto community, Stack has described the way in which poor black women work and live interdependently, sharing tasks and resources.[20]

Researchers who adopt a cultural perspective have suggested that, rather than changing children or their parents, school personnel should learn to value the culture of origin, foster multicultural education, and accommodate the culturally specific learning strategies that black children have acquired.[21] Education, in this sense, should become "culturally responsive."[22]

Research Experience and Findings

In my comparative study of child-rearing practices, I became uncomfortable with my role as observer and, wanting to relate to the adults in the setting in a more personal and honest way, I began visiting the preschool less frequently and spending more and more time at the center. I offered to keep notes and to be useful.

After some weeks, I realized that I had become a teacher: planning, instructing, cleaning, sharing chores, advising, and humoring. Though from the beginning I had been accepted as a peer at the preschool, such was not the case at the center. I was white, the teachers were black; I had been an observer, they the observed. Both role differentials have had a history of abuse. What ultimately was of consequence, however, was that we were all women, all single parents, all working hard each day to care for and to educate children, and to tend to the multifaceted duties essential to the program as it was defined. From being an observer, outside the action, I thus became a participant-observer and, for the first time, was able to begin to understand the classroom in terms of the implicit and explicit values and beliefs of the women who had constructed it.

Over time I became aware of larger patterns of beliefs, values, and norms that informed the teachers' actions by comparing what the teachers in each setting said about their practice with how they organized their activity and interacted with children. The two programs appeared to be different means to reach different ends. In both settings the beliefs that guided their actions seemed continuous with their experience outside the schools. The preschool teachers created a setting quite like that found within nuclear families, one in which women spend a great deal of time in child-centered interactions. They worked alone with children much of the time, encouraging children also to work alone, making "unique" products and fostering language that would enable the individual child to differentiate his/her experience from that of others. The Head Start teachers appeared to re-enact patterns of interaction that prevail within extended family networks,[23] working closely together, sharing tasks, decisions, and resources, and sharing also the perception of those outside as hostile to their interests and efforts.[24] They worked together much of the time, and, in their structuring of events, provided group-oriented activities that encouraged children to do what others did.

These different values were evident in the ways in which the teachers in the respective settings structured time and space, selected activities and

utilized materials, and in the way in which they patterned their interactions with children.[25] In their focus on individual children and in their
structuring of an environment that maximized individual choice and action, the preschool teachers encouraged children to be uniquely different
from others. "Free time" provided time for children to select activities of
interest. Time was a continuum through which both children and activities changed. Because children were perceived to "develop" over time the
teachers provided different materials for children of different ages and
separated the children into three different age groups for "develop-
mentally appropriate" activities.

For much of the morning, individuals moved in different directions,
at different rates of speed. The classroom space was highly differentiated, providing activities in distinct areas of the room. Transforma-
tional materials (sand, water, clay, paint) afforded opportunities for
children to have unique experiences, to make unusual products, to im-
pose their own order into things. Children frequently initiated conversa-
tions with the teachers, and they called them by their first names. The
classroom thus seemed to reinforce values of individuality and autonomy
and to promote positive feelings toward change.

In contrast, the Head Start teachers structured time, space, and activity so as to reinforce values of collectivism, authority, and traditional
(repetitive) modes of interaction that reinforced the group experience.
Children were required to wait until others were finished before they
could move on to the next activity. They were grouped together for much
of their time at school. Art projects were intended to result in multiple
examples of the same end product: the same jack-o-lanterns at Hallo-
ween or pictures of Martin Luther King all colored brown. The teachers
expressed a deep sense of fairness and equality, and demonstrated in
words and actions that they believed in treating children the same.

The teachers also believed that children should show respect and
deference to their elders. These beliefs seemed rooted in a traditional
respect but also reflected the teachers' perceptions of the behaviors they
deemed necessary for children to succeed in school. "Group time" was
seen as the time in which learning occurred. In the Head Start center the
teachers were called by their last names.

The Head Start teachers also spent much of their time working
together, engaged in a proliferation of tasks for which the preschool
teachers were not responsible but which were integral to the social service
demands of the Head Start program. Though teachers and children
shared the same space at the preschool, a separate "teacher space" was set
up to provide a place in which other responsibilities could be carried out
at the center.

In both settings, the teachers appeared quite intentionally to construct environments that were consonant with their life orientations. Though both classrooms were approximately the same size and had many of the same furnishings and materials, very different orders came to be constructed within them. Ultimately, the Head Start teachers appeared to socialize children to the preeminent values of a society in which the needs of the group prevailed over the needs of individuals, thereby to extend a collective orientation that has had both historic roots and contempoarary efficacy.

The Social Evolutionary Context

Theory and Assumption

By defining what he calls knowledge constitutive interests, Habermas has shown that knowledge can take a number of forms and serve a number of purposes.[26] In their introduction to critical theory and to the work of Habermas specifically, Bredo and Feinberg describe how Habermas both differentiates and integrates three types of knowledge, the methods they use, the explanations they imply, and the types of science which they support (See Table 1).[27]

According to Habermas, critical theorists strive to transcend the limitations of both positivism, with its focus on the individual and concern with sense data, and interpretivism, with its focus on the collective and concern with shared meanings. Critical theory suggests that social knowledge must be viewed in terms of its power to effect progressive social change.

> By placing knowledge in this broad social evolutionary perspective, the critical theorist in effect creates a hierarchy of contexts and types of knowledge, running from the narrowest individual context to the collective context to the social evolutionary context. Understanding the nature of social knowledge involves understanding these contexts and their interrelationships.[28]

It is through labor and communicative action, through the work we engage in and the sense that informs our action, that we acquire practical knowledge of the social order, how it functions, the roles the statuses we are assigned within it, and our intuitive sense of how "fair" or "practical" is the result. The interplay between these two forms of action creates the social evolutionary context; the contradictions inherent in situations over time generate the impetus for change.

Table 1 Knowledge and Human Interests

Types of Knowledge	Methods	Types of Science	Explanation
"Emancipatory"- needs to resolve contradictions between the two in the direction of greater autonomy	study of systematic distortions in learning and in commun- ication that result from contradictions between the first two types	critical sciences: psychoanalysis ideology critique	explanatory understanding -dialectically interrelated (seeks to explain systematic dis- tortions at the individual and social levels)
"Practical"- concern with the understanding and reaching of under- standing with others	hermeneutic methods	historical/hermen- eutic: history anthropology	reason (internal)
"Technical"- concern with the prediction and control of events	study of what can be detected, measured and manipulated - information received through our perceptual mechanisms	empirical-analytic: natural sciences systematic social sciences	causal (external)

Note: Summarized from Bredo and Feinberg, pp. 273–281.

Research Experience and Findings

In the course of comparing the classroom life of a preschool and that of a Head Start center, I came to understand how the teachers' practices were influenced by history and culture but also by structural factors which either empowered or constrained their actions in important ways.[29] Where the preschool teachers operated their program with relative autonomy, the Head Start teachers functioned within a stratified social order. At the bottom rung of a bureaucratic hierarchy, they constantly were made accountable to others outside the context of the classroom.

The preschool teachers, who chose to work part-time, appeared to exercise a good deal of control over their work situation. They had relatively free reign in terms of the curriculum they provided and the pro- gam they organized. I never observed either the pastor or his secretary enter the room while class was in session, likewise, the parents waited in the foyer outside the classroom and only entered when the children began singing or when the teachers otherwise indicated that activities were

winding down. In this "world-taken-for-granted" the teachers valued —
and granted the children in their care — freedom and choice, allowing the
children frequent opportunities to make their own decisions.

At the center, the demands on the teachers' time and energies were
multifarious and unpredictable. The telephone rang frequently, and it
was not uncommon for someone to arrive at the door unexpectedly: the
bus driver, the supervisor, someone from the central office, another
teacher, a member of the ancillary staff, a parent.

In the course of each day the teachers fed the morning children break-
fast, provided a program, and fed them lunch. They fed the afternoon
children lunch, provided a program, and gave the children a snack before
sending them home. Meal times frequently took one-third of each
group's total time at school. Organization and planning went into the
provision of meals. Teachers stocked the refrigerator, set the tables,
distributed food, and cleaned up four times each day. Each morning at
the Head Start center the remains of a principle meal: cereal, juice, paper
napkins, styrofoam bowls, and plastic utensils littered the tables, thus
juxtaposing the luxury of snack time at the preschool where children
might eat purple grapes one day and fresh pineapple the next.

Other constraints were manifested in numerous ways. First, the
teachers were expected to go for training frequently, training which was
unidirectional, rather than dialogic, and which presupposed middle-class
norms that violated strongly held values. Second, the supervisor would
drive by in the morning to scan the parking lot for the teachers' cars or
arrive unexpectedly to observe their teaching. The teachers' jobs were
defined by demands of the system, and they also were required to visit
the children's homes and to "rate" them. Their ambivalent relationship
with parents, at least in part, was created by this extension of the monitoring role. Finally, the teachers were responsible for maintaining extensive records: on absences, check-ups, shots, home visits, expert and ancillary personnel, etc. If records were not in order, I was told, they would
not be paid. This multifaceted bureaucratic structure created an atmosphere of vigilance and external control that had a sort of "ripple effect."
This appeared to unite the teachers against those who neither understood
nor participated in the life they shared.

The teachers came to organize the daily life of the classroom in line
with values and attitudes that were congruent with their experience outside of school but also to organize it *in opposition to* constraints that
were placed upon them.[30] Nowhere was this more evident than in their
dealings with the supervisor who came to be treated much as a landlord
or a social worker might be. The supervisor supported the official policy
of the metropolitan Head Start governing agency by advocating "play,"
variety and individual expression. Though she would tell the teachers

what to do, she never worked with them or with the children herself. Both her ideology and her attitude came to be deeply resented. Out of her presence the head teacher, in particular, argued that "play" was "just babysitting." She registered concern that children, after a year in her care, "wouldn't know anything," and she repeatedly interpreted situations in which children had "freedom" or "choice" as situations that were "out of control." In word and deed she defined her job as "getting the children ready to listen to the teacher."

Though the supervisor's power was acknowledged and surface attempts were made to do what she wanted, the plans on paper constructed for her benefit did little to regulate the daily life of the classroom. Over the years I was included in efforts to create a "smoke screen" that gave the appearance of conforming to her authority, while, behind the scenes, the teachers maintained a quite different order. At her arrival, easels would be set up, puzzles set out, and the teachers would sit with the children while they were being observed. At her departure, they would reorganize the classroom as they saw fit.

Like the adults who orchestrated their care, the Head Start children learned to become group members, but they also seemed to adapt to the type of authority structure that governed those who cared for them, and this became another world-taken-for-granted."

CONCLUSIONS

Forms of knowledge exist as alternative construction of reality. Choices can be made about how (or if) a problem is defined and a solution determined.

As shown in Table 2, meta-analysis casts in relief alternative constructions of social knowledge. Focusing as it does on individuals, much of the research in psychology and education can be seen to be overshadowed by a normative bias. Individuals exhibit valued personality, behavioral, and cognitive traits that are depicted either to be dichotomous with "negative" traits or to exist to a greater or lesser degree along a continuum. "Permissive-indulgent" parenting is seen to result in positive outcomes for children, while "authoritarian" parenting is placed at the opposite end of the spectrum.

Anthropologists have been critical of the fact that such work ignores the vastly different *contexts* in which people conduct their lives and work. The primary contribution of cultural studies of child rearing and of child development has been appreciation for the fact that people make collective sense of their life situations. By this rendering, behavior cannot be understood without reference to the meanings that people ascribe to

Table 2 Alternative Constructions of Social Knowledge about Child Rearing Practices

Social Evolutionary: Differing practices differentially rewarded in the broader society	"individualistic" _____ "collective"	
Collective: Differing practices based on different meaning systems—rooted in time and adapted to context	"collective"	"individualistic"
Individual: Differing practices depicted along a continuum	"authoritarian"——————"permissive"	

what they do and without recognizing that beliefs, values, and practices are both rooted in time and adapted to circumstances. Studies of culture demonstrate how different orders characterize the meaning systems of different groups at the collective level, with individual differences apparent within them.

Research indicates that, in the face of racial prejudice and rampant inequality, Afro-Americans, particularly women, have maintained values of equality and collective responsibility that stem from the African heritage. Poor black children appear to be reared to value equality, to have a sense of oneness with others, and to respect their elders.

Finally, from the broader social evolutionary perspective, social groups (frequently depicted by anthropologists as relatively distinct and autonomous, as patterned and integrated wholes) are seen as interlinked within larger, organized sytems. Different ways of thinking and behaving become differentially rewarded in the society at large, and membership in particular racial, ethnic, class, and gender groups has traditionally entailed the ascription of particular roles and statuses within a broader system of relations.

From this vantage point, questions of knowledge use and knowledge control are clarified. Clearly, social knowledge about the child-rearing practices of minority women has not been presented as discrete facts, as so-called "objective" data. Rather it has been guided by the methods that are employed and by the explanations that are assumed. As depicted in Table 3, the interpretive frame itself allows for both "problems" and "solutions" to be defined in particular ways.
"Technical knowledge lodges the problem in individuals and defines solutions through efforts to change "their" behavior. "Practical" knowledge places the problem in schools and in teachers who fail to value differences. Here understanding and valuing are presumed themselves to effect change.

Table 3 Types of Knowledge and the Definition of Problems and Solutions

Types of Knowledge	Nature of "Problem"	Nature of "Solution"
"emancipatory" needs to resolve contradictions between the two in the direction of greater autonomy	Inequality inherent in the systems of relations Specific problems defined by those whose lives are most affected	Problems addressed by raising practical understanding to the level of discourse Increasing awareness of how knowledge is both used and controlled
"practical" concerns with the understanding and of reaching an understanding with others	Problem resides in schools: teachers fail to recognize and support different cultures and cultural styles of learning	Multicultural education "Culturally-responsive education"
"technical" prediction and control of events	Problem resides in individuals	Training programs for adults Supplementary education programs for children

The positions are fundamentally contradictory. Where "technical" knowledge has been used to support change initiatives based on the supposedly "inferior" nature of child rearing practices, "practical" knowledge has been used to celebrate culture in a way that is perhaps overly supportive of the status quo.

Contradictions also exist in the way in which knowledge comes to be constructed and, thereby, in the roles which "scientists" come to play in its construction. People can be "observed" or "understood" through limited participation in their lives; yet, just as there are limitations to observing people from one's own cultural perspective, so there are limitations to participating in their lives in order to understand "them." Although the latter is somewhat more muted, it nonetheless implies a role differential and makes an implicit statement about knowledge and about who it is that has the right or privilege to "know."

Finally, in both conceptualizations, the complex means by which opportunities and resources are allocated to some and denied to others never come under scrutiny. Adults simply have different resources at their disposal, and schools have tended to educate children for different places in the social order. It is the task of critical theory to make apparent the systematic distortions that result from contradictions between these two types of knowledge in the direction of greater autonomy.

By 1992 it has been projected that one in every three workers in the nation will be from a racial minority.[31] With an aging population to support, a "permanent underclass" will no longer be economically viable.

How policies will be affected to meet this challenge — and how knowledge will be used to define and to address it — will become increasingly critical questions.

Public Law 99-457 (which will provide incentives to states to serve children from three to five and discretionary funds for programs for infants and toddlers) may be the first harbinger of things to come. It is an effort to mobilize resources but also, in important ways, to take public responsibility for what traditionally has been of private concern. Decisions that profoundly affect individuals and communities will be made in this broader (political) arena, and the use of control of knowledge will be crucial to the process.

It is as yet unclear how historically disenfranchised groups might organize to understand and effect change in this broader context. Friere and others have seen education as reciprocal exchange in which people with different kinds of knowledge, knowledge of the local situation and knowledge of the broader scene, each combine their partial renderings to provide a fuller account.[32] "Conscientization," according to Friere, is the process by which adults engage in critical analyses of the causes of their powerlessness. Others stress the need for large-scale organization and articulation. In their analysis of the racial state and the "politics of difference," Omi and Winant conclude that the collective subjectivity of minority groups must develop a new principle "that would articulate in a single framework the multiple grievances and the diverse historical experience of the groups involved and the vision this oppositional current would contain in a fundamentally reorganized society."[33]

In complex ways, behaviors and attitudes characteristic of any racial, class, or gender group are rooted in time, instantiated in thought, enacted in interaction with others, and systematized into roles and practices across time and space in the broader system of relations.[34] Conscious social change will require changes at all levels, active efforts to change the world out there, but equally active efforts to change the world structured within, the perceptions that separate us, the assumptions we act upon, the statuses we assign, the roles which we play. Such efforts will require the creative fusing of multiple perspectives and methods and continuing attempts to make the known problematic by moving reflexively to and from contexts large and small.

NOTES

1. The growing number of hybrid fields (social cognition, psychological anthropology, political economices, etc.) bears witness to this concern.

2. Sally Lubeck, *Sandbox Society: Early Education in Black and White America—A Comparative Ethnography* (London: Palmer Press, 1986); and "Kinship and Classrooms: An Ethnographic Perspective on Education as Cultural Transmission," *Sociology of Education* 57, (October 1984), pp. 219–232.

3. One needs to be sensitive to the fallacy of confounding race and class. However, in the year in which this study was undertaken, the average income for black American families was slightly more than half that of white families, and 45% of black children were living in families that were below the poverty line. The study explores two early education settings, one white, one black, settings not uncommon in integrated communities into which blacks have only been allowed to move in recent years. Parents paid to send their children to the preschool; the Head Start program was federally-funded (parents had to qualify on a sliding scale based on income and size of family), and children attended free of charge. Obviously there are social class (and other) differences in child-rearing practices among both whites and blacks. Within-group differences in families and in child-rearing practices among black Americans have been explored by Willie and by Clark. See Charles Willie, *A New Look at Black Families* (Bayside, N.Y.: General Hall, 1981); and *Black and White Families: A Study in Complementarity* (Bayside, N.Y.: General Hall, 1985); and Reginald Clark, *Family Life and School Achievement: Why Poor Black Children Succeed or Fail* (Chicago: University of Chicago Press, 1983).

4. The names of all people and places were changed.

5. Clifford Geertz, *The Interpretation of Cultures* (New York: Basic Books, 1973), p. 10. Geertz writes: "Believing, with Max Weber, that man is an animal suspended in webs of significance he himself has spun, I take culture to be those webs, and the analysis of it therefore not an experimental science in search of law but an interpretive one in search of meaning." (p. 5)

6. For example, A. Harnischfeger, J. Mullan, and D. Wiley, "Early Childhood Socialization and Social Class Environment," *Final Report to the National Institute of Education of the Family Influences on Children's Characteristics Project* (NIE-C-74-0032), 1975. An early review of the literature on "democratic" vs. "authoritarian" child training practices between 1928 and 1957 can be found in Urie Bronfenbrenner, "Socialization and Social Class through Time and Space," in Eleanor Maccoby, ed., *Readings in Social Psychology* New York: Henry Holt, 1958). For a broader perspective, see Robert LeVine, "Cross-cultural Study in Child Psychology," in Paul Mussen, ed., *Carmichael's Manual*

of Child Psychology Vol. 2, 3rd edition, (New York: John Wiley and Sons, 1970).

7. Robert Hess, "Social Class and Ethnic Influences on Socialization." in Mussen, ed., *Carmichael's Manual of Child Psychology* pp. 457–557. For a discussion of the fallacy of attributing the characteristics of black Americans to class alone, see John Ogbu, "Crossing Cultural Boundaries: A Perspective on Minority Education" (Paper presented at the symposium on "Race, Class, Socialization and the Life Cycle, University of Chicago, Chicago, Ill., October, 1983. Revised May 8, 1985).

8. A more recent history of such typologies and discussion of a fourfold scheme (the authoritarian-autocratic pattern, the indulgent-permissive pattern, the authoritarian-reciprocal pattern, and the indifferent-uninvolved pattern), can be found in Eleanor Maccoby and John Martin, "Socialization in the Context of the Family: Parent-Child Interaction" in Paul Mussen, ed., *Handbook of Child Psychology*, Vol. 4, (New York: John Wiley and Sons, 1985), p. 83. For an alternative interpretation, see Diana Baumrind, "An Exploratory Study of Socialization Effects on Black Children: Some Black-White Comparisons," *Child Development* (1972), pp. 261–267.

9. William Ryan, *Blaming the Victim*. (New York: Pantheon Books, 1971).

10. The classic reference is Daniel Moynihan, *The Negro Family: The Case for National Action, Report to the Office of Policy Planning and Reserach of the Department of Labor*, (Washington, D.C., 1965). There is an extensive literature on "cultural deprivation."

11. See, for example, David Weikart and Dolores Lambie, "Preschool Intervention through a Home Teaching Program," in J. Hellmuth, ed., *The Disadvantaged Child* Vol. 2, (Seattle: Special Child Publications, 1967); Merle Karnes, T. Teska, A. Hodgkins, and E. Badger, "Educational Intervention at Home by Mothers of Disadvantaged Infants," *Child Development*, 41 (1970), pp. 295–335; or Phyllis Levenstein, "Cognitive Growth in Preschoolers through Verbal Interaction with Mothers," *American Journal of Orthopsychiatry* 40 (1970), pp. 426–432.

12. Sara Harkness, "The Cultural Context of Child Development," in Super and Sara Harkness, eds., *Anthropological Perspectives on Child Development* (San Francisco: Jossey-Bass, 1980); and Alan Howard and Robert Scott, "The Study of Minority Groups in Complex Societies," in Robert Munroe, Ruth Munroe, and Beatrice Whiting, eds.,

Handbook of Cross-Cultural Human Development (New York: Garland Star Press, 1981), pp. 113–152.

13. Sara Harkness, "The Cultural Context of Child Development," in Super and Sara Harkness, eds., Charles, *Anthropological Perspectives on Child Development* (San Francisco: Jossey-Bass, 1980); and Alan Howard and Robert Scott, "The Study of Minority Groups in Complex Societies," in Robert Munroe, Ruth Munroe, and Beatrice Whiting, eds., *Handbook of Cross-Cultural Human Development* New York: Garland Star Press, 1981), pp. 113–152.

14. John Ogbu, "Black Education: A Cultural-Ecological Perspective," in Harriet McAdoo, ed., *Black Families* (Beverly Hills: Sage, 1981).

15. Robert LeVine, "Properties of Culture: An Ethnographic View," in Richard Schweder and Robert LeVine, eds., *Culture Theory: Essays on Mind, Self, and Emotions* (Cambridge: Cambridge University Press, 1984), p. 68.

16. Roy D'Andrade, "Cultural Meaning Systems," in Richard Schweder and Robert LeVine, eds., *Cultural Theory: Essays on Mind, Self, and Emotions* (Cambridge: Cambridge University Press, 1984), p. 68.

17. See Edward Franklin Frazier, *The Negro Family in the United States* (Chicago: University of Chicago Press, 1939/66); and Melvin Herskovits, *The Myth of the Negro Past* (Boston: Beacon Press, 1958).

18. Wade Nobles, "Africanity: Its Role in Black Families," *Black Scholar* 5 (June 1974), pp. 10–17; and Nina Sudarkasa, "Interpreting the African Heritage in Afro-American Family Organization," in McAdoo, ed., *Black Families*, pp. 37–53.

19. Robert Hill, *The Strengths of Black Families* (New York: Emerson Hall, 1972); and Robert Staples, "The Black Family Revisited: A Review and Preview," *Journal of Social and Behavioral Sciences*, 20 (1974), pp. 60–67.

20. Carol Stack, *All Our Kin: Strategies for Survival in a Black Community* (New York: Harper and Row, 1975).

21. For example, Janice Hale, *Black Children: Their Roots, Culture, and Learning Styles* (Provo, Utah: Brigham Young University Press, 1982).

22. A review of the theory on which "culturally responsive education" is based can be found in Courtney Cazden and Ellen Leggert,

"Culturally Responsive Education: Recommendations for Achieving Lau Remedies II," in Henry Trueba, et al., eds., *Culture and the Bilingual Classroom: Studies in Classroom Ethnography* (Rowley, MA: Newbury House, 1981), pp. 71–86.

23. See Hill, Stack, Nobles.

24. See the discussion that follows.

25. Lubeck, 1985.

26. Jürgen Habermas, *Knowledge and Human Interests* (London: Heinemann, 1971).

27. Eric Bredo and Walter Feinberg, "The Critical Approach to Social and Educational Research," in Eric Bredo and Walter Feinberg, eds., *Knowledge and Values in Social and Educational Research* Philadelphia: Temple University Press, 1982), pp. 272–291. See also Jürgen Habermas, *Communication and the Evolution of Society* trans. Thomas McCarthy (Boston: Beacon Press, 1979).

28. Ibid. p. 273.

29. In opposition to structuralism's excessive determinism, hermeneutic theorists (with ethnomethodologists being the most completely constructivist) proposed a form of radical voluntarism which merely played off the extreme of the other position without providing critical account of how human action can, in fact, be seriously constrained by a lack of resources or opportunity. Elsewhere we see educational ethnographers to be grappling with this issue in various unresolved ways. See Sally Lubeck and Craig Calhoun, "Structuration Theory and the Ethnography of Education," n.d.

30. Paul Willis, *Learning to Labour: How Working Class Kids Get Working Class Jobs* (Westmead: Saxon House, 1977), describes how the student culture is crucial to the reproduction of schooling, but he also succeeds in showing how the students are involved in active organized contestation with the school. Henry Giroux—"Theories of Reproduction and Resistance in the New Sociology of Education: A Critical Analysis," *Harvard Educational Review* 53, 3 (1983)—sees Willis's book as the basis for a new, "resistance theory." Willis contends that the students achieve only "partial penetration" or incomplete understanding of the causes of their oppression and thus rebel in a way that is counter to their interests.

31. Children's Defense Fund, *A Children's Defense Budget: An Analysis of the FY 1987 Federal Budget and Children* (USA CDF, 1986). The Report states that in 1950 there were 17 workers for every retiree; by 1992 there will be three.

32. Paolo Friere, *Pedagogy of the Oppressed* (New York: Herder & Herder, 1970); and *Education for Critical Consciousness* (New York: Seabury Press, 1973).

33. Michael Omi and Howard Winant, "By the Rivers of Babylon: Race in the United States, Part Two," *Socialist Review* 13:6 1983 p. 65.

34. Anthony Giddens, *The Constitution of Society: Outline of the Theory of Structuration* (Berkeley: University of California Press, 1984).

2

Hispanic-American Children's Experiences in Classrooms: A Comparison between Hispanic and Non-Hispanic Children

FLORA IDA ORTIZ

Several arguments have been raised regarding whether schools make a difference or not. The most consistent finding has been that for minorities and low socio-economic children, schools make the most difference. The studies reported by Rutter et al. and the effective schools literature have pointed to several aspects of schools which make for effectiveness.[1] In general, the definition of effectiveness has been that students perform well.

Three fundamental themes are covered in the effectiveness literature which have a bearing on the material presented in this chapter. First, the reserach shows that it is impossible to predict the effectiveness of a school or program on the basis of quantitative measures of the resources or "inputs" provided to it and substantial explanatory power is developed if process, climate, or "ethos" measures are used.[2] This literature demonstrates that schools become more or less effective as a result of the style or *manner* in which programs are executed rather than the quality of the raw materials they are given to work with.

The teacher effectiveness literature provides a second theme. This literature identifies the important characteristics of high-performing teachers. Among the many teaching and classroom behaviors which have been investigated, in general the most profound finding has been that teacher behavior is more strongly affected by immediate student actions than it is by gross demographic characteristics of the student populations.[3]

This third theme concerns the appropriate methods for studying teacher effectiveness. This literature highlights the complexity of teacher work behavior analysis and underscores the importance of methodological care and sophistication.[4]

The present chapter addresses the first theme by focusing on classroom processes and climate in describing the *manner* by which Hispanic and non-Hispanic children are taught. The second theme is addressed by identifying and analyzing teacher-student relationships and how the effectiveness is determined. The third theme is addressed by the manner in which the data upon which this chapter is based were collected. Observational and interview data were collected which focused on classroom processes. The intent is to identify those classroom and teacher variables which elude quantitative studies.

This chapter presents observational and interview data which compare the educational experiences of Hispanic, (usually Mexican-American) and non-Hispanic children (children whose ancestry is other than Hispanic) in two different contexts. One context is classrooms where most of the children are non-Hispanic and are usually engaged in bilingual education programs. These classrooms will be contrasted with classrooms where most of the children are non-Hispanic. The usual program is the traditional elementary grade level program.

The second context is where there are about equal numbers of Hispanic and non-Hispanic children in the classroom, or where a few Hispanic children are present in the classroom, but no official designation regarding their ethnicity is present. The comparison will be between the two groups' experiences in the classroom.

The research question in this study is: What is the quality of the educational experience of elementary children in a variety of classrooms? The associated question is: Does the quality of the educational experience differ for Hispanic and non-Hispanic children?

METHODOLOGY

This chapter is part of a much larger study, spanning six years of classroom observation in several southern California school districts. The larger study's focus is an investigaton of instructional systems for Hispanic children. A sample of ninety-seven elementary classrooms, both bilingual and non-bilingual were observed for periods of time varying from two weeks to three months. Since the original intent was to identify instructional systems, classrooms were first observed in regard to a particular program, unit of study, or special technique. After two years in the field, the researcher identified certain factors affecting instruction which appeared to be present in some classes and not in others. The unit of analysis was, thus, modified to include observation of traditional classes, observation of classrooms with different student composition, and observation of classrooms with different types of school personnel. The number of classrooms observed totaled ninety-seven. Some classrooms were observed continuously and others were returned to as analysis of the data dictated.

Data were collected primarily from three sources: documents, interviews, and observations. The procedure followed in the collection of data was to gain access to classrooms. At the beginning of the study most of the classrooms observed were those identified as bilingual. By the third year of the study, the selection of classrooms included non-bilingual classrooms. Justification for non-bilingual classrooms was to gain comparative data. After permission to observe certain classrooms was obtained, interviews were conducted with the school's principal, classroom teachers, aides and other school personnel, e.g., secretaries. In most cases, three individuals would be contacted per school, if only one classroom was involved. If more than one classroom was involved, the appropriate teacher and aide would be included. In a few instances, secretaries, custodian, truancy officer, bilingual education directors, psychometrist, and parents were interviewed. A total of 231 persons were interviewed. The interviews ranged from fifteen minutes to two hours in duration. Most interviews were forty-five minutes long. Some teachers were interviewed more than once.

Documents were collected. Since initially the focus was instructional systems, lesson plans and curricular material were collected. By instructional systems we mean the composite of programs, curricular offerings, activity sequences, and knowledge and skill areas systematically presented to children as part of their schooling experiences throughout the day, week, grading period, semester, and year. As the study progressed, student personal information became more critical and documents were collected. Other types of written information included the in-service material available to school personnel and descriptors of school and classroom expectations.

Observational data were collected in two different ways. One was intense observation of, e.g., two full consecutive days' observation of classrooms. All activities, interaction patterns, and events would be recorded. Students and teachers from that class would be observed from the moment they arrived on campus until they left. The intent was to obtain a "feel" for their "quality" of experience in the classroom.

The second way observational data were collected was by selecting a particular time period, a particular unit study period, or a particular activity. A few of these observations were filmed. For example, in order to triangulate the data of one teacher's two contrasting styles which appeared to be conditioned by the composition of the class, video-taping was conducted. A total of six classroom time periods were filmed in this way. In all instances these periods were selected as a follow-up of data previously collected.

Because this study spanned six years, it was possible to return to classrooms to verify teacher-classroom observational data. Of course, the students were different, but the classroom teacher, the aide, and the classroom remained constant. A total of fifteen classrooms were visited more than once a year or more later. Five classrooms were visited three times a year or more later.

THEORETICAL FRAMEWORK

The public school elementary classroom is a type of organization in which many students and few adults spend intense, continuous time together, presumably engaged in a limited number of endeavors. It is usually agreed that the children are to engage as students and the adults as teachers or instructors. It is also assumed that children will acquire knowledge, academic and social skills, and will develop attitudes conducive to the maintenance and improvement of our society. Thus, it is usually expected that schools will socialize the children to be good students and persons. The belief has been that the adults will provide a safe, rational, pleasant, and equitable environment for the children. Thus, the overall expectation is that upon visiting public school elementary classrooms one would see all participants engaged in some aspect related to instruction and skill acquisition.

Associated with the above expectations, it has been assumed that resources would be available to these classrooms in order that they be able to function. The literature reports that the most precious resources in the classrooms are of two types: material and personal.[5] The material resources include space, desks, tables, books, equipment, and the like. The personal resources include those aspects more likely under the control of the teacher. They are personal because they are related to how the teacher relates to the students. The first resource is time: How much time does a teacher devote to students? The second resource is interaction: How often and for how long does the teacher interact with students? The third resource is the quality of relationships between teacher and students, adults and students, and students and students. For example, does the teacher raise her/his voice and pitch when addressing a Hispanic child, but not when addressing a white child? Is the directness of the teacher's interaction more likely to be as part of a lesson or a disciplinary measure? The fourth resource is the choice teachers make in the types of lessons they deliver. For example, there are four types of lessons teachers normally engage in: verbal teacher-led, activity, drill, and test.[6] Teachers differed in the degree to which they preferred certain types of lessons and classrooms differed in the degree to which they engaged in certain lessons. The present study looks at whether classrooms differ in the type of lessons delivered according to the composition of students.

Public school elementary classrooms differ in the way the resources are allocated. In pursuing the issue of equity in classrooms the question to be answered is: Are resources, both material and personal, differentially allocated in classrooms according to ethnicity or race? More generally, is this a discriminatory practice which can be linked to the lack of success among Hispanic-American children?

ANALYSIS

Bilingual Classrooms

Hispanic American children are readily identifiable through their Spanish surnames. Once identified, many school districts have been directed to assess this group's proficiency in English. Several types of assessment instruments have been devised. A review of the items on these tests reveals an interesting similarity. They all address the issue of English proficiency by initially asking: Is another language besides English spoken in your home? This critical question is, then, used as the basis on which to decide whether the student belongs in one of several bilingual education programs. The general perception is that children who speak another language at home do not know English. That perception does not seem to change even when the children have been attending school for several years.

Goodrich, for ABT Associates and the National Institute of Education planning program of Bilingual Instructional Features Study in 1980, determined that 80 percent of bilingual education is Spanish/English in four major geographical areas—Southeast, Middle West, West and Southwest, and Northeast. The four other languages they included were: Navajo, French, and Chinese and one of the following Asian languages: Vietnamese, Filipino, or Korean were the proposed programs.[7]

In a 1985 study done by the California State Department of Education, approximately 525,000 students, one out of every eight public school students in California, were limited in their English proficiency. The largest group of these children were Spanish speaking, and most of these were Mexican. It is, then, mostly Mexican-American children who get placed in bilingual classrooms in California.[8]

The schools attended by Mexican-American children tend to be located in run-down, poor, and neglected neighborhoods. Because these schools are held in low esteem by the school district, their needs are not viewed as critical. Principals and teachers placed there tend to be the weaker school personnel of the school district. Additionally, these over-crowded schools are frequently also allocated less-than-adequate physical plant and grounds resources.[9]

Because most of the data for this study were collected during a period when bilingual education programs were federally and state sup-ported, it was expected that classroom and instructional materials and equipment would be plentiful. The data indicate that the bilingual educa-tion programs were supported with those components associated with personnel, such as a director's office and support staff, teacher aides and their training, and in-service training for other teachers and personnel. Some classrooms had equipment and materials such as audio-visual aids: films, records, ear phones, and language charts and easels. Curiously, there was an absence of textbooks, workbooks, teacher manuals for teaching fundamental skills, and technological equipment such as com-puters.

Bilingual education classrooms situated in schools where only a small portion of the students were Hispanic did not differ greatly from the ones described above. One important difference was that the school, in general, was a safe, pleasant one with landscaped grounds, and the school personnel appeared professional and in charge. The bilingual classrooms, however, differed from the rest of the classrooms in the following respects: Commonly portable, they might be distanced from the core of activity of the school. If they were in the same building they might be located far from the administrative offices and public en-trances. Though identical to all other classrooms in terms of size, shape, and general structure, bilingual classrooms differed in the materials and equipment they contained and the maintenance care they received. Books and technological equipment were sparse.

When the teachers were compared, teachers in bilingual classrooms were frequently young, inexperienced teachers who had perhaps chosen to specialize in bilingual education. These teachers arrived at the school with high ideals and expectations. Other teachers had been rejected from regular classrooms due to some incompetence, often classroom manage-ment. Others were Mexican-American or had a Spanish surname and were, thus, assumed to be competent to teach in these classrooms. Many of these teachers were teaching on emergency or special credentials. In general, most bilingual classrooms were staffed by teachers who had not specialized in bilingual education or in teaching children with particular needs. The data for this study show that, in general, bilingual teachers tend to be regarded as low status by the rest of the teachers. Many times when there is more than one bilingual teacher in a school, they may be asked to have their lunch and other breaks at different times from the rest of the staff. One principal explained,

> The other teachers came in here and told me they did not want the bilingual teachers eating with them. They would start speaking in Spanish and, maybe, talking about them and they didn't like that. They asked that I schedule two separate lunch and other breaks. I have and now we don't have a problem.

Thus, we see two distinct patterns of structuring which occur within school districts where Hispanic children are involved. One is that the school distrtict allocates special schools for these children. The other is that a school may allocate a special classroom for these children. In all cases, the differences between the two are apparent. In all cases, the quality is less for Hispanic children.

Three types of consequences occur. The first is with the school personnel and parents. The school personnel's status within the school is determined by the group of students they teach, that is, whether they teach Hispanic or non-Hispanic. The parents, likewise, are directed to take their children to the proper classroom, whether Hispanic or non-Hispanic. For example, one Hispanic neighborhood school has bused gifted children to the school to be taught by the outstanding teachers of the district. Upon close examination, however, it is apparent that the outstanding teachers have no occasion to deal with the other teachers and the gifted children have no occasion to be integrated with the Hispanic children. Thus the parents of the gifted enter the school through one side of the campus while the parents of the Hispanic children enter through another. The two groups have their own distinct areas of classrooms, playground, and activity centers. In this way, interracial intolerance and hostility are deterred, but integration is not likely. In the case of this study, the effect is that there is differential delivery of educational services to the two groups.

Teacher or instructional aides have been included as part of the bilingual programs funded through state and federal resources. Many times, other teachers resent bilingual teachers having aides. In the predominantly Hispanic schools where most of the teachers have aides, the resentment may be imperceptible, whereas in schools where only the bilingual teacher has an aide, the reverse may be true. Other teachers perceiving bilingual teachers as ineffective are insulted by having these teachers provided additional help. The insult is exaggerated when it is believed that in any case, the children are not going to learn. Thus, an area of conflict in schools attended by Hispanic children is teacher aides. Principals are particularly sensitive. One explained,

The rest of the teachers cannot see the logic of providing all of this help to these bilingual children. Why should Mrs. Sanchez have an aide while Mrs. Jones does not, particularly when Mrs. Jones is much better at managing children and planning new programs? Besides, aides are also viewed as a reward for those incompetent teachers.

The second consequence is with the students. Hispanic children are treated differently, are encouraged to stay together and separate from the rest of the students. The location and contrasts in classrooms provide the first context for this difference. The point raised here is that children learn to coexist, but do not feel obligated to interact or cooperate with other groups. Lunch, playground, and open areas display the structure of these parallel groups.

The third consequence is that the instructional program delivered to Hispanic children is remedial. It provides a basis for classifying the school personnel and the students. The classification is negative for both groups.

In conclusion, the data collected for this study show that material resources are differentially allocated to Hispanic and non-Hispanic children. The two major structures are through differing schools and classrooms. The differences tend to be justified on the basis of the types of students who attend. For example, a principal explained why barrio schools are as they are. He said,

Hispanic parents and children don't value education. They have to be coerced into attending. They don't know English and can't learn. They aren't very capable. Neighborhood schools reflect their communities. Dirty communities maintain schools of that sort. Better communities work to improve their schools.

The Quality of Participation in Bilingual Classrooms

Two major types of resources are available in bilingual classrooms. The material resources have been presented in the previous section. The personal resources are those directly controlled by the teacher. In bilingual classrooms, there is normally a teacher aide who fulfills several functions. The competence of aides varies across school districts. Some districts administer tests and other assessment instruments in order to select well-qualified aides; others appoint aides according to the various benefits which may be derived. For example, some aides were initially hired because they were vocal in calling attention to inadequacies in the schools. Being hired by the school district provided a means to reduce community conflict. In any case, the aides differ widely in their attitudes, knowledge, and skills. In all cases, however, they speak both English and

Spanish. Most aides are high school graduates, a few have attended the university, and in a few instances, aides have obtained teaching credentials and become teachers.

Consistent with the variety of competencies, aides are also utilized in different ways. Some aides carry a major burden of instruction, whereas others are primarily engaged in clerical, playground, and other support services.

The presence of aides, however, radically alters the traditional structure of classrooms with one adult and many children. When both the teacher and aide are bilingual, the teacher is likely to be reluctant to relinquish much of the instructional responsibility to the aide. Teachers trained specifically for bilingual classrooms are likely to maintain total control of the instruction in the classroom. This aspect of the classroom may be entirely different in the case of teachers who have been demoted to bilingual classrooms or teachers who are not bilingual. Many of these classrooms show the teacher relinquishing the instructional responsibilities to the aide. This is particularly true if the bilingual classroom contains a group of fluent English speakers. The teacher engages herself/himself with the proficient English-speaking students and relinquishes the non-English-speaking children to the aide. In this case, the aide may teach all of the subjects to these students during the day. Data for this report show that teachers sometimes do not teach these non-English-speaking children for periods as long as a week. The constant interaction for these children is with the aide rather than with the teacher. Thus, we see how the teacher's personal resources of time, attention, interaction, and lessons are denied these children. The consequences affect the students' perceptions regarding each other: they note that some students' teacher is the "Mexican" (aide) whereas the other's is the "real" teacher.

One consequence of teachers assigned to crowded bilingual classrooms is that tardiness and absenteeism generally increase. This is especially true of those classrooms run by teachers who have been transferred to these schools. So, another consequence for these children is that a great portion of their scheduled classes are taught by substitute teachers. In some instances, particularly when the classroom contains a small portion of English-proficient students, and the financial situation of the school district is precarious, the aide may serve as the substitute teacher. In most cases, substitute teachers relinquish the bilingual children to the aide. Hispanic children are denied personal resources, first because the teacher may be absent, second, because the teacher may relinquish her/his responsibilities to the aide, and third, because the teacher's time, attention, interaction, and lessons are turned elsewhere. In sum, the bilingual children in the bilingual classroom receive little teacher support.[10]

There are some bilingual classrooms which differ from the ones presented above; however, it must be recalled that bilingual education is perceived as remedial rather than enriching and most such classrooms consist of students believed to be incapable of learning. To illustrate, if bilingual programs were devised to teach content, we would find bilingual programs in Spanish in bilingual classrooms. There is no evidence of that in these data. Instead, the bilingual programs in and of themselves are of greater value to the administrators of those programs than are the students. For example, a principal described the bilingual program imposed upon her school in this way.

> The bilingual program in this district is primarily for the benefit of the minority administrators. They can be given an opportunity to advance from the classroom. They can be kept in their place and they can feel important by directing others.[11]

The examples of non-remedial bilingual programs are those in which children are taught by language specialists, Spanish teachers, through a regularly scheduled class of Spanish. The class is treated as any other part of the curriculum with children expected to learn Spanish as any other skill. Children from all types of families participate and succeed in learning the major aspects of the language. Most importantly, there is no stigma attached to the program, the school personnel, and the students who are involved in it.

The division of labor between teachers and aides in bilingual classrooms is important to understand. The non-bilingual teacher tends to relinquish the bilingual children to the aide. The aide teaches all the classes in Spanish and some of those in English. Most generally, the aide conducts the drill lessons. Other lessons, such as verbal teacher-led activities, drills, and tests, are differentially allocated. For Hispanic children, all classes in Spanish and activities and drills will be directed by the aide. The teacher assumes the English verbal teacher-led lessons and the testing of the content of those lessons. If the students are perceived to do poorly on tests, they may not be tested very frequently. Standardized tests may be denied this group. The teacher presents all types of lessons to the non-Hispanic students.

Another means of dividing the classroom tasks is to have the Hispanic students receive instruction in Spanish from the aide and then receive instruction in English from the teacher. This differentiation means that these students receive the same content information in two languages but may be denied new information because there is no time. A description of the opening flag salute ceremony will illustrate how this works. The children stand at attention facing the flag. The aide begins the flag salute in Spanish. The children join in. The teacher directs the flag salute in English. The children repeat it. The aide asks the students in Spanish to sing "America." They do. The teacher asks the students in English to sing, "America." The children repeat it. This form of instruction may proceed through several lessons, or the aide may take the bilingual children with her and the day proceeds. In any case, the content in English will either not be presented to the Hispanic children or the previously presented Spanish lesson will be presented in English, but new material may be denied them. The consequence is that the volume of information presented to Hispanic children will never be equal to that presented to others.

This division of labor also affects the management of student discipline. For example, if a student misbehaves, the teacher reprimands the child and the class continues. In the case of the Hispanic child, the student's misbehavior calls for a reprimand from the teacher aide in Spanish, another from the teacher in English, and possibly a mimic from a student in the class. The disruption to the lesson can be substantial, but the child's misbehavior has been highlighted through the use of the aide and teacher in reprimanding.

Another consideration is that bilingual education materials have not been developed to the degree that other materials have. The materials have not been synchronized with the general national testing programs and the sequencing is uneven. Because bilingual programs are generally conceived as remedial, they are designed to provide drill and practice, rather than challenge.

There is another consideration in bilingual classrooms. Students may be "pulled out" of the classroom for extra drill or different lessons. This "pull out" activity functions in several ways. First, students must move from their classroom to another location. Sometimes, if students are going to the library or a central media area, the child is likely to have to go across the campus. It may take as long as five minutes to move from one area to another. Most elementary lessons are twenty to thirty minutes long. Spending ten minutes moving from one area to another is costly for the Hispanic child. School personnel, however, see that period as a relief. Classroom teachers tend to be grateful to have these students leave. The aides or resource teachers view the passage time as relief time, since they will not have to subject the technological equipment to these children, or they will not have to instruct as long. Walking across the campus may become a pleasant experience. The consequence for children is that they are unable to maintain a normal production level.

For example, a teacher turned to the observer just before the bilingual group left the classroom and said,

Ah, it is time for that group to go. Now, I can concentrate with this group in this science lesson. I look forward to this period, because then I can do exciting things with the students who are left.

Another teacher commented when being interviewed:

It is hard to teach these children. You can't imagine the relief when I don't have to focus on drill, frustration, or doom. We can just get to go outside and walk! Walk across the campus!

Traditional Classrooms

Some Hispanic-American children attend school in regular and traditional and usually suburban classrooms. They may be bused from Hispanic neighborhoods, they may live in the suburb, or they may have requested special permission to attend these classrooms because their parents are professional, or their parents do not want their children in bilingual classrooms. Their success in these classrooms is dependent on the degree to which they can "blend in" with the total environment. If they do not appear "Mexican," and if their Spanish surname is not readily recognizable, they may be integrated to a greater degree.[11]

The data collected for this study indicate that the Spanish surname is the initial identifier. Some school personnel anxiously assess the children by asking such questions as, "Do you speak Spanish?" If the child uses an English form of a first name, the teacher may ask, "What is the Spanish form for Nick?" Or, they may ask, "Have you heard from your relatives in Mexico?" Goffman, in *The Presentation of Self in Everyday Life*, refers to this process as an initial attempt for the parties to determine their places.[13] Three major reactions on the part of teachers take place during this introduction of selves. Teachers accept the children and treat them as all others. These teachers seldom probe for information and seldom refer to these children by their ethnicity. This group is very small. The second group of teachers is certain they have dull children with whom to cope for a year. Their expectations are that these children will do poorly and embarrass them. The results with these children are justifiable on the basis of the children's attributes. The third group of teachers realizes that some of these children are quite capable if not better than most of the other students. Resentment of these children's abilities increases as the children do better. The teacher seeks several explanations such as cheating, help from parents, and accidents. Many times children are severely penalized for their performance. The most obvious cases are with bright Hispanic girls. Most teachers belong to these last two groups.[14]

Rist found that teachers determine the group to which students belong within the first week of school. Most importantly, he conlcuded that children were seldom able to depart from the initial placement and be advanced. The data for this study, likewise, indicate that teachers place their students as soon after the school year begins as is possible in one of the three categories just presented. The students are likely to remain in these categories for the remainder of the year.[15]

During the period in which this research was being conducted, many of these teachers attended cultural-awareness workshops and seminars. In most cases, the teachers' reactions to these events were negative. In some cases, teachers responded in attitudinal instruments that they understood children of other ethnic groups. This research never observed anyone assessing the changes in behavior of these teachers after the in-service efforts. The data for this report indicate that teachers' behavior was not modified. In most cases, the in-service events served to provide stronger justification for the continuation of existing practices.

For example, one teacher said,

> Here we go again. To be told that these minority children deserve all these special services and attention. Why don't the students get this in-service? They need to know they are in school. I have been teaching for twenty years and these minorities don't change. The Mexicans don't study; the Asians beat everyone else!

An analysis of the three different attitudinal instruments administered in three school districts to over 1,000 teachers revealed that the responses portrayed teachers who were informed about ethnic groups' characteristics and cultures. Most teachers were also willing to accept differences and adapt to different types of students. Seventy-five percent of the teachers who responded to the above-mentioned attitudinal instruments revealed as high a profile in tolerance and understanding as is possible. Of the remaining 25 percent, 20 percent were above the median ranking. The observer's sample of teachers was drawn out of this larger group. Thirty teachers scoring with the first 75 percent were identified in order to determine the consistency between classroom behaviors and the instrument's profile. Teachers' behaviors were consistent with their prior behavior and not with the profile generated in the instrument. When this was mentioned to principals in interviews, not one principal expressed any interest in the inconsistency. Teachers, on the other hand, openly acknowledged classroom practices and paper responses were quite different. For example, one teacher said, on the way back to the parking lot after completing a questionnaire,

I know what I'm supposed to do in that classroom. But I can't help myself, those kids are dull, dirty and their parents don't care. Why should I? I can't teach them and I know it. I don't like them, and I wish I didn't have to teach so many of them. But this is a job and so I show up and give these kids a pencil to push.

The allocation of material and personal resources is one way to examine the quality of participation of Hispanic and non-Hispanic children. As has been noted the traditional classroom will generally be directed by a competent teacher with certain perceptions regarding Hispanic children. The classroom will contain the fundamental materials and equipment necessary for instructing the children. The critical question is: do teachers allocate material and personal resources differentially to Hispanic and non-Hispanic children?

A comparison of Hispanic children and non-Hispanic children in bilingual classrooms has been presented. The comparisons are not completely parallel because student composition, programatic content, and school personnel differ at the outset. An opportunity to provide parallel comparisons of Hispanic and non-Hispanic children in elementary classrooms is when at the outset both programatic content and school personnel remain constant and the ratio of Hispanic children in the classroom is no more than half of the class.

The Quality of Participation in Traditional Classrooms.

Traditional classrooms differ from bilingual classrooms in some very important respects. First, the teachers tend to be competent. The more suburban the classroom, the better prepared, experienced, and trained is the teacher. Second, the teachers tend to be influential in acquiring the materials and equipment they need. Because of the suburban environment, it is important that the classrooms reflect recent developments and if the principal or the school district is reluctant to provide the necessary materials, teachers may appeal to the parents and ultimately have their requests fulfilled. Bilingual classrooms do not tend to have these kinds of mechanisms in place. The most likely advocates bilingual classrooms have are the bilingual program administrators. However, the data for this study indicate that these administrators' priorities are more closely allied to programatic than student needs.

Third, suburban elementary classrooms are furnished and equipped with textbook series which coincide with the district's testing program. Children are expected to master the material, do well in the tests, and thereby improve the district's image. In this manner, every student has his/her own textbook in the fundamental areas, such as a basic reader, speller, arithmetic text, and workbook. Moreover, teachers have access to the necessary manuals, guides, publishers' aides, and services in order to insure that the sequencing and appropriate content are covered for each level of testing.

Fourth, because of the above characteristics these teachers are able to conduct verbal teacher-led lessons in all of the content areas. One of the most obvious differences between these classrooms and bilingual classrooms is that bilingual classroom children appear to spend most of their time with worksheets, drilling, and filling in blanks. In contrast, the traditional classroom students appear to spend most of their time in verbal teacher-led and activity lessons. Note that both of these types of lessons lend themselves to teacher-student interaction.

Fifth, traditional classroom work norms are more closely allied to high expectations. Every child is expected to do well. If they do not do well, it is attributed to their unwillingness to work rather than to their deficient ability. These classrooms are more likely to reflect high expectations for all participants: teachers, students, and support staff. These expectations lead to pronounced role actualization. Teachers look and act professional. Students reciprocate, parents respond, and the community is pleased and supportive.

Sixth, traditional classrooms do not tend to have aides or other adult participation. Volunteer, special presentations, and periodic adult visitations occur, but the teacher is at all times in command of the classroom. There is no ambiguity about which adult is the teacher. Students are fully informed about who the teacher is and their relationship to her/him.

Many Hispanic children attend school in such classrooms. In some cases, these children receive excellent education and services, and many successful professionals are the products of such classrooms. These children's language is seldom referred to, their ethnicity is of minimal concern, and their integration may be almost total.[16]

Most of the cases, however, differ from those just mentioned. Traditional classroom teachers do not generally appreciate having to accept an Hispanic child. They may at worst view it as a form of punishment from the administrator or at best as an unlucky draw. In all cases, this attitude is based on the perception that Hispanic children just do not possess abilities and capacities for success. This attitude is persistent despite students who do well. Physical ability is more readily acknowledged than intellectual capacity. A few examples of this perception are:

One teacher was explaining how an Hispanic girl had been in her classroom for three months and hardly ever said anything. The researcher asked about the child's work. The teacher pulled out the grade book. Carlota has been getting A's and B's. The researcher said, "She seems to be a good student." The teacher looked over the grades. "Yes," she said, "it is probably a fluke. The next three months will tell."

Mr. Stone had just finished passing out the arithmetic tests. He asked the students to look over their papers and for those who received grades lower than B to plan an extra drill with him. He looked over at Roberto. He called out, "Roberto, don't forget." Roberto looked at his paper and said, "But I have an A-; I did OK." Mr. Stone went back to his grade book. "That could not be," he said. "Are you sure you did not copy? Let me see that paper again." Roberto handed the paper to Mr. Stone. Mr. Stone said, "I'm not satisfied. See me afterwards."

Later that day, Mr. Stone checked over Roberto's work during the past semester. Roberto's grades were A's and B's. In response to the researcher's questions regarding Roberto's consistency in test grades, Mr. Stone explained, "Something is wrong. A kid like Roberto doesn't get A's and B's without something fishy. I will have to check."

Roberto's test work was consistently scored A and B, but his activities and daily exercises were also consistently questioned. Mr. Stone resisted to the end of the year to acknowledge that Roberto was a good student who did well.

An example follows of how the belief that Hispanic children are not able or capable may be nurtured. The teachers were in the lunchroom discussing the introduction of fractions. They were exchanging ideas about how to explain how fractions work and how to demonstrate in several ways how fractions function and appear. One teacher said, "Adding and subtracting aren't much of a problem. Just wait till you have to teach multiplication and division to those three Hispanic students you have. Those kids don't know top from bottom, can't memorize their tables, and they'll just bring down your classroom's score." The rest of the teachers proceeded to give examples about how Hispanic children do not understand English, do not speak English, and as one summarized, "Can't do."

These teachers' perceptions condition the way they conduct their classroom lessons.[17] The most obvious indicants are the way resources are allocated. For example, if the class happens to be short a textbook, a puzzle, a desk, or something else, the child to be left out will be Hispanic. The teacher somehow does not "see" the child and everyone else gets materials. This Hispanic child will, then, share a textbook or whatever with someone else, preferably another Hispanic. The teacher explains that Hispanics are more cooperative than the other students, so it is all right. She says,

> Well, you see, Hispanics are cooperative children. They don't mind sharing things. These other students like to work alone and independently. With Hispanics it is all right to have students work together.

Another way in which the teacher's perceptions become evident is in the avoidance of eye contact, interaction, and physical closeness. One way in which Hispanic children are singled out is by having the teacher forget their names or be unable to pronounce them. Finally, students may be totally forgotten. There is no acknowledgment of their presence. This takes the form of having the child not asked to read aloud when everyone else is taking turns reading out loud. The child may be forgotten when the children are being selected for teams or groups or certain activities. One child declared in class, "Miss Andrews, Diego is always left out. Nobody chose him for a part in the play." Miss Andrews later explained that Diego is very shy and sometimes does not speak good English. That probably leads to his being left out. The data, however, show that Diego was gregarious in the playground and his mother was of Anglo descent. The family spoke English in the home and his father had an office job with an insurance company.

The perceptions teachers hold are more consistently revealed in the actual classroom endeavors. As stated previously, the lessons are often verbal and teacher-led, and organized so that teachers elicit student responses.[18] Various studies suggest that Hispanic children are often ignored.[19] If they are called upon, teachers do not wait as long for their responses as they do for other children's. If the teacher does call on them or provide help in the response, it tends to be in a voice louder and higher in pitch, often with note of irritation or impatience. Teachers in these circumstances do not tolerate stuttering, hesitations, and other verbal expressions. For example, in contrasting Hispanic children in the bilingual classrooms and middle-class Hispanic children the suburban schools, one behavioral difference is that the latter have learned to address and respond to the teacher directly in a clear, concise way and ask that the teacher look at them. Students in the bilingual classrooms may lower their heads, look away, and in some instances giggle. Teachers interpret that as "simple" behavior and their perception of the children is that they are not as able. Students who are bused into the suburban schools with traditional teachers may exhibit similar behaviors which are, then, severely penalized.

The data in the present study also show that Hispanic children behaving in a straightforward way may be perceived as arrogant and smart. Teachers are particularly sensitive to Hispanic girls who exhibit self-confidence and insist on teacher eye contact and person-to-person encounters. For example,

> Naomi went to ask the teacher at her desk how to pronounce a country's name. The child asked, "Miss Daniels, how do you pronounce this word?" Miss Daniels without turning to the book that contained the word or looking at Naomi, but continuing to write at her desk said, "I cannot hear you, Naomi." Naomi moved the book and her head forward and repeated her question in a much louder voice. Miss Daniels lifted her head and said, "I'm not hard of hearing. You do not have to shout. That word is pronounced Newfoundland." The child said, "Thank you, Miss Daniels" and left. Miss Daniels later said, "That Naomi is an arrogant little girl. This Mexican needs to learn to be patient."

Teachers, thus, restrict their interaction with Hispanic children during the verbal teacher-led lessons. The also tend to treat them differently during activity lessons. Two major ways are used to differentiate the Hispanic from non-Hispanic. The first is that if errands need to be run, if there is some task which requires leaving the room or delivering or picking up something, Hispanic children are likely to be frequent candidates. This is sometimes perceived as a reward, but in suburbia it is usually viewed as servant or maid work. Classrooms differ in the degree to which students volunteer to perform errands, but this researcher's data indicate that there has been a severe decrease in the amount of volunteer work in classrooms. Most children are more and more willing to have others run errands and do other things.

The second way in which Hispanic children are differentiated in activity lessons is in the selection of activities available for them. Verbal activities are rarely assigned to them. Stand-up and support activities are readily available to them. Physical activities tend to be relatively available. Activities involving abstractions and calculations such as puzzle works, games, and such, are reluctantly granted. The "cooperative" attribute is used many times to justify placing students in activities they have not chosen, while the rest are granted the activities they prefer. Solo performance and leadership activities are seldom granted to Hispanic children.

Teachers also differentiate between Hispanic and non-Hispanic children in the use of drill lessons. Hispanic children are expected to have more difficulty acquiring the content of lessons. Teachers follow two patterns: they may have for Hispanic children materials and equipment which are much simpler to master or they may have drill material such as worksheets rather than regular materials such as textbooks. Teachers may also allocate additional drill time for Hispanic children whereas other children are given new and/or different materials to work with. The effect is that Hispanic children begin to lag behind the rest of the students. In many cases, students and parents resist these practices. The data show that in many cases parents maintain a constant vigilance that their children engage in the same classroom lessons as all other students. This vigilance is carried out more successfully by professional parents who live in the suburbs because the students themselves speak about their work. Students who are bused in may not receive this support. Nonetheless, the tendency is for teachers to provide drill lessons for Hispanic children and verbal and teacher-led lessons for non-Hispanic children.

Finally, test lessons are also differentially conducted. As was indicated before, Hispanic children are perceived as being unable to perform adequately on tests. Tests, however, are perceived as critical elements in suburban schools. Mastery of content is generally determined by teacher-constructed tests, but the regular curricular guides and programs tend to include tests as well. Most importantly, standardized and, recently, competency tests are also part of this program. If teachers believe their classroom's rating will be jeopardized by the low scores received by Hispanic children, they may not administer tests to them, or more often, they may discount the Hispanic children's performance altogether. If the Hispanic children are in different curricular programs, then it is justifiable to deny the test lesson. The data for this study show that test results of Hispanic children were discounted in averaging classroom scores. Absenteeism, sickness, programmatic differences, and general cultural attributes are used as justifications for the practice.[20]

In those instances where Hispanic children performed above average and superbly, teachers were resistant to readily acknowledge this. Good test performances by Hispanic children, especially girls, remained suspicious to teachers. Monitoring and scrutiny were applied to the test-taking period and review of scoring was conducted in those cases where Hispanic children scored above the 90th percentile. Teachers were also at a loss to explain the results. For example, Mr. Hunt said,

> Herman cannot work this rapidly. He completed all of the mathematics section of this test. This is incredible. We have to go over this part of the test again. Mrs. Day is going to help me.

Mr. Layton advised Mrs. Jones about Sofia while she took the test at the end of the year. She said,

> Remember how Sofia did so well last year. We warned each other we'd check carefully to determine how she could have scored so high. Have you asked someone to help you monitor?

Mrs. Jones said she could not do that because the test was a standardized one and it had to be conducted for her class as for all others, but she promised to "keep an eye on Sofia." A similar incident was reported by the Office of Civil Rights in 1973.[21]

> One Chicano sat toward the back in a corner and volunteered several answers. At one point the teacher did not even acknowledge, much less reinforce, his answer. At another time he volunteered an answer which was perfectly suitable. Yet the teacher stated: 'Yes, but can anyone else put it in different terms?' An Anglo boy who gave the same basic response with very little paraphrasing was smiled at and told, 'Yes, that's it exactly.'[22]

A contrasting means of differentiating Hispanic from non-Hispanic children is to "praise" mediocre or low performance. This is consistent with what Dornbush and his associates found on the West Coast.

> Researchers at Stanford University found that San Francisco high school students with the lowest academic performance [particularly minority students] were most likely to say they were being praised by their teachers. Expressing warmth toward minority students without accompanying the friendliness with challenging academic standards is just as debilitating to students as expressing overt hostility.[23]

The net effect is that Hispanic students are unable to attribute their performance to their efforts.

CONCLUSIONS

This chapter has dealt with the differentiated delivery of educational services to Hispanic and non-Hispanic students in elementary classrooms. The differentiation is programmatic and interpersonal. The differentiation is due in part to the allocation of resources. Material resources provided to Hispanic children are not adequate or equal to those provided to others. Personal resources, or those resources under the control of teachers, are also denied.

The concern over the improvement of education for Hispanics has been based on providing a *different* educational program. Bilingual education programs have been intended to aid this group. This chapter shows how bilingual programs serve to separate Hispanic children from others. They also serve to justify the provision of inadequate material and personal resources. This chapter also displays an important consideration in the delivery of educational services which has been addressed to a certain degree in the school-effectiveness research. The critical point raised here is that educational experiences differ because both material and personal resources are allocated according to the initial design of the educational program. The design has been based on group attributes rather than on educational expectations. Remedial programs, which is how bilingual programs are normally conceived, prove to be inadequate because those resources necessary to the educational intent are absent. An example of program conception on the basis of group attributes is the description of the Master of Arts in Teaching (MAT) program which was presented in *Phi Delta Kappan*, September 1986, as a "program which fell on hard times in the 1970s because its emphasis on the liberal arts and its rather upper-class academic style did not fit the needs of inner-city minorities and urban schools as well as these features served students and schools in more affluent communities."[24] This chapter shows that education and educational experiences cannot be conceptualized as elite or non-elite, remedial or non-remedial. Instead, lessons and teacher-student interaction (the business of schooling) consist of very specific components which by their application determine the quality of the students' educational experiences. The challenge is thus presented that the schools' effectiveness with Hispanic children may be determined by the way material and personal resources are allocated. Hispanic children are not receiving the same material and personal resources as others and this discrepancy can be readily identified by the collection of classroom data which defines material and personal resources in specific terms. Ethnographic research thus provides a means to attend to the issues related to school effectiveness with Hispanic children.

NOTES

1. M. Rutter et al., *Fifteen Thousand Hours: Secondary Schools and Their Effects on Children* (Cambridge: Harvard University, 1979).

2. J. S. Coleman, *Equality of Educational Opportunity* (Washington, D.C.: U.S. Office of Education, 1966); and H. A. Averch, "Federal Role in Science Education: What's Inside NSF's Proposed Budget?" *Science Teacher* 43 (1975), pp. 40–43; and S. C. Purkey and M. S. Smith, "Too Soon to Cheer? Synthesis of Research on Effective Schools," *Educational Leadership* 40 (1982), pp. 64–69; and W. B. Brookover et al., "Elementary School Social Climate and School Achievements," *American Educational Research Journal* 15 (1978), pp. 301–318; and R. R. Edmonds, "Programs of School Improvement: An Overview," *Educational Leadership* 40 (1982), pp. 4–11; and L. R. Smith and E. M. Edmonds,"Teacher Vagueness and Pupil Participation in Mathematics

Learning," *Journal of Research in Mathematics Education* 9 (1978), pp. 228–232; and G. F. Madaus et al., "Sensitivity of Measures of School Effectiveness," *Harvard Educational Review* 49 (1979), pp. 207–230; and T. L. Good, "Classroom Research: A Decade of Progress," *Educational Psychology* 18 (1983), pp. 127–144; and D. E. Mitchell, F. I. Ortiz, and T. K. Mitchell, *Work Orientations and Job Performance: The Cultural Basis of Teaching Rewards and Incentives* (Technical Report, Washington, D. C.: U.S. Department of Education, NIE, 1983).

3. L. L. Baird, "Teaching Styles: An Exploratory Study of Dimensions and Effects," *Journal of Educational Psychology* 64 (1973), pp. 15–21; and N. A. Flanders, "Note on the Use of Flanders Interaction Analysis," *Journal of Educational Research* 58 (1965), pp. 222–224; and Ned A. Flanders, *Analyzing Teaching Behavior* (Reading: Addison-Wesley, 1970); and Good, "Classroom Research"; and A. C. Ornstein, "What Are We Teaching in the 1980's?" *Young Child* 38 (1982), pp. 12–17; and L. S. Shulman and E. Sykes, *Handbook of Teaching and Policy* (New York: Longman, 1983); and R. J. Shavelson, "Review of Research on Teachers' Pedagogical Judgments, Plans and Decisions," *Elementary School Journal* 83 (1983), pp. 392–413; and W. J. Tikunoff, D. C. Berliner and R. C. Rist, *Special Study A: An Ethnographic Study of the Forty Classrooms of the Beginning Teacher Evaluation Study Known Sample* (San Francisco: Far West Laboratory for Educational Research Development, 1975); and J. Brophy and C. Evertson, *Learning from Teaching: A Developmental Perspective* (Boston: Allyn & Bacon, 1976); and B. Rosenshine and N. Furst, "The Use of Direct Observation to Study Teaching," in *Second Handbook of Research on Teaching* (New York: Rand McNally, 1973); and G. Natriello and S. M. Dornbusch, "Bringing Behavior Back In: The Effects of Student Characteristics and Behavior on the Classroom Behavior of Teachers," *American Educational Research Journal* 20 (1983), pp. 29–43.

4. A. Simon and E. G. Boyer, eds., *Mirrors for Behavior: An Anthology of Classroom Observation Instruments*, Vol. 1–6 (Philadelphia: Humanizing Learning Program, Research for Better Schools, Inc., 1967; and Ibid., vols. 7–15, 1970; and S. Bennett, "Teaching Styles and Pupil Progress," *Times Educational Supplement*, 3178 (1976), pp. 19–20; and T. L. Good, B. J. Biddle and S. E. Brophy, *Teachers Make A Difference* (New York: Holt, Rinehart and Winston, 1975, Chapter 4; and C. M. Hook and B. V. Rosenshine, "Accuracy of Teacher Reports of their Classroom Behavior," *Review of Educational Research* 49 (1979); pp. 1–12.

5. Rutter et al., *Fifteen Thousand Hours.*

6. Mitchell, Ortiz, and Mitchell, *Work Orientations.*

7. R. L. Goodrich, ABT Associates, *Bilingual Instructional Features Planning Study*, Vol. 4 (Washington, D.C.: ABT Associates for NIE, 1980).

8. California State Department of Education, *California Schools . . . Moving Up Annual Report* (Sacramento, California: State Department of Education, 1985).

9. F.I. Ortiz, *Career Patterns in Education: Women, Men and Minorities in Public School Administration* (New York: Praeger, 1982); and E. M. Bridges, *The Incompetent Teacher: The Challenge and the Response* (London: The Falmer Press, 1986).

10. L. Steinberg, P. L. Blinde, and K. S. Chan, "Dropping Out Among Language Minority Youth," *Review of Educational Research* 54 (Spring 1984), pp. 113-132; and Bridges, *The Incompetent Teacher.*

11. Ortiz, *Career Patterns.*

12. J. D. Finn, "Expectation and Educational Environment," *Review of Educational Research* 42, 3 (Summer 1972), pp. 387-410.

13. E. Goffman, *The Presentation of Self in Everyday Life* (New York: Doubleday, 1959).

14. Finn, "Expectations"; and R. C. Rist, "Student Social Class and Teacher Expectations: The Self-Fulfilling Prophecy in Ghetto Education," *Harvard Educational Review* 40, 3 (August 1970), pp. 411-451.

15. Ibid.

16. P. Gandara, "Passing Through the Eye of the Needle: High Achieving Chicanas," *Hispanic Journal of Behavioral Sciences* 4, 2 (1982), pp. 160-167.

17. J. E. Brophy and T. L. Good, "Teachers' Communication of Differential Expectations for Children's Classroom Performance," *Journal of Educational Psychology* 61, 5 (October 1970), pp. 365-374; and J. D. Dusek, "Do Teachers Bias Children's Learning?" *Review of Educational Research* 45, 4 (Fall 1975), pp. 661-684; and T. L. Good, "Teacher Expectations and Student Perceptions: A Decade of Research," *Educational Leadership* 38, 5 (February 1986), pp. 415-422.

18. H. Mehan *Learning Lessons* (Cambridge: Harvard University Press, 1979).

19. J. Martin, L. M. Anderson, and D. J. Veldman, "Within Class Relationship Between Student Achievement and Teacher Behaviors," *American Educational Research Journal* 17, 4 (Winter 1980), pp. 479-490; and Tikunoff et al., *Special Study*; and T. L. Good, "Which

Pupils Do Teachers Call On?" *The Elementary School Journal* 70, 4 (January 1970), pp. 190–198.

20. Good, "Teacher Expectations"; and Rutter et al., *Fifteen Thousand Hours.*

21. U. S. Department of Education, Office for Civil Rights, *1980 Summaries of Elementary and Secondary Civil Rights Survey*, unpublished data (Washington, D.C.: Office for Civil Rights, 1982).

22. Ibid; U.S. Office of Civil Rights, *Mexican American Education Study: Report 5, Teachers and Students*, (Washington, D.C.: Report of U.S. Commission on Civil Rights, 1973) p. D-5.

23. S. Dornbusch, G. Massey and M. Scott, *Racism Without Racists: Institutional Racism in Urban Schools* (Stanford: Stanford University Publications, 1975).

24. F. Keppel, "A Field Guide to the Land of Teachers," *Phi Delta Kappan* 68, 1 (1986), pp. 18–23.

3

Gender Identity and the Technology of Office Education

LINDA VALLI

> Right now, I'm not thinking on the job, and that's
> the important thing. Otherwise you turn into a
> vegetable.
>
> — a COOP student

Granting academic credit for work experience is an established practice throughout the United States. Two variations generally can be found. One bears a course title like "Work Study" and is available mostly to students behind in credits needed for graduation. The other, regarded by educators as more legitimate and integral to vocational preparation, is called cooperative education. These programs claim to give job training in areas of students' career choice. Prerequisite courses are required.

As a business education teacher described it:

> In work study the kid just gets a job—any kind—not at all career related. They pump gas. Nothing jobs. There's little learning, no correlation to school, and no supervision. Maybe during the year the counselor will contact the employer one time and nine times out of ten the student isn't even there anymore. It's terrible. A sham.

By contrast, cooperative education programs are designed to give students in-school and on-the-job instruction through "a series of plan-

87

ned, meaningful" experiences matched with career objectives and regularly evaluated. Academic credt is given for both school and work components; students are also paid for their work experience.

This paper examines one cooperative education program in the business department of a comprehensive high school. Its specific focus is the technology of office education; what the program conveys as the knowledge and skills needed to do clerical jobs. A basic assumption is that these messages, like all school knowledge, are major regulators of experience which evoke certain kinds of identity.[1] In this sense, schools can be referred to as people-processing as well as knowledge-processing institutions. They tell students things about themselves as well as about the world of office work; they construct subjectivity as well as abstract knowledge.[2] By learning about the technical relations in production, about the machines, skills, technology, and scientific knowledge used in producing goods and services, the students learn not only about the nature of office work, but about themselves as office workers. Since office education students are almost always young women, and since office work is an expanding labor market sector with thirty-five percent of all working women currently employed in that sector, experiences in office education programs have profound gender identity implications.[3]

The site of this study was Woodrow High, a predominantly white, working-class, comprehensive senior high school in Macomb. This midwest city had a progressive political tradition: a major university, the state government, a food processing plant, and insurance companies were major employers. Though the social class division was not absolute, the south side of town had one other working-class high school besides Woodrow while the two middle-class high schools were on the north side.

Woodrow's Cooperative Office Occupation Program (commonly referred to as COOP), or general education courses, as well as the work related office education course, were taken in the morning. I spent one academic year with a cohort of sixteen students in their classes and on the job, observing their experiences and interviewing them, their teachers and supervisors, and a representative group of COOP graduates. Because my research approach was mostly one of non-participant observer, I was able to take extensive field notes during observation periods. Formal interviews were immediately typed and analyzed, curriculum materials and COOP documents collected and analyzed. Brief visits to gather comparative data were made to the Cooperative Office Education Programs in the city's other three schools.[4]

This case study approach opens up what is now commonly referred to as "the black box" of schooling, making possible a view of the in-use and socially constructed nature of the curriculum. As McNeil has argued, most school studies take assumptions like "schools exist to convey information" for granted.[5] They mistake the formal goals, content, and instructional materials of a course for the way school knowledge is actually created and distributed to students. A case study can avoid that problem by examining how the form and content of the curriculum-in-use and the social relations of the classroom (and in this case the work-place) produce particular types of learning environments which convey implicit and often profound messages.

As other ethnographic work has revealed, neither the in-use-curriculum nor the social construction of teacher and student roles is primarily a function of teacher personality.[6] My analysis led to the same conclusion. Observations of Mrs. Lewis, the COOP teacher, in her other classes revealed marked differences from her COOP teaching, which, from alumnae accounts, was consistent over the years. The type of learning environments Mrs. Lewis offered students was not the product of her personality, but the result of such intra- and inter-institutional factors as school work norms, departmental relations, course sequences, teacher isolation, notions about working-class students, relations with area employers, and the nature and availability of office jobs.[4] This strongly suggests that the COOP experience described here was not peculiar to this setting.

According to the official state handook, an advantage of COOP was providing *two* learning environments—"in school and on the job"—which enabled students to assess and develop interests and abilities, understand employment opportunities, and make intelligent life choices. While all students participated in the same COOP learning environment in school (they were all required to take the office education course), their work environments varied. Students were employed in four distinct office occupations: file clerk, typist, clerk typist, and account or credit clerk. These occupational categories proved to be primary determinants of the workplace learning environment.

I will argue that important dimensions of the in-school and on-the-job instruction severely restricted learning opportunities for many students. These restrictions often caused COOP to resemble the work-study positions disparaged by vocational educators, heightened work dissatisfaction, and marginalized the young women's "career" orientations. Ironically, although COOP's explicit goal was to reproduce the clerical work force, it actually helped reproduce another generation of women who identified more with unpaid domestic labor.

IN-SCHOOL INSTRUCTION

An analysis of fieldnotes kept specifically on the COOP class generated ten categories germane to the overall learning environment: teacher planning, class activities, curriculum orientation, type of learning materials, deadlines, homework, monitoring, feedback, perception of students, and teacher role. Further analysis indicated that the most important aspects of the curriculum-in-use could be described under the two areas of course content and use of class time.

Course Content

The formal content of the COOP class comprised units on checkbook reconciliation, typing, letter styles, proofreading, dictaphones, payroll, income tax, vocabulary, grammar, and communications. Most topics were given two to five weeks of class time. Other activities which took place during class time were planning an appreciation banquet for work supervisors, organizing a fund-raising candy sale for the banquet, inventorying the room's equipment, reading and summarizing office-related magazine articles, and doing typing and mailing for various clubs and organizations. The candy sale occupied a part of each class throughout November and banquet preparations took much of April and May.

Students, however, rarely knew from day-to-day what they would be doing in class. They were not given a syllabus, nor was a plan of study discussed with the group.[8] Students would ask one another, "What are we going to do today?" "Do you know what we're going to do next?" Content uncertainty was particularly prevalent in intervals between pre-packaged units when, without prior notice, students were given seemingly-random worksheets to do. March 10th fieldnotes contain the comment, "There's a definite feeling of lack of planning. What happens, happens."

Curriculum units in COOP focused on technical knowledge: learning how to do the work of a payroll clerk, how to balance a checkbook, how to pay income tax. With the exception of the magazine articles discussion, the official curriculum concentrated on the development of specific skills. While some of these articles dealt with work issues like "office troublemakers," the secretarial shortage, and sexual harassment, others stressed technical aspects: office layout, furnishings, etc. The two units on income tax and checkbook reconciliation, which occupied approximately two months of class time, did not directly relate to office occupations. They had a personal rather than an occupational orientation, covering basic living skills, not occupational skills.[9]

The technical knowledge conveyed in the curriculum was found in authoritative sources. Logic systems behind them were seldom explained so students could neither become independent of the external source nor determine whether their own knowledge was faulty. During an exercise on "Words Frequently Confused" neither the students nor the teacher knew some of the answers. This twenty-five sentence exercise sheet asked students to choose one of two works which completed the sentence. The words for each sentence were homonyms or words that sounded similar, (e.g. This writing is 'eligible' or 'illegible'). Because Mrs. Lewis had no answer key and had not done the exercise in advance, answers sometimes had to be found in the dictionary or sentences skipped. In response to one student's answer she said, "All right, I'll take your word for it." Students were similarly left to transform wordy passages during a proof-reading unit without input on how these passages could be identified and changed.

Many of the units were self-instructional, pre-packaged materials which contained the necessary information for motivated students with the right background knowledge to complete them. Unmotivated or confused students could also complete the work by getting answers from others. On the payroll test, for instance, most questions asked for information directly from the exercises. If a student had correctly copied all the information onto her exercise sheets, she could pass the test with no trouble. If the student did not finish the exercises or forgot to bring her materials to class, she could not answer the questions.

Use of Class Time

Classes at Woodrow generally ran fifty-five minutes, but the principal had agreed to a forty minute COOP class so students, particularly those dependent on public transportation, could eat lunch before leaving for work. This provision was necessary for only a small fraction of the class, however, since many of the students had or shared cars, skipped lunch, or started work later than the originally scheduled time.

Since self-instructional units provide students with directions and information, functions normally attributed to teachers, Mrs. Lewis seldom had to engage in whole-group instruction.[10] Rather than being in the front of the room, she could often be found in her back office on the telephone, talking to other teachers or students, or doing paperwork. In fact, a notable characteristic of the classroom was Mrs. Lewis's absence.

A pattern of student absence quickly followed. If students did not miss class entirely, they often came late, left early, wandered in and out, or were mentally elsewhere. Because no syllabus, deadlines, or home-work patterns were established, students could easily slow down the work pace in the course. Mrs. Lewis's absence from the classroom encouraged this pattern. As one student said toward the end of the year:

> I didn't learn as much as I wanted to in school. I thought school would have been a lot harder. I thought I'd learn more, especially in COOP class. I mean we hardly do anything in there. Like today. We just came in and she let us go. That's why a lot of kids don't come.

Patterns of student time use can be seen in this compilation of field-note observations.

> only five of the students are doing the assigned work. . . . only three of them had their work ready to turn in. . . . Cindy comes late every day . . . . few are working today. . . . Terri (who works steadily) is on Exercise 11, most others haven't finished Exercise 6 yet. . . . class was dismissed again today. . . . between December 1st and January 21 little class activity occurred. . . . Kris, Nancy, Doris, Josie, and Carolyn are talking about their favorite bar again.

Days when most students worked on assignments were so rare they generally warranted fieldnote comment. On one such day Mrs. Lewis dismissed them early because of an overlapping obligation.

Well into the second semester Mrs. Lewis gave the students an overnight assignment for the next day to be ready to answer questions at the end of a chapter. However, as they were leaving, she responded to those going to a pep rally that they could leave their reading material behind. When students arrived for class the next day without the questions answered, Patti asked if they "couldn't just have class time to do it." That had been, and continued to be, the dominant instructional mode. The only other time I observed Mrs. Lewis give homework, she dismissed class the following day and never again referred to the assignment.

Because Mrs. Lewis did not monitor assignments she had little control over work pace and little opportunity to assess and assist comprehension. Student bewilderment was evident to someone observing their "helping relations" from the back of the room and hearing their "I don't understand" remarks. It was also evident to Mrs. Lewis when students turned in incomplete or inaccurate assignments after several days or weeks of work. This was generally the only time instructional feedback was given. On the last day of the fall semester, for example, when students were turning in proofreading assignments which had required substantial typing, Mrs. Lewis gave them pointers about spacing, tabulating, spelling, and initializing, mechanics she had not pointed out in advance. Nor did she notice that students were doing them incorrectly during the month-long unit.

This curriculum pattern of providing students with unmonitored activities rather than with information to increase knowledge and skills meant that students spent most of their class time in ways which had little to do with learning. COOP students socialized, tried to find a pattern to follow from a previous exercise though they did not understand its logic, copied answers from the answer book, relied on previous knowledge, or asked each other for answers. When Josie, perhaps the weakest grammar student in the class, complained, "I don't feel like doing all these sheets,"

Mary Jo offered, "Here, just copy mine." This procedure had been implicitly sanctioned by Mrs. Lewis. While checking a punctuation exercise with the whole class, Mrs. Lewis had responded to a student's comment, "I didn't know a comma belonged there" with "Well, just look it up in the book."

COOP class time was spent moving through an exercise, not being engaged in an instructional event. The exercise was done in class; once completed there was no purpose in students staying. Brief, whole group, direct instruction was given at the start of a unit followed by individual work on activities and check-in at the end. Mrs. Lewis's role was primarily one of giving students activities to do. These were more like *work* activities than *learning* activities, since students lacking prerequisite knowledge could do little to be successful. If they already had the knowledge, they would learn little from the activity. As Maureen said about the proofreading unit, "It's just doing the same thing over and over. It's not helping me get better at it." If students did not already have the knowledge to reproduce in their written work, the only way they could accomplish the task was by copying the answer from another student or from the answer book, which was readily available.[11]

Messages about Office Work and Workers

What did the COOP class teach the students about office work and office workers? The fundamental message seemed to be that legitimate work knowledge is technical, with the range of the "how to" restricted to equipment and material processing. Office work knowledge excluded social relations, only peripherally referring to bosses, co-workers, or clients. When students voiced complaints about supervisors and managers, they were promptly redirected to technical matters. Issues of safety, worker rights, pay, unions, the personal and social impact of technology, etc. were apparently beyond the scope of the curriculum.

An elaboration of this basic message was that the technology of office work is simple, reducible to the few easy tasks of typing, filing, bookkeeping, editing, and proofreading. This message was created by the formal course content containing non-office work material (balancing checkbooks and filing personal income tax) and by the non-rigorous use of time. If class is dismissed, teacher and students absent, late, or not engaged in instructional activities, the message is that there is little work knowledge to learn and few skills to acquire.

The message created about the students' identities as office workers is based on this image of technical skill. Students were implicitly told that they already had the technical skills necessary to perform entry-level office jobs. The fact that class time was not used to further skill development meant one of two things: either office jobs did not require more skill or the students were incapable of acquiring it. In either case, further office education was irrelevant for them. Office work was a natural, unchangeable reality to which they had to adapt, using the technical knowlege they had so far acquired.

ON-THE-JOB INSTRUCTION

The second site of learning for COOP students was on-the-job training. As will be seen in the descriptions of work sites as learning environments, students placed in jobs as file clerks and typists received messages remarkably congruent with their in-school instruction: that work knowledge is limited to simple technical matters. Once this knowledge is obtained, time is spent unvaryingly repeating its use.

The four clerical categories in which students found employment were not official designations but classifications derived from ethnographic observation and data gathering. On their mid-term and final examinations, students were asked to describe what work they performed on a daily, weekly, or monthly basis. Observations of students on the job verified and expanded their accounts. When summarized as ten basic production functions and organized into occupational categories, as in Table 1, the range of technical work knowledge the jobs provided can be ascertained.

As Kusterer argues "jobs vary in the range of potential learning situations that they present to the job holder." This variation is determined to a great extent by the degree to which a job is specialized and routinized. Specialization refers to "the number of producton functions assigned to the job; routinization to "the degree of variation in the performance of each function."[12]

As seen in Table 1, the jobs of file clerks and typists were far more specialized than those of clerk typists or account/credit clerks. The range of skill typists and file clerks could develop was restricted by the nature of their jobs. Their work schedules involved only three or four production functions whereas the work schedules of clerk typists included ten production functions and those of account/credit clerks nine. Students employed in one of the latter two categories had a more varied work schedule and greater opportunity to gain work knowledge.[13]

Degree of job routinization is an even more salient indicator of learning possibilities than specialization. Because certain production functions are less routinized than others, a person could be employed in a job which required more knowledge and skill even though the job comprised fewer production functions *if* those functions were less routine.[14] If, for example, the only task credit clerks performed was handling credit data, their jobs would require higher levels of skill than most clerk typists

Table 1 Number of Students Who Used the Various Production
Functions According to Occupational Categories

	File Clerk	Typists	Clerk Typists	Account Credit Clerks
Filing/sorting/ alphabetizing	4	1	8	3
Typing	2	2	8	1
Photocopying/collating	1	2	7	1
Stuffing/mailing		1	8	3
Answering phones/ taking & delivering messages			6	3
Record keeping			3	1
Handling credit/ account data			1	2
Greeting people/ making appointments			4	1
Giving directions/ running errands			6	
Using word processor			3	2
N =	4	2	8	3

whose jobs consisted of more, but more routine, functions. Because job specialization and routinization are independently varying dimensions, four occupational classifications are possible. Relative to one another, COOP jobs fell into three of them. (See Figure 1).

Figure 1 Office Occupations Classified along Dimensions
Routinization and Specialization

	Specialized	Non-Specialized
Routine	file clerks typists	clerk typists
	1	2
	3	4
Non-Routine	account/credit clerks	

File clerks and typists are in area 1, representing the most routine/specialized jobs. These are office jobs from which the least can be learned, with opportunities for file clerks less than those for typists. Area 2, which characterizes clerk typists, represents routine but relatively non-specialized jobs. In area 3 are the account clerks and credit clerks. Their jobs are specialized but non-routine. No COOP student was placed in an area 4 job (e.g. secretary) which potentially would have offered the most learning opportunity. The day-to-day work activities in these three different categories indicate the variation in the students' opportunities to learn.

File Clerks are responsible for maintaining company documents: they sort and file correspondence, records, and other data.[15] Although classification is officially within their job description, file clerks seldom determine the way a system is organized. More often their time is spent creating, coding, copying, distributing, purging, updating, and retrieving files. None of these sub-divisions of filing, however, was viewed by the students as a reprieve from the daily grind. Filing was tedious, time-consuming, and often backbreaking work because of the bending and lifting involved.

All the COOP students spent significant amounts of time filing; some were file clerks the entire year. Typical work days for those students involved typing name/number tabs for claimants; coding files by affixing self-adhering color labels to folders; sorting by color, name, number, or date; photographing documents for microfiche; pulling files for another department; searching for lost or misfiled folders; and removing old or outdated information from individual folders. At one COOP site, filing involved bending over rows of waist-high metal tubs where microfiche were numerically stored. Rotation around the tubs was the primary source of variety built into the labor process.

So even though file clerks do more than sort and file (their work has ten or eleven "sub-functions"), the task from which they would learn the most, classification, is generally outside their purview. Their remaining tasks are routine in nature, with variation being either trivial (being rotated to a different set of files) or a source of frustration (trying to locate a document improperly filed).

File clerks' dissatisfaction and unofficial designation as the "bottom of the office social scale"[16] was reflected in student remarks:

> I'm still purging files. . . . .I sometimes get sick of it, but it's usually not too bad. I don't have to concentrate on what I'm doing. It's pretty automatic. But I would like something to do that required more concentration. . . . .I would like it better if it were harder.
>
> I don't care if they paid me $10.00 an hour. I would not sit and file all day. I'd go nuts! When I told you I was running off those papers, I thought I was going to cry I got so bored.

Typists are machine operators who transfer rough copy into printed form by means of a typewriter. For those who work with correspondence and reports, comprehension and communication skills are of great importance. None of the COOP students, however, were responsible for those tasks. They spent their days instead doing highly standardized, straight-copy typing of insurance forms, transferring information onto the appropriate form. Sometimes the information was in a form which closely approximated the final typed version; other times it was buried in more extensive information and had to be searched for.

But even the most minimal, standardized typing such as transferring a name and address onto a pre-printed form was a richer learning environment than filing. Although it entailed fewer production functions, each function contained a greater degree of variation. The mere process of typing (coordinating materials and machinery to transcribe numeric and alphabetic symbols) includes more variables than all the sub-functions of filing. This higher level of skill is recognized in the practice of schools offering several semesters of typing but not filing, and in employers advertising for typists who can produce so many words a minute.

Clerk Typist is an amorphous category for which the specific combination of tasks is largely dependent on the organization's size and number of clerical employees. Production functions can include filing; compiling and typing documents; operating duplicating equipment; sorting, delivering, stamping, and addressing mail; operating a switchboard; computing accounts; running errands; and receiving clients. Although COOP students who were clerk typists performed a much broader range of production functions than the file clerks or typists, most of the tasks were no less routine, taking only a few hours or days to learn.

Many of the functions did, however, involve use of equipment or personal interactions not encountered in the other two categories. These elements called upon additional skill and judgment if the clerk typists were to satisfactorily accomplish their work. Good receptionists, for instance, needed both human relations and organizational skills since their work was constantly interrupted. Operating a switchboard demanded good communication skills, speaking and note-taking, and knowledge of the multi-line equipment. Mail handling required the ability to differentiate business, personal, and junk mail; distribution decisions (since mail is often not addressed to a particular person); and the successful operation of cumbersome stamping machines.

Account/Credit Clerks are technically two distinct categories. They are combined here because they are both specialized, non-routine jobs which primarily deal with monetary symbols. Account clerks perform routine calculating, posting, and typing duties related to accounting procedures. Their typical responsibilities include recording such business transactions as allotments, disbursements, payroll deductions, pay and expense vouchers, checks and claims; totalling accounts; computing and recording interest, refunds, charges, and rentals; and collecting data from sales slips, invoices, check stubs and inventory records.

Since the work of the account/credit clerks is woven into the multiple operations of a given office, their production functions, particularly in small firms, are often indistinguishable from those of clerk typists. The primary difference is that they spend far less time typing and photocopying and far more time processing accounts. What this quantitative difference does not reveal, however, is the qualitatively less-routine nature of the account/credit functions these workers performed.

The two COOP students employed as credit authorizers worked mostly on account approvals. This seemingly routine job was actually the most difficult of the COOP jobs, having the most sub-functions and the most variables. Mrs. Lewis attested to this by sending only her brightest students to interview for these positions. The difficulty of the position also became apparent when Evelyn, an academically high-ranking student, told her supervisor she could not handle it and might have to quit. Four factors contributed to the job's complexity: the variety of forms; the various types of equipment (phones, computer terminals, and printers); the speed at which messages came in, requiring the ability to work quickly and handle multiple calls at once; and the numerous codes and computer formats which had to be memorized.

Work Messages and Restricted Learning Environments

Coupled with the in-use-curriculum of the related class, these on-job experiences constituted one-tenth of the academic credits students needed for graduation. Yet students with jobs as file clerks and typists fulfilled those credits in environments which placed extreme limitations on learning opportunities. According to Mrs. Lewis's own description, these jobs more closely resembled the "nothing jobs" of work study than the "career-related" jobs supposedly intrinsic to cooperative education.

Students employed as file clerks and typists basically learned only a limited range of routine processing procedures: how to use a particular organization's file system (they already knew alphabetic and numeric filing); how to transcribe onto various forms, etc. Those employed as clerk typists and account/credit clerks not only dealt with a broader range of routine procedures, but also had to learn more variable material properties, machine aspects, and client behaviors.[17] Typists and file clerks regularly worked with the same materials and machinery. By contrast, clerk typists and account/credit clerks greeted clients; made appointments; contacted sales personnel; used switchboards; spreadsheets, adding and stamping machines, computer print-outs, complex printers and computer terminals, etc.

The messages conveyed to students in area 1 jobs (typing and filing) were consistent with those of the COOP class: office work requires minimal skills, those skills are basically processing material and operating machinery, little school knowledge is needed to do the work, and learning does not happen on the job. For these students, work becomes the unvarying repetition of fragmented production functions.

In contrast, the more complex jobs of clerk typist and account/credit clerks conveyed messages which contradicted those from school. Students employed in these job categories realized that they did not have the necessary skills, that there was more to learn. On occasion work experience led these students to believe they were incapable of mastering the job requirements. But with time and supervisory assistance this message was transformed into one stressing the challenge of learning new things: "You never come to the end of learning. It's fun to know you know the machines like the back of your hand and yet there's always more to learn." A message to COOP students in these jobs was about the power knowledge gave them. They could confront and be victorious over complex office technologies. These victories were a source of deep satisfaction and self-affirmation.

Obviously then, the more schools prepare students for and place them in routine and specialized jobs, the more their learning opportunities are blocked. As one perceptive alumna commented about COOP placements:

> If a girl gets the opportunity to learn the different things the department does, that's great. If she doesn't, I don't see how it can help her in terms of experience. Anyone can file or copy. I hope there aren't any girls who do just that. I hope they're given opportunity at their work. I definitely think everyone has the ability to do more than file or copy. And if that's all they do, what about the ones who don't stay full time? Their work on that job hasn't benefited them at all. One COOP student I knew just handled microfiche all day. She wrote down what was past due and how long and that's all. How can that help her?

But placing students in the more routine and specialized file clerk and typing jobs was not a random process or a matter of simply matching student qualifications with job requirements. It was, in part, a function of the clerical job market. As has been documented in much of the labor market literature,[18] traditional white-collar skills have become increasingly redundant under conditions of advanced capitalism. This process of deskilling, which occurs most often in large bureaucracies, is the result of management attempts to increase efficiency, control workers, and lower the cost of labor, conditions which are pursued by fragmenting and routinizing the labor process. Braverman has argued that offices needed only to become sufficiently large to make the rationalization of the labor process worthwhile for management.[19] This proletarianization theory was born out in Macomb, where routine and specialized jobs were most prevalent in large state government offices and insurance companies.

LEARNING, WORK DISSATISFACTION, AND GENDER

From a young worker's perspective, learning is one of the most important aspects of a job. When the COOP students and alumnae were asked what aspects of their jobs were most satisfying, a challenging workplace with a lot of variety (along with good pay) emerged as the most important characteristic. Boring, repetitive work was the most dissatisfying work experience. As is evident in Table 11, these experiences were highly correlated with job type.[20]

Table 2 Number of Students and Graduates Who Expressed Job Satisfaction or Dissatisfaction by Job Type

	Satisfaction	Dissatisfaction
File Clerk	1	7
Typist	1	4
Clerk Typist	8	
Account Clerk	7	

When workplaces provided learning, COOP students extolled their experience:

> My evaluation of my supervisor is very high. She is always there to explain anything to me. Almost everything that I do is new to me, so she helps out a lot. . . . She helped me learn so many things that I never knew before.

When learning environments were absent, student disappointment and frustration were evident:

> The hour in school seemed wasted. We didn't discuss problems at work and what we were doing. That's what I thought it would be like, saying what problems we had at work and discussing what we could do about them. . . . There were problems I would have brought up in class. . . . There were times when I was getting too much shit work.

This experience of having the work day filled with "shit work," work which was boring and routine, from which little learning could be derived, had the effect of marginalizing the young women's wage-labor identities.

The young COOP workers seemed to quickly grasp the reality that, as Evelyn's supervisor so cogently stated, "The longer you stay at a place, the more it owns you." COOP students placed in area 1 jobs (file clerks and typists) were particularly dissatisfied and eager to limit their time in those jobs, which were more difficult than clerk typist and account/credit clerk jobs to humanize, to infuse with a sense of meaning and purpose.[21] These students quickly began to disengage themselves from the work environment in attempts to prevent the market economy from controlling their gender identities.

Nancy is a case in point. Regarded by the COOP teacher as capable and attractive, she was sent to interview and subsequently was hired by one of the town's most sought after employers. Upon graduation, Nancy was offered a full-time file clerk position, about which she later commented, "I always felt like I was going to fall asleep. . . .it was the same stuff over and over." She promptly rejected this offer in favor of continued part-time employment. A glamorous young woman, Nancy preferred to seek out a second part-time position at a local shopping mall where she would be more visible and more central to the source of fashion distribution. This choice of a second job site was not random; it was deeply embedded in cultural notions of social places appropriate for women and by the ideology of "the glamorous woman" perpetuated even in the COOP program, where students were encouraged to model themselves after fashion magazines in preparing for job interviews and to highlight their bodily image rather than their work knowledge.[22]

COOP students dissatisfied with the minimal challenge of office jobs did not, like middle-class young women, decide to pursue higher education. Even though many of them were clearly capable of college success, their working-class backgrounds exerted a strong influence on their life plans. Instead of college they projected part-time or temporary futures in beauty shops, travel agencies, nursery schools, and shopping malls. Nor did they, like working-class boys, have culturally-defined monetary reasons for staying in dissatisfying work environments.[23]

Part-time work, temporary work, and changing work places are strategies women use, not only to manage family responsibilities, the explanation most often found in the literature, but to prevent the workplace from exerting excessive control as well.[24] These strategies do offer young working women more control over their time and expand the physical space in which they develop their subjectivities. The long-term trade off, however, is the self-distancing from the market economy which eventually forces dependence on someone, generally a husband, who earns a family wage.[25]

Since this distancing is in part a function of job proletarianization, simple exhortations for the school to provide better placements, or for young women to be more career oriented will do little to change their tendency to distance themselves from wage labor. As studies of the transformation of office work have indicated, electronic work cubicles, worker isolation, machine monitoring, and pacing are pervasive trends.[26] Nonetheless, by conveying the impression that all office jobs can be performed with minimal entry-level skill, that this is all working-class women can expect from wage labor, and that these job characteristics are natural and immutable rather than socially constructed and contestable arrangements, COOP increases the probability that these students will adopt strategies which will reproduce their subordination and dependency.

Obviously, initial work experience is not the only factor which marginalizes women's wage-labor identity. The ideology of domesticity and the culture of romance remain powerful forces in predisposing women to become unpaid domestic workers, as does the prevalent expectation that women, not men, do housework, and child-care. Office education and initial work experience could, however, offset some of this tendency if they were not so technically oriented, minimal, and dissatisfying; if they provided young women with a learning environment in which they could experience meaning and power.[27]

NOTES

1. See Basil Bernstein, "On the Classification and Framing of Educational Knowledge," *Class, Codes and Control*, Vol. 3, 2nd edition (London: Routledge and Kegan Paul, 1977). The COOP program also conveyed messages about the social relations in production. In *Becoming Clerical Workers* (London: Routledge and Kegan Paul, 1986) I analyze what COOP taught about exchange relations, authority relations, and gender relations in the workplace. Obviously, these messages also have implications for the formation of gender identity. Because of space limitations, I am not able to deal with those here. See Linda Valli, *Becoming Clerical Workers* (London: Routledge and Kegan Paul, 1986).

2. See Michael W. Apple, *Ideology and Curriculum* (London: Routledge and Kegan Paul, 1979).

3. *Race Against Time: Automation of the Office*, Report by Working Women, (Cleveland: National Association of Office Workers, 1980).

4. For a more extensive discussion of the research methodology see *Becoming Clerical Workers*.

5. Linda M. McNeil, "Defensive Teaching and Classroom Control," in Apple and Weis, eds., *Ideology and Practice in Schooling* (Philadelphia: Temple University Press, 1983), pp. 114–142.

6. See Steven T. Bossert, "Classroom Structure and Teacher Authority," *Education and Urban Society* 11, 2 (November 1978); Linda McNeil, "Defensive Teaching and Classroom Control"; and Reba Page, "Lower-Track Classes at a College-Preparatory High School: A Caricature of Educational Encounters," in G. Spindler, ed., *Interpretive Ethnography at Home and Abroad* (New York: Lawrence Erlbaum and Associates, in press).

7. For more analysis of these factors and a discussion of the study's generalizability see Valli, *Becoming Clerical Workers.*

8. This was in stark contrast to Macomb's two middle-class schools where syllabi, assignments, and deadlines were mimeographed and distributed to students.

9. While living skills might be perfectly appropriate high school curriculum content, its inclusion in the office-related capstone class is of analytic interest.

10. Not all prepackaged materials are self-instructional. In-depth analysis of different uses and effects of prepackaged materials can be found in Michael W. Apple, *Education and Power* (London: Routledge and Kegan Paul, 1982) and Andrew Gitlin, "School Structure and Teachers' Work," in Apple and Weis, eds., *Ideology and Practice in Schooling*, pp. 193–212.

11. Borko et al. refer to this mode of instruction as a teaching, as contrasted with a learning, paradigm. See Hilda Borko, Margaret Eisenhart, Martha Kello, and Nancy Vandett, "Teachers as Decision Makers versus Technicians," *Changing Perspectives on Research in Reading, Language Processing and Instruction* (Rochester, N. Y.: 33rd Yearbook of the National Reading Conference, 1984).

12. Ken C. Kusterer, *Know How on the Job: The Important Working Knowledge of 'Unskilled' Workers* (Boulder: Westview Press, 1978).

13. Studies with larger samples confirm these findings. See Michael Crozier, *The World of the Office Worker* trans. David Landau (Chicago: The University of Chicago Press, 1965); David Lockwood, *The Blackcoated Worker: A Study in Class Consciousness* (London: George Allen & Unwin, 1958); and Fiona McNally, *Women for Hire: A Study of the Female Office Worker* (London: Macmillan, 1979).

14. The term production function is quite vague since virtually any function can be further subdivided. See Karl Marx, *Capital: A Critique of Political Economy*, Vol. 1, ed. Frederick Engels, trans. Samuel Moore and Edward Avening (New York: International Publishers, 1967) pp. 342–343. I am using a broad definition of the term, making it synonymous with the common-sense notion of work task. As an example of the extent to which office jobs can be subdivided, some organizations now have positions where the sole function is proofreading.

15. See the *Dictionary of Occupational Titles*, p. 158.

16. Crozier, *The World of the Office Worker*, p. 80

17. This is based on Kusterer's five categories of work knowledge. See *Know-How on the Job*, pp. 138–145.

18. For proletarization analyses of labor process changes see Harry Braverman, *Labor and Monopoly Capital: The Degradation of Work in the Twentieth Century* (New York: Monthly Review Press, 1974); Michael Burawoy, "Toward a Marxist Theory of the Labor Process: Braverman and Beyond," *Politics and Society* 8, 4 (1978), pp. 247–312; Evelyn Nakano and Roslyn L. Feldberg, "Proletarianizing Clerical Work: Technology and Organizational Control in the Office," in A. Zimbalist, ed., *Case Studies on the Labor Process* (New York: Monthly Review Press, 1979), pp. 51–72.

19. Braverman, *Labor and Monopoly Capital*.

20. Studies using large samples of workers reveal similar perspectives. Interesting work and the opportunity to use one's mind rank high in desirable work criteria, while being underutilized is a source of serious job dissatisfaction. See Henry Levin, *Education and Work* (Stanford: Institute for Research on Educational Finance and Governance, 1982); McNally, *Women for Hire*; and *Work in America. Report of a Special Task Force to the Secretary of Health, Education and Welfare.* (Cambridge, MA: MIT Press, 1973).

21. Because these higher level jobs had more variation and more client contact, students could more easily overcome alienating properties of wage labor by taking pride in their learning and special contributions, and by experiencing work as service to others. File clerk and typist jobs did not provide these opportunities.

22. See Linda Valli, "Becoming Clerical Workers: Business Education and the Culture of Femininity," in Apple and Weis, eds., *Ideology and Practice in Schooling*, pp. 213–234.

23. Lillian Breslow Rubin's *Worlds of Pain* (New York: Basic Books, 1976) provides a thoughtful contrast of working- and middle-class girls' relation to college. For an illuminating analysis of the way shop floor culture and the wage packet create "manhood" and how this contrasts with the construction of women's identities, see Paul Willis, "Shop Floor Culture, Masculinity and the Wage Form" in J. Clarke, C. Critcher, and R. Johnson, eds., *Working-Class Culture: Studies in History and Theory* (New York: St. Martin's Press, 1979).

24. McNally, *Women for Hire.*

25. Michele Barrett and Mary McIntosh, *The Anti-social Family* (London: Verso, 1982).

26. See, for example, Evelyn Nakano Glenn and Roslyn L. Feldberg, "Proletarianizing Clerical Work: Technology and Orgnaizational Control in the Office," in Andrew Zimbalist, ed., *Case Studies on the Labor Process* (New York: Monthly Review Press, 1979), pp. 51–72; Peter Perl, "Monitoring by Computers Sparks Employee Concerns," *Washington Post* (September 2, 1984); and *Race Against Time: Automation of the Office.* Report by Working Women (Cleveland: National Association of Office Workers, 1980).

27. For more specific recommendations for office education see *Becoming Clerical Workers*, Ch. 11.

4

Tracking in Mathematics and Science Education: A Structural Contribution to Unequal Schooling

National statistics on academic achievement, high school completion, acquisition of college degrees, occupational status, and income all reveal substantial inequities in the accomplishments and representation of racial and ethnic minorities, and the poor. That these discrepancies are most extreme in science and mathematics attainments has been eloquently detailed in several recent reports.[1]

While it is tempting to lay blame for low achievement and participation in mathematics and science on the disadvantages that poor and many minority students bring with them from home, their school experiences contribute to these disappointing outcomes as well. Schools often respond to race and class in ways that exacerbate the difficulties of minorities and the poor. Assessments of students' ability and their assignment to ability groups and curriculum tracks is one of the most obvious examples of this nexus of student characteristics and school experiences. Judgments about academic ability often lead to the placement of

*Jeannie Oakes is a social scientist at The RAND Corporation. This paper draws on experience in a Rand project funded by the National Science Foundation, "Monitoring National Progress in Mathematics, Science, and Technology Education" and on work conducted under the auspices of the Laboratory in School and Community Education, University of California, Los Angeles. The views expressed in this paper do not necessarily reflect those of the NSF, the RAND Corporation, or UCLA.

students in separate elementary and middle school classes and to enrollment in different senior high school courses. These placements, in turn, mediate students' opportunities to learn science and mathematics. This paper explores the proposition that the limited success of minorities and the poor in mathematics and science is linked to these school tracking practices.

DISPARITIES IN SCHOOL ATTAINMENT

Note these current trends:

1. Blacks and Hispanics consistently perform below the levels of whites on measures of end-of-high-school achievement in mathematics and science. Poor children do less well than their more affluent peers. Not only is the overall pattern of differences disturbing, even more distressing is that the greatest continuing disparities are found on measures of higher-level skills and problem solving.[2]

2. Minority low achievement in mathematics and science is undoubtedly more profound than test scores imply, considering the disproportionate number of poor, black, and Hispanic dropouts not represented in measures of high school achievement. High School and Beyond (HSB) data reveal higher sophomore-to-senior dropout rates for blacks and Hispanics than for whites — 16.8, 18.7 and 12.2 percent, respectively — and 22.3, 13.2, 10.7, and 7.0 percent from the lowest to highest socioeconomic (SES) quartiles.[3] Even these statistics underestimate the differences since many minority youth leave school before the sophomore year. Census data from 1982, for example, show high school dropout rates for twenty- to twenty-four-year-olds as 23 percent for blacks, 40 percent for Hispanics, as compared to 15 percent for whites.[4] These differences in dropout rates undoubtedly exacerbate the achievement differences reflected in test scores, since those students leaving school before graduation are typically among the lowest achievers.

3. Black and Hispanic high school graduates are less likely than whites to enter college. Further, those who do enroll are more likely than whites to attend two- rather than four-year colleges. A pattern of disproportionate school attainment is reflected at every juncture in post-secondary education. Ever-widening gaps exist in the percentages of blacks, Hispanics, and whites completing four-year college programs, and entering and completing graduate school.[5]

4. Blacks and Hispanics are underrepresented as college majors in science, mathematics, and engineering and as recipients of bachelor's, master's, and doctoral degrees in these fields. These groups of students decreasingly choose quantitative fields of study as they

travel through the educational pipeline and are decreasingly represented at succeedingly advanced levels. Between 1981 and 1984, blacks, who represent approximately 12 percent of the population, received for smaller percentages of science- and mathematics-related doctoral degrees—1.2 percent in physics and astronomy; 1.3 in chemistry; 1.21 in mathematics; 1.2 in computer sciences; 1.4 in engineering; and 1.4 in biological sciences. Hispanics, about 6.5 percent of the population, showed similar underrepresentation— 1.2 percent in physics and astronomy; 1.7 in chemistry; 1.5 in mathematics; 0.5 in computer sciences; 0.9 in engineering; and 1.3 in biological sciences.[6]

5. Non-Asian minorities, as a consequence of all of the above, are significantly underrepresented in science-, mathematics-, and technology-related careers. In 1984, for example, blacks, Hispanics, and American Indians (20 percent of the total population) constituted less than 7 percent of this sector of the workforce.[7]

Trends in adult attainments in scientific and technical fields (in college study and occupational choice) reflect equally disturbing trends in elementary and secondary school enrollment and attainment. Patterns of lower achievement and underparticipation for minorities and poor children begin early in the educational process. And perhaps most troublesome is that discrepancies among groups grow larger the longer children remain in school.

Race and socioeconomic differences in mathematics and science *achievement*, for example, are evidenced at age nine, are clearly in place by age thirteen, and continue to increase during senior high school.[8] Race and class discrepancies in science and mathematics *participation* appear in junior and senior high school.[9] Minority and poor high school students typically take fewer courses in science and mathematics, and their achievement scores are often quite low in these subjects.[10] Thus, the striking differences in college enrollments, choice of fields for study, and adult participation in the math, science, and technology workforce appear to have their roots in precollegiate education.[11]

Of course, evidence of unequal participation and outcomes is, in itself, insufficient to establish schooling inequities as their cause. However, the existence of these discrepancies *does* document that schools have been considerably less successful with *some groups* of students than with others. Moreover, such substantially unequal participation and achievement among groups and the significant increases in outcome discrepancies over time in school provide noteworthy signals that schooling factors may contribute to them. A critical look at the actual experiences of poor and minority students—both in and out of school—suggests how the schooling may itself help create these disparities.

INFLUENCES BEYOND SCHOOL

Socioeconomic Influences

It is easiest, of course, to attribute differences in school and adult attainments solely to the influence of negative out-of-school factors on poor and minority students. Students' socioeconomic status is, of course the most obvious and frequently noted consideration. Recent analyses of High School and Beyond data, for example, show that with other school and home factors controlled (including race and ethnicity), students' socioeconomic status (defined by education levels of parents, father's occupation, family income and household possessions) accounted for a substantial amount of the difference in students' mathematics achievement.[12] Parallel findings emerge from the SAT.[13]

Data on Asian-American students illuminates this rather clearly. Asian-American students are often considered a puzzling anomaly among racial and ethnic minorities. They have the highest rate of educational participation and achievement in quantitative fields of any of the racial and ethnic subgroups of American students (including whites) and are significantly overrepresented in mathematics-, science-, and technology-related careers.[14] Coupling race/ethnicity data with SES statistics, however, begins to explain *part* (although not all) of the differences between Asian and other minorities. The high levels of achievement and participation for Asian-American students are paralleled by distinct advantages in their home backgrounds. Asian-American students in the HSB sample participated most in out-of-school educational activities (music lessons, travel, museum experiences), and were most likely to own microcomputers. Only whites equaled Asians in the educational resources their families owned — books, newspapers, calculators, etc. Other minority groups lagged far behind on all these measures of home advantages. Asian achievement and involvement become less mysterious in light of these data.[15]

Family income is probably less important in itself than for its clear connection to the level of education students' parents attained; and parent education is an important predictor of minorities' school success.[16] This relationship can be found, for example, in minority students' participation in mathematics and science. Unlike first generation college students, minority college freshmen whose parents were college educated choose quantitative majors with about the same frequency as whites.[17] Closely connected to levels of parent education are parents' expectations and aspirations for their children and the amount of encouragement they provide.[18]

Much of the educational difference between minorities and whites disappears when family income and parent education are controlled.

Nevertheless, even though SES is central to the typically poorer performance of minorities, it does not *fully* explain it. Some evidence of differences in science and mathematics achievement between minority and white senior high students remains, even with SES, school experiences, and prior achievement controlled.[19]

Attitudes and Self-Perceptions

A few seemingly-plausible attitude, motivation, and self-perception factors have been investigated as reasons for these "unexplained" influences of race and class. Speculation about the relevance of these factors arises from work suggesting that individuals pursue areas that they value and in which they expect success. Among the hypothesized factors for minorities' lower achievement and participation in quantitative fields are race-linked differences in the following: liking for math and science; relative interest in "people" and "things" generally;[20] perceived utility of science and mathematics; stereotyping of these subjects as the purview of white males.[21] Few of these factors have been researched extensively, however, and results about most are as yet inconclusive.[22]

We do know, however, that attitude and interest differences accrue in a social context. For minorities and the poor that context may promote attitudes and self-perceptions that lead away from school participation and achievement. Important evidence exists that, as minorities have gained greater access to education, their overall economic and social position has improved substantially.[23] But historically, even well-educated minorities have been unable to market their achievements in the workplace of returns equal to whites. For example, minorities (including high-achieving Asian-Americans) have been unable to translate school attainments into commensurate employment or salary rates.[24] These social and economic realities are likely to affect race, class, and gender differences in parent aspirations, attitudes, and self-perceptions. Anticipation of employment discrimination may play a significant role in shaping these "negative" attitudes.[25] The perceived utility of mathematics and science, and the stereotyping of these subjects as the purview of white males, for example, flow logically from these social conditions. Thus, background factors and societal conditions are likely to interact and interfere with minorities' achievement and participation.

The disadvantages that poor and minority children bring to school with them are obvious and cannot be dismissed. Economic, social, and attitudinal differences among minorities and the poor undoubtedly play a significant role in race and class differences in measured school aptitude, achievement, and participation. But viewing race and class characteristics as the *cause* of these differences often obviates the need to examine schooling characteristics for sources of inequalities. More likely, family and attitudinal influences on the achievement and participation of the poor and minorities *interact* with what students experience at school. While theory and research evidence about this interaction are sketchy, at best, it is in this interaction that educational effects are most directly produced and where the school's contributions to inequality are found.

SCHOOLING MAKES A DIFFERENCE

Consider these typical paths to end-of-high-school achievement and adult attainments:

1. Achievement and interest in mathematics and science in elementary school affects ability-group placement in junior high or middle school, particularly in mathematics.[26] Often students exhibiting high levels of interest, prior achievement, and/or ability are placed in middle school or junior high school classes that prepare for (and often begin) high school course content. Indeed, many junior highs offer pre-algebra, algebra, and, a few, geometry for high-achieving students.[27] Students exhibiting little interest and/or low levels of achievement are often assigned to remedial, review, or practically-oriented math and science classes.

2. End-of-junior-high or middle school achievement influences high school course enrollments. High-achieving students enroll in college-preparatory or academic programs that require them to take both a greater number of courses in mathematics and science and more sequentially-ordered courses. These courses typically cover advanced concepts and processes. Lower-achieving students enroll in vocational or general curricula that typically require fewer math and science courses.[28] Moreover, non-academic courses in these subjects are most often non-sequential, low-level, or remedial.[29]

3. Upon completion of often-minimal high school graduation requirements, student enrollment in science and mathematics courses is dependent upon their interests, attitudes, and prior achievement.[30] Teacher and counselor encouragement (usually based on these characteristics) may also influence students' decisions to persist.

4. High school course completion—both the number and level of mathematics and science courses—exerts the strongest influence on students' end-of-high-school achievement, and preparation for college.[31]

5. For non-college-bound students, high school course completion and achievement influence their adult level of scientific and mathematics literacy.

6. For college-bound students, end-of-high-school mathematics achievement is the strongest influence on choice of major. Mathematics preparation may be particularly critical since admission to many science and quantitative fields requires readiness for college-level calculus.[32] And, finally, the choice of college major leads directly to attainment of degrees in quantitative fields and participation in mathematics-, science-, and technology-related careers.

While these patterns may appear obvious, they hold the keys to successful schooling. In particular, three seemingly-interrelated factors appear to be critical to high levels of accomplishment: 1) access to math and science instruction; 2) early achievement in math and science which, in turn, leads to further instructional opportunities; and 3) the development of attitudes such as confidence, interest and willingness to study mathematics and science. Moreover, high expectations and encouragement from parents and school adults and contacts with academically-oriented peers at school appear to be important influences on these factors. That poor and minority students may follow patterns that distance them from these critical factors is explored in the following section.

RACE, CLASS, AND ABILITY INTERACT TO LIMIT ACCESS

Growing evidence indicates that school judgments of students' intellectual abilities play a major role in differential allocation of learning opportunities to students.[33] In elementary and middle schools, students who appear to be slow to "catch on" are often placed in "slow" classes or remedial programs; students who learn more easily, to high-ability classes. This practice appears to lead to lower levels of achievement for students who are not in the "top" classes.[34] At the senior high level, judgments about students' ability influence decisions about curriculum track enrollment — whether students take college preparatory, general, or vocational courses of study. Curriculum track enrollment, in turn, is a critical factor in both course-taking and achievement,[35] and in the quality of the curriculum content, instructional practices, and classroom learning opportunities.

Diverging Curriculum Paths

Assessments of mathematics and science ability and placements in different classes appear to be particularly relevant to the educational experiences of poor and minority students. In elementary and middle schools these students are most likely to have initial difficulties and be placed in the low-ability and remedial classes or in special education programs.[36] Whites and upper-SES elementary students are more likely to be identified as able learners (and more often as "gifted and talented") and placed in enriched or accelerated programs.[37] Thus, the first signs of black and Hispanic students' divergence from successful curriculum paths appears early in elementary school. These differences are paralleled by differences on standardized achievement tests; by age nine minority students score substantially lower than whites in both mathematics and science.[38]

The paths of many poor and minority children continue to veer off-course in junior high school. As a consequence of their poorer elementary school performance, these students are often placed in remedial programs as they begin their secondary education. During these middle school years they have little access to the topics and skills that would prepare them for academic sequences in senior high mathematics. Neither do non-Asian minorities (and most probably the poor as well) close the mathematics-achievement gap with whites, even in those low-level topics and skills that have been the focus of their remedial instruction.[39] This pattern appears in science as well since junior high schools often differentiate science curriculum for high- and low-achievers, frequently basing these grouping decisions on students' mathematics achievement.[40] Again, non-Asian minorities and the poor are more likely than others to be placed in low-achieving groups.

These patterns continue into senior high school with blacks, Hispanics, and poor students enrolling more frequently in vocational and general (non-academic), whites and high SES students more frequently in academic curriculum tracks[41] and high-ability classes.[42] These curriculum differences lead to quite different course-taking in mathematics and science, as the following data from High School and Beyond make clear.

Variations in Course Taking

Largely as a result of these differences in curricular paths, science, mathematics, and computer science course-taking patterns vary considerably by race and class. As Table 1 shows, substantially lower percentages of poor and non-Asian minorities complete academic courses of study in mathematics and science (either concentrating or completing four-year college-entrance requirements in these subjects). Differences were also substantial in computer science course-taking.

The largest differences in course-taking appear among students who differ in their socioeconomic backgrounds. These differences are somewhat larger than are differences among students from various racial groups. For example, the largest gaps are between high- and low-SES students' completion of academic preparation in mathematics and science, with the high-SES group completing these course sequences at almost three times the rate of the low. Racial differences are substantial as well, however, with whites completing academic preparation at a rate only slightly less than twice that of blacks and Hispanics. Of course, these two categories — SES and race — cannot really be considered separately. Undoubtedly, many, although not all, of these low-SES students were also black and Hispanic. Similarly there is probably considerable overlap between the high-SES and white categories. Regretably, few data sets have included sample sizes adequate to examine patterns among students within SES or racial groups (e.g., to contrast the course-taking of high-, average-, and low-SES black students).

These High School and Beyond data parallel findings about differential course participation from the NAEP. NAEP data indicate that in 1980 only 15 percent of black and Hispanic students had completed trigonometry as compared with 27 percent for whites and 50 percent for Asians.[44]

For minorities, the influence of these lower levels of participation on achievement is clear. Analyses of NAEP data have found that the differences in number of high school courses taken by black and white students accounts for a considerable part of the differences between black and white seventeen-year-olds' mean achievement scores.[45] But the number of courses taken is not likely to be sufficient to explain the full impact of course-taking. Minority-white differences are also found in the level of courses taken.[46] As we have seen, blacks and Hispanics are (with lower achievement at high school entrance) disproportionately found in low-level high school mathematics and science courses, white in advanced.[47] The level as well as the number taken is an important factor in subsequent achievement and postsecondary participation in mathematics and science.[48]

Table 1 Students Exhibiting Academic Course–Taking Patterns by SES and Race
(Percentages of Students Exhibiting Pattern)

	High SES	Middle SES	Low SES	White	Black	Hispanic
Academic Math	69.1	45.7	25.1	51.5	28.1	28.9
Academic Science	58.3	36.9	19.6	40.7	26.1	23.8
Computer Science	17.4	12.4	8.4	13.8	10.5	8.0

Source: National Center for Educational Statistics[43]

Findings that course-taking is critical to the performance of minorities should come as no surprise, since, as noted above, for all students course-taking is the most powerful school-related predictor of achievement, particularly in mathematics.[49] Understanding precollegiate course-taking patterns is clearly a key to unlocking fundamental discrepancies in race and class differences in science and mathematics attainments. The evidence we have suggests that blacks and Hispanics fall behind in achievement early in their school careers. Thus they are less likely to have *access* to learning experiences that might prepare them for more advanced course-taking in high school.

Different Course Offerings

Obviously, the courses available to high school students will also limit what they actually take. Minorities are likely to attend schools with more limited offerings in mathematics and science. Advanced courses in mathematics and science are less likely to be taught at predominantly poor and/or minority schools.[50] These findings parallel NAEP data that show course-taking patterns vary among schools with the ethnic make-up of their student population. At schools with substantial black populations the average number of mathematics courses taken is lower than at schools with substantial white populations.[51] These patterns of course offerings and course-taking are undoubtedly influenced by the lower levels of achievement typically found at these schools.[52] The result, however, is that even those poor and minority students who *do* achieve in mathematics and science may attend schools where advanced courses are simply not offered.

Clearly course offerings and course-taking patterns represent a critical interaction of student background characteristics (race, class, and ability as assessed by schools), school performance, and schooling opportunities. How these factors come together in poor and minority schools serves to restrict the chances these students have to learn science and mathematics.

Conventionally, these class and track placements, the course offerings at poor and minority high schools, and the subsequent differences in learning experiences are explained as appropriate, given quite apparent differences in students' ability to learn. However, growing evidence suggests that these differences may in part be artifacts of schooling experiences. The typical ways elementary schools respond to students' performance may help to "fix" students' perceptions of their ability to learn and, over time, may actually exaggerate initial differences among them.[53] Further, national data suggest that, at the high school level, whether a student is enrolled in an academic (college-preparatory) or non-academic program has an independent effect on achievement. Students who are initially similar in background and aptitude exhibit increased achievement differences resulting from their placements in higher and lower tracks.[54] The net effect of schooling on achievement appears to be cumulative, since judgments of students' ability and their consequences tend to be quite fixed and long-term. Students placed in low-ability groups in elementary school are likely to continue in these tracks in middle schools and junior highs; in senior high they typically are found in non-college-preparatory tracks.[55]

These data raise the possibility that, in their efforts to accommodate differences in ability with different educational experiences, schools may actually exacerbate the differences among students by limiting some students' opportunities to learn. Assessments of low academic ability and placements in non-academic programs occur more frequently among poor and minority students. Thus the combined effects of background characteristics, ability assessments, and consequent school placements are of special importance in attempts to uncover factors related to underachievement and low participation among these groups.

Uneven Classroom Opportunities

But understanding the interaction of race, class, and school opportunities requires consideration of factors far more complex than simply group and track assignment or the course offerings available to students in various schools. These characteristics at the *school level* are important largely because they influence the conditions under which teaching and learning occur. To fully understand students' actual opportunities to learn science and mathematics, classroom characteristics themselves must be examined as well. Even similar course titles at secondary schools can represent quite different classroom learning experiences, just as similar amounts of time allocated to instruction in elementary schools can include substantial variation in how that time is spent.

Obviously, how well students learn science and mathematics and how long they sustain an interest in these subjects will be most influenced by their day-to-day experiences in classrooms. The quality of these experiences will be determined to a large extent by a number of factors: the quality of the teacher's background, training, and experience; the support and resources available to teachers; what instructional goals and objectives teachers hope to accomplish; what knowledge and processes teachers make available for students to learn; what books, materials, and equipment are used to aid student learning; what classroom learning activities teachers arrange; and the complex teaching and learning interactions between teachers and students.

Considerable evidence suggests that these day-to-day classroom experiences are likely to differ both between schools and between students within the same school. This evidence suggests that the distribution of actual classroom experiences, resources, and opportunities to students with different race, class, and ability characteristics may be an important schooling contribution to unequal outcomes.

NAEP data, for example, indicate that black students have fewer science experiences in their classrooms.[56] Other studies document inequities in the number of microcomputers available for student use at different schools, and the ways computers are used vary for different subpopulations of children.[57] For example, the following are telling differences in microcomputer use: Only about 40 percent of middle schools in low-socioeconomic communities had as many as fifteen microcomputers, in contrast to high-socioeconomic communities where two-thirds of the middle schools had at least this number.[58] Fewest microcomputers were found to be available in elementary schools serving predominantly poor children and/or minority children, and at these schools, smaller percentages of children actually used the computers. Additionally, fewer poor and minority schools had teachers who were computer specialists. Schools of this type were more likely to use their computers for "drill and practice" and less likely to use them for instruction in computer programming.[59]

Further, some case-study evidence suggests that the curriculum content within subjects taught to students in predominantly poor and minority schools is essentially different from that taught to white and middle- and upper-class children. These content differences suggest that advantaged children are more likely to learn essential concepts (as opposed to isolated facts) and to be taught that academic knowledge is relevant to their future lives.[60] There are also critical differences in the opportunities to learn *science and mathematics content* in classrooms enrolling different groups of students within the same school. Recent studies of the distribution of classroom experiences among academic (college-preparatory or "high-ability") and non-academic (general or "low-ability") classes in science[61] and mathematics[62] show considerable differences in the opportunities afforded these two groups.

In the data from A Study of Schooling,[63] for example, students in mathematics classes at different levels were exposed to substantially different topics and skills.[64] Students in upper-level classes focused primarily on mathematical concepts; low-level classes focused almost exclusively on computational skills and math facts. Marked differences in the use of class time and the quality of instruction were also noted. Teachers of high-track classes got more instructional time in class and were expected to spend more time doing homework. High-track teachers were more enthusiastic, and their instruction was clearer. They used ridicule and strong criticism less frequently. Moreover, the climates of high- and low-track classes differed in ways likely to limit the opportunities of students not in the highest groups. Students were less friendly to one another; teachers were more occupied with matters of discipline and control. In these data, there appeared a pattern of classroom experience that seemed to enhance the possibilities of learning for those students already disposed to do well and to inhibit the learning of those students most likely to have difficulties.

Obviously, the content teachers decide to teach and the ways in which they teach it are greatly influenced by the students with whom they interact. And it is unlikely that students are passive participants in the tracking process. It seems more reasonable that students' achievement, attitudes, perceptions of themselves (growing increasingly disparate over time) help produce some of the effects of tracking. Thus when those students who, by conventional school standards, seem less able and less eager to learn are grouped together, they very likely affect a teacher's ability or even willingness to provide the best possible learning opportunities. The result for the students seems to be less exposure to curriculum content and lower-quality teaching. Under these circumstances, we can not expect them to get the full benefit from their schooling.

INTERACTING CHARACTERISTICS AND RESPONSES: THE NEED FOR FURTHER INQUIRY

The data presented above reveal patterns of curricular inequality that are disturbing under any circumstances. In fact, many white, middle-class, suburban schools appear to consign a good number of their students to mediocre schooling with their tracking systems. Yet these patterns are particularly distressing in light of the prevailing pattern of placing disproportionate numbers of poor and minority students in the lowest-level classes. In the organization and distribution of the school curriculum, a self-fulfilling prophecy can be seen to work at the institutional level to prevent schools from providing equal access to high levels of participation and achievement in mathematics and science. Few students and teachers can defy those expectations.

The evidence about tracking calls into question the widely-held view that schools provide students with the "right stuff" (usually defined as ability) with a neutral environment in which they can rise to the top. In the data about curriculum paths, course offerings, and track-related classroom differences, we find that the differentiated structure of schools often throws up barriers to achievement and participation of poor and minority students. Measures of ability work against them, which leads to minimal course offerings at their schools and these students' disproportionate placement in groups identified as "slow." Once in these classes, their success seems to be further inhibited by the type of knowledge they are taught and by the quality of the learning experiences they are afforded.

Recent work has called attention to the fact that research must address issues of race, class, and gender as fundamentally inseparable and interactive characteristics.[65] But to unravel the problems of "at risk" groups we must go further. We need to examine how students' race, class, and gender characteristics interact with school judgments about ability to produce their schooling opportunities.

We have long been aware of the links between race, class, and typical school measures of academic ability (even if they have been little understood). But too little attention has been given to how schools actually respond to combinations of students' race, class, gender, and academic ability characteristics. This inattention probably stems from the fact that while race, class, and gender are generally viewed as illegitimate criteria on which to base the distribution of educational experiences, ability has been relatively unquestioned as *the most legitimate basis for differentiation*. And the consensus generally has been, that as long as ability "explains" most of the outcome differences that result, the concomitant existence of class and race relationships seem less troublesome.

The data presented here suggest that this conclusion warrants further scrutiny. They raise the strong possiblity that, as schools attempt to accommodate differences in ability with different educational experiences, they may actually limit students' opportunities to learn and contribute to lower outcomes. Schools often respond to poor and minority students with assessments of low academic ability and placements in non-academic programs. When these decisions are lifted from the race- and class-blind status usually accorded them, we can begin to understand how they may interact to create a non-neutral basis for distributing opportunities. This interaction and the resulting distribution provide promising keys to understanding and interrupting the typical patterns of underachievement and low participation of poor and minority students in science and mathematics.

NOTES

1. See, for example, Achievement Council, *Excellence for Whom?* (Oakland, Ca: The Achievement Council, 1985); American Association for the Advancement of Science, *Equity and Excellence: Compatible*

Goals, (Washington, D.C.: American Association for the Advancement of Science, 1984); Sue Berryman, *Who Will Do Science?* (New York: The Rockefeller Foundation, 1983); Susan F. Chipman and V. Gail Thomas, *The Participation of Women and Minorities in Mathematical, Scientific and Technical Fields,* (Washington, D.C.: Howard University, 1984); Linda Darling-Hammond, *Equality and Excellence: The Status of Black American Education,* (College Entrance Examination Board, New York, 1985); National Alliance of Black School Educators, *Saving the African American Child,* (Washington, D.C.: National Allicance of Black School Educators, 1984); Scientific Manpower Commission, *Professional Women and Minorities,* (Washington, D.C.: Professional Manpower Commission, 1983).

2. National Center for Educational Statistics, *The Condition of Education, 1985 Edition,* (Washington, D.C.: U.S. Department of Education, 1985).

3. National Center for Educational Statistics, *The Condition of Education, 1985 Edition.*

4. U.S. Department of Commerce, *Current Population Report,* Series P–, (Washington, D.C.: United States Department of Commerce, 1982).

5. National Center for Educational Statistics, *The Condition of Education, 1985 Edition.*

6. Commission on Professionals in Science and Technology, *Professional Women and Minorities,* (Wasington, D.C.: Commission on Professionals in Science and Technology, 1986).

7. National Science Board, *Science Indicators: The 1985 Report,* (Washington, D.C.: The National Science Foundation, 1986).

8. T. P. Carpenter et al., "Achievement in Mathematics: Results from the National Assessment," *The Elementary School Journal* 84 (1984), pp. 485–495; S. J. Hueftle, S. J. Rakow, and W. W. Welch, *Images of Science: A Summary of Results From the 1981–82 Natinal Assessment in Science* (Minneapolis: University of Minnesota, 1983); Lyle V. Jones, "White-Black Achievement Differences: The Narrowing Gap," *American Psychologist* 39 (1984), pp. 1207–1213.

9. National Center for Educational Statistics, *High School and Beyond: An Analysis of Course-Taking Patterns in Secondary Schools as Related to Student Characteristics,* (Washington, D.C.: U.S. Department of Education, 1985).

10. John W. Newfield and Joseph M. Wisenbaker, "Student Selection of A Challenging High School Program of Studies." (Paper presented at the Annual Meeting of the American Educational Research Association, Chicago, 1985); Donald A. Rock et al., *Excellence in High School Education: Cross-Sectional Study, 1972–1980*, Final Report, (Princeton, N.J.: Educational Testing Service, 1984); Donald A. Rock et al., *Excellence in High School Education: Longitudinal Study, 1980–1982*, Final Report, (Princeton, N.J.: Educational Testing Service, 1985).

11. For a more elaborated discussion of this argument, See Jeannie Oakes, "The Distribution of Excellence: Monitoring Race, Class, and Gender Equity in Precollegiate Science and Mathematics Education," in R. Shavelson, L. McDonnell, and J. Oakes, eds., *Toward a System of Indicators of Precollegiate Science and Mathematics Education* (Santa Monica: The Rand Corporation, in press).

12. Donald A. Rock et al., *Excellence in High School Education: Cross-Sectional Study, 1972*–1980, Final Report.

13. Darling-Hammond, *Equality and Excellence.*

14. Berryman, *Who Will Do Science?*; National Center for Educational Statitistics, *The Condition of Education, 1985 Edition.*

15. National Center for Educational Statistics, *Factors Associated With the Decline of Test Scores of High School Seniors, 1972–1980*, (Washington, D.C.: U.S. Department of Education, 1985).

16. Berryman, *Who Will Do Science?*; Shirley Malcom, Y. S. George, and M. L. Matyas, *Summary of Research Studies on Women and Minorities in Science, Mathematics and Technology*, (Washington, D.C.: American Association for the Advancement of Science, 1985).

17. Berryman, *Who Will Do Science?*

18. Malcom, George, and Matyas, *Summary of Research Studies.*

19. H. H. Walberg, B. J. Fraser, and W. W. Welch, "A Test of A Model of Educational Productivity Among Senior High School Students," *Journal of Educational Reserach* 79 (1986), pp. 133–139.

20. Chipman and Thomas, *The Participation of Women and Minorities.*

21. W. Matthews, "Influences on the Learning and Participation of Minorities in Mathematics," *Journal of Research in Mathematics Educa-*

tion 15 (1984), pp. 84–95; M. L. Johnson, "Blacks in Mathematics: A Status Report," *Journal for Research in Mathematics Education* 15 (1984), pp. 145–153.

22. Malcom, George, and Matyas, *Summary of Research Studies.*

23. James P. Smith and Finis R. Welch, *Closing the Gap: Forty Years of Economic Progress for Blacks* (Santa Monica: The Rand Corporation, 1986).

24. United States Commission on Civil Rights, *Social Indicators of Equality for Minorities and Women* (Washington, D.C.: United States Commission on Civil Rights, 1978).

25. Chipman and Thomas, *The Participation of Women and Minorities.*

26. James E. Rosenbaum, "Special Implications of Educational Grouping," in D. C. Berliner, ed., *Review of Research in Education* 8 (1981), pp. 361–401.

27. Jeannie Oakes, *Keeping Track: How Schools Structure Inequality*, (New Haven: Yale University Press, 1985).

28. Larry F. Guthrie and Constance Leventhal, "Opportunities for Scientific Literacy for High School Students" (Paper presented at the Annual Meeting of the American Educational Research Association, Chicago, 1985.)

29. Oakes, *Keeping Track.*

30. A. E. Lantz and G. P. Smith, "Factors Influencing the Choice of Nonrequired Mathematics Courses," *Journal of Educational Psychology* 72 (1981), pp. 825–837.

31. Walberg, Fraser, and Welch, "A Test of A Model of Educational Productivity," Wayne W. Welch, Ronald E. Anderson, and Linda J. Harris, "The Effects of Schooling of Mathematics Achievement," *American Educational Research Journal* 19 (1982), 145–153.

32. Lucy Sells, "Leverage for Equal Opportunity Through Mastery of Mathematics," in S. M. Humphreys, ed., *Women and Minorities in Science: Strategies for Increasing Participation* (Washington, D.C.: American Association for the Advancement of Science, 1982).

33. Guthrie and Leventhal, "Opportunities for Scientific Literacy," Valerie Lee, "The Effect of Curriculum Tracking on the Social Distribution of Achievement in Catholic and Public Secondary Schools" (Paper presented at the Annual Meeting of the American Educational Research

Association, San Francisco, 1986); Oakes, *Keeping Track*; Jeannie Oakes, "Limiting Opportunity: Student Race and Curricular Differences in Secondary Vocational Education," *American Journal of Education* 91 (1983); pp. 328–355; Jeannie Oakes, "Secondary School Tracking: A Contextual Perspective," *Educational Psychologist*, (in press).

34. Robert Slavin, *Ability Grouping in Elementary Schools: A Best Evidence Synthesis* (Baltimore: The Johns Hopkins University, Center for Effective Elementary Schools, 1986).

35. Lee, "The Effect of Curriculum Tracking"; Rock et al., *Excellence in High School Education: Cross-Sectional Study, 1972–1980*, Final Report; Rock et al., *Excellence in High School Education: Longitudinal Study, 1980–1982*, Final Report.

36. Carolyn H. Persell, *Education and Inequality: The Roots and Results of Stratification in America's Schools* (New York: The Free Press, 1977); Rosenbaum, "Social Implications of Educational Grouping."

37. Darling-Hammond, *Equality and Excellence*.

38. Carpenter et al., "Achievement in Mathematics"; Hueftle, Rakow, and Welch, *Images of Science*.

39. National Assessment of Educational Progress. *Third National Mathematics Assessment: Results, Trends, and Issues* (Denver, Co: Education Commission of the States, 1983).

40. Oakes, *Keeping Track*.

41. Rock et al., *Excellence in High School Education: Longitudinal Study, 1980–1982*, Final Report.

42. Oakes, *Keeping Track*.

43. National Center for Educational Statistics, *High School and Beyond*.

44. J. M. Armstrong, "Achievement and Participation in Mathematics: An Overview," (Washington, DC: The National Institute of Education, 1981).

45. Jones, "White-Black Achievement Differences."

46. Ibid.

47. National Center for Educational Statistics, *High School and Beyond*; Samuel S. Peng, Jeffrey A. Owings, and William B. Fetters, "Effective High Schools: What Are Their Attributes?" (Paper presented at the Annual Meeting of the American Statistical Association, Cincinnati, Ohio, 1982).

48. Sells, "Leverage for Equal Opportunity"; Peng, Owings, and Fetters, "Effective High Schools."

49. Wayne W. Welch, Anderson, and Harris, "The Effects of Schooling of Mathematics Achievement."

50. Matthews, "Influences on the Learning and Participation of Minorities in Mathematics."

51. Jones, "White-Black Achievement Differences."

52. It should be noted, however, that recent analyses of *High School and Beyond* data, reveal no discrepancies in course-taking when schools with 10 percent or greater black or Hispanic enrollment are compared with schools enrolling fewer than 10 percent minorities. However, these HSB data are likely to be misleading, since 1980 data show three-quarters of all black students attend schools where minority enrollments exceed 30 percent. See, for example, Lyle V. Jones, "White-Black Achievement Differences: The Narrowing Gap." Lumping together all schools with 10 percent or more minority enrollment may obscure important differences in course offerings and course-taking among those schools.

53. Susan J. Rosenholtz and Carl Simpson, "The Formation of Ability Conceptions: Development Trend or Social Construction?" *Review of Educational Research* 54 (1984), pp. 31–63.

54. Karl A. Alexander and Edward L. McDill, "Selection and Allocation Within Schools: Some Causes and Consequences of Curriculum Placement," *American Sociological Review* 41 (1976), pp. 969–980; Karl A. Alexander, Martha Cook, and Edward L. McDill, "Curriculum Tracking and Educational Stratification: Some Further Evidence," *American Sociological Review* 43 (1978), pp. 47–66; Adam Gamoran, "The Stratification of High School Learning Opportunities" (Paper presented at the Annual Meeting of the American Educational Research Association, San Francisco, 1986).

55. Oakes, *Keeping Track*; Rosenbaum, "Social Implications of Educational Grouping."

56. Jane B. Kahle, "Can Positive Minority Attitudes Lead to Achievement Gains in Science?" *Science Education* 66 (1982).

57. Henry J. Becker, *School Uses of Microcomputers: Reports from a National Survey* (Baltimore: Johns Hopkins University Center for the Social Organization of Schools, 1983); Henry J. Becker, *Computer Survey Newsletter* (Baltimore: Johns Hopkins University Center

for the Social Organization of Schools, 1986); J. D. Furr and T. M. Davis, "Equity Issues and Microcomputers: Are Educators Meeting the Challenge," *Journal of Educational Equity and Leadership* 4 (1984), pp. 93-97; John D. Winkler, et al., *How Effective Teachers Use Microcomputers for Instruction* (Santa Monica: The Rand Corporation, 1984).

58. Becker, *Computer Survey Newsletter.*

59. Darling-Hammond, *Equality and Excellence.*

60. Jean Anyon, "Social Class and School Knowledge," *Curriculum Inquiry* II (1981), pp. 3-40; Martin Carnoy and Henry Levin, *Schooling and Work in the Democratic State* (Stanford: Stanford University Press, 1985).

61. Guthrie and Leventhal, "Opportunities for Scientific Literacy."

62. Oakes, *Keeping Track.*

63. John I. Goodlad, *A Place Called School* (New York: McGraw-Hill, 1984).

64. The following paragraphs present only a brief overview of these findings. The data are presented and analyzed fully in Oakes, *Keeping Track.*

65. Carl A. Grant and Christine Sleeter, "Race, Class, and Gender in Educational Research: An Argument for Integrative Analysis," *Review of Educational Research* 56 (1986), pp. 195-211; Malcom, George, and Matyas, *Summary of Research Studies on Women and Minorities.*

5

Hispanic Student Retention in Community Colleges: Reconciling Access with Outcomes

AMAURY NORA AND LAURA RENDON

The extraordinary diversity of the American higher education system assures that those who graduate from high school or earn a GED, regardless of academic preparations, race, class, age, or sex, will be accepted for admission at some institution. However, there is evidence that a student's educational choice tends to be delimited not only by academic preparation, but by race and social class.[1] Community colleges, the capstone of American equal opportunity, have evolved as the primary access to higher education for ethnic minorities and students from low social class origins. A controversy presently exists that community colleges may have a negative effect on ethnic minorities, who represent their primary source of students (particularly Hispanic students), and that the colleges may actually serve to perpetuate race and class inequities in the American society. The controversy stems from the fact that Hispanic students are differentially concentrated in the nation's community colleges, but that their educational achievement, retention, and transfer rates to senior institutions have been less than satisfactory.[2]

HISPANICS IN COMMUNITY COLLEGES

Hispanic students are largely dependent on community colleges to initiate college-based programs of study. In the fall of 1984, 54.3 percent of all Hispanics enrolled in public and private postsecondary institutions

126

were found in two-year colleges, compared to 42.7 percent for blacks and 35.9 percent for whites.[3] The disproportionate presence of Hispanics, ethnic minorities, and students of low to modest social origins in two-year colleges raises concern about the type and extent of the educational opportunities afforded to selective students in the stratified hierarchy of postsecondary institutions. Economically and academically disadvantaged students appear to be primarily attending colleges which rank at the bottom of a stratified institutional hierarchy, have the most modest resources, and have had the lowest levels of student achievement and persistence. The limitations inherent in the structure and nature of community colleges only serve to exacerbate the problems associated with these institutions' high Hispanic and ethnic minority student attrition and low transfer rates to senior institutions.

Hispanic Student Retention

The academic achievement of Hispanic students in community colleges has been less than satisfactory, and is marked by low retention and transfer rates to senior institutions. Data are available to suggest that the uneven flow of Hispanic students through the postsecondary educational pipeline maybe due to the cohort's disproportionate enrollment in community colleges. In a survey taken two years after 1980 seniors enrolled in postsecondary institutions, 50 percent of the Hispanics were not enrolled in college.[4] In a study of minority student participation in higher education, the Commission on the Higher Education of Minorities[5] indicated that one of the most important reasons that Chicanos, Puerto Ricans, and American Indians are underrepresented in graduate programs is their greater-than-average attrition from undergraduate colleges, particularly community colleges.

Data from the National Longitudinal Study indicated that of the students who entered college in the fall of 1973, 47 percent of the Hispanic two-year college students, compared to 28 percent of four-year college Hispanics had withdrawn by 1977.[6] Further, a National Longitudindal Study of the class of 1972[7] established race/ethnicity differences in educational attainment. Seven-and-one-half years after high school, Hispanics had the greatest proportion (38%) of persons with only a high school diploma and the lowest proportion (8%) with a baccalaureate degree. In a separate study, Haro[8] found that in seven states with the largest enrollment of Hispanics there is "an average college attrition rate for the Spanish-surnamed student population of 80.4 percent, compared to 62.3 percent for the majority population." The state of California, which accounts for nearly one-third of all Hispanic enrollments in higher education,[9] had a five-year college graduation rate of 15.4 percent for

Mexican-Americans, 34.2 percent for white, non-Hispanics, and a three-year graduation rate of 27.9 percent for Mexican-Americans and 38 percent for white, non-Hispanics.[10]

Transfer Rates to Senior Institutions

Slippage in the educational pipeline also occurs during student transition from a two- to four-year institution. Estimates on baccalaureate degree intentions of community college students range from a low of 52 percent to a high of 74 percent.[11] However, it is estimated that only 5 to 25 percent actually achieve this initial goal.[12] A case in point is illustrated by the state of California, which has the largest number of Hispanics in the largest system of community colleges in the country. In California, community colleges experiencing the largest transfer losses tended to be those with a very high proportion of Chicano or black freshman students.[13] Affirming that initial intentions of community college minority students rarely translate to reality are figures which substantiate their gross underrepresentation in the share of college degrees earned. In 1980 Hispanics comprised approximately six percent of the U.S. population. Yet, they earned only 2.3 percent of the bachelors, 2.2 percent of the masters, 1.4 percent of the doctorates, and 2.2 percent of the first professional degrees.[14]

The factors associated with poor Hispanic student retention are varied. The problem of minority and low-SES student underrepresentation really begins at the precollege level. Hispanics have lower high school graduation rates than whites. In 1982, only 40.3 percent of Hispanics graduated from high school. Exacerbating this problem is the fact that Hispanic high school graduates are less likely to attend college than whites. About 32 percent of white students attend college, compared to 29.9 percent for Hispanics. Factors which may be attributed to high dropout rates and low levels of college participation among Hispanics include: poverty, unemployment, poor quality of education at inner-city schools, infrequent student/faculty interaction, the absence of role models, lack of commitment to educational goals, institutional right-to-fail policies, declining literacy demands, and lack of academic preparation in reading, writing, and math.[15]

Student financial aid has recently received attention as a determinant of student retention. Astin,[16] Voorhees,[17] Brooks,[18] and Herndon[19] have found that student financial aid has a positive effect on student persistence. However, a study of Olivas[20] on Hispanic financial aid recipients found that not only were students uninformed about their parents' income, but that half of all Hispanic students in the study overestimated their actual income. In a separate study on financial aid packaging policies and Hispanics in higher education, Olivas[21] found that over 60 percent in a representative sample of over 16,000 Hispanic students reveived only single-source aid and that this one source of aid was "almost exclusively Basic Educational Opportunity Grants (or BEOGs, known as Pell Grants since 1981)." Even when multiple-source aid was awarded to Hispanic students, 95 percent of all multiple sources in the study included a Pell Grant award, a non-campus-based grant. If Hispanic community college students, who may qualify for financial assistance, are overestimating actual income on financial aid forms and being denied financial aid, not only are the students having to bear the entire cost of a college education, but their chances of succeeding and attaining some form of credential may be reduced.

In summary, Hispanic students may be enrolling in institutions which limit their ability to attain their educational goals and reduce their chances to move up the social and economic ladder. Despite open access, Hispanic retention, academic achievement, and transfer rates remain inadequate. Equal opportunity, the democratic ideology which fueled the community college movement, appears to be contradicted by the social reality that gross education achievement inequities persist between majority and minority student cohorts. The net effect is that individuals from selective ethnic backgrounds and social classes are granted a prolonged social niche, at the bottom of a diversified class structure.

Factors Affecting Hispanic Student Retention: Two Research Studies

To what extent do community colleges have a negative effect on Hispanic students? Critics of community colleges contend that the colleges ill serve minorities, serve as tracking mechanisms that divert students from more prestigious institutions, restrict opportunities to earn baccalaureate degrees, and perpetuate the existing hierarchical class structure. In short, community colleges are viewed as academic graveyards for ethnic minorities. These are serious indictments against community colleges which more often than not are based on perceptions and observations unsupported by empirical evidence. The research literature has been deficient in explaining how multiple student- and institution-related factors limit Hispanic student achievement and persistence in community colleges. Given that community colleges are not research-based institutions and have been poorly studied, they remain most vulnerable in terms of being targets for adverse criticism and for responding to disparaging accusations. Nevertheless, enough evidence exists to question whether or not community colleges, the vehicles of egalitarianism, perpetuate inequities in access and educational achievement for Hispanic students who are disproportionately concentrated in these institutions. This critical issue serves as the major basis for analyzing the complex factors which may account for the differential progress of Hispanic students in community colleges.

Two retention studies[22] employing a structural equation model[23] provide the most recent empirical information about Hispanic student retention in community colleges. The first study[24] examines student and institution-related determinants of Hispanic student retention. The second study[25] addresses the relative effects of student financial aid on Hispanic student retention. Both studies modified Tinto's[26] student attrition model to explain the effects of student background characteristics and academic and social integration on retention.

Determinants of Retention among Chicano Community College Students

Nora tested the hypothesis that high levels of congruency between students and their environments lead to high levels of credential attainment, hours earned, and goal satisfaction. Through the modification of Tinto's[28] attrition model, the study examined how six constructs affected student retention. These constructs were: grades, parents' education, encouragement, institutional/goal commitments, academic integration, and social integration. The model examined the direct and indirect effects of background characteristics and initial commitments on academic integration and social integration; and direct and indirect effects of background characteristics and initial commitments on retention; and the direct effects of academic integration and social integration on retention. Structural equation modeling[29] was used to examine the structural coefficients and measurement model of the hypothesized causal model.

Population and Sample

The study population was drawn from 3,544 first-time Chicano students who were enrolled full- or part-time in 1977 or 1978 in each of three South Texas community colleges. The colleges were: Laredo Junior College (Laredo), Texas Southwest College (Brownsville), and Del Mar College (Corpus Christi).

A systematic random sample of every other Chicano student was taken to arrive at a total N of 1,786. To gain longitudinal data between 1977 and 1982, a South Texas Student Survey (Rendon, 1982) was mailed to the sample population. After three mailing efforts, the final number of respondents was 227. Proportions from the mailings were tabulated to yield a conservative, estimated response rate of 23.71 percent.

Results

The mean age of the sample population was 23.57 with 59 percent of the sample being females. Although the mean was twenty-three, 77 percent of the student population was under twenty-three years of age. The sample population was relatively young and was unmarried (72.85%). Over half (56.44% of the students were in the third quartile of their graduating class, but eighty-six percent of the total student population graduated in the third quartile or above. The two largest categories for grades were Mostly A's and B's (28%) and Mostly B's and C's (36.44%). Most of the students (89%) reported having made Mostly B's and C's and above. The mean number of years for mother's education was 8.30 and 8.62 for father's education. Moreover, 54.95 percent of the student population initially wanted to attend a two-year college. Among the reasons given for selecting a community college over a four-year institution were: (1) close to home (11.41%), (2) cheaper (13.69%), (3) work while studying (10.50%), (4) "try out" college work (10.50%), and (5) take courses for self-improvement (13.24%). Those students who graduated (or received some form of credential) represented 29.91 percent of the population. In the four-year period from 1977–1978 to 1981–1982, the mean total number of hours enrolled by students was 65.17. It is important to note that with sixty-five hours or less, students could have received some form of two-year credential.

Although the measures used in testing the fit of the model reflected the overall strength of the causal model (see Table 1), the findings were not entirely supportive of Tinto's model. Both academic and social integration did not have the significant direct effects on retention which have been reported in other studies[30] testing Tinto's model. Tinto's model specifies effects which are mediated through academic and social integration.

Table 1 Measures of Goodness of Fit for the Whole Model

Measures	Test of Significance
Goodness of Fit Index	.920
Adjusted Goodness of Fit Index	.840
Root Mean Square Residual	.093
Total Coefficient of Determination for Structural Equations	.341

Students entering an institution with higher levels of institutional/goal commitments will have higher levels of academic and social integration at their respective institutions and consequently higher levels of retention. For Hispanic community college students, however, institutional/goal commitments not only have a significant direct effect on retention, but are considerably more important in determining retention (see Table 2). The total effect for academic integration was only .218, while the total effect of social integration (.092) on retention signified that there was no causal path between these two variables. The effect coefficieny for institutional/goal commitments, on the other hand, was .904, significantly higher than the two integration variables. There were no significant direct effects of grades, parents' education, and encouragement on retention rates, but two of the three variables, grades and encouragement, directly affected initial institutional/goal commitments.

Institutional/goal commitments. Although the effect of parents' education on institutional/goal commitments[31] was hypothesized to be positively related, the strength of the structural coefficient (gamma = .019) was not what had been expected. Students' initial commitments to the institution and to their educational goals were not affected significantly by their parents' education. It was believed that for most Mexican-Americans education was highly valued, whether it was because parents who had not themselves earned a college degree provided strong incentives for their children to "succeed" where they did not[32] or because it was expected by parents who had "succeeded" in earning a college degree.

Social integration. None of the hypothesized direct effects of the background characteristics on social integration were supported in the findings. More importantly, though, was the positive direct effect (.683) which initial institutional/goal commitments had on social integration. Students who entered college with higher levels of commitment to the institution and to their educational goals had more informal interactions with faculty members, met more often with counselors, and attended and participated more in peer-related activities.

Acadeamic integration. The direct effects of students' initial institutional/goal commitments on students' academic perceptions about the faculty, counselors, and administrators and about their academic experiences (including career preparation) was supported by the findings and substantiates research conducted by Fox[33] and by Pascarella, Terenzini, and Wolfle.[34]

Retention. The last structural equation examined the direct and indirect effects of grades, parents' education, encouragement, and institutional/goal commitments, academic integration, and social integration on the dependent variable, retention. Students whose parents had higher levels of education were more likely to enroll in more semester hours, to be more satisfied with their present goal attainment, and to have earned

Table 2 Effect Coefficients of Exogenous and Endogenous Variables

Variable	Direct Effect	Total Effect
Retention		
Grades	.059	.170
Parents' education	.134	.138
Encouragement	−.052	.092
Institutional/goal commitments	.651	.904
Academic integration	.218	.218
Social integration	.092	.092
Institutional/Goal Commitments		
Grades	.138	.138
Parents' education	.019	.019
Encouragement	.157	.157
Social Integration		
Grades	−.154	−.059
Parents' education	−.146	−.133
Encouragement	.029	.137
Institutional/goal commitments	.683	.683
Academic Integration		
Institutional/goal commitments	.871	.871

some form of credential. Although this direct effect was hypothesized, and the findings supportive (gamma = .134), it was expected to have had a smaller impact on retention. The direct effect of academic integration on retention was the second largest structural coefficient in the equation (beta = .218).

One precollege variable, high school grades, and one endogenous variable, social integration, had direct effects on retention as hypothesized; however, even with total effects taken into account, the strength of the relationship was minimal. Although it was hypothesized in the causal mode, the degree (strength) of the direct effect of institutional/goal commitments on retention was unexpected, the direct effect on the latent variable was .651, the effect coefficient .904. Students with higher levels of commitments to the institution and to educational goals enrolled in more semester hours, were more satisfied with their present educational goal attainment, and graduated with some form of credential.

Fox[135] has consistently found that high levels of academic integration have more of an impact on persistence than any other variable in Tinto's model. The findings in the present research, however, revealed that for a community college Chicano student population, neither academic integration nor social integration affected retention rates significantly more than academic and social integration measures.

Student Finances and Retention Rates

A causal model examining the effect of campus- and noncampus-based financial aid on Hispanic community college student retention was employed by Nora.[36] Campus-based financial program included Supplemental Education Opportunity Grants (SEOG), College Work Study (CWS), and National Defense Student Loans (NDSL). Non-campus-based resources were Pell Grants. The paradigm represented a multi-equation model with five endogenous variables. The five endogenous variables included academic performance, three campus-based resources (National Direct Student Loans, College Work Study, and Supplemental Educational Opportunity Grants), and the dependent variable, retention. Exogenous variables included non-campus-based resources, high school grades, and student financial need. Background characteristics were examined to determine the direct effects and indirect effects (through intervening variables) these factors had on minority retention rates and the direct and indirect effects of campus-based resources and academic performance on minority retention rates. Based on Tinto's[37] model of student retention, the LISREL[38] model in the study incorporated a modification of the measurement model made earlier by Nora[39] and included measures of student finances examined by Voorhees.[40]

Population and Sample

The study population (N = 170) was drawn from a total population of 883 first-time Chicano students who were enrolled full- or part-time in 1982 in a community college (Laredo Junior College) in South Texas.

Results

The mean financial need for the sample population was $3560, ranging from a need of $180 to a high of $12,227. The mean high school grade for financial aid recipients was 83.38. The mean for non-campus-based awards (Pell Grants) was $1617 with only twelve (6.31%) students not receiving this particular form of financial assistance. Once enrolled in the community college, students were enrolled for a mean of 6.17 semesters (including summer sessions), earned a mean of 55.26 semester hours, and received a mean GPA of 2.524. Although the mean number of semester hours earned would indicate that many students could have received a community college certificate or associate degree, only 17.64 percent of the sample population received some form of credential from the two-year institution in which they were enrolled; a total of 140 (82.38%) students did not. The means for campus-based resources (Supplemental Educational Opportunity Loans, College Work Study, National Direct Student Loans) were $811, $674, and $51, respectively. However, 29.47 percent, 70.52 percent, and 96.84 percent of the students in the sample population did not receive Supplemental Educational Opportunity Loans, College Work Study, and National Direct Student Loans, respectively. These findings are supported by Olivas[41] in that, among Hispanic college students, financial aid is restricted to Pell Grants almost exclusively.

The effect coefficients for the structural model are included in Table 3. The Goodness of Fit Index for the causal model was .970, the Adjusted Goodness of Fit Index .949, and the Root Mean Square Residual .07. The total Coefficient of Determination for the overall model was .805; the squared multiple correlations (R^2) for the latent constructs (campus-based resources, academic performance, and retention) were .524, .216, and .764. All the measures of the overall strength of the structural model indicated that the modified model in the study represented a plausible model of retention.

The results indicated that two factors had a significant impact on Hispanic community college retention rates: non-campus-based resources (Pell Grants) and campus-based resources (Supplemental Educational Opportunity Loans, College Work Study, National Direct Student Loans), total effects being .774 and .402, respectively. The im-

Table 3 Effect Coefficients of Exogenous and Endogenous Variables

Variable	Direct Effect	Total Effect
Retention		
Non-campus based resources	.613	.774
Grades	.110	.189
Need	−.132	−.084
Campus-based resources	.197	.402
GPA	.208	.208
Campus-based resources		
Non-campus based resources	.700	.441
Need	.179	.113
GPA		
Non-campus based resources	−.076	.114
Grades	.381	.381
Need	.017	.065
Campus-based resources	.271	.430

pact of compus-based resources on retention, however, was enhanced when it was mediated through academic performance; the direct effect of campus-based resources was only .197, the effect coefficient (direct and indirect effects) was .402. Moreover, the findings indicated that these factors had a significantly larger effect on retention than GPA as reported by Fox [42] and Voorhees.[43]

Other variables in the model which were significant included the direct effect of high school grades on the student's academic performance in the two-year institution (gamma = .381) and the direct effect of campus-based resources on academic performance (B = .271). More importantly, the direct effect of high school grades on retention, although significant, was only .110. Even when the total effects were examined, the effect coefficient was .189. Another direct effect which was significant was that of need on retention (gamma = −.132). Again, however, this effect was negated by the intervening variables (total effects = −.084). There were no significant direct effects of need (gamma = .017) and non-campus-based resources (gamma = −.076) on academic performance.

In sum, Hispanic community college students who received higher levels of non-campus and campus-based financial aid award were enrolled in more semesters, earned more semester hours, and received some form of credential. Moreover, Hispanic students who received higher levels of campus-based resources earned higher grade point averages. Although the direct effect of campus-based resources on retention was not as large as that of non-campus resources or academic performance, students who received Supplemental Educational Opportunity Loans, College Work Study, and National Direct Student Loans did considerably better in their academic performance and, consequently, had higher levels of retention.

DISCUSSION, IMPLICATIONS, AND RECOMMENDATIONS

The key findings of Nora's[44] study of Hispanic community college student retention indicated that the largest impact on retention was of high levels of student institutional and goal commitments. Hispanic students who were committed to attending a two-year institution and who had strong commitments about their educational goals tended to enroll in more semester hours, were more satisfied with their educational goal attainments, and earned some form of college credential. Unlike other studies[45] social integration was not found to be a determinant of retention. Academic integration had only a slight effect on retention.

The results of Nora's[46] regarding the relationship between campus and non-campus financial aid resources and student retention indicated that the largest effect on retention was Pell Grants. The second largest effect was produced by Supplemental Education Opportunity Loans, College Work Study, and National Direct Student Loans; the third largest effect came from student GPAs. Nora's study contradicts those of Voorhees[47] which have indicated that campus-based resources (Supplemental Educational Opportunity Loans, College Work Study, National Direct Student Loans) have the most effect on retention.

The implications of these findings must be viewed in the context that the results come from studies which, although confirmatory in nature, have only begun to explore how diverse variables operate in complex ways to influence Hispanic dropout decisions in community college settings. Nonetheless, Nora's studies do shed additional light on the debate about whether or not community colleges are having a negative effect on Hispanic students.

A pronounced contradiction appears in both of Nora's studies that awaken doubts about the true opportunities afforded to Hispanic students in community colleges. In both studies, a substantial number of students earned enough credit hours to earn a college credential. In the first study, the mean credit hour earned was 65.17; in the second, 52.25. However, only 29.91 percent of the students in the first study had earned some form of credential, and only 17.64 percent received a degree or certificate in the second study. In short, while Hispanic students do enroll and earn enough credit hours to make them eligible for some form of college credential, relatively few graduate or earn degrees or certificates.

This contradiction may be explained through an analysis of the finding that students with strong institutional and goal commitments tended to earn more college credit hours and to earn college credentials. Many students may be enrolling in community colleges without a clear conception of what their educational goals are. Some may attend to get a Pell Grant because they don't have a job; those who have a job or family problems may have external preoccupations that preclude institutional affiliation and commitment to studies; others may attend for personal satisfaction as opposed to earning a college degree. Still others may have spent most of the time taking remedial courses, paying more attention to "catching up" than to developing other educational goals. In any case, having unclear, diffuse goals appears to work against Hispanic student retention and ultimate graduation. Students with uncertain goals may never develop strong goal commitments and may consequently never finish their program of study.

This generalized finding has important implications for Hispanic students who indicate they wish to transfer to earn baccalaureate degrees. Nationwide, as many as 74 percent of community college students indicate they wish to earn a four-year degree, yet only a small fraction actually transfer to achieve this goal.[48] Explanations for poor student transfer rates may be attributed to lack of commitment to the goal of transferring, or to the setting of educational goals based on a lack of information about what it takes to complete a four-year degree, and a misconception about the structure of higher education.[49] The implication is that community colleges need to do more in the way of providing assistance and information to help students develop clear, realistic educational goals at an early enrollment point.

"Front-loading"[50] is a proposal that would give top priority for the allocation of faculty and institutional resources to first- and second-year undergraduate students. In community colleges, students need early counseling and advisement about setting realistic educational and career goals, getting serious and committed to studying, selecting proper course sequences, and acquiring materials and information about transferring to senior institutions. Assigning students to a faculty mentor who can provide consistent advisement and follow-through can provide students with a contact person who can help them to shape their goals as well as to become actively involved in the studying and learning process. Transfer centers, staffed with special transfer counselors, can provide supplemental information about the transfer process. These centers can help early-identified, potential transfer students with proper course selection and sequence, the selection of an appropriate curricular program at a senior institution, and the completion of admissions, financial aid, and housing forms.

On the issues of financial aid, one must consider the nature of the Hispanic community college student. Most students come from low socioeconomic status background and from families where the precedent of attending college is not established. Because both campus- and non-campus-based resources have been found to have a significant impact on retention rates among Hispanic community college students, two-year institutions need to do more than simply meet a student's financial need. The colleges need to develop a comprehensive financial aid advisement program that reaches out to students and their parents before they graduate from high school. Hispanic parents need to understand and appreciate the higher education system, as well as its costs and the financial assistance available for their children. Parents and students also need information about the cost of going to college and about diverse financial resources available to them. Parents and students can also be educated about the importance of completing IRS and student financial aid applications in a correct and timely fashion, making correct estimates about their income and selecting a comprehensive financial aid package.

Although campus- and non-campus-based resources are deciding factors in whether or not Hispanic students stay in college, the fact remains that the majority of Hispanic students receiving Pell Grants do not necessarily earn degrees. This fact creates some fundamental questions. Does simply staying in college (for whatever reason) define retention, even if students don't earn some form of credential? Why aren't Hispanic students earning comnmunity college credentials? Are they merely escaping a poor job market, wasting time, or uninterested in earning a credential? Are other factors such as poor advisement and lack of involvement with the college community operating to negate student achievement? Too many unanswered issues force one to conclude that more research needs to be conducted on the diverse and complex factors which may be operating to impact Hispanic student achievement in community colleges.

Do community colleges short-change Hispanic students? In some ways they do, in others they don't. Clearly community colleges have done more than any other postsecondary sector to increase access for Hispanics. And, to their credit, many two-year colleges are doing more with regard to affirmative action policies and strategies to not only attract Hispanics to their campuses, but to retain them, assist them to complete their program of study, and facilitate transfer to senior institutions. However, the weight of the evidence does more to challenge the dubious nature of equal opportunity than it does to confirm true equity. For example, the present flow of Hispanic students through the educational pipeline suggests that Hispanics have made few appreciable gains in either their particiation or achievement in community colleges. The fact remains that few Hispanics earn college credentials, graduate, or transfer to senior institutions.

Community colleges need to do more to provide demonstrable evidence that they are more than the "end-of-the-line" for Hispanic students. A crucial lesson learned from the expansion of higher education and the provision of equal opportunity for all students through a differentiated system of higher education is that increased access does not automatically lead to reduced social and economic inequalities between majority and minority groups. In the end, the critical issue is not how many gain access to higher education, but rather what happens to students once they get there. This is true for community colleges as it is for other postsecondary sectors. That community colleges can make systemic reform and devise interventions to turn the present condition of Hispanic education around remains to be seen.

NOTES

1. Commission on the Higher Education of Minorities. *Final Report on the Higher Education of Minorities.* (Los Angeles: Higher Education Research Institute, Inc., 1982); J. Karabel and A. W. Astin,

"Social Class, Academic Ability and College Quality," *Social Forces* 53 (1975), pp. 381–397; J. Karabel, "Community Colleges and Social Stratification," *Harvard Educational Review* 42(4) (1972), pp. 521–558; and J. Karabel, "Open Admissions: Toward Meritocracy or Democracy?; *Change* 4 (1972), pp. 30–44.

2. Amaury Nora, "Determinants of Retention Among Chicano College Students: A Structural Model," *Research in Higher Education* 26(1), (1987), pp. 31–59; Laura Rendon, *Chicanos in South Texas Community Colleges: A Study of Student and Institutional-Related Determinants of Educational Outcomes.* (Unpublished doctoral dissertation, University of Michigan, 1982); Commission on the Higher Education of Minorities, *Final Report*; A. W. Astin, *Minorities in American Higher Education* (San Francisco: Jossey-Bass, 1982); and Michael Olivas, *The Dilemma of Access* (Washington, D. C.: Howard University Press, 1979).

3. S. Jaschik, "States Called Key to College Gains for Minorities," *The Chronicle of Higher Education* July 23, 1986.

4. V. Lee, *Access to Higher Education: The Experience of Blacks, Hispanics and Low Socio-Economic Status Whites.* (Washington, D.C.: American Council on Education, 1985).

5. Commission on the Higher Education of Minorities, *Final Report.*

6. R. Wilson and S. Melendez, *Minorities in Higher Education.* (Washington, D.C.: American Council on Education, 1982).

7. H. J. Burkheimer and T. P. Novak, *A Capsule Description of Young Adults Seven and One-Half Years After High School.* (Research Triangle Park, Center for Educational Reserach and Evaluation, 1981).

8. C. M. Haro, "Chicanos and Higher Education: A Review of Selected Literature," *Aztlan* 14:1 (1983), pp. 35–76.

9. Michael Olivas, "Financial Aid and Self-Reports by Disadvantaged Students: The Importance of Being Earnest," *Research in Higher Education* 25(3), (1986), pp. 245–262.

10. The California State University and Colleges, *Those Who Stay —Phase II: Student Continuance in the California State University and Colleges.* Technical memorandum No. 8 from the Office of the Chancellor, California State University and Colleges, 1979.

11. R. C. Richardson and L. W. Bender, *Students in Urban Settings: Achieving the Baccalaureate Degree* (Washington, D.C.: Association for the Study of Higher Education, 1986).

12. Ibid; E. M. Bensimon and M. J. Riley, *Student Predisposition to Transfer: A Report of Preliminary Findings* (Los Angeles: Center for the Study Community Colleges, 1984); and Astin, *Minorities in American Higher Education.*

13. California State Postsecondary Education Commission, *Update of Community College Transfer Student Statistics, Fall 1984.* Commission Report 85-21 (Sacramento: CSPEC ERIC Document No. ED 256399, 1979); and G. Hayward, *Preparation and Participation of Hispanic and Black Students: A Special Report* (Sacramento: California Community Colleges, Office of the Chancellor ERIC Document No. ED 254285, 1985).

14. Wilson and Melendez, *Minorities in Higher Education.*

15. Rendon, *Chicanos in South Texas.* Nora, "Determinants of Retention"; and Wilson and Melendez, *Minorities in Higher Education.*

16. Astin, *Minorities in American Higher Education.*

17. Richard A. Voorhees, "Student Finances and Campus-Based Financial Aid: A Structural Model Analysis of the Persistence of High Need Freshmen," *Research in Higher Education* 22:1 (1985), pp. 65-91.

18. J. W. Brooks, "Academic Performance and Retention Rates of Participants in the College Work Study Program and Recipients of National Direct Student Loans" (Doctoral dissertation, Indiana University, 1980). *Dissertation Abstracts International* 40, 3440-A. (University Microfilms No. 8103407).

19. M. S. Herndon, "A Longitudinal Study of Financial Aid Persister, Dropouts, and Stopouts: A Discriminant Analysis" (Doctoral dissertation, University of California, Los Angeles, 1981). *Dissertation Abstracts International* 42, 4736A-4737A. (University Microfilms No. DA8206026).

20. Olivas, *Financial aid.*

21. Olivas, "Financial Aid and Self-Reports".

22. Nora, "Determinants of Retention"; and Amaury Nora, *Campus-Based Aid Programs as Determinants of Retention Among Hispanic Community College Students* (Paper presentation at the American Educational Research Association, Washington, D.C., 1987).

23. Structural equation modeling combine a measurement model and structural (causal) model into a complete model and are analogous to a combination of factor analysis and path analysis. The measurement

model is similar to factory analysis; however, it is confirmatory in nature, unlike traditional factor analysis. Confirmatory factor analysis does not have the rotation problems found in exploratory factor analysis and unique variables (residuals) can be correlated (see note 47). The structural model is similar to path analysis (simultaneous regression equations) except that these regression equations are based on latent (unobserved) variables and there is the possibility of correlated residuals.

24. Nora, "Determinants of Retention".

25. Nora, "Campus-Based Aid Programs".

26. Vincent Tinto, "Dropout from Higher Education: A Theoretical Synthesis of Recent Research," *Review of Educational Research* 45:1 (1975), pp. 89–125.

27. Nora, "Determinants of Retention".

28. Tinto, "Dropout from Higher Education".

29. P. M. Bentler, "Multivariate Analysis with Latent Variables: Causal Modeling," *Annual Review of Psychology* (1980), pp. 419–456; P. M. Bentler and G. Speckart, "Attitudes 'Cause' Behaviors: A Structural Equation Analysis," *Journal of Personality and Social Psychology* 40:2 (1981), pp. 226–238; P. M. Bentler and J. A. Woodward, "A Head Start Reevaluation: Positive Effects Are Not Yet Demonstrable," *Evaluation Quarterly* 2 (1978), pp. 493–510; Karl G. Joreskog and Dag Sorbom, *LISREL: Analysis of Linear Structural Relationships by the Method of Maximum Likelihood* (Version VI) (Chicago: National Ed. Resources, 1981); D. Kenny, *Correlation and Causality* (New York: Wiley, 1979); J. Scott Long, "Estimation and Hypothesis Testing in Linear Models Containing Measurement Error," *Sociological Methods and Research* 5:2 (1976), pp. 157–203; and Elazar Pedhazur, *Multiple Regression in Behavioral Research: Explanation and Prediction* (2nd ed.) New York: Holt, Rinehart & Winston, 1982).

30. J. Fox, *Application of a Conceptual Model of College Withdrawal to Disadvantaged Students* (Paper presented at the annual meeting of the American Educational Research Association, Chicago, Ill., March 1985); and Ernest Pascarella, Patrick Terenzini, and Lee Wolfle, *Orientation to College as Anticipatory Socialization: Indirect Effects on Freshman Year Persistence* (Paper presented at the annual meeting of the American Educational Research Association, Chicago, Ill., March 1985).

31. This variable measured the initial institutional commitment that students had upon entering a community college for that particular in-

stitution. Secondly, it was a measure of the students' initial goal commitments when they first entered their community college.

32. W. Sewell and V. Shah, "Parents' Education and Children's Educational Aspirations and Achievements," *American Sociological Review* 33:2 (1968), pp. 191–209.

33. Fox, *Application of a Conceptual Model.*

34. Pascarella, Terenzini, and Wolfle, *Orientation to College.*

35. J. Fox, "Effect Analysis in Structural Equation Models," *Sociological Methods and Research* 9:1 (1980), pp. 3–28; and Fox, *Application of a Conceptual Model.*

36. Nora, "Campus-Based Aid Programs".

37. Tinto, "Dropout from Higher Education."

38. Joreskog and Sorbom, *LISREL.*

39. Nora, "Determinants of Retention".

40. Voorhees, "Student Finances."

41. Olivas, "Financial Aid and Self-Reports".

42. Fox, *Application of a Conceptual Method.*

43. Voorhees, "Student Finances."

44. Nora, "Determinants of Retention".

45. Ernest Pascarella and Patrick Terenzini, "Interaction Effects in Spady's and Tinto's Conceptual Models of College Dropout," *Sociology of Education* 52 (1979), pp. 197–210; and Pascarella, Terenzini, and Wolfle, *Orientation to College.*

46. Nora, "Campus-Based Aid Programs".

47. Voorhees, "Student Finances"; and Richard Voorhees, "Financial Aid and Persistence: Do the Federal Campus-Based Aid Programs Make A Difference?" *The Journal of Student Financial Aid* 15:1 (1985), pp. 21–30.

48. Richardson and Bender, *Students in Urban Settings.*

49. Bensimon and Riley, *Student Predisposition to Transfer.*

50. Study Group on the Conditions of Excellence in Higher Education, *Involvement in Learning* (Washington, D.C.: National Institute of Education, 1984).

6

A Rationale for Integrating Race, Gender, and Social Class

CHRISTINE E. SLEETER AND CARL A. GRANT

Since the late sixties, radical theory has undergone tremendous development in the social sciences as intellectuals have sought to understand how and why social stratification is reproduced, and how it might be reduced or eliminated. As members of oppressed gender and racial groups, we applaud this development. Yet at the same time, we are troubled by a direction taken by many radical theorists: the tendency to subsume multiple forms of oppression under a class analysis.

Marxist theory has gained a rather recent popularity among American intellectuals. Aronowitz has termed Marxist theory a "refreshing antidote" to those "reared in the pluralist traditions of American social science."[1] Intellectuals found it refreshing because of its power to question the ethics of social stratification, its interest in the lives of the oppressed, and its focus on control of the means of production as the primary site for social inequality. In contrast to functionalist theory, Marxism provided a conceptual tool for examining social inequality for the purpose of changing it rather than accepting it.

However, its focus on control over the means of economic production gives rise to a fundamental problem in the theory: the tendency to give primacy to class relations over race or gender relations. As a result, much of the neo-Marxist social science literature either ignores race and gender, or pays them only cursory attention. As Giroux put it, "The failure [of neo-Marxist work] to include women and racial minorities. . . has resulted in a rather uncritical theoretical tendency to romanticize ᵐᵒᵈᵉˢ of resistance even when they contain reactionary racial and gender ᵖ" He pointed out that ironically much of this work, "although

144

allegedly committed to emancipatory concerns, ends up contributing to the reproduction of sexist and racist attitudes and practices."[2]

In a review of a sample of seventy-one journal articles dealing with race, social class, and gender published between 1973 and 1983, we found only one article to integrate these three forms of oppression, giving equal attention to all three. A second integrated race and class, a third integrated race and gender, and a fourth integrated gender and class. But the great majority of articles treated these as separate forms of oppression, and did not acknowledge relationships among them.[3]

There is a need for the continued development of theory and research that emphasizes social justice and emancipation. Such theory must, however, see race, gender, and class as equally important and as enduring forms of oppression that are interrelated but not reducible to one form. In this paper we will argue the persistent importance of race and gender in the U.S., and point out some problems inherent in reducing these to a class analysis. We will argue for collaboration in theory-building among those interested in race, class, and gender, aimed toward the construction of a more universally liberating conceptual framework than that offered by Marx. Although this paper will not offer a theory, it takes a first step by arguing for a need to do this.

Racism in Relationship to Social Class

People of color, especially blacks, are facing less racial discrimination today than they once were in achieving some jobs — the jobs most readily open to them paying a low income (minimum wage level). This has caused several researchers to question whether race is still a primary factor in inequality today, and to assert that social class counts more than race in determining one's opportunities.[4] People of color, the argument goes, have become trapped disproportionately in lower levels of the class structure, and experience the same material, class-based factors as whites preventing upward mobility. But we argue that race is still a major determinant of opportunity, and an analysis of inequality cannot be reduced to an analysis of social class.

Racist thinking reflects a philosophical conception of reality which holds that life forms exist on a hierarchy with humans at the top. As "superior" life forms, humans are viewed as having the right to use and even destroy other life forms for their own benefit, based on the rationale that the "superior" human brain knows what is best. Acceptance of this hierarchy has led to a conception of human groups as also existing on the hierarchy. Gould has described and critiqued a history of craniometric and psychometric research that has attempted to document the genetic superiority of Caucasians in the evolutionary chain.[5] This hierarchy, which is almost always expounded by the group that sees itself on top, suggests the same rationale for human exploitation of nature: those with "superior" brains or "superior" culture know what is best, and therefore have a right to exploit and assume authority over people they view as lower on the hierarchy. Thus, racism has legitimated and made psychologically okay the conquest, enslavement, and exploitation of people of color, and is an integral part of the self-definition and feeling of self-esteem of most whites in western societies, *regardless* of class.

The philosophical worldview underlying racism is *intertwined* with class relations, but not *the same as* class relations, nor a *subset* of class relations. In the United States and increasingly in England, in order to understand social class, racism and race relations have to be taken into analytical schemata. Racism, as a dominant ideology that supports and encourages a stratified economic structure, impacts daily upon people (both as individuals and as groups) in our society. Racism is ever present, widespread, and definitely influences the work roles, goals, and the privileges people receive. Because the receipt of privileges is directly connected to one's race, we argue that there exists a strong, direct correspondence between race and social class. This correspondence demands that an examination of one necessitates the examination of the other. An examination of some of the privileges that a person receives because of race will help to illuminate our argument.

Racist ideologies were developed to provide a rationale for the social, economic, and political domination which Europeans initially established over people of color to enhance their own resources and privileges. The ideology of white race superiority was developed to establish "structured-in privileges" that are still present today. Williams has noted that the protection of white privileges is critical to discriminatory practices: "Whenever a number of persons within a society have enjoyed for a considerable period of time certain opportunities for getting wealth, for exercising power and authority, and for successfully claiming prestige and social difference, there is a strong tendency for these people to feel that these benefits are theirs 'by right'."[6]

Historically, racism contributed to the development of a stratified economy, and it continues to contribute today. As Kushnick pointed out, "Racism has enabled the bourgeoisie to establish race-stratified labor forces in the metropole, which facilitates the super-exploitation of racially oppressed workers and the continuing exploitation of white workers as well."[7] Modern economic structures rest in part on racial and ethnic prejudice. In fact, capitalism itself has taken its shape in part because of the belief that people of color and certain white ethnic groups are inferior: this belief in a hierarchy of human ethnic and racial groups contributed to the development of an economic system in which different racial and ethnic groups occupied different strata.

Collins, in his analysis of the rise of the credential system in this country, observed how oppression based not only on race but also on ethnicity promoted class stratification. He wrote, ". . .ethnic divisions shaped the lines of class stratification. Administrative jobs were reserved whenever possible for Anglos. Immigrant ethnic groups were confined to manual labor or, at best foremen of labor gangs."[8] He pointed out that various ethnic groups fought for positions within the labor force. For example, the Irish gained control over skilled work, the Italians and Slavs dominated unskilled labor positions, and blacks were confined to service work. He further noted:

> Even if ethnic differences were completely to disappear today, this institutional structure would still be with us and still occupy a central place in our stratification. The fact that ethnic diversity does still exist and that Chicanos, Puerto Ricans, blacks, Asians, and various white ethnic groups (even self-conscious, backlashing Anglo-Protestants) make demands for precedence within the credential system today merely *accelerates* that pattern of development of that system in channels laid down several generations ago.[9]

In the past, people of color were limited to a relatively small number of jobs, and many employers refused to hire them. Today employers may not refuse to hire on the basis of color, but because of racism most of these jobs still tend to be low-level, or peripheral to the hierarchy of positions open to upwardly-mobile whites. Based on a study of racism in the labor force, Reich concluded that:

> The shift from exluding blacks from industry to incorporating them into the working class has not by itself resulted in racial equality. Racial inequality is now reproduced by bureaucratic structures in large modern corporations that organize jobs and workers hierarchically and by the farming out of a portion of production to small-scale low-wage employers in competitive market structures.[10]

For example, an aspiring minority professional is often promoted to the position of Affirmative Action supervisor — often a dead-end position — rather than sales manager. This situation has allowed the white worker and especially the white male worker to have some privileges over workers of color, in that white male workers have greater access to higher-paying jobs.

However, relegating workers of color to lower-level jobs has prevented the development of working-class solidarity, which ultimately has benefited wealthy whites. As Kushnick put it, "racism has functioned to retard, and in a major sense to prevent those who make up the working class from becoming conscious of the centrality of that identity in opposition to the identity and interest of those who exploit them, the capitalist class."[11] Racial stratification continues to leave poor people less powerful in their struggle for better pay and more control over their lives than they could be *if all* working-class people worked *together*. For example, an excellent description of the relationship between race and social class is provided by Hill in a report on race and labor. Hill observed that, "the white electrician, by virtue of the exclusion of blacks from the trade, does not have to compete with an entire class within the working population."[12] This exclusion of blacks perpetuates privileges for the whites, and provides them with "higher status." In this way, "white" and "high status" have become synonymous and interdependent. Hill went on to explain that, "In certain desirable occupations in industrial plants, white workers are also exempted from competition with blacks, they are assigned to classifications which have a higher wage base (supported by the payment of lower wages to blacks) and have access to better paying, higher skills jobs, not open to blacks."[13]

The removal of previous unfair practices against workers of color is currently causing increased tensions between white workers and workers of color. Hill explained, "It is, in fact, the removal of the preferential treatment traditionally enjoyed by white workers at the expense of black earners that is now at issue. These self-generated factors — the result of the historic dual labor system based on race — account for the maximum resistance by labor unions to change in the status of the black labor force."[14] White racist attitudes, and the benefits white workers gained from reducing their competition against blacks by relegating them to lower positions, led to exclusion of blacks from unions. As Hill noted, discriminatory unions and segregated seniority and promotional lines in labor agreements have directly contributed to the privileged position of white workers.[15] Hill then noted what this racist discriminatory practice realistically means. "In reality, employment discrimination, either as total exclusion of blacks from a craft or as limitation to inferior classification, has been a form of subsidization to the white worker and his union. Thus, organized labor and employers have jointly created a highly exploited class of black labor, rigidly blocked from advancing into the all-white occupations."[16]

 What this has done has been to divide the working class based on race. White workers gain privileges relative to workers of color, but also reduce the size and potential power of the working class itself. Lacking a well-developed class consciousness and sense of unity, the working class is less able to resist demands of management or capital, which ultimately hurts the entire class. At the same time, however, it should be recognized that capital simultaneously unites class fractions by treating workers as workers, regardless of race. As Weis puts it, "The tendency for capitalism to transform all labor into a pure commodity means that on one level at least, there is a tendency to treat black labor power like white labor power, and one class fraction like any other."[17] The important point is to recognize that relationships between capital and labor, among laborers, are formed in the context of both race and class relations, which have a dialectical interplay; neither can be reduced to the other.

Education has historically served as a means of allocating people to jobs, and as a vehicle for social mobility. For this reason, people of color have fought for a right to an education, and have dramatically closed the gap with whites in educational attainment. For example, in 1969 the average white adult had completed three more years of schooling than the average black adult. By 1983, the average white completed 12.6 years and the average black completed 12.2 years of schooling.[18]

Because of racism, however, education has had less pay-off for people of color than for whites. For one thing, increased educational attainment has not closed the black-white unemployment gap. Since 1948, although unemployment rates for all races have fluctuated, the black unemployment rate has consistently been a little more than double the white rate.[19] In 1984, the unemployment rate among white high school graduates was 8.3 percent; among black high school graduates it was 28.1 percent, over three times as high. Only 3.9 percent of whites with some college were unemployed, while 13.0 percent of blacks with some college were unemployed.[20]

If race were not a factor, once employed, we would expect people with similar levels of education to hold similar paying jobs. Let us compare the experiences of blacks and whites today. In 1978, black men earned less than white men with the same level of education, regardless of what that level was, as Table 1 shows.
Furthermore, white men had a better chance than black men with the same level of education to hold better jobs, and black men were more likely to hold lower-paying, lower-class jobs than white men with the same level of education. Table 2 illustrates this for the year 1980.

As a result of higher unemployment rates, higher rates of underemployment, and lower pay, the income of black families today is no better relative to that of whites than it was two decades ago. In 1969, black families were earning on the average 58 percent of the earnings of white families; in 1983 that figure had fallen to 56 percent.[21]

Even though people of color may face less racial discrimination than they used to in attaining low-income jobs, they have far less of an opportunity than whites to earn an income greater than $12,000 and even less

Table 1 Mean Earnings of Black and White Men

Years of Education	Mean Earnings of White Men	Mean Earnings of Black Men	Percent of Black to White Men's Earnings
Less than 8 years	$11,303	$ 9,305	82.3
8 years	13,322	9,893	74.3
9–11 years	14,183	11,221	79.1
12 years	16,026	12,813	80.1
1–3 years college	17,626	14,611	82.9
4 years college	22,975	18,242	79.4
5 years or more college	27,476	19,945	72.6

Source: Treiman and Hartman, 1981, p. 15.

to earn an income over $25,000. For example, a recent survey found that only fifteen out of 340 congressional employees earning more than $30,000 annually were black.[22] In 1982 in the U.S. as a whole, 25 percent of all white men were earning at least $25,000, but only 8 percent of all black men were.[23] Jones posited it thus:

> Affirmative action has assisted blacks and other minority persons in entering the white-collar world of middle management, particularly within the government sector. But what must remain clear to all is that black Americans and other racial and ethnic minority groups of color have not made a serious dent in the corporate, entrepreneurial world of business. Institutional racism includes the upper as well as the lower spectra of income and economic opportunity.[24]

Race is a determinant of opportunity in areas besides jobs and income. For example, blacks and whites of the same social class do not

Table 2 Employed Males by Years of High School Completed, Occupation Group, and Race

Race, Years of High School Completed	Percent White Collar	Percent Blue Collar	Percent Service
White			
Less than 4 years	15.5	64.0	13.6
4 years or more	53.0	37.6	6.5
Black			
Less than 4 years	8.5	65.4	20.2
4 years or more	32.6	51.9	14.6

Source: U.S. Department of Commerce, 1981.

share the same housing opportunities. In 1976, 66 percent of all black families in the U.S. who were below the poverty level were living in poverty housing areas; only 31 percent of all white families in the same economic condition lived in poverty areas. In the same year, 41 percent of all black families above the poverty level lived in poverty areas, while only 13 percent of all white families above the poverty line lived there.[25] This was hardly because black families *chose* to live in poorer housing areas more often than white families; racist attitudes on the part of whites are the more likely cause. Recent studies of racial attitudes report that white attitudes towards blacks are much less negative than they were three-and-one-half decades ago;[26] nevertheless, white stereotypes of blacks are no less prevalent,[27] and positive white attitudes are not necessarily associated with positive behavior.[28] A 1978 survey conducted by *The New York Times* and CBS, designed to replicate the study conducted by the Advisory Commission on Civil Disorder in 1968, summarized the recent new attitude of whites very appropriately. The study reported that there are indeed new attitudes about race relations and new understanding among whites, but perhaps not the new will to take the bitter medicine the remedies may require.[29]

Finally, people of color have not yet attained their share of political power. Between 1971 and 1986 there has been only one black U.S. senator, and the number of other senators of color has fluctuated between two and three. The number of black congresspersons ranged during those years between twelve and twenty. At present there are twenty black congresspersons, only one of whom is female. That represents just 4.6 percent of the House, in spite of the fact that approximately 12 percent of the U.S. population is black. Other people of color in the House of Representatives currently number sixteen (none are female). Although nonwhites have been elected to state level offices in greater proportion, only one state governor is not white (he is Hispanic).

Ultimately the Marxist agenda is to replace capitalism with collective ownership of the means of production. Theorists hope that this will result in a more equitable distribution of goods, power, and privilege, and one that will last. If there is no simultaneous and equally powerful assault on racism, why should we believe such an economic revolution will diminish racist practices such as those cited earlier, or that whites will not create another economic structure or recreate capitalism to resubordinate people of color?

SEXISM IN RELATIONSHIP TO SOCIAL CLASS

Sexism is rooted in biological reproductive differences and, like racism, is intertwined with class. Generally, sexism rests on the idea that men and women by nature have different roles to perform. Historically many have also viewed women as genetically inferior to men, but whether or not the sexes are seen as genetically unequal, they *are* seen as genetically *different*. This difference has served as the basis for exploitation.

Sexism is usually subsumed under a class analysis as follows. Owners of the means of production require laborers who can commit most of their waking time to labor. However, laborers are not machines and require physical and emotional needs to be met, as well as requiring their children to be raised until they are old enough to enter the workforce. As Oakley has pointed out, "Industrial capitalism requires *somebody* to buy the food, cook the meals, wash the clothes, clean the home, and bear and bring up the children. Without this backup of domestic labour the economy could not function."[30] Since women bore and nursed children, they became servants to laborers, and their unpaid labor at home produced the laborers required by capital. While the requirement that women do the reproductive work is less fixed today, in large part they have remained responsible for this type of work. The idea follows that if capitalism were to disappear, so would sexism since there would be no need for workers to work full-time away from home, and thus no need for a class of people whose primary role is domestic service of workers.

This analysis fails to account for several aspects of the oppresison of women. One problem it does not account for is why *women* are relegated as a group to domestic service. Biology dictates that women bear children, but that is all. If workers require clean clothes, meals, clean houses, care for their children, and so forth, why do women perform these tasks? It might be more profitable for the capitalist to hire workers of both sexes who are best at performing the tasks capital requires, while people of either sex who are good at cooking, cleaning, and child-care do the domestic work. Marxist theory offers an explanation for why somebody does unpaid labor in the home, but not for why women consistently do it, regardless of their potential usefulness in the labor force.

Furthermore, Marxist analyses do not explain why employed women still perform most of the domestic labor. Oakley has noted research data that have found little difference between the amount of domestic work done by husbands of unemployed wives and husbands of employed wives. In fact, as Davis has pointed out, the notion that workers require somebody else at home taking care of them ignores not only the experience of today's employed women, but also the experiences of lower-class women and women of color who of necessity have always worked outside as well as inside the home.[31]

Woman's primary place is still in the home, regardless of whether this is the most profitable arrangement for the business owner seeking the most productive workers, regardless of women's employment status, and regardless of technological developments. Technology has changed many aspects of society, but not the oppression of women. In the workplace, technological advances have simplified and even eliminated many jobs. In the home, technological advances have tended to make "women's work" more complex without making it less time-consuming. Vanek has noted that in spite of recent technological innovations purporting to simplify housework, women in the 1970s were spending as much time on it as they were in the 1920s.[32] (During World War II, women's time on domestic labor fell as women were needed in the labor market, but rose again when men returned to the labor market and to the home.) What technology does is elevate standards of domestic cleanliness and open up new demands to place on women. For example, towels now must not only be clean, but also soft and fluffy, which requires knowing which additional products to buy and when to add them to the wash cycle. Whether or not towels are soft and fluffy has nothing to do with most capitalist profits—although it has much to do with profits of softener manufacturers—but it is a comfort that requires additional, not less, effort on the part of those who do wash—women.

Another problem with class analyses is that they do not account for the subordination of women in the labor force. On the average, the earnings of full-time working women of all races today are about 63 percent of those of full-time working men of all races. Black men are concentrated in lower-paying jobs than white men, but females of all races are concentrated in lower-paying jobs than men. For example, in 1982, 25 percent of all white working men and 8 percent of all black working men earned at least $25,000; this level of income was earned by only 4 percent of white working women and 2 percent of black working women. Incomes of less than $10,000 were earned by 35 percent of white males, 54 percent of black males, 68 percent of white female workers, and 72 percent of black female workers.[33]

A number of studies have examined human capital factors (e.g., education, work experience, evidence of work commitment) that might explain this differential, but taken together these "factors usually account for less than a quarter and never more than half of the observed earnings differences."[34] After reviewing studies of employment patterns of both sexes in an effort to explain differences in earnings, Treiman and Hartman have concluded that:

> ...an additional part of the earnings gap results from the fact that women are concentrated in low-paying jobs. Job segregation by sex is quite pronounced and shows few signs of substantially diminishing.

Women are concentrated in low-paying occupations and, within occupations, in low-paying firms.[35]

These authors pointed out that women end up in jobs with low pay, low job security and little opportunity for advancement due to a combination of three factors.[36] First, women tend to choose certain kinds of jobs based on cultural factors such as prior socialization, perceptions of what is available, lack of training for other higher-paying jobs, and anticipated family commitments. Second, women are often excluded from occupational opportunities at the hiring and promotion levels, on the basis of sex. The persistence of exclusion due to sex stereotypes that permeate our culture is underscored by Oakley who reported that:

> One recent British survey of managers formulating and implementing personnel policy discovered that more than a third of managers (in 213 establishments) believed that women are not career-conscious; half thought women belonged at home and were inferior employees because of their high absenteeism and turnover rates.[37]

Third, Treiman and Hartman believe that "women's work is underpaid because women do it." They have found that "several documented cases of pay rates were shown to have been influenced by the sex composition of the work force as well as by the content of jobs."[38] The same point is made by Janssen-Jurreit who examined a study using U.S. Labor Department statistics. Comparing the relative numbers of men and women entering different fields, and comparing the sexes in terms of profession, education, and income, the following result was found: "The more the amount of female labor power in a professional group rose, the more the relative income of the women dwindled in the last twenty-five years."[39] Treiman and Hartman pointed out that over a period of time as wage rates become customary for certain jobs in which there is a concentration of women—jobs like teaching—these low wage rates come to be accepted as standard for that job and thereby institutionalized on a nationwide scale.

Thus, institutional job segregation which concentrates men and women into different jobs at different levels of pay—regardless of the comparability of the work being performed—effectively maintains male privilege in the workplace. While Marxist analysis explains why *someone* gets the low-status, low-pay work, it fails to explain why *women* make up the lower ranks. In a critique of sociological theories of women and class, West pointed out that:

> Conditions in the labour market, deskilling and other such factors do not explain why *women* are drawn in rather than migrants, or school

leavers, or indeed men displaced from other sectors of the economy. We want to know, for instance, why it is precisely *women's* labour that can be hired more cheaply.[40] (Emphasis ours)

By subordinating women in the labor force, men have accrued some advantages, although this has weakened the potential of workers to unite to combat their collective exploitation. In the latter half of the nineteenth century when the labor movement was consolidating its own power, Davis pointed out that women were excluded from most of the ranks of organized workers. She noted that "the influence of male supremacy was so powerful that only the Cigarmakers and Printmakers had opened their doors to women."[41] We pointed out earlier that blacks had also been excluded from the mainstream labor movement; the black National Colored Labor Union, unlike its white counterparts, admitted women as members and demonstrated commitment to advancing the interests of both sexes. But, since most white women refused to associate with blacks, they did not join forces with their black working-class sisters. This left the working class split on the basis of both race and sex, and thereby weakened its power to advance common class interests. In fact, women were not only virtually excluded by the white labor movement; they were exploited by it. According to Janssen-Jurreit:

> Only by delegating housework and childcare responsibilities to women could the male worker—in the little time that remained after a twelve- or ten-hour workday—have any chance at all to develop his class organizations—trade unions, parties, and cooperative buying associations.[42]

Still today, sexism continues to inhibit class consciousness and consolidation of power in the working class. Oakley pointed out that in the U.S. only 12 percent of employed women are union members, and about 25 percent of all unions have no female members.

> The view prevails that women are difficult to organize because they are apathetic and/or concerned only with the next wage packet. But the male-dominated trade unions have done little to accommodate their organization and timetabling to the needs of women workers, whose work also includes running homes and servicing husbands and children.[43]

By continuing to subordinate women, even when it inhibits class formation, men can maintain their perception of women as sex objects and servants, and have a class of people to whom to relegate some of the jobs they see as distasteful.

Finally, the notion of class itself is essentially based on the male experience, and the analytic frameworks used to define and examine social class do not adequately capture or lend themselves to an understanding of the female experience. Historically, as both Oakley and West have pointed out, official and sociological definitions of social class have been based on the assumption that women derive their social class status from men. Official statistics have assumed that families all have a head and that this head is usually male, and have proceeded to classify the entire family's social class based on his income or occupation. Sociological studies have often defined a family's social class in the same way, since "male occupationally based social class proves to be a powerful indicator of life chances in many fields."[44] However, since women rarely hold the same jobs as their husbands, make the same income, experience the same promotions, and so forth, feminist sociologists are beginning to question whether traditional conceptions of social class accurately take account of women. For example, Oakley noted that it is usually assumed that both husband and wife share the same social class position, but argued that, "unity cannot be assumed, especially within the family. The wife's work and the man's wage may complement each other from a theoretical point of view, yet pragmatically this lack of symmetry causes division and difference."[45] Oakley and West pointed out that assumptions of family unity and derived social class fail to account for problems such as different interests of men and women within the same family; women's lower status within the family; separated, divorced, or single women who hold considerably lower-paying jobs than their former husbands or fathers; and how unpaid domestic labor should fit within a social class structure. Based on problems such as these, they argue that our conceptions of social class need to be reformulated giving equal attention to women's experiences, rather than simply adding women onto conceptions of social class based on the experiences of men.

Marxist theory suggests that a more equitable distribution of material goods will eliminate or at least greatly reduce other forms of inequality including sexism. We would argue that the basis of women's oppression is only partially economic; it also rests on psychological and material advantages one sex maintains over the other on biological grounds. Although sexism is related to classism, like racism, it cannot be reduced to a class analysis.

CONCLUSION

Social theory that criticizes unequal relationships among groups, and that illuminates how oppressive structures are reproduced and can be changed, is needed. Marxism has brought us a fair distance in such theory-building. But it is not sufficient, and theories of racism and sexism cannot simply be grafted onto it. There is a need to build a theory that integrates racism and sexism with class relations, and that does not treat two of these as subsidiary to the third.

We believe that such theory-building should be done collectively by a group representing diverse race and class backgrounds and both sexes. Individuals in the group will need to prepare themselves by familiarizing themselves with the historic and contemporary experiences of their own race/class/gender groups, and of one or two other groups, paying particular attention to what they have written about themselves. During this preparation, individuals should seek answers to the following questions: Under what conditions has one group oppressed another group? Exactly what were the group boundaries? What strategies or power bases did a group use to subordinate another group, how was that relationship maintained, and how did the subordinate group respond? For example, one may discover that groups start competing for power when a social system reaches a certain size, but that in very small societies this is minimal. If so, why? One may find various mechanisms used for maintaining distance between groups, enabling "good" people to accept putting others down; geographically distancing oneself from others allows one to forget them; distancing them by "proving" them biologically different seems to be another strategy. Then one is ready to try sketching a theory that explains the experiences of the few groups studied. If all members of a theory-building group do this preparation, collectively there should be enough of the pieces to be able to construct a theory of race, class, and gender.

NOTES

1. Stanley Aronowitz, *The Crisis in Historical Materialism* (New York: Praeger, 1981), p. 4.

2. Henry A. Giroux, "Theories of Reproduction and Resistance in the New Sociology of Education: A Critical Analysis," *Harvard Education Review* 53 (1983), pp. 257–293.

3. Carl A. Grant and Christine E. Sleeter, "Race, Class, and Gender in Education Research: An Argument for Integrative Analysis," *Review of Educational Research* 56 (1986), pp. 195–211.

4. See for example, W. J. Wilson, *The Declining Significance of Race* (Chicago: University of Chicago Press, 1978).

5. Stephen Gould, *The Mismeasure of Man* (New York: Norton, 1981).

6. Robin M. Williams Jr., "Prejudice and Society," in J. P. Davis, ed., *The American Negro Reference Book* (Englewood Cliffs: Prentice-Hall, 1966), p. 727, cited by J. R. Feagin and C. B. Feagin, *Discrimination American Style* (Englewood Cliffs: Prentice-Hall, 1978), pp. 8–9.

7. L. Kushnick, "Racism and Class Consciousness in Modern Capitalism," in B. P. Bowser and R. G. Hunt, eds., *Impacts of Racism on White Americans* (Beverly Hills: Sage, 1981), p. 193.

8. Randall Collins, *The Credential Society* (New York: Academic Press, 1979), p. 100.

9. Collins, *Credential Society*, p. 103.

10. Michael Reich, *Racial Inequality* (Princeton: Princeton University Press, 1981), p. 267.

11. Kushnick, "Racism and Class Consciousness," p. 192.

12. Herbert Hill, "The AFL-CIO and the Black Worker: Twenty-five Years after the Merger," *Journal of Intergroup Relations* 10 (1982), p. 57.

13 Ibid.

14. Ibid., p. 50.

15. Ibid., p. 57.

16. Ibid. The example we cited of the electrician field is not isolated. For example, information on the exclusion of blacks from the New York City Plumbers Union in the 1970s and 1980s can be found in Herbert Hill, "The New York City Terminal Market Controversy: A Case Study of Race, Labor and Power," *Humanities in Society* 6 (1983), pp. 351–391.

17. Lois Weis, *Between Two Worlds* (London: Routledge and Kegan Paul), p. 141.

18. U.S. Department of Commerce, Bureau of the Census, *Statistical Abstract of the United States 1985*, 105th ed. (Washington, D.C.: U.S. Government Printing Office, 1985), p. 134

19. Ibid.

20. Ibid., p. 458

21. Ibid., p. 446.

22. "Constitutional Law – Equal Employment Law – Discrimination in Employment on Capitol Hill: Some Alternative Solutions," *Harvard Law Journal* 23 (1980).

23. U.S. Department of Commerce, 1985, p. 452.

24. J. M. Jones, *Prejudice and Racism* (Reading, Mass: Addison-Wesley, 1972), p. 38.

25. U.S. Department of Commerce, Bureau of Statistics 1979. *The Social and Economic Status of the Black Population in the United States: An Historical View, 1890–1978.* Washington, D.C.: Government Printing Office.

26. See, for example, D. G. Taylor, P. B. Sheatsley, and A. M. Greeley, "Attitudes toward Racial Integration," *Scientific American* 238 (1978), pp. 42–49.

27. See M. Karlins, T. L. Coffman, and G. Walters, "On the Fading of Social Stereotypes: Studies on Three Generations of College Students," *Journal of Personality and Social Psychology* 13 (1969), pp. 1–16.

28. Tinto, "Dropout from Higher Education."

29. *The New York Times* (February 26, 1978).

30. Annie Oakley, *Subject Women* (New York: Academic Press, 1981), p. 167.

31. Angela Y. David, *Women, Race, and Class* (New York: Random House, 1981).

32. Joann Vanek, "Time Spent in Housework," *Scientific American* 231 (1974), pp. 116–120.

33. U.S. Department of Commerce, 1985, p. 452.

34. D. J. Treiman and H. I. Hartman, *Women, Work, and Wages: Equal Pay for Jobs of Equal Value* (Washington, D.C.: National Academy Press, 1981), p. 42.

35. Ibid.

36. Ibid., pp. 53–61.

37. Oakley, *Subject Women*, p. 158.

38. Treiman and Hartman, *Women, Work, and Wages*, p. 56.

39. M. Janssen-Jurreit, *Sexism: The Male Monopoly on History and Thought* (New York: Farrar Strauss Giroux, 1982), p. 182.

40. Jackie West, "Women, Sex, and Class," in A. Kuhn and A. Wolpe, eds., *Feminism and Materialism* (London: Routledge and Kegan Paul, 1978), p. 247.

41. Davis, *Women, Race, and Class*, p. 137.

42. Janssen-Jurreit, *Sexism*, p. 119.

43. Oakley, *Subject Women*, p. 305.

44. Ibid., p. 285.

45. Ibid., p. 289.

Part II

CULTURAL FORMS IN SCHOOL

7

Class Stratification, Racial Stratification, and Schooling

JOHN U. OGBU

INTRODUCTION

There is a long-standing debate over the relative influence of social class background and racial-group membership on school experiences and outcomes of black Americans and similar minorities. A major question is whether the relatively low academic performance of black students is due to the fact that the students come from lower-class backgrounds or because they belong to a racial minority group. Although race is recognized as a variable, the dominant view is that the low school performance is due to the children's lower-class background.

The question about how much social class background shapes the school experiences and outcomes of black children is becoming increasingly significant these days because of recent developments in the analysis of the class structure within the black population in the United States. These developments have led to the claim, for instance, that the black population is now divided into two unequal, distant, if not antagonistic classes: the successful middle class and a depressed underclass.

Students of black education who have traditionally favored explanations of black academic performance patterns in terms of social class backgrounds have not been immune from the new conception of black class structure. Indeed, the underclass concept has generated so much interest among researchers that race as a significant variable has increasingly receded into the background.

There are several approaches to the study of the relationship between class and education among blacks, but in this presentation I will focus on only two. One is the correlational approach; the other is the cultural reproduction or resistance theory approach. The purpose of my paper is to show that these class analyses are limited by the fact that they are primarily concerned with instrumental relations and situations. I will suggest that in a racial stratification of castelike type, expressive factors are also very important and cut across class boundaries. For this reason, racial stratification has its own unique influence on the school experiences and outcomes of black children and similar minorities which is not explained by reference to socioeconomic factors or class struggle. Before I go on to suggest how racial stratification uniquely influence black school experiences and outcomes I will discuss briefly the emerging conception of black class structure and the two approaches to class and education among black Americans.

THE NEW CONCEPTION OF BLACK CLASS STRUCTURE

At the moment there is a tendency to more or less arbitrarily divide the black population in the United States into two camps: the middle class and the underclass. However, I think that Wilson, one of the originators of the underclass concept, is right when he points out that there are also other classes in the black community, namely, the working class and the lower class.[1] According to Wilson's model of black class structure, at the top is the *middle class* which he initially thought was made up primarily of college-educated blacks. He later modified his view to say that the middle class included black white-collar workers and those in the skilled crafts and foremen positions. Next is the *working class*, which consists of semi-skilled operatives. Below the working class is the *lower class*, consisting of unskilled laborers and domestic workers. At the very bottom is the *underclass*, a group that is highly heterogenous. The underclass includes employed lower-class people who do not earn enough to be above the official poverty level, permanent welfare recipients, long-term unemployed, and official dropouts from the labor force. The underclass segment, according to Wilson, is characterized by female-headed households, street-loitering males with no fixed addresses, and people lacking in skills for employment above lower-class jobs. But what ultimately distinguishes the underclass from other classes is that it consists of poor blacks living below the official poverty line: the key criterion is income level.[2]

By defining the underclass population in terms of income level we can see that this segment of the population is likely to be unstable: its size can vary from one month to the next and from year to year, depending on trends in the economy. For example, on July 19, 1982, Dan Rather reported on the CBS Evening News that in one year, 1981 to 1982, more than two million Americans "fell" below the official poverty line. This, according to the above definition, would mean that 2 million Americans joined the underclass in that one year period because their income slipped below the official poverty level. But in doing so would they really assume the attributes of the underclass within that period? This seems unlikely, knowing from other sources that some of the two million people were middle-class retirees who, because of inflation, had become short of funds; but the fact that they became short of funds did not mean that they also lost their middle-class values and other middle-class characteristics. Others of the two million people were temporarily unemployed skilled workers whose unemployment benefits ran out; they, too, I suspect, would return to their former lifestyles when the economy improved and they regained their former jobs and wages. On the whole, then, it seems that classifying people as belonging to different classes, particularly to the underclass, because of their income is not very satisfactory.

I am, therefore, skeptical of the current view of the black class structure, as one polarized into middel class and underclass because of income differences. Furthermore, as noted earlier, there are other social classes within the black population, namely, the working class and the lower class. Unfortunately, as will be pointed out below, current analysis of the educational problems of black Americans tends to emphasize the dual-class polarization and the negative influence of underclass background.

SOCIAL CLASS AND SCHOOLING

1. Correlational Studies

Denial of Racial Stratification

Amost a decade ago I pointed out that Americans who study the education of blacks and similar minorities seemed to avoid analyzing the problems of schooling in terms of racial stratification,[3] This was evident in major works which influenced social policies and programs in the 1960s and in the 1970s. Although these works recognized race as a variable, they ignored racial stratification. In fact, the concept of racial stratification rarely appeared in their indexes. The preferred view of American society is one stratified by social class in which all racial groups and all ethnic groups participated in the same class system.

The preference for analysis of minority education terms of class stratification and the denial of racial stratification can be seen from reactions to my suggestion that black Americans are involved in a racial or castelike stratification and that such a stratification system both co-existed with class stratification and appeared to have a distinctive influence on black schooling.[4] Indeed, I suggested that where castelike stratification or racial stratification co-exists with class stratification, as in the United States, it is the former that is more basic to social structure and therefore the ultimate determinant of inequality in school outcomes and in adult socioeconomic status between the racial minorities and the dominant group.

The reaction of those in favor of class analysis was predictable. Some responded by saying that the ultimate cause of inequality in American society is corporate capitalism; consequently, class is more fundamental since it is based on economic differences. In their view racism is merely an expression of economic or class inequality.[5] Others note that poor people everywhere (e.g., Britain) have been shown to have lower IQ scores and to do poorly in school; therefore, they insisted that the lower IQ test scores and poor academic performance of black American children are due to the fact that a disproportionate number of the children come from lower-class or poverty backgrounds.[6] Still other critics asserted that racial stratification, if it ever existed, had disappeared from American society because of changes in the structure of opportunities available to black Americans and similar minorities. And using the emerging conception of black class structure, they claimed that the problem of lower academic performance is primarily a problem of the "underclass." According to them, with declined significance of race as a factor in the economic marketplace and in American society in general, middle-class blacks are now making it just like middle-class whites, while underclass blacks are not making it just like underclass whites are not making it.[7]

The Reality of Racial Stratification

The insistence that only class stratification is real is an illusion for a number of reasons. In the first place, racial stratification or castelike stratifications, hence "racism" or "castism" has been found in pre-corporate capitalist and pre-capitalist societies. Examples of such societies are the pre-colonial Ibos of Nigeria,[8] the Nupe of Nigeria, and Beni Amer of East Africa, and the Tira of Sudan;[9] in pre-colonial Rwanda in Central Africa,[10] the Senufo of West Africa,[11] and among the Konso of Ethiopia.[12]

Not only can castelike or racial inequality or stratification exist in the absence of corporate capitalism, but it can also exist alongside a class system under corporate capitalism, as has been the case in the United States. Under corporate capitalism, members of different castes or racial groups who have similar social class backgrounds are not treated alike in the economic marketplace or for social positions. This differential treatment under corporate capitalism has been long and well documented in the case of blacks and white in the United States.[13]

A good example of the differential treatment of black Americans as a subordinate group in a racially stratified society is found in Thernstorm's study of blacks, the Irish, Italians, and Jews residing in the metropolitan Boston area between the late nineteenth century and 1970. The study showed that over the entire period large gaps between blacks and the white immigrant groups (i.e., the Irish, Italians, and Jews) remained in employment, wages, and other socioeconomic conditions.[14] The persistence of these gaps led Thernstorm to ask: "What accounts for the overwhelming concentration of (black) males in the most menial and ill-paid occupations from the late nineteenth century down through the Great Depression and the persistence of substantial economic inequality between the races even after the major advances made between 1940 and 1970?" After analyzing the impact of rural background, education, the ghetto, family patterns, discrimination, and black culture, Thernstorm concluded that *racial barriers* were the main cause of lack of economic progress among blacks. He summed up the problem caused by the racial barriers by saying that in nearly every area of the economy, including efforts by blacks to establish their own business,

> it appears that the main barriers to black achievement have not been internal but external, the result not of peculiarities in black culture but of peculiarities in white culture. For three quarters of a century following Emancipation there was a pervasive (white) belief in inferiority (of blacks) that fostered overt discrimination in many industries, and left most blacks with little choice but to accept traditional "Negro jobs." (p. 203).[15]

Thernstorm's conclusion is that racial barriers, not class barriers to employment, were the main cause of the relative lack of black economic advancement.

The point to emphasize is that the United States is characterized by the existence of multiple stratification systems. This was pointed out long ago by Myrdal when, with reference to black Americans, he said that:

> Upper class people in all countries are accustomed to look down upon people of the laboring class as inherently inferior. But in the case of Negroes the deprecation is fortified by the elaborate system of racial beliefs, and the discrimination are organized in the social institutions of rigid and not only of flexible social class.[16]

Each system of stratification—class, gender, caste/race—has its own educational consequences. And the academic problems and achievements of each category cannot be fully understood or explained in terms of social class or SES analysis alone. Furthermore, each racial group, such as blacks and whites in the United States, has its own class differentiation but the classes are not necessarily equal, as I have shown elsewhere.[17]

It is true that changes have occurred in the opportunity structure of black Americans, particularly since the 1960s. But these changes have been distributed unevenly by the powers that be. Thus, through deliberate government policies backed by legislation, and through government encouragement of the private sector, college-educated or middle-class blacks have been given increased access to high-level jobs or jobs more appropriate for their educational attainment than was previously the case. For the college-educated or middle-class blacks, the job ceiling under racial stratification has been raised, though not completely eliminated. One consequence of raising the job ceiling for middle-class blacks has been to establish among them appropriate linkage between school credentials on the one hand and, on the other, jobs and earnings, such as apparently has usually existed among the white middle class. Thus, if college-educated or middle-class blacks are making it in school and in the job market, it is partly because of deliberate societal policy used to break employment barriers under racial stratification and the fact that the resulting connection between school credentials and post-school rewards which these middle-class blacks now experience may generate positive perceptions of schooling and positive responses to school on their part and on the part of their children.

For the non-college-educated blacks, i.e., for the working-class, lower-class, and underclass blacks, there has been no comparable official policy to increase their employment opportunities; no affirmative action of equal strength. Thus, if members of these classes—the working class, the lower class, and the underclass—are not doing well in the job market it is partly because there has been no comparable policy to help them break employment barriers under racial stratification. Most of them continue their traditional marginal participation in which the linkage between schooling, work, and earnings is relatively weak.[18]

In summary, in the changes in opportunity structure that have occurred since the 1960s, middle-class blacks have been helped to achieve positions in the economic and related marketplace appropriate for their educational attainment. This experience has undoubtedly had positive effects on their perceptions of and responses to schooling. The other classes have not received such a help and have not experienced this appropriate linkage between educational attainment and jobs and related benefits in life. They have, therefore, no new basis for changing their perceptions of and responses to schooling. But, as I will try to show later, instrumental factors, such as opportunities for better jobs and wages, are not the only ones shaping the school experiences and academic outcomes of racial minority students.

Academic Problems of Blacks are Beyond the Underclass

Another difficulty with the correlational studies is that among blacks the academic lag is not restricted to the underclass or to the lower classes. It is true that within the black population middle-class black children do better in school than children from the working-class, lower-class, and underclass backgrounds. But middle-class black children are not necessarily doing as well in school as their white middle-class counterparts. As many studies have shown, black children, on the average, do less well in school than white children from similar social class or socio-economic backgrounds.

Some examples will help clarify the problem. One is a comparison of the test scores of black and white candidates taking the S.A.T. in the 1980–81 season. According to a report in the New York Times of October 24, 1982, black candidates from homes with annual incomes of $50,000 or more had a median verbal score at about the same level as white candidates from homes with average annual incomes of $13,000 to $18,000. Furthermore, black candidates from homes with average annual incomes of $50,000 or more had a median math score slightly below the median math score of white candidates from homes with average annual incomes of $6,000 or less.[19] Another example is reported by Kriston Anton who studied the academic records and college admissions of some 4,000 California high school graduates of 1975. She found that among blacks and Hispanics, "children from affluent and well-educated families are not benefiting from their parents' achievement and, like children from poorer families, have trouble getting into college."[20] Other studies point to similar lower performance of black students from various social class backgrounds when compared to their white counterparts.[21]

Correlational studies do not provide a satisfactory explanation for the gaps in the academic performance of black and white students of similar social class or family backgrounds. At best they attribute the difference to "race." But, as I have shown elsewhere, membership in different racial groups does not necessarily result in differences in school performance; nor does membership in the same racial group lead to similar school performance.[22] Gaps in school performance appear and persist only when racial groups are stratified in a castelike form.[23] The challenge is to explain why middle-class blacks do not perform as well as their white counterparts and why underclass or lower-class blacks do not perform as well as their white counterparts.

2. The Cultural Reproduction and Resistance Theory

A more useful approach to the class analysis is that of the cultural reproduction school which emphasizes the element of resistance or opposition in the dynamic relationship between the culture of the schools and those of the students. This approach, like the correlational approach, sees the situation as one involving essentially lower-class and underclass children. As formulated by Willis in his British study and adopted by American researchers, the resistance theory holds that working-class youths and minority youths consciously or unconsciously reject the meaning and knowledge taught by the schools and turn to working-class adults or to street people as a source of materials for resistance and exclusion. That is, it is said that they repudiate the schools by forming countercultures which eventually impede their school success and employability in the more desirable sector of mainstream economy.[24] Why do they reject school knowledge and meanings? Working-class and minority students reject school knowledge and meanings because they seem to understand that the kind of education they are receiving cannot solve their collective problem of subordination.[25]

However, Weis has shown in her excellent ethnographic study of black students in a community college, as I have shown in my own research in the public schools in Stockton, that the situation for black students is paradoxical.[26] Black youths do not consciously reject school meanings and knowledge. In fact, black youths say emphatically that schooling is important to them and that they want to get an education in order to escape from poverty and other problems in their ghetto community.[27] But although they verbalize a strong desire for education, black youths tend to behave in ways that will not necessarily lead to school success. For example, they tend to be excessively tardy, lack serious attitude toward their schoolwork, and not to persevere in doing their schoolwork. In addition, as black children get older some drift into drug use and sale and pursuit of other non-academic activities. Consequently, many do not do well enough in school to obtain the educational credentials they need for employment in mainstream economy.

Weis has made a significant effort to interpret the paradoxical situation. She says that both white working-class students and black students produce "oppositional cultural forms"[28] in school but that the oppositions are coded differently because *black workers* have had a different historical struggle and blacks have had a different place (e.g., as a castelike minority) in the class structure.[29] For instance, blacks initially had to fight for a positive collective identity and life as a racial minority and then they began to fight for equality of status. Under this circumstance it is possible that blacks developed high educational aspirations and initiated a long history of collective struggle for equal education *as a form of opposition* against white people who denied them access to education and equality of educational opportunity. If it is true that black educational aspirations and their collective struggle for equal education developed as a part of their opposition to the dominant whites, then, since education did not work for them in the same way as it did for the whites historically, there is apparently no contradiction between the fact that black students accept the process and content of education but at the same time behave in a manner that ensures that they do not succeed, i.e., "they drop in and out of school, arrive late to class, exert little effort, and engage in extensive drug use that serves to distance them from the process of schooling."[30] Weis sums up by saying that, "While (black students) do not (consciously) reject the form and content of schooling (this — i.e., the non-rejection — must be seen as historically oppositional in and of itself), their own lived culture (e.g., dropping in and out of school, etc.) reveals these impulses."[31]

I find Weis's analysis exciting and very helpful. It throws much light on the problem. However, I think that the paradoxical situation cannot be adequately resolved or explained through an analysis cast essentially within the framework of class struggle. For although Weis repeatedly points to the importance of racial struggle, her ultimate reference seems to be to the material conditions of the group, i.e., blacks. In my earlier writings on the subject I also emphasized the importance of material conditions, especially of lack of technoeconomic opportunities; but over the years it has become clear that the relationship between racial stratification and schooling involves more than instrumental factors. Expressive factors are equally important and their nature and role need to be explored and clarified. Furthermore, as indicated earlier, the academic problems of blacks are not limited to the lower classes involved in a class struggle. And it is my impression from reading some ethnographic studies as well as from personal communication with researchers, teachers/educators, and parents, not to mention students themselves, that the paradoxical situation of high educational aspirations and low effort investment and counter-academic behaviors cut across class boundaries. The issue appears, therefore, to involve more than class struggle. It involves, in my view, the problem of racial stratification which is broader than that of class stratification.

Finally, it seems to me that the school or academic behavior of black students or the "lived culture" is not merely an on-site production.

Historical and ethnographic studies appear to indicate that other blacks in other settings and other contexts manifest similar behaviors. It seems to be a part of an evolved cultural pattern characteristic of the communities from which the students come.

I will now turn to indicate some of the ways in which racial stratification *qua* racial stratification or castelike stratification makes some unique contributions to the problem of black school performance and to the paradox of affirmation of school knowledge and meaning and rejection of standard practices of the school.

RACIAL STRATIFICATION AND SCHOOLING

I should point out from the outset that in studying groups like black Americans we are dealing with a particular form of racial stratification, one which involves a non-immigrant minority group. Thus, a very significant factor is that blacks did not come to occupy their subordinate relation to white Americans voluntarily in the belief that this was a starting point of a new opportunity to achieve a better life for themselves and/or for their children. Rather, blacks were initially forced to occupy their subordinate position involuntarily through slavery, relegated to menial status, and after emancipation from slavery were denied material resources for advancement and denied true assimilation into the mainstream of society. Moreover, under this circumstance blacks had no "homeland" to return to like immigrant minorities; nor could they easily "pass" physically to escape their subordination.

I have described in detail elsewhere the treatment of blacks by whites historically; here I will focus, though briefly, on black responses to their treatment relevant to their current academic performance pattern. But to put the latter in its proper context I will also note the relation of blacks to the class system of the mainstream society and also the expressive exploitation of blacks by whites historically.

I have shown elsewhere that blacks were excluded from participating in the same class system as the whites even after blacks were emancipated from slavery. A lower-class black person could not expect to rise in the class system like a lower-class white person because the black was not allowed access to the resources with which to achieve higher class status, was not given access to education or to other strategies for achieving higher class status, and was not even recognized or expected to do so. The education of blacks, when it was permitted or provided, was tailored to prepare them for their more or less ascribed positions in adult life. This situation lasted well into the present century.

While in my earlier writings I emphasized this instrumental exploitation of blacks by whites throughout their history, it is equally important to point out that there was also an expressive exploitation, whereby white Americans used blacks as scapegoats and projected onto blacks undesirable traits. These projections which relieved whites of their intrapsychic stresses in times of economic, social, or political crisis often became institutionalized as "cultural solutions" for similar future needs.[33] Consequently, blacks have not only had to respond instrumentally to instrumental exploitation, in order to improve their material conditions, they have also had to respond expressively in order, for example, to achieve a sense of identity.

I will use Figures 1 and 2 below to summarize the complex historical developments and the resulting present situation with regard to black school experiences and outcomes. Fig. 1 summarizes the dynamic relationship between white treatment of blacks and black responses. Column B in Fig. 1 shows various forms of white treatment or what I call the "collective problems" that blacks have faced historically at the hands of the whites. In column C are the responses of blacks or their "collective solutions" to the collective problems indicated in column B. These collective solutions were institutionalized in the course of black history and have come to form a part of the black folk system and cultural frame of reference or beliefs and practices of the black community. The folk system and the cultural frame of reference also embody the attitudes, knowledge, and competencies transmitted to and acquired by black children as they grow up and form a part of what the children bring to school pertaining to schools, schooling, and white people who control the schools (see Columns E and F in Fig. 1).

Fig. 2 shows three aspects of black responses that I consider most pertinent to their school perceptions and responses. The first set of responses are instrumental, and these are the ones I emphasized in my earlier writings on the problem.[34] They also appear to be the ones that figure prominently in the conceptual framework of resistance theorists. The instrumental domain shown in column 1 of Fig. 2 indicates that because blacks have faced a job ceiling or technoeconomic barriers, they have evolved a folk theory or folk theories of making it which do not necessarily emphasize strong academic pursuit. Moreover, blacks also developed alternative or survival strategies, i.e., other ways of making it outside the strategy of mainstream education and jobs. These survival strategies, I have suggested, may divert the interest and efforts of blacks into non-academic pursuits, and they may also promote personal attributes or competencies that are not necessarily congruent with standard school practices for academic success. Finally, black youths know from

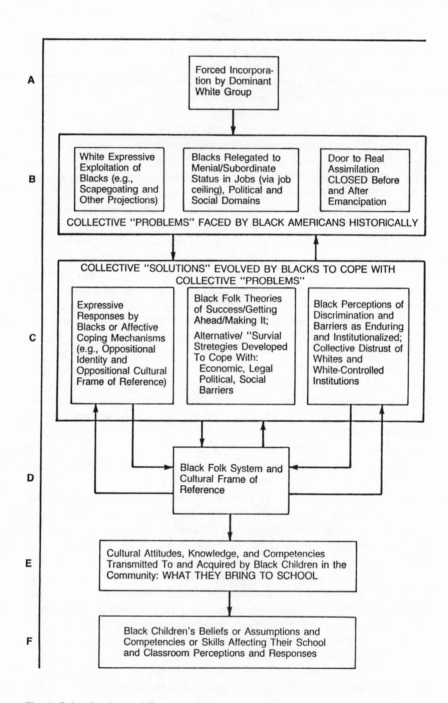

Fig. 1. Subordination and Response in Racial Stratification

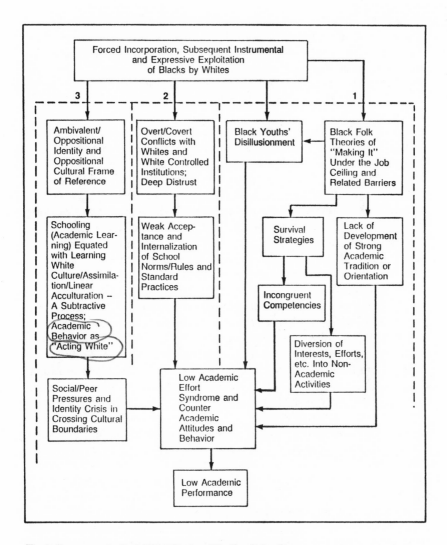

Fig. 2: Responses to Racial Stratification Affecting Schooling

observing their parents' situation and that of other adults in their communities that their chances of making it through education and mainstream jobs are not very good. They, therefore, often become increasingly disillusioned as they get older and consequently try less and less to do their schoolwork seriously.

Another type of response which I have identified is a deep distrust for the schools and white people who control them or their minority representatives. This distrust arose out of a long history of conflict between blacks and the public schools as well as between blacks and white authorities. I have suggested that this distrust is apparent in the black community and that it is communicated to children from an early age. Furthermore, as the children learn to distrust the schools and the people who control them, as their parents do, it is probably difficult for them to accept, internalize, and follow school rules of behavior for academic achievement.

Column 3 of Fig. 2 shows another set of responses which have only recently begun to be recognized and are not yet well understood. The responses are oppositional social or collective identity and oppositional cultural frame of reference. Both are expressive and are intimately related. They differ from the opposition of white working-class youths insofar as the latter arises from the material conditions of the working class and insofar as the oppositional cultural forms of the working-class youths are an on-site production in school. The oppositional identity and oppositional cultural frame of reference of black students are continuous with the same phenomena historically and contemporarily outside of a school setting.

Comparative and historical analyses of relationships between dominant groups and subordinate groups in castelike stratifications, such as between blacks and whites in the United States, indicate that these subordinate minorities usually react to their subordination and exploitation by forming ambivalent or oppositional identities as well as oppositional cultural frames of reference. That is, the minorities like blacks often develop an identity system or sense of peoplehood which they *perceive and experience* not merely as different but more particularly as in opposition to the social identity system of their dominators or, in the case of blacks, "white oppressors." In the area of behavior the racial minorities often come to define certain attitudes and ways of acting as *not appropriate* for themselves because these are attitudes and ways of members of the dominant group, or the "white ways." And the minorities define opposing attitudes and behaviors as more appropriate for themselves. Thus, from the point of view of black Americans and similar minorities, there co-exist two opposing cultural frames of reference or ideal ways of behaving, one for white Americans and the other for black Americans (or other minorities). Individual blacks who step into what their peers and the black community regard as the "white cultural frame of reference," i.e., individuals who try to cross cultural or language boundaries, may experience both internal opposition or identity crisis and external opposition or peer and community pressures.

Not every Black American is affected by the oppositional process (i.e. identity crisis and peer/community pressures to conform) to the same degree or all the time. In fact, some blacks consciously disassociate themselves from black collective identity and from a black cultural frame of reference and prefer to "assimilate" or follow the white ways. However, for a large segment of the black population, whether living in the ghetto or in the suburb, there exists a distinct black social identity or sense of peoplehood and a distinct black cultural frame of reference that guides their relationship with whites and that guides their behavior, especially in white-controlled institutions.

The oppositional or ambivalent social identity and the oppositional cultural frame of reference becomes particularly important in the school context because black Americans (like similar minorities) generally equate school learning with the learning of the culture of the dominant group, or white culture. Furthermore, it is believed that such learning can only result in giving up black culture. (See Fig. 2, column 3). Specifically, blacks and similar minorities (e.g., American Indians), believe that in order for a minority person to succeed, academically, in school, he or she must learn to think and act white. Furthermore, in order to think and act white enough to be rewarded by whites or white institutions like the schools, a minority person must give up his or her own minority-group attitudes, ways of thinking, and behaving, and, of course, must give up or lose his or her own minority identity. That is, striving for academic success is a subtractive process: the individual black student following standard school practices that lead to academic success is perceived as adopting a white cultural frame of reference, as emulating white, or as "acting white" with the inevitable outcome of losing his or her black identity, abandoning black people and black causes, and joining the enemy, namely, white people.

The perception or interpretation of emulating whites as a betrayal to black people or as joining the enemy consciously and/or unconsciously arouses criticisms and opposition among blacks, especially among peer group members. It also probably leads to personal crisis or an identity crisis, since the individual learning to "act white" is not really sure that he or she would be accepted or rewarded by white people if he or she succeeded.[35] Therefore, individuals are discouraged from acting white or behaving in a manner regarded as acting white in the school context (e.g., doing one's schoolwork seriously) by both internal and external factors.

The definition of certain behaviors and attitudes as white, including the standard practices of the school and classroom, poses some serious problems for black students and for similar racial minority students. The reason is that the behaviors designated by these students as "white" include many that are essential for school success. For example, in one study where the researcher made an attempt to study the problem of acting white, interviews with black high school students yielded no less than seventeen behavioral categories that the students identified as "acting white" or white ways. These included speaking standard English, working hard in school to get good grades, getting good grades, being on time, and so on.[36] The study also found that students who elected to "act white" faced a real burden. This supports my own findings in Stockton and also the finding of Petroni among black high school students.[37] The consequence is that many potentially good students avoid doing their schoolwork seriously for fear of being accused by their peers of acting white. Those who ignore the threat and act white find themselves punished by being rejected as not being black or not thinking of themselves as black. Finally, students who do relatively well in school while still accepted by their peers are those who are either simultaneously successful in sports and other activities regarded as black or students who have found ways to camouflage their academic efforts and outcomes. The point I would like to stress is that the burden of acting white seriously affects the academic efforts and outcomes of black children of all social classes or socioeconomic backgrounds, although children from some segments of the black community may be more affected than the others. But it cuts across social class boundaries.

Nor is the burden of acting white limited to black adolescents in high school or to black youths in college. The problem is also found among blacks who have made it in school and are now situated in what were traditionally "white positions" in the corporate economy and mainstream institutions. For some of these adult blacks and middle-class blacks the burden of acting white has led to "dropout problems"; for some others it has even resulted in suicide.[39]

CONCLUSION

I will conclude by restating the problem. Among black Americans as among white Americans, students from middle-class backgrounds do better academically in school than students from lower-class, working-class, or the so-called underclass backgrounds. However, in comparing black and white students, black students, on the average do not do as well academically as their white counterparts at a given social class level. Correlational studies do not explain satisfactorily why this gap exists in academic performance of black and white students of similar social class backgrounds. I do not believe that this lag in academic performance of black students in adequately accounted for in terms of class struggle and class oppositional process, if social classes are defined in economic terms.

If, however, we take racial stratification seriously as a distinct type of stratification, we see that it generates its own oppositional process that cuts across class boundaries because it is tied to the minority-group members' sense of peoplehood or collective social identity. Thus the oppositional process may remain even after economic and other instrumental barriers have been removed. That is why some black students from middle- and upper-class backgrounds may still express their opposition to "acting white" in school just as black students from working-class, lower-class, and underclass backgrounds may do. The problem is, of course, more serious in some segments of the black population. But, on the whole, the phenomenon is in large part responsible for the academic lag of black students.

NOTES

1. W. J. Wilson, *The Declining Significance of Race: Black and Changing American Institutions* (Chicago: University of Chicago Press, 1978); and W. J. Wilson, *Race, Class and Public Policy in Education* (Unp. Lect., prepared for the National Institute of Education, Vera Brown Memorial Seminar Series, Washington, D.C. 1980).

2. Wilson, *Declining Significance*, p. 181; and Wilson, *Race, Class and Public Policy*.

3. J. U. Ogbu, "Racial Stratification and Education: The Case of Stockton, California," *IRCD Bulletin* 12: 3 (1979), pp. 1–26.

4. J. U. Ogbu, *Minority Education and Caste: The American in Cross-Cultural Perspective* (New York: Academic Press, 1978).

5. E. W. Gordon and C. C. Yeakey, "Review of Minority Education and Caste," *Teachers College Record*, (1980); pp. 526–529; and C. C. Yeakey and G. S. Johnson, "Review of Minority Education and Caste," *American Journal of Ortho-Psychiatry* 49: 2 (1979) pp. 353–359.

6. G. C. Bond, "Social Economic Status and Educational Achievement: A Review Article," *Anthropology and Education Quarterly* 12: 4 (1981), pp. 227–257.

7. P. van der Berghe, "A Review of Minority Education and Caste," *Comparative Education Review* 24: 1 (1980), pp. 126–130; and Wilson, *Race*, 1980.

8. J. U. Ogbu, "Education, Clientage, and Social Mobility: Caste and Social Change in the United States and Nigeria," in *Social Inequality: Comparative and Developmental Approaches*, C. D. Berreman, ed., (New York: Academic Press, 1981) pp. 224–306.

9. S. F. Nadel, "Caste and Government in Primitive Society," *Journal of Anthropological Society of Bombay* 8:9 (1954), p. 22.

10. J. J. Maquet, *The Premise of Inequality in Ruanda* (London: Oxford University Press, 1961).

11. D. Richter, "Further Consideration of Caste in West Africa: The Senufo," *Africa* 50:1 (1980), pp. 37–54; and D. M. Todd, "Caste in Africa?" *Africa* 47: 4 (1977), pp. 398–412.

12. C. Hallpike, *The Konso of Ethiopia* (Oxford: Clarendon Press, 1972).

13. B. Harrison, *Education, Training and the Urban Ghetto* (Baltimore: Johns Hopkins University Press, 1972); and G. Myrdal, *An American Dilemma: The Negro Problem and Modern Democracy* (New York: Harper, 1944); and P. H. Norgren and S. E. Hill, *Toward Fair Employment* (New York: Columbia University, 1964), "U.C. Study on Minorities in College," *Oakland Tribune* (7 Aug. 1980), p. 1; and J. U. Ogbu, *The Next Generation: An Ethnography of Education in an Urban Neighborhood* (New York: Academic Press, 1974) and J. U. Ogbu, *Minority Education*; and S. Thernstrom, *The Other Bostonians: Poverty and Progress in the American Metropolis, 1880–1970* (Cambridge: Harvard University Press, 1973); and P. Wallace, ed., *Equal Employment Opportunity: The AT & T Case* (Cambridge: MIT Press, 1976).

14. Thernstrom, *Bostonians*, p. 203.

15. Ibid.

16. Myrdal, *American Dilemma*, p. 209.

17. Ogbu, *Racial Stratification*; and *Minority Education*.

18. D. K. Newman, et al., *Protest, Politics and Prosperity: Black Americans and White Institutions, 1940–1975* (New York: Pantheon Books, 1978); and D. K. Newman, "Underclass: An Appraisal" in *Caste and Class Controversy*, Charles V. Willie, ed., Bayside: General Hall, 1979) pp. 92–97; and J. U. Ogbu, *Minority Education* and J. U. Ogbu, *Education, Clientage*; and C. V. Willie, "Relative Effect of Race and Social Class on Family Income," in *Caste and Class Controversy*, Charles V. Willie, ed., (Bayside: General Hall, 1979) pp. 50–68; and W. J. Wilson, *The Declining Significance of Race: Black and Changing American Institutions* (Chicago: University of Chicago Press, 1978); and W. J. Wilson, "The Declining Significance of Race: Revisited But Not Revised" in *Caste and Class Controversy*, Charles V. Willie, ed., (Bayside: General Hall, 1979) pp. 159–176.

19. M. Slade, "Aptitude, Intelligence or What?" *New York Times* (24 Oct. 1982).

20. "U.C. Study on Minorities in College," *Oakland Tribune* (7 Aug. 1980), p. 1.

21. R. Haskins, *Race, Family Income and School Achievement* (Unp. Ms., 1980); and C. Jencks, *Inequality* (New York: Basic Books, 1972); and A. R. Jensen, "How Much Can we Boost IQ and Scholastic Achievement?" *Harvard Educational Review* 39 (1969), pp. 1–123; and A. R. Jensen, *Bias In Mental Testing* (New York: The Free Press, 1980); and R. A. Mickelson, et al., *Brown and Black in White: The Social Adjustment and Academic Performance of Chicano and Black Students in a Predominantly White University*, in press (1986); and U. S. District Court for Northern California, Larry P. vs. Wilson Riles: Opinion (San Francisco: Unp., 1979) DOC #C–71–2270 REP; and A. K. Wigdor and W. R. Garner, eds., *Ability Testing: Uses, Consequences, and Controversies* Part I: Report of the Committee (Washington D.C.: National Academy Press, 1982).

22. Ogbu, "Racial Stratification," p. 2; and Ogbu, *Minority Education*; and Ogbu, *Understanding Community Forces Affecting Minority Students' Academic Effort* (Oakland: Unp. ms. prepared for the Achievement Council of California, 1984).

23. Ogbu, "Racial Stratification," p. 1.

24. P. Willis, *Learning to Labor: How Working Class Kids Get Working Class Jobs* (Westmead: Saxon House Press, 1977).

25. L. Weis, "'Excellence' and Student Class, Race and Gender Cultures" in Philip Altbach, Gail Kelly and Lois Weis, eds., *Excellence in Education: Perspective on Policy and Practice*, (Buffalo: Prometheus Press, 1985), pp. 217–232.

26. L. Weis, *Between Two Worlds: Black Students in an Urban Community College* (Boston: Routledge and Kegan Paul, 1985); and Weis, "'Excellence'."

27. Weis, *Between Two Worlds*; and Ogbu, *The Next Generation*.

28. Weis, *Between Two Worlds*; and Weis, "'Excellence'."

29. Weis, Personal Communication, 1985.

30. Weis, "'Excellence'," p. 224.

31. Ibid.

32. Ogbu, *Minority Education*.

33. G. A. DeVos, *Ethnic Persistence and Role Degradation: An Illustration From Japan* (New Orleans, unp. paper, presented at the

American-Soviet symposium on Contemporary Ethnic Processes in the USA and the USSR, 1984, april 14–16).

34. Ogbu, *The Next Generation*; and Ogbu, *Minority Education*; and Ogbu, *Understanding Community Forces*.

35. DeVos, *Ethnic Persistence*.

36. S. Fordham, Personal Communication, 1985.

37. F. A. Petroni, "'Uncle Tom': White Stereotypes in the Black Movement," *Human Organization 29: 4 (1970), pp. 260–266*.

38. B. M. Campbell, "To Be Black, Gifted and Alone," *Savy* (December 1984), pp. 67–74.

8

High School Girls in a De-Industrializing Economy

LOIS WEIS

Previous studies suggest that working-class high school females elaborate, at the level of their own culture, a private/public dichotomy which emphasizes the centrality of the private and marginalizes the public. Home/family life becomes central for adolescent girls and wage labor secondary. As many studies have shown, working-class girls elaborate what Angela McRobbie has called an "ideology of romance," constructing a gender identity which serves to encourage woman's second class status in both the home and workplace. Studies of McRobbie and Valli, in particular, have been important in terms of our understanding of the way in which these processes work upon and through female youth cultural forms.[1]

Such cultural forms have serious implications for the position of women in both the family and the workplace in the sense that they represent parameters within which struggles will take place. By defining domestic labor as primary, women reinforce what can be called the Domestic Code, under which home or family becomes defined as women's place and a public sphere of power and work as men's place. The reality, of course, is that generations of working-class women have labored in the public sphere, and that labor also takes place in the home, albeit unpaid. Yet, as Karen Brodkin Sacks points out, "the Domestic Code has been a ruling set of concepts in that it did not have to do consis-

I would like to acknowledge the helpful comments of Hugh Petrie and Sheila Slaughter on an earlier version of this paper. Ava Shillan and Craig Centrie acted as my research assistants and provided valuable help during the data collection phase of this research. My sincere thanks to them as well. These data will be reported in full in Lois Weis, *Working Class without Work* (New York: Methuen, forthcoming).

tent battle with counterconcepts. It has also been a ruling concept in the sense that it 'explained' an unbroken agreement among capitalists, public policy makers, and later, much of organized labor, that adequate pay for women was roughly 60 percent of what was adequate for men and need be nowhere adequate to allow a woman to support a family or herself."[2]

The Domestic Code is being challenged on a number of fronts, but it is not my intention to elaborate them here. It is important to note, however, that the Domestic Code in its strict sense of *separate* spheres no longer characterizes any segment of the society. As of 1982, 53 percent of all employed women were married, and 51 percent of married women were employed. Fifty-six percent of married mothers were in the paid labor force, rivaling the 61 percent of divorced or single mothers who were in the paid labor force.[3] Young females tend to elaborate a Domestic Code, marginalizing wage labor, but the fact of the matter is that they will almost certainly engage in such labor. This is even more the case for working-class females. It is not, then, the case that women live out the separate spheres envisioned when they are young. These concepts, however, set the parameters within which later lives tend to be lived. Women who do not envision the primacy of wage labor, for example, may not prepare themselves, or argue for the right to be prepared, for well-paying jobs with career ladders. If women see the domestic sphere as *their* responsibility, they may not struggle for the high quality day care centers which would allow them to maintain involvement in the paid labor force to the extent necessary for a career. In point of fact, the lines between the public and private spheres have blurred considerably in recent years and issues ostensibly "private" are now debated in the public arena. Action in the public sphere also impacts on the private increasingly, as more and more women work. This might be even more the case, however, if the lines were not so clearly drawn at a young age.

Internalized elements of the Domestic Code combined with the reality of women working outside the home has led to what can be called "women's double bind." Women define themselves primarily in terms of home and family but, in fact, work outside the home. Rather than alter social interactions and labor processes within the home, a "double day" was institutionalized in which labor in the home was simply added to hours spent in wage labor.[4] As Ferree notes, "Women are more and more likely to be in the paid labor force but experience little change in the division of labor at home. Employed women continue to do 4.8 hours a day of housework compared to the 1.6 hours their husbands do."[5]

There have been a number of explanations put foward that could potentially explain male dominance in both the home and workplace, and the debate rages regarding the extent to which capitalism and/or patriarchy contributes to these outcomes. Hartmann has emphasized the interlocking systems of capitalism and patriarchy, and stresses that job segregation by gender is *the* primary mechanism that maintains the superiority of men over women because it encourages lower wages for women in the labor market, thus encouraging women to marry and ultimately live out the double bind described earlier.[6] Hartmann's argument is powerful, but it is not my intention to focus on it here. Rather, it is my intention to focus on the conditions under which female youth cultural forms might change, thus opening up the possibility of breaking the cycle of female subordination in both home and workplace.

THE DE-INDUSTRIALIZING OF AMERICA

Studies suggest that patriarchy takes a particularly virulent form in working-class communities. The home is defined as "women's sphere" even though working-class women have always worked outside the home. Data collected in studies by Ferree, Rubin, and others suggest that women lack power in both the home and the workplace, and that there is a sharp demarcation of male and female spheres of activity and authority. Since husbands perceive housework as demeaning and unmasculine, working-class women have an even more difficult time than middle-class women negotiating a more favorable division of labor within the home.[7]

This model of the working-class family is based on an economy that provides working-class men with access to jobs that enable these constructions. Working-class men have had access to jobs recently that, although alienating and often dangerous, have paid relatively well as a result of union struggles. Skilled, semi-skilled, and even unskilled laborers have been able to establish middle-class consumption patterns in the home, and their wages have often exceeded those of middle-class semi-professionals such as teachers. This has changed recently with the de-industrialization of the American economy. Working-class men simply do not have access to the wages that they did in the past. This raises the question of the degree to which patterns of gender domination and subordination will be maintained given that such patterns are at least encouraged by the sex-segregated labor force noted by Hartmann and men's ability to obtain relatively high-paying jobs within this labor force.

This is undergoing change due to current de-industrialization of the economy. At the end of World War II, American corporations dominated world markets. The American steel industry, for example, was virtually the only major producer in the world. By the 1960s, Germany, Japan, Italy, France, and Britain had rebuilt their steel industries, using the most advanced technology and becoming highly competitive with American industry. By the 1970s, the American industry was in decline relative to other countries, and this has led to numerous factory closings.

Factory closings are not restricted to the steel industry and, while more common in the northeast of the United States, are not confined to this area. Gone are many of the jobs in basic production—jobs in steel, automobiles, and manufacturing. The largest growth sector in the economy is now service, not production. Jobs in the service sector demand retraining, provide less security and money, and often demand relocation. De-industrialization means a less secure, generally lower, standard of living for working-class Americans.

Barry Bluestone and Bennett Harrision argue that "when the employment lost as a direct result of plant, store, and office *shutdowns* during the 1970s is added to the job loss associated with runaway shops, it appears that more than 32 million jobs were destroyed. Together, runaways, shutdowns, and permanent physical cutbacks short of complete closure may have cost the country as many as 38 million jobs.'"[8] Many displaced workers remain unemployed today; others obtained jobs in the lower-paying service sector. From all indications, de-industrialization is not temporary. It represents a radical shift in the nature of the American economy and the way in which workers intersect with this economy.

Given that gendered subjectivities have taken their shape and form historically in an economic context that is underoing radical change, what is happening to cultural forms? In particular, for this chapter, what is happening to female youth cultural forms given that forms noted in previous investigations are linked to patterns of male employment which are being eroded? Data reported here are not to be construed as a strict empirical test of a hypothesis regarding the primacy of the economy in any sense. However, data *were* gathered on youth cultural forms in a school in an area which is undergoing intense de-industrialization. The question is, are youth cultural forms, in this case, female cultural forms, different from those noted in previous investigations? Such data can be indicative at best since they were not gathered under strict hypothesis testing conditions. However, there is no apparent evidence that Freeway —the community in which data were gathered—is any different from other working-class communities in which previous investigators did their work except that de-industrialization and associated job loss are current. In other words, the speculated long-term trend of the American economy is being enacted right before the eyes of today's youth.

FREEWAY

Data reported here were gathered as part of a larger ethnographic investigation of Freeway High. I spent the academic year 1985–1986 in the high school, acting as a participant-observer for three days a week for the entire year. Data were gathered in classrooms, study halls, the cafeteria, extracurricular activities, and through intense interviews with over sixty juniors, all teachers of juniors, the vice-principal, guidance counselors, and others. Data collection centered on the junior class since this is a key point of decision when PSATs, SATs, and so forth must be considered.[9] In addition, this is, in the state where Freeway is located, the time when the bulk of a series of state tests must be taken if entrance to a four-year college is being considered.[10] I focus on the high school both as a way of gaining access to adolescents and to discuss, at a later point, the possible relationship between within-school processes and cultural production.

Freeway is an ideal site in which to conduct this investigation. Examination of data gathered for the Standard Metropolitan Statistical Area (of which Freeway is a part; data for Freeway per se not available) confirms a number of trends which are reflective of Bluestone and Harrison's argument. Occupational data for 1960–1980 (see Table 1) suggest that the most striking decreases in the area are found in the categories of "Precision; Craft and Repair" and "Operators, Fabricators, and Laborers." These two categories constitute virtually all of the so-called "blue-collar jobs." When combined, data suggest a relative decline of 22.3 percent in the "blue collar" category from 1960 to 1980. A look at some of the more detailed sub-categories reveals more striking decline. Manufacturers, for example, have experienced an overall decline in the area of 35 percent between 1958 and 1982.

Data also suggest an increase in the "Technical Sales and Administrative Support" category. These occupations constituted 22.8 percent

Table 1 Occupations by Year for Freeway Area SMSA*, All Persons

Occupation	% of All Occupations			Absolute Change	Net % Change
	1960	1970	1980		
Managerial and professional specialty occupations	19.2%	21.9%	21.7%	+2.5	+13.0%
Technical, sales, and administrative support applications	22.8%	25.4%	30.7%	+7.9	+34.6%
Service occupations	10.1%	12.9%	13.9%	+2.8	+37.6%
Farming, forestry, and fishing occupations	1.0%	0.6%	.9%	−0.1	−10.0%
Precision production, craft, and repair occupations	16.8%	15.4%	12.5%	−4.3	−25.6%
Operators, fabricators, and laborers	25.3%	23.6%	20.2%	−5.1	−20.2%
Occupations not reported	5.1%				

*Standard Metropolitan Statistical Area

of the total in 1960 as compared with close to 31 percent in 1980, representing an increase of over one-third. Increases in "Service" and "Managerial and Professional Specialty" categories also reflect a shift away
from industries and toward service occupations.

Although data on occupational trends in Freeway per se are not
available, the 35 percent loss in manufacturing noted above is due in part
to the closing of the Freeway steel plant. The plant payroll in 1969 was at
a record high of $168 million dollars, topping 1968 by $14 million. The
average daily employment was 18,500. Production of basic oxygen fur-
nace and open hearth was at a near record of 6,580,000 tons.[11]

In the first seven months of 1971, layoffs at the Freeway Plant
numbered 4000 and decline continued into the 1980s. From 18,500 jobs
in 1970, there were only 3700 production and 600 supervisory workers
left in 1980, with 3600 on layoff.[12] At the end of 1983, the plant closed.
All that remains of close to 20,000 are 370 bar mill workers.

This provides an ideal site in which to investigate the relationship between youth cultural forms and the economy. Here I will explore one
piece of the larger project in which data were gathered. I focus specifically on female cultural form and the extent to which girls in a de-industrial-
izing area construct a culture similar to that noted in previous studies.
Data presented here are based on in-depth interviews with twenty white
working-class juniors.

WORK OUTSIDE THE HOME

The most striking point about female culture at Freeway High is that
there is little evidence of a marginalized wage-labor identity. In fact,
these girls have made the obtaining of wage labor a *primary* rather than
secondary goal. Almost without exception the girls desire to continue
their education and they are clear that they intend to do so in order that
they can get their own life in order. The girls below exemplify this point.
It is noteworthy that only *one* girl interviewed mentioned marriage and a
family first when talking about what they wish to do after high school.
All the rest of the students stressed jobs or "careers," and college or some
form of further education was specifically discussed. It is only when I actually inquired about a family did most of the girls mention this at all. I
will return to this point in the next section.

The first set of interviews below details the responses of girls in what
is known as the "advanced" curriculum. These students were selected in
ninth grade for accelerated work. Only thirty out of a class of approximately 300 are so accelerated. Students in this group generally want to attend a four-year college and girls talk in terms of actual careers, often
non-traditional ones. Girls in the "regular classes" also talk about contin-

uing their education after high school, but generally focus on the two-year college, business institutions, or schools for hairdressing. Both groups of girls, however, stress job or "career" ahead of family, although the form of work desired tends to differ.

Judy, Rhonda, Jennifer, Jessica, and Liz are members of the advanced class. With the exception of Rhonda, who wants to become a medical technician, all intend to pursue careers which demand at least a four-year college degree. Some, like Jennifer, intend to go to graduate school. It must be clear that these are responses to a question about ,post–high school plans. I have chosen to quote at length here in order to let the students speak for themselves.

Judy: I'm thinking of [State University] for electrical engineering. I know
    I'm going to get into that.
LW: How did you pick electrical engineering?
Judy: Cuz my brother is an electrical engineer. . . .He works for General
    Electric. He has a BA.

· · ·

Rhonda: (I'll) probably go into medicine.
LW: Any particular area?
Rhonda: Medical technician, maybe.
LW: Would you consider being a nurse or doctor?
Rhonda: I considered being a nurse. But with all the strikes and them
    saying they're underpaid. I read alot about the job.

· · ·

Jennifer: [I want] to go to college but I'm not sure where. And I want
    to go into psychology, I think.[13]

. . . .I'd love to be a psychiatrist but I don't think I'll ever make it through medical school. So I was talking with a guidance counselor and she said you could get a Ph.D. in psychology and there are a lot of good jobs that go along with that.

. . . .I think I'm forced [to go to college]. I don't think I have a choice.

· · ·

Jessica: My mother wants me to be in engineering like my brother cuz he's so successful. . . .I have an interest with the behavior of marine animals. Which is kind of stupid cuz we don't live anywhere near an ocean so I was thinking of going to Florida State. My parents don't want me to go to any other school but [State University] so I haven't brought this up yet. I figure we can wait awhile.

· · ·

LW: What are you going to do when you leave high school?
Liz: College
LW: Do you know which college?
Liz: I'm thinking of [State University] in Physical Therapy.

Aside from Jennifer, whose father is head of the chemistry lab at a local hospital, these girls are not from professional families. On the contrary, they are the daughters of industrial laborers and they are thinking of obtaining a four-year college education and gaining some type of career. It is noteworthy that two of these girls are being encouraged by their families to go into engineering, one of the most non-traditional fields for women.[14] It might be hypothesized that as working-class individuals do obtain professional positions, they are disproportionately in areas such as engineering which are seen as having a direct relation with hands-on laboring processes. Obviously, I cannot prove this, but it is noteworthy that two girls are being encouraged by their families to pursue this end.[15]

The excerpts below are statements of girls in the regular classes. They too are, without exception, planning to pursue jobs, although most are those associated with two-year colleges or business institutes. They also tend to be jobs in sex-segregated ghettos.

Lorna: Well I go to (a cooperative vocational education program] for food service and I think I want to be a caterer. I don't want to be sitting down all the time. I like to be on my feet moving [she does not wish to go into business even though her shorthand teacher says she has "potential."] I like to cook and stuff (but) you get to do everything, not just stay in the kitchen.

. . . .[Suburban Community College] has got a two-year course and then if I want to I can transfer my credits and stuff and go to a four-year college. My mother's got a friend, she teaches food service in a college and she was telling me about it. Like what to do and stuff.

• • •

Loretta: [I want to go to] [State University].
LW: . . . .When you get out of [State University], what do you hope to do?
Loretta: Become a lawyer, have a family, I guess, but not until I graduate from college. . . A lot of my friends want to go to college.

• • •

Susan: I'll go to [the community college]. I don't want to go four years to school. I can just go two years and become a registered nurse and get a

job. I volunteer at [the local hospital] so I'm hoping to have a foot in
the door when it comes time for a job.

LW: When you leave high school, what do you want to do?

Carol: A lot of things. I do want to go to college for fashion design.
I don't know how good I'll do.

LW: Where do you want to go?

Carol: I haven't thought about it. But as soon as I graduate [from high
school] I want to get my New York State license [for hairdressing] and
get a job and then save money so that I have money when I want
it. . . . I want to have my own salon but first of all I want to start off
in somebody else's salon so I get the experience.

• • •

Valerie: I didn't really think I was going to go to college, unless business
courses. I'm going to try for a job [after high school] and if I can get a
good job out of it then I won't go to college. If it requires college training, then I'm going to go.

LW: What kind of job?

Valerie: Something with word processing.

• • •

Avis: I want to [go to] college around here. . . . They [business institute]
have medical secretary; they have a lot of business stuff and that will
help out. And they could get you a job. . . .

LW: What do you think you'll be doing five years from now?

Avis: Hopefully working. A medical secretary or something.

• • •

Gloria: [I'll probably] go to [State University] or [State College]. Become
a registered nurse specializing in pediatrics.

With the exception of Loretta and Gloria, all the girls in the non-
advanced curriculum wish to attend two-year colleges, business institutes, or schools for hairdressing. In addition, most are thinking in terms
of sex-segregated occupations. Avis and Valerie are thinking of being
secretaries; Carol wants to be a hairdresser; Lorna, a food service
worker; and Susan and Gloria, nurses. This is in contrast with the girls in
the advanced curriculum, where there appears to be some desire to break
out of these ghettos.

The predominantly male pattern of going into the armed forces has
little appeal to these girls, despite the fact that the armed forces has opened
up for women. Chris, below, is the only white female interviewed who in-

dicates a desire to go in this direction. She gives lip service to attending college, but it is clear that she is not truly interested in pursuing this option.

Chris: I either want to go to college or go into the air force. . . . .The air force because they say it's the best education around if you want to go into any of the military services.

     . . . .College is like another school to me. Like I have to go five years to college or something and then I have to go out and look for a job. It seems like another high school to me. Like the air force it seems like you're going somewhere. It seems like an adventure, kind of. . . . .See, my cousin, she's in the air force, and she's doing really well, and she likes it a lot. It's just that basic training is really hard. She says you have to pick a field, though. You can't just go there for the money.

     . . . .Like whatever they [air force] offer me, I could go for nursing. It's [college] not like a high school; I mean you could leave and do whatever you want to do, but it [college] just seems like another school.

Chris is clearly not interested in just "another school" and the air force seems to offer her a way out. It is interesting that she, too, has selected a traditionally female field — nursing.

Unlike previous studies the students think first of continuing their education and a career or job. Students in the advanced curriculum tend to think more in terms of four-year colleges and training leading out of a sex-segregated occupational ghetto, whereas the students in the non-advanced class tend to think largely in terms of two-year colleges, business institutes, cosmetology, and so forth, leading ultimately to sex-segregated jobs. This relationship is not perfect, however, and there are students in the advanced class who are intending to prepare themselves for jobs that can be obtained with two-year college degrees. Not all students in the advanced classes are thinking outside of the sex-segregated labor market and not all within the other classes think within its boundaries. The relationship does exist, however, even though it is far from perfect.

Two important points should be noted here. One is the lack of primacy for a home/family identity. These girls are thinking first and foremost of obtaining jobs and the further education necessary to get these jobs. Second, it must be noted that some of these girls are, in fact, thinking of non-traditional jobs: marine biologist, engineer, psychologist, and so forth.

Given the primacy of a wage-earning identity, the question must be raised, do they envision a home/family identity at all? If so, what shape does it take? I will now turn to this point.

MARRIAGE AND FAMILY

The fact that students do not marginalize a wage-labor identity contrasts sharply with data collected by Valli, McRobbie, Gaskell, and others.[16] Wolpe, for example, argues

> By the time teenage girls reach school leaving age, they articulate their future in terms of family responsibilities. They reject, often realistically, advice about pursuing school subjects which could open up new avenues; the jobs they anticipate are not only within their scope, but more importantly, are easily accessible to them and in fact in conformity with their future familial responsibilities.[17]

The girls in Valli's study similarly had notions of the primacy of family responsibilities; raising children, and possibly working part-time. As Valli notes,

> Experiencing office work as either secondary to or synonymous with a sexual/home/family identity further marginalized these students' work identities. The culture of femininity associated with office work made it easier for them to be less attached to their work and their workplace than men, who stay in paid employment because they must live up to masculine ideology of male-as-provider. Women's identities tend to be much less intrinsically linked to wage labor than are men's.[18]

> . . . .By denying wage labor primacy over domestic labor they inadvertently consented to and confirmed their own subordination preparing themselves for both unskilled, low-paid work and unpaid domestic service.[19]

Angela McRobbie's research on working-class girls in England also examines the role of gender as it intersects with class in the production of culture and ideologies. In spite of the fact that the girls in McRobbie's study know that marriage and housework are far from glamorous simply by virtue of the lives of female relatives and friends, they construct fantasy futures and elaborate an "ideology of romance." They create a specifically female anti-school culture which consists of interjecting sexuality into the classroom, talking loudly about boyfriends, and wearing makeup. McRobbie casts the culture in social control terms as follows:

> Marriage, family life, fashion and beauty all contribute massively to this feminine anti-school culture and, in doing so, nicely illustrate the contradictions inherent in so called oppositional activities. Are the girls in the end not doing exactly what is required of them — and if this *is* the case, then could it not be convincingly argued that it is their own culture which itself is the most effective agent of social control of the girls,

pushing them into compliance with that role which a whole range of institutions in capitalist society also, but less effectively, directs them towards? At the same time, they are experiencing a class relation in albeit traditionally feminine terms.[20]

The Freeway youth are markedly different. Although some assert that they wish to have some form of home/family identity, it is never asserted first, and generally only as a possibility "later on," when their own job or career is "settled." Some of the girls reject totally the possibility of marriage and children; many others wish to wait "until they are at least thirty." The primary point, however, is that they wish to settle *themselves* first, go to school, get a job, and so forth before entering into family responsibilities. Only one of the twenty girls elaborates a romance ideology, and this girl is severely criticized by others. Significantly, they do not construct fantasy futures as a means of escape.

It is important to point out that few of the girls discuss the possibility of marriage without considering divorce. The attitude toward marriage and children does not differ between the advanced and non-advanced students. Although these students tend to differ in terms of type of envisioned relationship to wage labor and future schooling, they do not differ at all with respect to the fact that they assert the primacy of a wage-labor identity over that of the home and family. The language of wanting to be "independent" is often used in discussions about home/family and the wage labor force. It must be noted here that the initial probe questions revolved around what they wanted to do after high school, what they wished to do in five years, and in ten years. Many times the issue of family never even was mentioned. It is only at that point that I asked the girls, *specifically*, whether they wished to get married and/or have a family. Again, I quote at length here in order to give the full flavor of the girls' perspectives. The perspectives of the advanced students are presented first.

LW: Why not just get a man to support you and then you can stay home?
Penny: Cuz you can't fall back on that.
LW: Why do you say that?
Penny: Cuz what if I get a divorce and you have nothing to fall back on.
LW: Does your mother encourage you to get a job because, 'What if I get a divorce'? [Her father is no longer alive.]
Penny: No
LW: So, where did you get that?
Penny: Just my own ideas. Just how things are today.

• • •

LW: Do you want to get married?

Jessica: Gee, I don't know. After I see all the problems that go on now, I just don't know. All the divorce. Just how can you live with somebody for forty years? I don't know, possibly. . . .You see it [divorce] all over. I'm not living to get married.

．　．　．

Judy: I want to go to college for four years, get my job, work for a few years, and then get married. . . .I like supporting myself. I don't want my husband supporting me. I like being independent.

LW: You're doing something very different from your mother. Why? [Mother was married at nineteen, went back to work when Judy was in grade 3.]

Judy: I think I have to. . . .What happens if I marry a husband who is not making good money? My dad works at Freeway Steel. He's switching jobs all the time (although the plant is closed, there is still piece work going on and workers are called back according to seniority rules). He used to work at the strip mill; now he's not. Now everything is gone, benefits and everything.

．　．　．

LW: Do you want to get married?

Pam: I want to and I don't. I'd like to have a child but not get married. . . . I would like to have a child just to say it's mine. Just to be able to raise it. . . .If you get married, like my mother and father are two different people. I would be afraid that my kids would come out like me and my sister. Like I can't talk to my father. . . .And if I did get married I'd want to be sure it would last if I had kids cuz I wouldn't be able to get a divorce. They say that it's 'ok' if you get a divorce and have children, but the kids change. I wouldn't want kids to go through that, cuz I, like, see the people around me.

．　．　．

LW: Do you think you'll get married?

Rhonda: I always thought that if I get married it would be after college.

．　．　．

LW: Do you hope to get married; do you hope to have children?

Liz: After college and everything's settled.

LW: What do you mean by 'everything's settled'?

Liz: I know where I'm going to live. I know what I'm going to be doing; my job is secure, the whole thing. Nothing's open. Everything's going to be secure.

• • •

Carla: Oh, I'm going to do that later [get married; have children]. I'm going to school to get everything over with. I wouldn't want to get married or have kids before that.

LW: Why not?

Carla: It'd be too hard. I just want to get my school work over with, get my life together, get a job. . . . I want to be independent. I don't want to be dependent on him [my husband] for money. Then what would I do if I got divorced fifteen years, twenty years, you know how people are in marriages. Twenty years down the line you have kids, the husband has an affair or just you have problems, you get divorced, then where is that going to leave me? I want to get my life in order first, with my career and everything. . . . Maybe it has something to do with the high divorce rates. Or the stories you hear about men losing their jobs and not have any job skills and you see poverty and I just don't want that. I want to be financially secure on my own.

All the above girls in the advanced class express the desire to get their "own lives in order before marrying." They all say that they will get married eventually, however. Only Suzanne, below, says she will never get married.

LW: Tell me a little bit about whether you want to get married.

Suzanne: [interrupts me] No. No marriage, no kids!

LW: Why not?

Suzanne: I don't like that.

LW: Why?

Suzanne: I don't think you can stay with somebody your whole life. It's dumb. . . . Like this one kid says, 'Marriage was invented by somebody who was lucky if they lived to twenty without being bit by a dinosaur.' It's true. It started so far back and it's, like, people didn't live long. Now people live to be 80 years old. You don't stay with one person for 80 years. It's, like, impossible.

LW: What makes you say that?

Suzanne: A lot of divorce. A lot of parents who fight and stuff. I couldn't handle the yelling at somebody constantly cuz I wanted to get out. I just don't want to be trapped. . . . Back when they [parents] were kids, girls grew up, got married, worked for a couple of years after graduation, had two or three kids, had a white picket fence, two cars. Things are different now.

LW: How so?

Suzanne: Girls don't grow up just to be married. They grow up to be people too.

LW: And that means they don't want these other things?

Suzanne: Not that they don't want them. A lot of girls in school, they're like, 'Hey, you're [Suzanne] crazy. I want to be married sometime, I want to have kids,' [but] they all want to wait. They all want to get into a career first; wait until they're thirty. It's [marriage] only 'if' though, and it's going to be late.

. . . .You've got to do it [make a good life] for yourself. I don't want to be Mrs. John Smith. I want to be able to do something.

I mean just from what I've seen a lot of people cheat and that. I don't want that. . . .You can't rely on them [men]. You just can't rely on them. . . .[Also] drinking a lot. It's like, I know a lot of older guys, they drink all the time.

The girls in the advanced class all suggest that they have to get themselves together first before entering into home/family responsibilities. Only Suzanne says she does *not* want to get married, but the rest of the girls clearly want the economic power to negotiate terms within the marriage. It is very clear from these excerpts that the conditions of their *own* lives mediate their response to family and paid work. Numerous students note the high divorce rate. Penny, for example, says, "What if I get a divorce and you have nothing to fall back on?" Jessica states, "After I see all the problems that go on now, I just don't know. All the divorce." Carla also states, "Then what if I get divorced fifteen years, twenty years, you know how people are and marriages. Twenty years down the line you have kids, the husband has an affair or you just have problems, you get divorced, then where is that going to leave me?" The lack of male jobs is also brought out by the students. Judy, for example, says, "What happens if I marry a husband who is not making good money? My dad works at Freeway Steel. He used to work at the strip mill, now he's not. Now everything is gone, benefits and everything."

The students assert that men cannot be counted on for a *variety* of reasons—high divorce rate, drinking, lack of jobs, lack of skills, affairs, and so forth. They respond to this aspect of their lived experience by establishing the primary of wage labor in their own lives in order to hedge their chances. They are attempting to control the conditions of their *own* lives in a way that previous generations of women did not.

The issue of a home/family identity and the degree to which girls in the advanced curriculum embrace an identity as a wage laborer first is highlighted in the following discussions. Amy has decided to drop the advanced curriculum in order to pursue cosmetology. She has done this as an assertion that, for her, a home/family identity *is* primary and she articulates this below. Jennifer, also an advanced student, is very critical of Amy's decision, as are the other girls. It must be clear here that Amy

has decided to go into cosmetology in order to work around envisioned
family life in much the same way as girls in previous studies envisioned
their lives. She is the *only* girl interviewed in this study who takes this
position and she sees herself as an outsider. It is the "outsider" nature of
her previously "normal" female position that is so interesting here.

Amy: They [my friends] don't want to get married. They just want to go
    out and get richer.
LW: The kids in the honors class?
Amy: *Everybody* [emphasis hers] I talk to. . . .They jsut want to be free.
    They're all going to college [some form of continued education],

    Everybody in my class is . . . They have a lower opinion of me [be-
    cause I don't want to go on to some form of school].

    . . . .They talk about it [marriage] as 'maybe some day.' But they
    don't really care whether they do or don't. They won't do it in the near
    future.

    . . . .They [outside the honors class] want to go to college too. They
    say, 'Why do you want to get married so young?' [twenty, twenty-one]
    They don't want to get married until they're thirty.
LW: Why do you think that's the case?
Amy: They don't want to be tied down.
LW: What does that mean? Why not?
Amy: They think that if they get married they're going to have to be told
    what to do. The won't be able to do what they want to do and they
    don't, like, want nobody dictating to them; nothing like that.

    . . . .Like if my girlfriends want me to come somewhere with them
    and I say, 'I'm coming with him [boyfriend]', they just say, 'You can
    come with us, let him go by himself. . . .Why do you let him tell you
    what to do?' I go with him everywhere. That's how they are.

At a later point Amy says:

Amy: I want to get married and have kids and I want to be at home. It's
    [cosmetology] a good thing to do at home so I don't have to go out
    and work and leave my kids with a babysitter or nothin'. I just don't
    like the whole idea.
LW: When are you thinking of getting married?
Amy: Three years. We figure we'll get married as soon as he finishes
    college.
LW: Is having kids something you want to do right away?
Amy: Yeah.
LW: And you're going to stay home with those kids?

Amy: Yeah, I guess I'm old fashioned. . . .When I tell my friends about that they look at me funny. Like, why would I want to do that? They want to go out and work, not get married and not have kids. They think I'm crazy or something. I'd just rather stay home, have kids and be a beautician on the side, at home. Have a shop in my home.

LW: How long do you think you should stay at home?

Amy: Depends on the money situation. Things like that. If we need extra money, I could go out and work. But if we didn't, whatever I felt like doing.

. . . .I'm just like her [my mother]. I want to do exactly what she did. She started working seven years ago. She's a clerk at a drug store and she hates it cuz she's not making much money at all. A little above minimum. Seven years and she can't get raises. They won't give her a raise and she complains. She wishes she went to college. She can't get any kind of good jobs.

Amy articulates the Domestic Code and, at the same time, notes the contradictory nature of that code in the real world. She says she wants to be "just like her mother" who is currently having difficulty getting a job that pays above minimum wage or provides a career ladder. It is exactly this Domestic Code which is being challenged at the cultural level by working-class females.

The tension over this code is articulated by Jennifer, below, who refers to Amy in her comments:

LW: Do most of the kids in the advanced curriculum plan to go to college?

Jennifer: All except for one who plans to get married and have kids.

LW: What is your perception of that one?

Jennifer: We've all told her on many occasions, 'It's crazy.' She's always been in our group and now she is taking cosmetology and she thinks she's just going to get a small job somewhere to help support when she gets married. She's all planned out. She's going to get married when he finishes college. She's been with this guy for a while. Her whole life is all planned out and it's like, 'ok, fine, you get married, what happens if you get a divorce?' 'My God [she says] that would never happen.' 'It might, you know; what if he dies, then what are you going to do?' You have to support yourself some way. Even if you do get married and you're happy now, something could happen tomorrow. You could have an unhappy marriage and get divorced. You can't say I'm gonna have a happy marriage, it might not work.

. . . .Maybe we think it's such a waste. I mean you have the opportunity, it's such a waste. I mean civil rights have come so far. If it were

100 years ago, I can see saying that, when you were being a rebellious women if you wanted to go out and get a job. I mean, now we have that opportunity; to relinquish that and say, I mean, I'm a cautious person and thinking of the future and saying what if something does happen. She isn't even thinking of that.

This same challenge is exhibited by the girls who are not in the advanced curriculum. Although they are preparing themselves for jobs in largely sex-segregated ghettos, they nevertheless challenge the Domestic Code as strongly as the others. *None* of the girls place home/family responsibilities before wage labor.

LW: Do you want to get married?
Chris: Yeah, eventually. Once I'm settled down with myself and I know I can handle myself.

· · ·

LW: Do you want to see yourself getting married: do you think you'll have children?
Valerie: Yeah, but not right away. I'll wait until I'm about twenty-four . . . .I just feel that I want to accomplish my own thing, like getting a job and stuff.
LW: Why not find a guy and let him support you?
Valerie: Feels like I have a purpose in life. Like I can do what I want.
LW: As opposed to?
Valerie: Feeling like *he* [emphasis hers] has to support me, and *he* has to give me money.
LW: Is that bad?
Valerie: I don't know.

· · ·

Carol: Well I know I'm not going to get married until I'm at least 30 and have kids when I'm around 31, 32.
LW: Why?
Carol: Cuz I want to have my own freedom to experience life, everything, to travel, to go out places without having to have a babysitter or worry about kids. Plus with a beauty salon [her envisioned job] it would be hard to have kids to take care of and do that at the same time.

· · ·

LW: Do you want to get married?
Susan: Yes.
LW: When do you think you'll get married?

Susan: I want to prove to myself if I can be on my own. I don't want no man to have to take care of me.

LW: Why?

Susan: Because my mother told me that, I don't know what the statistics are anymore, but for every marriage that lasts, every marriage doesn't, so. . . .

Women, when they go into a marriage, they have to be thinking, 'Can I support myself?'

. . .

LW: When you think about your life five years from now, what do you think you'll be doing? Do you think you'll be married?

Lorna: I'm trying to get all my education so I can support myself. Why put effort and then let somebody support you?

. . . .I saw my friends getting pregnant so young. If you get married young, you're going to get pregnant young and it's going to ruin the rest of your life. That's the way I see it.

. . . .Five years from now I'll just be able to go out to a bar. I'll be 21. And I don't want to ruin my life in just five years. Cuz as soon as you get married you're going to starting having kids; then you're going to have to stay home and raise them and stuff. I don't want to have to do that.

LW: Why not?

Lorna: I like to do things. I don't want to have to sit around all the time. . . .I just don't want to stay home all the time.

LW: Does marriage mean you're going to have to stay home all the time?

Lorna: Well, that's what I think of. You get married; you got to stay home. You can't just go out with other people. . . .I like to go out with my friends when I want to. I like to be able to make my own decisions and if you're married, you have to sort of ask the other person, 'Can I spend the money here, can I do that?' It's, like, you got to ask permission. Well I been asking permission from my parents all my life, you know. I don't want to just get out of high school and get married, and then have to keep asking permission for the rest of my life.

LW: . . . .Will you ever get married?

Lorna: I was just talking about that today. Probably when I'm thirty. Then I'll take a couple of years to have kids.

Although the girls in the non-advanced class tend to exhibit the same themes as the advanced class girls, there is some tendency on their part to elaborate the theme of "freedom" and, in contrast, the restrictions imposed by marriage. This is true for the earlier set of interviews as well, in that a number of girls stressed "independence." Non-advanced girls, however, seem a bit more strident about it. Lorna, for example, states that, "As soon as you get married, you're going to start having kids; then you're going to *have* (my emphasis) to stay home and raise them and stuff." She then states, "You get married; you got to stay home. You can't just go out and go out with other people. . . .I like to make my own decisions and if you're married, you have to sort of ask the other person, 'Can I spend the money here; can I do that?' It's like you got to ask permission." Valerie, too, notes that she doesn't want to feel that "*he* (emphasis hers) has to support me, and *he* has to give me money." Carol states that she wants "to have [her] own freedom to experience life," implying that marriage means that she forsakes such freedom. This point cannot be pushed too strongly since both groups stress the importance of their own independence. The non-advanced students tend to stress the possibly oppressive conditions of marriage in that you have to "ask permission," whereas the advanced students tend to stress the high divorce rate and the possibility that their husbands may leave them or not be able to get a good job. This is, however, not an overwhelming difference.

I have argued here that the girls' culture exhibits a challenge in many ways to the Domestic Code and its current manifestation in women's "double bind." They are definitely envisioning their lives very differently from girls in previous studies, and very differently than investigators such as Lillian Beslow Rubin and Glen Elder suggest that their mothers and grandmothers did.[21] In the next section I will speculate as to the meaning of this challenge and the way in which patriarchal forms may be challenged and reinforced at one and the same time.

CULTURAL FORM AND PATRIARCHY

The working-class girls examined here exhibit a challenge to patriarchal structures. They are, at least in terms of the ways in which they envision their lives, breaking down the Domestic Code. For them, the domestic is *not* primary; wage labor is. If patriarchy rests on a fundamental distinction between men's and women's labor, and currently the domination of women in both the home/family sphere and the workplace, these girls challenge that. They understand, to the point of being able to articulate it, the fact that too many negative consequences result if you depend on men to the exclusion of depending on yourself, and that this means you must engage in long-term labor. They do not suggest the "part-time" work solution and/or flights into fantasy futures offered by girls in previous studies.

In this sense, then, they challenge a fundamental premise of patriarchy—that women's primary place is in the home/family sphere and that men will, in turn, "take care" of them.

In another sense, however, the girls only partially challenge patriarchy, and it is the partial nature of their challenge which may result in so many girls ending up exactly as their mothers have. Many of the girls express the desire to obtain jobs in the sex-segregated ghettoes. This is not to denigrate such jobs in any way, but simply to acknowledge, as Hartmann has, that such jobs do not usually pay enough to allow women to exist outside the bounds of marriage. In other words, one reason why the girls want to have a job/career is the high divorce rate. They suggest the fact that they do not want to be in a bad marriage simply because of money. In fact, as they point out, the husband might drink, have an affair, or simply leave, in which case the wife needs to have a source of her own support. Yet the jobs many of the girls envision for themselves will not give them that level of support. A secretary cannot, for the most part, support herself and her children should anything happen to her marriage.[22] In this sense, then, the "selection" of traditionally female jobs limits their own chances to escape patriarchal structure despite their intentions.

This may be too simple an analysis, however. Given that girls selecting these jobs do so in order to escape patriarchy in some sense, it is likely that they will organize at some point to ensure that such jobs pay them a living wage. At least part of the reason that females in occupational ghettos are not as organized as males in laboring jobs is precisely because women have lived out a marginalized wage-labor identity—thus making organization within the workplace less likely. This is not to deny sheer male power in the workplace and in the home, but to suggest that women's own marginalized wage-labor identity has encouraged oppressive conditions to persist. The girls in Freeway do not marginalize their wage-labor identity and it is the very centrality of this identity that may encourage greater organization and political activity among female workers, most of whom are in the occupational ghettos. If Hartmann is right, that it is the sex-segregated labor force which encourages male dominance in both the workplace and the home, then the sex-segregated workplace must be dismantled before patriarchy can be seriously challenged. This may well be. It is also the case, however, that female workers who have a central wage-labor identity may move to organize traditionally female occupational ghettos in a way not yet imagined. I tend to agree with Hartmann and, therefore, see the overwhelming selection of jobs in the ghetto as ultimately serving patriarchy even though the girls intend otherwise. It may not, in fact, work that way, however, and the time may soon be ripe for this form of political activity, given the nature of gender culture described here.[23]

The girls who select careers outside of the occupational ghetto have a better chance at actually controlling the conditions of their own lives in that they may earn enough money to do so. In other words, they might actually be able to determine the conditions under which they marry, stay married, and so forth because the economic constraints will not be the same for them as for the others. My point here is not that middle-class women are traditionally more "free" than working-class women. They are not, in fact, necessarily less constrained than their working-class sisters as Ferree, Stephen Bahr, and others point out.[24] The girls in Freeway, however, elaborate a primary wage-labor identity and the question then becomes, to what extent will they be able to enact this identity and what power will it give them over their own family life? Those opting out of the sex-segregated ghettos and actually working in relatively high-paying positions have a better chance, I would argue, simply because they control greater personal/financial resources.

One last point needs to be made here. The girls' culture represents a challenge to patriarchy in the sense that emphasizing paid labor may allow women to negotiate the conditions of family life. Ferree points out that husbands in working-class families base their claims for family consideration and special treatment on the fact that they work hard at often dangerous, tiring, and certainly alienating jobs. Women will often say, "He works hard, he's earned it," in order to justify consideration of his needs for quiet, "time with the boys," and so forth.[25]

When women enter the wage-labor market they also have a claim potentially to special consideration because the family also needs *her* paid labor. As Ferree notes, "When an employed woman demands consideration for her needs—quiet, escape, leisure and the like—for the family to respond to these demands will mean a shift in responsibilities greater than introduced by her simply taking a job."[26] If and when these working-class girls enter into marriage, they do so with potential bargaining power. They may have the leverage to attempt to negotiate the conditions of family life, division of domestic tasks, financial arrangements, and so forth. If the family needs her paid labor in the same way as the family needs male labor, the *conditions* are there for readjustment in family authority and responsibilities. This is likely to be even more the case since traditionally well-paid male working-class jobs are being eroded. Although the girls do not articulate this directly, their insistence on not wanting to be "supported," on being independent, and maintaining paid work even after marriage and children, indicates that this may, at least, be in the back of their minds. The concern among some of the girls for not having to "ask permission," not being told where to go and so forth, suggests that they wish a more equitable arrangement in the home than in their own lived experiences suggest in this case.

The solutions posed thus far by the girls tend to be individualistic, however, in that they, individually, intend to get more education, continue working, and so on. Collective solutions are, as yet, not envisioned. Only one girl stressed that she would press for good day care at work, for example. In order to truly press for change, individual problems must be seen as shared and needing collective solutions. In other words, these girls have not yet seen themselves as sharing certain problems emanating from patriarchal structures — problems that necessitate collective struggle and solution. At present the culture appears to be a fractured one in the sense that each girl is trying to negotiate individually the power to lay at least some of the conditions to negotiate her own life. As these girls move into the work force, however, the need for individual solutions could easily encourage collective action in order to reduce male dominance in both the workplace and the home/family sphere.

The question of the extent to which the de-industrialization of the economy is responsible for this, in the final analysis, should be discussed. Although I have no way of testing this in any strict sense, it is possible that as well-paying male laboring jobs are phased out, the "good" points of patriarchy can no longer be seen and the "bad" become only too apparent. It is a certain set of lived realities on the cultural level that Freeway girls are responding to. Almost all note the high divorce rate, and many note the oppressive nature of male authority and dominance. This is, in their own words, what they wish to escape. The bargin of "male as provider" in return for female domestic labor breaks down when there is no paid work for the traditional working class. The harsh realities of patriarchial structures are then laid bare, and the Freeway girls are moving to dismantle these structures.

The challenge to patriarchy in the broader culture cannot be dismissed, however. The high divorce rate, harsh male authority, and emotional violence noted by the Freeway girls are not limited to the working class. Women throughout the class structure have challenged patriarchy in a variety of ways. The challenge exhibited by the Freeway girls should properly be seen as stemming both from a shift in the economy which erodes traditional working-class jobs as well as broader challenges to patriarchy in the society as a whole. What the girls live, however, on a day-to-day basis, is economic change and the way in which this change alters their lives and perceptions of men. Jobs are not there for men, and men are unreliable because of it — they drink, walk out on you, and have affairs. Girls cannot count on any return for occupying the traditionally female sphere of activity and they want the power to at least negotiate the conditions of their own domestic lives—whether to marry or not, stay married or not, what goes on within the family, and so forth.

This process of challenge is linked fundamentally to de-industrialization in the case of the working class. Similar processes of challenge are occurring throughout the class structure but they tend to be lived out gender challenges linked to class fractions. The Freeway girls are not, for the most part, linking up to a women's movement per se, but rather, responding to the lived experiences of their own working-class lives which, given de-industrialization, lay bare the brutal aspects of patriarchy.

NOTES

1. Angela McRobbie, "Working Class Girls and the Culture of Femininity," in Women's Studies Group, ed., *Women Take Issue* (London: Hutchinson, 1978); Linda Valli, *Becoming Clerical Workers* (Boston: Routledge and Kegan Paul, 1986).

2. Karen Brodkin Sacks, ed., *My Troubles Are Going to Have Trouble With Me.* (New Brunswick: Rutgers University Press, 1984), pp. 17-18. See also Alice Kessler-Harris, "Where Are the Organized Woman Workers," *Feminist Studies* 3: 1-2, pp. 92-110, as cited in Sacks, p. 18.

3. U.S. Bureau of Labor Statistics, "Earnings of Workers and their Families," *News* (November 1982) as cited in Myra Marx Ferree, "Sacrifice, Satisfaction, and Social Change: Employment and the Family," in Sacks, pp. 61-79.

4. See B. Berch, *The Endless Day: The Political Economy of Women's Work* (New York: Harcourt Brace Jovanovich: 1982), as cited in Ferree, p. 63.

5. Myra Marx Ferree, "Sacrifice, Satisfaction," pp. 63-64.

6. Heidi Hartmann, "Capitalism, Patriarchy and Job Segregation by Sex," *Signs* 1: 3 (pt. 2), pp. 137-170.

7. I do not mean to imply here that middle-class men engage in domestic laboring tasks whereas working-class men do not. The degree to which a negative valuation is assigned such tasks differs to some extent, however.

8. Barry Blueston and Bennett Harrision, *The De-Industrialization of America* (New York: Basic Books, 1982), p. 26.

9. The Preliminary Scholastic Aptitude Test (PSAT) and Scholastic Aptitude Test (SAT) are tests administered by Educational Testing Service in Princeton. Most four-year colleges require the SAT for entrance.

10. The governing body of the state administers a series of tests which must be taken if entrance to a four-year school is desired. Not all students take these tests, however, and track placement often determines whether the tests are taken.

11. Freeway Evening News Magazine Section (June 5, 1983).

12. Freeway Evening News Magazin Section (June 5, 1983).

13. Jennifer is the only daughter of professional parents. Her father is head of the chemistry lab at a local hospital. As one of the central office workers put it, "He [Jennifer's father] was almost too smart in high school, you know what I mean?" (she had gone to school with him).

14. See Lois Weis, "Progress But No Parity," *Academe* (November /December 1985), pp. 29–33.

15. One of the machine shop teachers also had a daughter in engineering. He was the person who initially pointed out to me that a number of students from manual laboring families who do become professionals go into engineering.

16. See Valli, McRobbie, and work by Jane Gaskell. See, for example, Jane Gaskell, "Gender and Class in Clerical Training" (Paper prepared for session on "Work and Unemployment as Alienating Experiences" at World Congress of Sociology in New Delhi, August 1986). Jane Gaskell "Gender and Course Choice" *Journal of Education* 166: 1 (March 1984) pp. 89–102.

17. Ann Marie Wolpe, "Education and the Sexual Division of Labour," in Annette Kuhn and Ann Marie Wolpe, ed., *Feminism and Materialism: Woman and Modes of Production* (London: Routledge and Kegan Paul, 1978), pp. 290–328, as cited in Valli, *Becoming Clerical Workers*, p. 77.

18. Linda Valli, "Becoming Clerical Workers: Business Education and the Culture of Femininity," in Michael Apple and Lois Weis, ed., *Ideology and Practice in Schooling* (Philadelphia: Temple University Press, 1983), p. 232.

19. See Madeleine MacDonald, "Cultural Reproduction: The Pedagogy of Sexuality," *Screen Education* 32/33 (Autumn/Winter 1978/80), p. 152, as cited in Valli, p. 232.

20. McRobbie, "Working Class Girls," p. 104.

21. Lillian Breslow Rubin *Worlds of Pain* (New York: Basic Books, 1976); and Glen Elder, *Children of the Great Depression* (Chicago: University of Chicago Press, 1974).

22. Linda Vallil argues in this volume that 35 percent of all working women are currently employed in office education, for example.

23. Linda Valli argues in *Class, Race and Gender in U.S. Schools* that it is the experience of office work itself that encourages women to marginalize a wage-labor identity since such work is repetitive and alienating. This may be the case but the ideology of the primacy of a home/family identity for women enables this to occur, I would argue. If such an ideology is attacked to begin with, the chance of this happening on the job is lessened. In other words, the Domestic Code enables this to occur for women and not for men.

24. See Myra Marx Ferree and Stephen Bahr, "Effects on Power and Division of Labor in the Family," in Lois Wladis Hoffman and F. Ian Nye, eds., *Working Mothers. An Evaluative Review of the Consequences for Wife, Husband, and Child* (San Francisco: Jossey-Bass, 1975).

25. Ferree, "Sacrifice, Satisfaction and Social Change" p. 69.

26. Ferree, "Sacrifice, Satisfaction and Social Change" p. 70.

9

Black Visibility in a Multi-Ethnic High School

JAMES STANLAW AND ALAN PESHKIN

The linguist George Lakoff and the philosopher Mark Johnson have argued that metaphors are not only instrumental in our everyday lives, they also structure our thinking in various direct and subtle ways.[1] Regardless of whether or not Lakoff and Johnson have overstated their case, the metaphor of "invisibility" characterizes the status of blacks in America. Though early black writers used the term[2], it was Ralph Ellison's novel *Invisible Man* that brought the notion of black invisibility into the popular parlance:

> I am an invisible man. . . .I am invisible, understand, simply because people refuse to see me. Like the bodiless heads you see sometimes in circus sideshows, it is as though I have been surrounded by mirrors of hard distorting glass. When they approach me they see only my surroundings, themselves, or figments of their imagination—indeed everything and anything except me.[3]

What we choose not to see, we need not deal with: if blacks are invisible, we can ignore their plight. Black anthropologist John L. Gwaltney[4] alludes to this on a broader scale when he speaks of how "Euro-American culture, for a plethora of conscious and unconscious considerations, has often chosen to deny the very existence" of black culture, black heritage, and black genius. It has been argued[5] that much of the unrest in the 1960s was an attempt by blacks to force whites not just to acknowledge social injustice, but to recognize their existence as legitimate and sentient beings.

Among educators, Rist has used the term invisibility, though in somewhat different fashion. He describes how a well-intended white school administration in Portland, Oregon, tried to achieve integration through racial assimilation. Ironically, by ignoring black cultural differences and personal individuality—by taking a "colorblind" approach to integration—the administration only perpetuated an insidious kind of invisibility:

> Day after day . . .Black students came off the bus to a setting where the goal was to render them invisible. And the more invisible they became, the greater the satisfaction of the school personnel that the integration program was succeeding![6]

Other images of invisibility have been used elsewhere in the literature to describe, for example, the problem of black families in America,[7] the plight of the elderly in a Jewish retirement home,[8] and the psychology of the pariah caste in Japan[9]. Rarely found, however, are instances of a favorable, visible minority or ethnic presence. In our study of Riverview High, a multiethnic integrated high school in northern California, we found not merely nonblack acceptance and tolerance of blacks, but a true black visible presence, as well.

At Riverview, integration has occurred without the assimilating invisibility (as Rist describes) that so often happens when different ethnic and racial groups are thrust into a mainstreaming school. In fact, we will argue that blacks are more than a visible presence at Riverview High School; they are a group to emulate. Concerning music, fashion, communicative style, and the general persona students carry, blacks seem to be the pacesetters. In what follows, we will describe this particular positive black visibility, how and where it occurs, and the different ways it is manifested. Though the "whys" of Riverview's black visibility—the causes of their unusual social presence—can not be definitively established, we will explore several possibilities. Since any of the reasons for black visibility are necessarily connected to the particular place of Riverview, we will begin by describing the town and the high school, their history and interrelationships, after first briefly describing the composition of the study.

THE STUDY

This ongoing research is the fourth in a series of investigations of American communities and their high schools.[10] Riverview was chosen because of its size and ethnic mix. Specifically, the research hopes to answer questions about how a school with a diverse ethnic composition operates, e.g., How and why do students get along? Is ethnic identity an issue in deciding what to teach? How do teachers respond when they face a class of Asians, blacks, and Hispanics?

The methodology used was naturalistic inquiry, augmented by questionnaire and interview data. We attended classes, teachers' meetings, and school assemblies. We also attended outside-school activities, such as football games, dances, and field trips. About fifty teachers (out of a faculty of around eighty) were formally interviewed using a standard set of items; approximately 125 students were interviewed using a slightly different schedule. In addition, a questionnaire was given to 458 students, almost a quarter of the student body, asking about their ethnic or racial heritage, the background of their best friends, and their attitudes towards being in a multiethnic high school.

Besides the data-gathering means mentioned above, we talked informally with students and teachers in various situations. All available documentation, such as the yearbook, newspapers, and school board transcripts, were also examined.

Since a high school does not exist in isolation from its community, our research agenda included interviews with parents, older residents, and other townspeople. We attended community meetings, and participated in most local festivities and celebrations. Both in and out of school, however, our research remained strongly ethnographic, open-ended, and qualitative, with no loyalty to any particular theory or paradigm.

RIVERVIEW: THE TOWN AND THE HIGH SCHOOL

The Town

Riverview is a town of approximately 34,000 people in northern California, located near a large city. The region was explored and claimed by a number of nationalities and groups, but in the late nineteenth century Sicilian fishermen and their families began to settle in the area. The town has a legendary ancestor, Vincenzo Vitiello, who supposedly founded the town in 1875 and to whom many of the Sicilian residents trace their lineage. By World War I, a thriving, predominantly Italian, fishing village had attracted several canneries. These original settlers and their families ran the town until after World War II. Some of the older folks in Riverview even today still speak a dialect of Sicilian Italian.

To say that World War II drastically changed Riverview is an understatement. First, wartime jobs in the local steel mills attracted thousands of southern blacks, vastly altering the composition of the town. Second, the United States Army built an embarkation center nearby that also brought new jobs and new faces. Moreover, after the war, many Filipino soldiers in the United States armed services were discharged at, or assigned to, this camp; this led to the establishment of a significant and still growing Filipino presence in the town.

As everywhere in California, a former possession of Mexico, Hispanics are a sizable minority in Riverview. However, besides a 14 percent Mexican-American population, continental Spaniards (who have farmed northern California since the 1930s) also comprise a countable part of the population.

The 1980s have seen a major increase in two groups: (1) non-Filipino Asians (especially Indians and Southeast Asian refugees), and (2) unaffiliated, non-ethnic whites. Family ties and federal agencies are sponsors of the first group, and affordable housing attracts the second.

The 1980 U.S. Census figures for Riverview are shown below in Table 1.

Table 1 1980 U. S. Census Data for Riverview

	Population	Percentage
Whites	20,280	61%
Italians	4,512	14%
Other Whites	15,768	48%
Blacks	6,671	20%
Asians	2,241	7%
Filipino	1,681	5%
Other Asians	560	2%
Hispanics	3,699	11%
American Indian	245	<1%
Total	33,034	

The High School

An independent Riverview High School was formally established around 1925. Riverview was never a segregated school, though black and Hispanic enrollments were significantly smaller than they are today. There are currently 1500 students and about eighty teachers at Riverview. The twenty-acre campus contains a dozen buildings, several swimming pools and gymnasiums, and a major football field.

Academics

Riverview High has had to fight a poor scholastic reputation. As one teacher said, "Academically, Riverview High is better known for its sports." This facetious remark encapsulates beliefs about the town that go back to the 1930s: Riverview is a rough, working-class, ethnic town; those Sicilians (later, blacks) are tough athletes, but mediocre students; no one with any intellectual ability could ever benefit from attending Riverview High.

Though never as bad as its reputation, until lately Riverview's academic achievement was one of the lowest in the country. There has been substantial improvement in the last five or ten years. The high school, in particular, has benefited from some rigorous new programs.

Perhaps the plan that will have the most far-reaching consequence (because it re-introduces tracking by default) is the EXCEL program. EXCEL will take about twenty-five of the top students from each class and place them in special accelerated courses for half of the school day. EXCEL is more than just advanced classes for the college bound; its students are expected to be the academic exemplars of the school.

Students who plan to attend college but are not in EXCEL also benefit from the renewed interest in academic achievement at Riverview. For example, last year all students in college-prep English spent three weeks training for the annual SAT examination. Further, all seniors received special drilling and motivation for taking the required state-wide California Assessment Program proficiency test. Voluntary after-school classes are also offered on a variety of topics ranging from critical thinking to non-Western arts.

Riverview High has made sincere attempts to serve the needs of its large non-college-bound population. Besides demanding demonstrable academic competence from all students (using required proficiency tests), no one can participate in school activities unless they have a minimal grade-point average and no failures for the quarter. Extensive vocational training is provided in the school's large shops and business and computer laboratories.

Though the high school is improving its quality for all students, and more minorities are continuing their education at local four-year or community colleges, equal academic achievement has yet to be obtained by all ethnic groups. Tables 2, 3, and 4 show that for both regular-track students and those intending to go to college (as evidenced by their taking the SAT), black students performed more poorly than others at Riverview. As will be discussed shortly, while blacks may be a highly conspicuous presence on campus, it is not as scholars that they are making themselves visible. In other words, black visibility does little for them in terms of promoting academic success.

Table 2 Distribution of 1984 Riverview High School GPAs by Student Ethnic Group[1]

Asian	2.03
Filipino	2.50
Hispanic	2.31
Black	2.19
White	2.59

[1] These GPA's are based on a four-point scale, and are averaged together for all classes, freshman through senior.

Table 3 Average SAT Scores and GPAs of Seniors Taking the SAT, by Ethnicity, 1984

Ethnic Group	n	GPA[1]	SAT Total	Math	Verbal
Asian	4	3.58	810	590	220
Filipino	5	3.08	756	404	352
Hispanic	11	3.00	767	416	352
Black	14	2.85	746	373	373
White	37	3.12	832	454	382
Total	71[2]	3.07	798	436	364

[1]GPA's are based on a four-point scale.
[2]Only 71 of several hundred seniors took the SAT.

Table 4 Enrollment of Ethnic Groups in Selected College-Related Courses, 1984

Ethnic Group	Advanced Math Percent	Chemistry Percent	Physics Percent
Asian/ Filipino	9.7[1]	72.2	27.3
Hispanics	6.4	16.7	14.8
Black	3.5	17.89	6.8
White	12.6	38.4	21.2
Total	8.1	31.4	15.9

[1]Numbers equal percentages of juniors and seniors of that ethnic group. For example, 9.7% of all Asian/Filipino students are enrolled in Advanced Math.

The Ethnic Diversity

The exact ethnic make-up of students is difficult to determine simply because they do not classify themselves consistently and unambiguously. For example, the 1984 yearbook gave the following ethnic breakdown:

Table 5 Percentage of Riverview High School Students by Ethnic Group, 1984[1]

Ethnic Group	Percent
Asian	3
Filipino	12
Hispanic	20
Black	33
White	33

[1]Data taken from *Riverview High School Yearbook*, 1984.

However, in the spring of 1986 we administered a questionnaire to approximately 25 percent of the Riverview High students, asking them about their ethnic identity and their parents' ethnic background. Ours was a representative sample having approximately equal representation of all classes and both sexes, and including students from the regular, college-prep, and ESL tracks. Sample statistics are in Table 6 below:

Table 6 Percentage of Riverview High School Students by Ethnic Group, 1986[1]

Ethnic Group	Percent
Asian	6
Filipino	15
Hispanic	24
Black	22
White	24
Mixed	8

[1]Data taken from questionnaire administered in 1986.

Many students who answered the questionnaire also were questioned in a follow-up interview. It was then we could see that having either/or notions of ethnic identity was simplistic. First, there is substantial miscegenation in Riverview. Though no confirming data are available, our questionnaire suggests that 10 to 15 percent of the Riverview population will soon consist of those persons who are half-black/half-white, half-Hispanic/half-Filipino, and so on. When or if these people consider themselves to be just white, black, Hispanic, or Filipino is problematic. Individuals may or may not differentially choose one ethnic identity over the other. Also, as we will discuss later, there seems to be a tendency for students at Riverview to publically adopt the "most ethnic" of two given alternatives: e.g., choosing black or Hispanic if the person if half-black/half-white or half-Hispanic/half-white. Second, the ethnic identity of whites is such an idiosyncratic parameter that comparison is almost impossible. Some people may consider themselves "Italian" if they have any Italian blood in them at all. Others may have immigrant parents, but feel no empathy whatsoever for their ethnic ancestry.

The Ethnicity of the High School and the Town

Even a cursory look at the census figures for the town and the high school indicates an obvious discrepancy: the white population of Riverview stands at 60 percent, while white students in the high school comprise only about 30 percent of the student body. There are three reasons for this difference. First, many of the newcomers to Riverview are young white families seeking affordable homes (while still staying within commuting distance of major metropolitan areas). As their children are still in elementary school, their presence is not yet reflected in the current high school tabulations. Second, the census data indicate that Black, Hispanic, and Asian families are larger than White families. Finally, there are several parochial schools in the area, and some of the older Sicilian families have a tradition of sending their children to them. For example, St. Ann's, the Riverview Parish local Catholic school, is predominantly (though not exclusively) White.

The Unity of the High School and the Town

Riverview is an ethnically diverse working class town surrounded by predominantly White upper class communities and takes pride in, and identifies with, its high school. Approximately twenty percent of the faculty and staff were themselves graduates of Riverview High. In sports, where inter-community jealousies and hatreds can be symbolically battled out, the Riverview residents support their team with an enthusiasm and loyalty granted only to the most blessed major professional franchises. It seems that the high school, the town, and the team are all great unifying symbols: whatever differences individuals might have among themselves, be they personal or racial, are set aside when confronted by outside challenges.

BLACK VISIBILITY AND INVISIBILITY

As mentioned, the image of "Black invisibility" is common in the literature. However, the hold fast to this notion without qualification is somewhat simple-minded. Any black man would probably feel quite visible walking down the streets of Beverly Hills, as indeed he would be. It is likely that he would be noticed by the neighbors, stared at by children, followed by the police. Sometimes there are positive aspects to being invisible or not being out of the ordinary. If you are black and you have no special "place" in your town, you can operate normally and unselfconsciously, with no feelings of pressure. It is not a simple matter, then, to look only at visibility or invisibility; we must also look at their positive and negative consequences as well. As a heuristic device, the following schematic might be used:

	Negative	Positive
Invisibility		
Visibility		

We have already mentioned the common theme of negative invisibility as described by Rist, Ellison, and others. We will now look at its antithesis — positive visibility — which we claim is a predominant theme of Riverview High School.

THE POSITIVE VISIBILITY OF BLACKS

Blacks are outstanding at Riverview High, both literally and figuratively. They wear their FILA shirts, caps, and sweats.[11] They play basketball at lunch on four outdoor courts, and rap with friends in class. Black students exude confidence, class, and style. If any one group sets the styles for others to follow, it is the blacks. Among Riverview black teenagers, there are few invisible young men and women.

A rough indication of just how visible blacks are on the Riverview campus can be seen from our interview data. As Table 6 shows, blacks probably comprise about 25 to 30 percent of the student body. Among those questioned about what the percentage of black students at Riverview might be, no student ever underestimated the number of blacks: many even claimed the school was at least half black, with whites and other ethnic groups being noticeable fractions, but nonetheless definitely a numerical minority. Black students, too, gave similar answers, inflating the black population (though none ever guessed that the school was half black or more). When questioned in both the formal and informal interviews as to who generally set the pace on campus, students answered — if at all — that it was "the blacks."

Black visibility was not just a matter of blacks being the most outlandish or conspicuous in appearance; several other groups contended for these honors. Among these groups were mods, punks, or new wavers (who dressed, to varying degrees, in black or loud, antique, used clothing, with teased, dyed hair, and heavy make-up), thrashers (hardcore skateboarders, oblivious to pain or the idea that clothes need not necessarily have holes), or *cholos* (an Hispanic subgroup whose males are especially known for driving "low-rider" cars with modified suspensions).

Particular areas where blacks are especially visible include:

Music

If Black culture truly dominates any one aspect of life at Riverview High School it is in musical taste. Top 40[12] black artists, like Whitney Houston or Lionel Richie, of course are popular. Also popular, however, are particularly black music idioms such as rap, beat, and soul. Such artists as Dougie Fresh or Run-DMC, who are usually not heard on top 40 radio and are not too popular in the surrounding areas, have a great following among both black and non-black Riverview students. Primarily black-influenced music is played at school dances, assemblies, and other school functions. All the school dances we attended were hosted by a black DJ,[13] playing mostly black-style music.

Fashion

There are perhaps a dozen or more labelled and readily identifiable groups of students at Riverview. These include "jocks" and "cheerleaders," "preps," "nerds," "brains," as well as largely ethnically-based groups such as Hispanic *cholos*, Filipino "hoodies," or white "stoners." Though each particular group at Riverview has its own special clothing, the influence of blacks on the general fashion scene is substantial. Stirrup pants, mega shirts, FILA sweatshirts, and painter's caps were all popularized by black students; black students also promote the general acceptance of exercise wear as everyday apparel.

Slang Expressions

Sociolinguists have long recognized the major influences of the black spoken vernacular on white speech; some scholars even claim that upwards of eighty to ninety percent of the common idiomatic expressions in white speech have black origins.[14] Also, the emphasis on stylistics and performatives in the black speech community has been well documented.[15] Riverview substantiates these findings, and, if anything, extends them. Many white students use particular black vocabulary items such as "blood" (a black man, but generalized by white males to refer to any other male), "touch your toes" (a metaphor for sexual intercourse), "freak" (fuck), or "fly-girl" (a girl of questionable morals). Many of the grammatical rules of the black-English vernacular (as described by Labov) were incorporated into the speech pattern of non-black students. For example, the first day of school in a general freshman English class we heard a white teenage male say to his half-Hispanic/half-white friend, "Dang, blood, what was you doin'? You be trippin' with her?" Depending on the intonation, in more typical white slang this might be rendered as "Hey, man, what was going on? Were you two really hanging out?"

Communicative Style

Kochman has shown that white and black speakers differ not just in dialect (the formal code) but also in the way their dialects are used (the communicative style). For example, Kochman claims that in a classroom setting, whites debate an issue as impersonally as possible, stressing objective ideas detached from whoever expressed them. Black students, however, engage in more personal arguments. They consider "debate to be as much a contest between individuals as a test of opposing ideas. Because it is a contest, winning the contest requires that one outperform one's opponents: outthink, outtalk, and outstyle them."[16] The latter form of argumentation was certainly most pervasive at Riveview.

The attitude of Riverview students, then, towards the black dialect and black rhetorical style is not just one of tolerance (i.e., "non-rejection") but one of acceptance and prominence. Non-black students do not criticize blacks for speaking "black," nor are blacks assertive about their right to talk black. White parents sometimes complain that "black talk comes home," but the students give it the label of normality and place the burden of understanding on mom and dad.

Stance: Being Cool

Associated with the above discussion on communicative style is the idea of "being cool." An attempt at a definition will not even be made, but as everyone knows, being cool is not a way of life for teenagers, it *is* life. Whether deserved or not, black students, especially males, exude the social confidence, the savvy, and the street-corner poise needed to be appropriately cool. Admittedly, this is one of the more subjective evaluations we made, but it is hard not to notice the distinctly black swagger in a Filipino or white boy's walk.

Leadership and Activities

Because of the effort of a number of key individuals, blacks were among the outstanding leaders at Riverview High School in the 1985–1986 academic year. Blacks had more than ample representation on the cheerleading squads, student council, and yearbook staff. The Black Student Union had about fifty members and took an active part in most school functions. One black student leader also read the daily announcements over the intercom in the mornings. Riverview's earlier yearbooks indicate that blacks have been a dynamic and felt presence for at least the past decade and a half.

Homecoming King and Queen

Two popular blacks students were elected homecoming king and queen at Riverview during our 1985–1986 fieldstay, no small achievement given that non-blacks predominate. No teacher or student indicated that it might be unusual to have both these positions filled by blacks, and when it happened it was thought to be a rather ordinary and natural occurrence, unworthy of comment. The significance of this event is further highlighted when we remember that a homecoming king or queen is not necessarily a school's best scholar, most talented athlete, or most active leader; these are positions of *pride*. Students select those whom they want to be a symbol of their class and their school.

Sports

Considering the interest in sports and the size of the population, it is not surprising that Riverview High School blacks are well represented on all JV and varsity athletic teams (save the new soccer and tennis organizations).[17] The first-string varsity football team was more than half black, and the varsity basketball team had only one white member. The men's and women's track teams were predominantly black, and fielded several champion black runners.

Though blacks were not the majority of the cheerleading squads, they were well represented. More important than that, however, was the fact that black dance styles, and sometimes even cheers in Swahili, were used and readily accepted by both fans and cheerleaders. As one black teacher commented in class after a big victory, "Our ladies know how to GET DOWN!"[18]

Blacks as a Symbol of Riverview High School

There has been a fifty-year rivalry between Riverview and its immediate neighbor, Jericho. Though Jericho shares a common history, similar economic backgrounds, and family ties with Riverview, it does not have a significant black population. This difference makes the animosity between the towns passionate, perhaps irreconcilable.

Each fall this friction is symbolically vented in the annual Big-Little Football game ("little" in that it is not necessary for the conference championship, but "big" in that it is just as important). This event attracts thousands of spectators, and requires the presence of the police departments from both towns. Tempers are hot, not just among the students but among the parents as well. Old newspapers and alumni are full of accounts of past fights, vandalism, and vendettas.

The 1985 game was enacted with all the usual competitive festivities, but one incident stands out which is germane to the argument here. Midway through the third quarter some Jericho fans held up a banner making derogatory remarks about the Riverview team. It included a black football player riding in a Cadillac convertible holding a watermelon. In response, some white and Filipino Riverview residents walked up and down the sidelines with a sign depicting the black epithet "Yo' Momma!" (with the back saying, "And yo' Daddy, too!").[19]

Outsiders view Riverview as little more than a crime-ridden black ghetto. Insiders view it as something different, of course, but they also know about the images folks "over the hill" have of them. The response (whether by white or black) to the discrimination and denigration afforded to all people from Riverview is a kind of "black pride." This underdog role often takes the form of coming on rough, macho, or "bas ass."[20]

FAVORABLE BLACK INVISIBILITY

It would be wrong to assume that blacks are always outstanding, are always a visible presence, at Riverview. This overstates the case; furthermore, such a situation could never occur in a town that is truly integrated. At Riverview High, black students are usually thought of simply as "persons," as opposed to "black persons." The high school no longer teaches any black history or black culture courses; for the new special accelerated college-prep EXCEL program, race is particularly specified *not* to be a factor in the selection of candidates. Students told us that the fights which occur at school are due to personal disagreements rather than to racial differences. The fact that a white student would even think of starting a fight with a black student without being thought a racist clearly testifies to how far integration has come at Riverview.

These attitudes, of course, are not simply confined to the school. One black teacher told us how strange it felt when he first came to Riverview. In contrast with his native Texas, blacks in Riverview had no special "place" in the community. A white woman could even talk to him on the street without fear of chastisement. Older white residents sometimes speak of the blacks they grew up with as being just "dark-skinned Italians": "Lamar Robinson didn't know he was black until he was ten-years old, and then *we* had to tell him." Of course, whether these blacks felt the same way is not always clear; Lamar Robinson, however, is the current mayor of Riverview.

WHY RIVERVIEW?

The social situation just described may not be unique, but it certainly is far from typical in American schools, where physical integration is underway but true equality for blacks and other minorities remains to be achieved. In fact, some observers[21] fear that with rising minority populations, declining economic opportunities, and a new influx of immigrants, trouble-free integration may be even more ephemeral in the 1980s and 1990s than in the 1970s. The questions are, then, what happened in Riverview? What did Riverview do, if anything, that was right? Are there lessons to learn from Riverview and its high school? We propose three general explanations: (1) a "magic" population ratio, (2) the particular history and development of Riverview, and (3) similarities in communicative styles of the black and non-black communities.

A "Magic" Population Ratio

This hypothesis argues that there are optimal numbers of a minority population in a town or school which maximize the possibilities for cooperation, friendship, and mutual trust and respect. If the minority is too few in number, they cannot help but feel threatened and alone. A fortress mentality of "them" vs. "us" sets in, and it is hard for the minority to feel comfortable interacting with the majority. Much time is spent "circling the wagons" and little, if any, real communication takes place. However, if the minority is *too* present, it is the ever-decreasing majority that feels threatened, often responding aggressively, harshly, and without thinking. What exactly this magic number might be is very difficult to guess, but St. John[22] suggests that between 15 and 40 percent minority enrollment is optimal in a school.

While this explanation has some merit, it certainly fails even to begin to depict the situation found at Riverview. First, there are other schools in America with similar demographies, but (at least as reported in the literature) their racial/social integration is not like that found at Riverview. Second, as described before, there are a variety of different ethnic groups in Riverview, all within the optimal "magic" range, but why is it that it is the blacks who have become the style-setters, the group to emulate, the notably *visible* people?

The Particular Historical Development of the Riverview Community

The inadequacies of the first hypothesis suggest the second: there must be something unique in the Riverview experience that has created this distinctive social matrix. Once again, however, it is difficult to specify what this might be. Historical explanations for the contemporary black visibility are certainly possible. However, the real increase in the black populations, and, thus, the present of blacks as a potential influence, did not occur until after World War II. Also, in the late 1960s Riverview suffered from racial unrest, as did many towns and cities in America at that time. The phenomenon of black visibility, then, seems to be something that has happened in the past ten or fifteen years. But what has happened in these fifteen years?

Non-forced Integration, and a Generation of Peace

The students we saw at this year's high school graduation ceremony are the first to have thirteen years of relatively trouble-free education. In the sixties and seventies Riverview experienced some unpopular attempts at busing, but this never profoundly affected things at the school or in the town. The natural plurality of the community has kept Riverview High from being a "rich school," a "black school," or any special kind of school at all. Accordingly, children have attended school for thirteen years with *everyone* in town. This is an ordinary, everyday event.

Thus, either through intent or accident, integration was never something that "occurred" at Riverview High. How the racial interactions that developed in this kind of setting differ from those which develop when integration is forced or artificial can only be guessed at. However, the literature strongly suggest that in most cases of forced integration, the resulting interracial social relationships are strained, cautious, or even hostile.[23] In Riverview, integration is a natural and stable fact of life. It occurs without substantial busing, magnet schools, or any of the other devices communities use to desegregate their school districts. Thirteen years of this kind of interaction culminates in a homecoming ceremony where the crowning of a black king or queen is a mundane, almost unnoticed, event.

Black Leadership

Riverview has been fortunate in having politically astute black leaders who possess the proper qualities to facilitate compromise and cooperation. For example, Lamar Robinson, the current mayor, is a black man trusted by both the black and white communities. Having been born and raised in the old Italian section of town, he has the virtue of being looked upon as a neighbor by whites. Though a peacemaker, blacks know Robinson has never bought the status quo: they expect him to earnestly represent and fight for black interests. It is hard to estimate the effect of such an individual on race relations in town. Certainly, the presence of men like Robinson can only be a beneficial influence, both in times of trouble and calm.

Minority Representation

While the country was suffering from racial unrest in the late 1960s, Riverview blacks and others formed effective political organizations which successfully challenged the old guard and its nepotism. Thus, while no minority feels totally comfortable with the way things are, most believe that the local political structure offers a viable forum for their grievances.

The School Board

It is commonly assumed in Riverview that there is a certain kind of rationality and common sense on the school board; its members are thought to be well-intended and sensitive to the needs of the total com-

munity. Though not revolutionary, they are perceived as being sufficiently responsive to minority requirements. Again, the presence of certain key individuals may be significant. Oswald Davis, an articulate and
educated black man, has been on the board since the troubled times in
the early seventies; Tony Messina, the son of one of the older influential
Italian families, has been on the board almost since his high school
graduation fifteen years ago. Both men are accepted and trusted by the
black and white communities, and can act as bridges when divisive issues
arise.

The School Administration

The Riverview community seems to have similar kinds of feelings about
the school administration as it does about its school board. Both the
district superintendent and the high school principal are locals, products
of the Riverview school system. They are generally thought to be
available, responsive, and sympathetic to minority needs. Their own
statements reflect this concern. Both have said that they invariably assess
the effect of their decisions on minority students, and they consider how
the minority community might interpret their actions.

Housing

It is well known that one of the biggest obstacles to school desegregation
is residence patterns. Thus, if a district boundary does not contain sufficient numbers of a certain kind of people, artificial steps must be taken
to alter the ethnic or racial mix. In the 1960s, Riverview was no better
(though probably no worse) than any other town in America as having
segregated housing. Urban renewal, with all its implications, was a fact
of life in Riverview, too. Most important, however, Riverview had
several ambitious developers who built more houses than there were
white people available to buy them. This meant that if blacks had the
financial means, they could disperse rather readily throughout the town,
thereby moderating the ghetto effect often associated with black neighborhoods.

Communicative Style

Another possible explanation concerning black visibility in the Riverview
community is communicative style. Kochman[24] claims that, generally,
black rhetorical devices are diametrically opposed to white methods of
communication. Thus, in many places, when blacks and whites interact
frustration or intransigence occurs. For instance, one of Gwaltney's informants mentions that

There are probably many white people who are as honest as we [blacks] are. Well, there certainly are some. I guess there can't be many or the country would not be as rotten as it is. Anyway, *since I can't tell the good ones from the rest, I have as little to do with any of them as I can.*[26] [Emphasis added.]

It was argued previously that most students in Riverview High share a common mode of argument, one that is similar to the rhetorical devices found in black speech. If all students indeed share a common style of communication, it is possible, and even likely, that such conflicts and attitudes can be avoided.

BLACK VISIBILITY OUTSIDE OF SCHOOL

Before the war, some Italian families would not let their daughters talk to a black boy on the street, even though these people might have sat next to each other every day in high school, or danced at the homecoming ball. An analogous situation occurs today upon graduation. What happens, say, to the highly visible black football star after graduation when he goes to work in town? Does black high school visibility become real-world invisibility?

In political and social terms, the answer is no, though blacks and non-blacks clearly mix less, and blacks enjoy less prominence. In economic terms, the answer is yes, both inside and outside of Riverview. When jobs and economics become the issue, whites have the advantage. Black unemployment is double that of white unemployment in town, even though federal and state monies have been granted to provide temporary and permanent jobs for minorities. As one white teacher said about several of his black students who were tossing paper on the floor, "I tell them, I don't care if you throw that shit on the floor now, because you're just going to be coming back here a couple years from now and picking it up every day."

In light of these facts, we asked teachers and townspeople if they felt that Riverview gave black students a false sense of security. In other words, did they think that blacks got the wrong impression of the rest of the world? Did they generalize from how their life was in Riverview High School? Many thought this not to be the case. They said that blacks realized Riverview was different and would expect more indifference, prejudice, or discrimination elsewhere.

In spite of this, however, Riverview High presents a number of dilemmas for both white and black students. There is a certain "party line," an unwritten code of conduct, among students: "Don't trip off people's color." It is un-cool to be prejudiced, and it is discouraged in all kinds of subtle and obvious ways. Perhaps in a place as ethnically diverse as Riverside this is not only a sensible way to behave, it is necessary. But to say that it is un-cool to be prejudiced is not to say that it is cool to be ethnic, that it is cool to be black. In one sense, blacks need to be somewhat bicultural in order to leave the Riverview environment: "I know I got to behave different when I go to Jericho or over the hill," says one black football player. "I got to be a little less, you know, *intense.*" But how can he learn what being "less intense" is if he attends a school where his intensity is encouraged, if not emulated, by those around him?

The problem, then, is this: Riverview High School students have created a world relatively free of overt prejudice, a world full of ethnic pride that celebrates ethnic diversity. But the cause that they celebrate is, in real-world terms, lost. Once outside of school, other norms apply for both black and white students. It is not clear how, or if ever, these contradictions can be reconciled.[26]

WHERE DOES RIVERVIEW GO FROM HERE?

Riverview is an interesting case study if for no other reason than its current population mix roughly corresponds to what America's national average will be like fifty to one-hundred years from now. Ironically, it is not clear how long Riverview's own current demographic statistics will remain as they are. First, because Riverview's location—being just far enough away from large metropolitan areas to have relatively inexpensive housing, while still being within commuting distance—has brought in many middle-class whites. Generally, these new people are ethnically nondescript, and have salaries higher than the Riverview norm. They also have none of the ties or allegiances to either the town or the high school that current residents have.

Second, non-black minority populations are growing in Riverview. An expanding number of Vietnamese, Cambodian, and other Southeast Asian refugees are settling in Riverside. More relatives of currently-residing Filipino families are coming over. And the Hispanic population is increasing.

Third, cross-ethnic marriages in Riverview are producing large numbers of mixed children of all combinations. Currently, the number of children in high school who have parents of different backgrounds is around 8 to 10 percent, which background they choose to identify with, and, subsequently, which background their children will choose to identify with, complicates the ethnic picture of an already diverse town.

These factors seem to indicate that the future of black student pre-eminence may be in doubt. Much will depend on how the newcomers become incorporated into the current social fabric, or on the degree to which they choose to become incorporated. As more and more new people move in, the more political clout they can wield, and the more changes they can make in the town and its schools. There already have been attempts by some to change the name of the town, in hopes of creating a more positive image of Riverview.

One of the things that could irrevocably change the structure of the town would be the building of a new high school. A single high school is the great amalgamator of Riverview: it is the one place that brings all ethnic groups together. If a new high school were to be built, its likely location "south of the tracks" would separate non-ethnic students from ethnic, rich from poor, and "educable" from "non-educable."[27] As a black teacher said overdramatically, "If there were two high schools in this town, it would have burned down a long time ago."

For the time being, blacks are visible: they are seen and are dealt with—at least while in school. In Riverview, and elsewhere in the United States, their economic disadvantage casts a long shadow on their future.

NOTES

1. George Lakoff and Mark Johnson, *Metaphors We Live By* (Chicago: University of Chicago Press, 1976).

2. Frederick Douglass, *Autobiography of Frederick Douglass* (New York: Fawcett, 1845 [1963]). W. E. B. DuBois, *The Souls of Black Folk* (New York: Fawcett, 1962), pp. 343–345.

3. Ralph Ellison, *Invisible Man* (New York: Vintage, 1947), p. 3.

4. John Gwaltney, "Common Sense and Science: Urban Core Black Observations," in D. Messerschmidt, ed., *Anthropologists at Home in North America* (Cambridge: Cambridge University Press, 1981), pp. 46–61.

5. H. Rap Brown, *Die Nigger Die* (New York: Dial, 1969). Richard Gregg et al., "The Rhetoric of Black Power," in A. Smith, ed., *Language, Communication and Rhetoric in Black America* (New York: Harper & Row, 1972).

6. Ray Rist, *The Invisible Children: School Integration in American Society* (Cambridge: Harvard University Press, 1978), p. 244.

7. Herbert Guttman, *The Invisible Fact: Afro-Americans and Their Families* (New York: Pantheon, 1976).

8. Barbara Myerhoff, *Number Our Days* (New York: Harper and Row, 1979).

9. George DeVos and Hiroshi Wagatsuma, *Japan's Invisible Race: Caste in Culture and Personality* (Berkeley: University of California Press, 1966).

10. Alan Peshkin, *Growing Up American* (Chicago: University of Chicago Press, 1978); *The Imperfect Union* (Chicago: University of Chicago Press, 1982); *God's Choice: The Total World of a Christian Fundamentalist School* (Chicago: University of Chicago Press, 1986).

11. FILA is a popular brand of sports clothes.

12. "Top 40 Radio" refers to the current forty most popular records that are being listented to at any given time.

13. "DJ" refers to "disk jockey," or someone who plays records on the radio or for a live audience.

14. William Labov, *Language in the Inner City* (Philadelphia: University of Pennsylvania Press, 1972); Thomas Kochman, ed., *Rappin' and Styling Out: Communication in Urban Black America* (Urbana: University of Illinois Press, 1972); J. Dillard, *Black English* (New York: Vintage, 1972).

15. Roger Abrams, *Talking Black* (Rowely, Mass.: Newbury House, 1976); Kochman, ed. *Rappin' and Styling Out*; Claudia Mitchell-Kernan, "Signifying and Marking: Two Afro-American Speech Acts," in J. Gumperz and D. Hymes, eds., *Directions in Sociolinguistics* (New York: Holt, Rinehart and Winston, 1972), pp. 161–179.

16. Thomas Kochman, *Black and White Styles in Conflict* (Chicago: University of Chicago Press, 1981), p. 24.

17. "JV" means "junior varsity," or the junior-level sports team. There seems to be some association between certain sports and ethnic groups: Hispanics and Asians with soccer, Filipinos with tennis, and blacks with basketball and football. However, these are not strict pairings, and all ethnic groups can play in any sport they desire.

18. "Get down" is slang for dancing well, with much enthusiasm.

19. "Yo' momma" is a slang expression which translates as "[Fuck] your mother" or "motherfucker."

20. It might be argued that the reasons for the particular social configurations found in Riverview are due to whites, rather than blacks, being a minority. Other minority groups may join with blacks in a solid

front against the mainstream "majority" (i.e. white) culture, which happens at this time to not be in a position of strength. We found little evidence to support this view. If anything, there may be more rivalry between the minorities (e.g., blacks vs. Hispanics, Filipinos vs. Hispanics, all vs. Southeast Asians) over school resources, social prestige, and so on.

21. Marvin Harris, *American Now* (New York: Torchstone, 1981).

22. N. H. St. John, *School Desegregation: Outcomes for Children* (New York: Wiley, 1975).

23. Raymond Mack, ed., *Our Children's Burden: Studies of Desegregation in Nine American Communities* (Chicago: University of Chicago Press, 1968); John Egerton, *Education and Desegregation in Eight Schools* (Evanston: Center for Equal Education, 1977); Rist, *The Invisible Children.*

24. Kochman, *Black and White Styles of Communication.*

25. Gwaltney, "Common Sense and Science," p. 53.

26. In a similar vein, Lois Weis (personal communication) asks, What is the role of the high school in such a situation? Is the school being racist if it insists on conformity to mainstream culture? Or is the school being negligent if it succumbs to the easy (though ultimately detrimental) temptation to indulge minority non-mainstream behavior? These questions, obviously, are no less difficult to answer than those posed in the text.

27. Milton Schwebel, *Who Can Be Educated?* (New York: Grove Press, 1968)

10

Urban Appalachian Girls and Young Women: Bowing to No One

KATHRYN M. BORMAN,
ELAINE MUENINGHOFF,
AND SHIRLEY PIAZZA*

INTRODUCTION

This chapter examines the relationship between the nexus of family, neighborhood, and school-based experience and students' cultural identities. The analysis is based on several related studies conducted by the authors in a low-income, predominantly urban Appalachian neighborhood. Although experiences and outcomes for boys and young men will be considered, the principal focus is upon how sex-specific avenues to social identity within the urban Appalachian community influence school and work-related outcomes for girls and young women. These concerns are inherent in more general gender-specific and class-based issues in both the labor market picture and in related social-psychological processes. Consistent with the perspective of other chapters in this volume, we contend that a class-based analysis of urban Appalachian culture as it shapes the identity of girls and young women is necessary for understanding their particular realm of experience.

Our argument is that women suffer inequalities and that girls and young urban Appalachian women are particularly at risk as they face the possibilities and limitations of their current roles as student and future work roles. This, we contend, is a result of patterns of social reproduc-

*The authors gratefully acknowledge the helpful comments on earlier drafts by Patricia O'Reilly and Lois Weis and the assistance of Celia Petty in preparing the manuscript.

tion begun in the home but later developed and resisted in neighborhood, school, and work-related training settings. One of the ways to understand the institutions of the family and school is in their relationships to workplace and labor-market success. These relationships whether defined by human capital theories,[1] reproduction theories[2] or more recent social-psychological theories of the commercialization of human feeling[3] emphasize the ways families, schools, and training programs reproduce social relations in the workplace and larger society. Gaskell[4] has pointed to the failure of most of this literature to adequately address the experience of women.

> Most . . . [analyses of labor-market-related processes are] based on the experience of men in school and at work. Women have been studied much less, partly because male researchers are simply less interested in women and partly because researchers have addressed women not as members of the paid labor force, but rather as wives and mothers. Women, as we know, have a very different experience of work from men. The labor market is highly segregated by gender. Women's participation in the paid labor force is more often intermittent and part time, the wages they are paid are lower, and the jobs they do involve less power and authority.[5]

Because an emphasis on male experience fails to provide an understanding of women's interest, it is clear that their relationships in social contexts must be made the centerpiece of ongoing analyses of the institutional relationships that matter in women's experience.

Following an overview concerning gender development and an exploration of the role of women in Appalachian culture, the remainder of the chapter is divided into two major sections. The first part highlights the findings of a series of studies concerning Appalachian families, their expectations, and their values and concerns for their children's futures. The second part reviews the influence of social roles and relationships in school in addition to broader social relationships. In this section ethnographies of classrooms and other settings are reviewed to analyze the experiences of urban Appalachian girls and young women in school and neighborhood contexts. In our analyses throughout we drew upon materials that allowed us to take the perspective of research participants. Our reliance upon literary sources and single-case ethnographic studies reflects a strong belief that these materials take us to the heart of the experience of women to comprehend their worlds with more clarity than data drawn from survey research and other types of quantitative research.

Frequently, survey research studies have either excluded women or seen them as peripheral to men's experience. Moreover, it is our belief that such methodologies, though mathematically sophisticated, frequently distance us from empirical reality, and thus fail to demonstrate the differential meanings experiences may have for participants.

However, it is also true that qualitative researchers have similarly been biased in their work, reflecting the tendency in ethnographic studies to identify women with positions of little status in the prestige structures of virtually all societies. This tendency derives from the fact that in most traditional societies studied by ethnographers, a large part of women's adult lives is spent giving birth and raising children, while men's adult roles are more public, less person-centered and "selfish," and hence accord men higher status in the larger community. Even with the advent of technology and capital, it can be argued that women's roles are still primarily relegated to "social production," a realm viewed as more circumscribed and less valued than the public sphere occupied by men. Thus "anthropologists in writing about human culture have followed our own culture's ideological bias in treating women as relatively invisible and in describing what are largely the activities and interests of men."[6]

It seems clear to us that women researchers must actively engage in research on women's cultures. Moreover, this research must utilize nontraditional methods and sources in order to capture the full context of women's experience. Although our concern here is primarily with the social and economic outcomes of their experiences in an alienating culture, there is also a need to understand their experiences in the more subjective domains of personal relationships.

THE SOCIAL CONSTRUCTION OF GENDER

Young Americans growing up in the 1980s are likely to be familiar with the term "women's movement." As they prepare for the job market they will see in print "equal opportunity employer." However, few are likely to understand the complexities surrounding the barriers which hinder some and allow others to go ahead regardless of personal effort, achievement, or talent. The major differences in advantage reside within the parameters of social roles by which people are categorized. Roles are either "achieved" through one's efforts as a doctor, mother, or student, or "ascribed" through attributes over which one has no control as infant, black, Italian. Although a young urban Appalachian woman has no control over her ascribed roles, they may influence her labor-market opportunities more than any other variable, including talent.

Pink ribbons and blue bows, symbols used from the time of infancy, separate girls and boys from birth onwards. Young children begin to formulate their views of themselves as boys or girls, males or females at a very early age. After the age of three most children have learned what it means to be a boy or a girl, and most importantly that this is a permanent aspect of one's life. Additionally, children learn to appraise and either appreciate or denigrate feelings, behaviors, and activities which are seen as "appropriate" for their gender. Thus, certain types of feelings, behaviors, and activities are deemed acceptable for those who are "female" and other types for those who are "male."

In the Caribbean community of St. Croix, Gibson found that contrasting school success patterns for boys and girls were best explained by examining sex-role differences in performance expectations. She related school performance and attainment differences between the sexes to sex-specific value systems in the society. While women earned "respect" through adhering to a pattern of behavior of regular church attendance, sexual restraint, and "proper" social manners, men gained "reputations" by withdrawing from women's respectability and gaining personal recognition for acting and talking tough, gambling, showing off, and generally taking a socially active role. Thus girls and young women persisted in school while boys and young men withdrew.[7]

In our society, stereotypic behavior is not only tolerated but is expected and reinforced. Certain socially constructed traits characterize men and women. Men are perceived as stronger and more aggressive. Women are passive and helpless. The culture in which we live tends to reinforce such myths despite the massive attempts to eradicate them.

Certain traits and skills are seen to assist the individual in pursuing and attaining various types of jobs and careers. Managerial roles, typically held by men, are assumed to require complex social skills such as supervising, negotiating, and mentoring and appear to be intergenerationally transmitted. Working-class females are seen to be at a particular disadvantage because they are less likely to have had experience in these areas than either middle-class males or females. Moreover, according to Hochschild's analysis of the work life of airline flight atttendants, most characteristically "feminine" occupations, while demanding personal service and nurturing attention to customers, clients, and bosses, are organized by job technologies to denigrate the emotional work carried out by these workers. Office work, though more cognitively complex and less obviously service-oriented than waitressing or hostessing, is no exception.[9] As Gaskell and others have pointed out, the gendered character of clerical work has implications for how the job is defined and subsequently for how the person occupying the role is perceived and treated.[10] As Gaskell notes:

> Secretarial work is low in status and pay, a condition that is tied historically to its association with women. The training it requires is

widely available and short, not protected by associations of workers. The wages are substantially less than those in manufacturing, blue collar trades or other technical areas. It offers few chances for promotion to more respected jobs, a characteristic that is tied to its historical association with women, who were expected to leave the labor force after a few years' employment to look after their families. Even those women who did stay on at work were prevented from promotion to responsible positions through a variety of gender specific regulations. While secretaries often did responsible work, it was seen to be done by the male boss, leaving women as the invisible power behind the throne, a traditional piece of female mythology which prevents women from getting recognition and pay for the skills and responsibility they have.[11]

These same skills and similar outcomes are prefigured in peer interactions in the classroom and in less formal settings with others in school and community contexts in childhood and throughout the life course.

Although more women are entering the labor force today, the kinds of jobs that are open to them remain limited. Smith notes that "the female labor force in the United States consists of more than 40 million women from diverse backgrounds, family situations and income levels," but that the "work they are doing . . . is . . . uniform [and] . . . consists largely of employment that is separate from jobs held by men, and is less remunerative."[12] Clearly, gender identity presents either advantages or disadvantages to those entering the market place. This chapter addresses the question of how these gender inequities begin, where they are particularly supported, and how they become entrenched.

APPALACHIAN CULTURE AND ITS IMPACT ON WOMEN

Young Appalachian women possess a strong cultural heritage emphasizing their identification with place, their emotional strength, and their ability to manage family and other social relations with particular ability and energy. Ganim describes the Appalachian woman as "naturalized within the inescapable presence of the mountains."[13] Such an environment contributes to the image of the strong, independent woman "sentimentally aligned with the hills."[14] Women in Appalachian literature are repeatedly pictured as strong and earthbound, life-giving and nurturing, passive and accepting. The novelist Emma Bell Miles, for example, "sees the woman as passive, internal, deep, reflective, stable," an individual who also knows her life is dedicated to service and inevitably to suffering.

Harriette Arnow in *The Dollmaker*[16] portrays the most widely-known female heroine of this literary genre, Gertie, who must leave her beloved home in the Kentucky hills at the outbreak of World War II to join her husband Clovis in Detroit where he has found work. For Gertie, leaving Kentucky is devastating because she can only find her identity "in her specificity of place." Gertie is terrified of her new surroundings after deferring the dream of buying her own land back home. To her this land had represented a foundation upon which she could love and nurture her family. In her new urban environment Gertie loses her strength, power, and authority as a contributor to the household economy, becoming completely dependent on Clovis as the only provider. The plight of Gertie centers upon

> . . . the loss of her status as worker, the one who cultivates the land, tends the garden, and milks the cows, who contributes to the family by means of her special relationship to the earth as woman and nurturer, . . . [making] . . . her angry and increasingly more dispossessed.[17]

Repeatedly, like Gertie, contemporary urban Appalachian women are described as "displaced" and "trapped by their world."

Young, contemporary urban Appalachian women, though rooted in their family's culture and history, must locate themselves in an unfamiliar, often hostile, city landscape. Appalachian women historically have identified with mountain landscapes and have understood their roles and identities in these terms. With migration away from the mountains to urban settings, a process affecting more than 3 million residents of the Appalachian region during the peak years of outmigration from 1945 to 1970, employment opportunities for women became minimal. The usual pattern was for young male workers to leave for the city by himself to find work, much as Clovis does in *The Dollmaker*.[18] If he were married, family and children would be sent for once he became established and found work.

Families relied upon complex networks of relatives and friends to ease the transition from a rural to an urban setting. A primary role taken on by Appalachian women in this process was the creation and maintenance of supportive collectivities of kin and near-kin, much as was true in communities of black migrants whose South to North migration paralleled that of the mountaineers.[19] Thus, the construction of kin-based social support networks appears to be a class-linked phenomenon, developed by black and white migrants during the post-war period and in earlier periods in urban American immigrant communities. There is evidence that family-based strategies for survival in new locales figure as well in the Chicano experience. In her study of seasonal cannery workers in the Santa Clara Valley, Zavella found that friendship networks created in the workplace provided patterns of support similar to those developed in Southern black and urban Appalachian migrant communities among kin and near-kin. Women assisted one another in managing child-care issues, marital problems, and housekeeping dilemmas. Zavella further saw these supportive linkages as potentially fostering a political consciousness among women whose recognition of their collective circumstances as workers and family members might lead to their active resistance of patriarchal arrangements in both the workplace and home.[20]

Despite the frequently successful experiences of many Appalachian families, feelings of displacement continue to be deep-rooted. The pull of the mountains and family left behind represents a strong force in the conflict between mountain and urban values. Because the lure of the city and possibilities for "making it" tug at the other end, second or third generation Appalachian urban migrants may feel uprooted in the urban environment. This tension is expressed by middle-aged Hannah Morgan, who lived in Dayton, Ohio at the time of her interview with behavioral scientists Jane and Robert Coles, and wishes both to reproduce mountain culture and to allow the creation of an occupational identity associated with success in the city for her daughter Pauline. The advice she provides her daughter is both traditional and liberating. When asked about the dreams she held for her daughter, Hannah replied that she has told her daughter

> 'You stay here and become a nurse. You be a proud woman of Harlan County who has learned to become a proud woman of Dayton. You bow to no one.' In my dreams, the ones I have just before I wake up and have to go to work, I see myself on top of my grandmother's favorite mountain, standing as tall as I can on my tiptoes to see more; bowing to no one; taking big gulps of thin air the way you have to when you're up high and you're tired, but feeling good, real good. When I do wake up, I say to myself what my grandmother used to say to me: 'Don't bow to anyone, not in your heart.' A mountain dream like that will carry a person right through a day working at that supermarket.[21]

Because an Appalachian heritage is so deeply rooted, it may be difficult for young urban Appalachian women to preserve a culturally-consistent sense of identity and positive self-regard while at the same time accommodating to values and concerns of an urban white middle-class culture as manifest in such institutions as the school and workplace. Some acceptance of middle-class values and experience while "standing tall" and "bowing to no one" is a challenging prerequisite for achieving well-paying jobs and professional careers. In the final outcome, young urban Appalachian women may sacrifice cultural heritage for success in the job market.

Some, perhaps most, may never consciously make a decision of choosing between value systems because the patterns begun early in their lives never allow them such freedom. "Family" as an organizational structure may remain so strong that early relationships to mother, father, sister, brothers, cousins, aunts, uncles, grandparents may both nurture the soul and constrain personal ambition. A pattern of extended family relationships reinforces this tradition. Children who are raised in urban settings frequently return to their mountain homes where members of their families still live. Thus, family and Appalachian tradition overwhelmingly influence the young child growing up.

URBAN APPALACHIAN FAMILIES IN A NEIGHBORHOOD CONTEXT

In a recent study, Borman and Mueninghoff looked closely at the daily activities of urban Appalachian children living in a port-of-entry neighborhood in Cincinnati.[22] In an earlier study of twenty-four working-class and poor parents in the same setting, Borman had determined that young children of both genders receive a mixed message from parents about their futures.[23] Persistent Appalachian values of independence and individuality were expressed in their child-rearing goals alongside urban working-class values of obedience to authority, the desire to maintain an aura of respectability, and the like. In this sense poor and blue-collar urban Appalachian families may be characterized as caught between two spheres, neither fully accommodating to either urban middle-class or working-class value profiles. However, viewed from a perspective that allows more active engagement with and resistance to environmental contraints than do social reproduction theories, these families more likely may be expressing their desire to "stand tall" and bow *only* if the personal cost is not too great.

In a similar and seemingly contradictory manner, while parents did not value studiousness in their children, they did hope their children would complete high school. Most expressed the view that an active engagement with life was more important in the end than personal self-sacrifice in pursuit of a professional career. For example, one parent proudly described his seven-year-old youngster's Evil Knevel-like exploits on a nearby freeway ramp with his bicycle in a manner that would have chilled the hearts of most middle-class parents. Although many held the desire for thier children to complete college degrees and enter professional employment, most felt these aspirations were unrealistic. When asked about the nature of work they actually expected their children to undertake, most mentioned employment as a craftsman in an industrial trade such as construction or electrical work. Approximately 30 percent mentioned such employment while fewer than 15 percent felt that their children would enter professional jobs.

Because family dependencies are strong, it may be difficult to break traditional long-established patterns of family reciprocities in order to achieve middle-class success. In addition, most parents seemed unwilling to see their children sacrifice a sense of adventure, individualism, and independence. It is not surprising that conformity and passivity, norms of school life, appeared distasteful to most.

Given the cultural discontinuities between family and school, it may be that more powerful and enduring socialization effects are experienced by children in neighborhood-based social centers and through child-organized games and activities. Thus, local cultural values instituted in the home become reinforced and validated by neighborhood folkways.

Borman, Mueninghoff, and Piazza investigated the use of neighborhood social services by children in the same urban Appalachian neighborhood that had served as the community context for the preceding research. The purpose of this study was to determine to what extent children took advantage of particular social services and activities established for them by both local residents and more formal municipal service agencies. Their patterns of involvement in informal activities with friends were also examined. It was assumed that children who took an active role in neighborhood life were building positive feelings about their culture since the neighborhood itself was predominantly populated by first, second, and third generation Appalachian migrants, most of whom were employed in blue-collar jobs or were out of work.[24]

The researchers discovered kin groups and informal friendship networks were important in determining children's knowledge of various social service programs. Thus, involvement in neighborhood life reflected children's perception of benefits derived from these services, but also was highly dependent upon their integration into neighborhood networks required to get information about neighborhood events and activities.

The most frequently used services were those created by neighborhood family groups as opposed to outside social service or city agencies. In fact the most frequently utilized "service" by seven-to-twelve-year-olds in the neighborhood was the Bible Center, a storefront recreational setting in which religious instruction was never observed to occur. Instead, children colored pictures in coloring books, hung out, or used the ping pong and pool tables available in the center, which was itself supported by a politically prominent neighborhood woman who, according to local legend, was the neighborhood's leading "fence." This family's third-eldest daughter was the most frequent Bible Center "supervisor."

Children apparently learned about less formal, more spontaneously organized activities in the neighborhood by word of mouth. Children met up with other children at predictable hours of the day to begin games, visit in each other's homes, and the like. Frequently, cousins, siblings, older and younger children interacted. One child when asked with whom he played in the neighborhood responded that, with respect to age, "Some is. Some ain't [my own age]. Sometimes I'm with babies like my baby brother."

SCHOOL AND PATTERNS OF SOCIAL REPRODUCTION AND RESISTANCE

As we have seen, Appalachian parents present a mixed message to their children about the value of school success via conformance to school norms. However, public schools do not. Their message is direct and clear. Urban Appalachian students perform poorly on standardized tests used to classify and sort students throughout their academic careers, and their dropout rates are dramatically high.

Belowitz and Durand, and Wagner examined rates of dropout and general alienation among Appalachian students in the Cincinnati Public Schools. Berlowitz and Durand identified high absenteeism, high suspension, and low reading and math achievement as variables linked with high dropout rates of Appalachian students enrolled in public secondary schools. As in most U.S. cities, dropout statistics vary by neighborhood. In Cincinnati, according to 1980 census data, dropout rates ranged from a high of 66.2 percent in a predominanely black neighborhood near Lower Price Hill to a low of 2.2 percent in a racially mixed upper-income neighborhood on the city's east side. Lower Price Hill's high dropout rate (57.8) was consistent with the pattern of association between neighborhood income level and school leaving. However, the dropout rates in other Appalachian neighborhoods were even higher than their socioeconomic status characteristics would predict. Thus, in addition to the socioeconomic status factor, there appears to be a strong ethnicity factor at work in the process of alienation from school.[25] Not surprisingly, given these data, Wagner showed that Appalachian youths in the schools he investigated did not identify with academic goals. Furthermore, they were non-participants in extra-curricular activities, indicating alienation from social programs sponsored by the school.[26]

In a highly intensive ethnographic study of three white sixth grade girls, each attending one of three schools in the Cincinnati metropolitan area, Mueninghoff and Borman focused on conceptions of power, roles, and rules girls were likely to learn in their everyday social interactions.

Conversational interactions centering on power negotiations, strategies, and outcomes in classrooms and on playgrounds were studied by analyzing sets of audio-taped and transcribed records and accompanying field notes. The primary purpose of the research was to examine the degree to which power negotiations varied among the three socially diverse school settings.[27] Based on earlier, related work conducted by Anyon[28] the researchers anticipated that middle-class girls would likely be presented with a greater number of options articulated by the teacher in a classroom code of control that emphasized individual autonomy, control over the environment, and the linkage between current school learning and later educational and occupational success. In contrast, it was assumed that urban Appalachian girls would be provided with fewer options, a rigid authority-based system of control, and a denigrating view of the links between their current school work and later educational and occupational outcome.

In the predominantly working-class urban Appalachian school in Lower Price Hill included in the study, Cheryl, a sixth grader, worked within a highly regulated environment where adherence to teacher authority was stressed and little opportunity was provided for informal discussion and elaboration of the power arrangements underlying both stated and less obvious classroom rules and roles. The teacher's method of social control, illustrated in the example below, emphasized her authority at the expense of student autonomy and dignity.

Ms. O: All right, boys and girls. . . .You can't do your work if you're talk so much you get warm air in the room.
Ms. O: Uh, fellas and girls . . . last warning . . . sit down . . . . You talk so much you get warm air in the room.

At Covedale, the college preparatory school, Colleen, a sixth grader, worked in an atmosphere structured to provide small group discussion, the type of social interaction supportive of the development of an understanding of how things work in a context free of the teacher's authoritarian supervision. Although they are allowed to work cooperatively on class projects, girls were observed to take a back seat to their male classmates.

Colleen: What does this go on?
Girl: I don't know. (They watch the boys maneuver parts.)
Boy 1: There's a whole bunch of gadgets.
Boy 2: (Directs operation)
Colleen: And she's missing a screw.

Boy 2: Go tell her we're missing some parts.
Girl: (Does)
Colleen: Here, I'll put the screws in here

Even in the middle-class school setting, girls were relegated to roles of passive dependency requiring them to "look on," fetch information, and "clean up."

Since the function of schooling in American society is ostensibly to provide an avenue of mobility for those who learn the "proper" attitudes and skills reflected in the schools' predominantly middle-class standards, Appalachian youth who are reluctant to give up their own cultural heritage will remain alienated. Even if they see an advantage in acquiring school-related standards for success, by the time they reach secondary school the processes of testing, labeling, sorting, and placement are likely to aim them toward academic careers set up for failure.

Mueninghoff studied the academic careers of fifty-two urban Appalachian secondary students, all of whom resided in the Lower Price Hill neighborhood and who were enrolled in a mixed-class high school outside their community.[29] In this investigation the purpose was to review patterns of achievement, school attendance, and other factors related to placement in either academic or comprehensive curricular tracks in tenth grade. Findings suggest a decreasing relevance of schooling for the majority of these students regardless of track placement. Absenteeism was pronounced for both high-achieving academic track students and students enrolled in the comprehensive program. One top-ranked high school sophomore enrolled in the academic tract missed more than twenty-six days during the school year, yet managed to receive a grade of B or better in English and other major subjects for all marking periods.

Other results in this same study indicated that the number of students doing poorly in their school-related studies greatly increased from ninth to tenth grade. This decline occurred in the so-called "nonacademic" or comprehensive classrooms in the school, where the work atmosphere exhibited frequent opportunities to participate in lengthy clean-up and preparation rituals. In fact, a similar pattern was exhibited across the board, even among students in academic classrooms characterized by intense learning and low levels of frustration. In the entire group studied, only eighteen of the fifty-two urban Appalachian students were in the academic program. Only three were doing well, earning grades of B or better. Interestingly, all three of these students were girls. Their descriptions of relationships at school and in their neighborhood revealed that their closest friendships were with girls from outside their neighborhood. Although they still resided in Lower Price

Hill, their social contacts in that neighborhood were limited. time after school and during the weekend was invested in hanging out with their middle-class friends who lived in the immediate school neighborhood, at a social and physical distance from the Lower Price Hill community.

Most (thirty-four) students in the study were enrolled in the comprehensive program. Only two performed well, achieving grades of B or better during the year. Twenty-five of the thirty-four performed poorly, earning grades of D or worse. By March, twenty-eight students had dropped out. When interviewed, students cited adjustment problems, changing interests, and added responsibilities at home as factors contributing to their difficulties in school. The perceived irrelevance of school weighed greatly in the decision of many who left. In summary, it seems clear that for many urban Appalachian students enrolled in public schools, the school holds few rewards. These students, both male and female, drop out of school at persistently high rates and prior to leaving school entirely, manifest high rates of absenteeism, nonparticipation in school activities, and low achievement.

High-achieving girls in their early high school careers saw their options for continued successful school performance as tied to their active pursuit of friendships with girls who lived outside this neighborhood. These friendships were likely to be costly. One remarked that she saw little of her old neighborhood friends, and found their ways of dressing and acting around school a source of embarrassment.

Two aspects of female cultural identity in the urban Appalachian milieu of Lower Price Hill compete against the formation of a commitment to stay in school for many girls and young women. The first is gaining the status and recognition of male peers by "becoming a woman." Maureen Sullivan, a long-time activist and community worker in Cincinnati's Appalachian neighborhoods, has explained the relationship between an identity as a woman and a commitment to the student role based upon her own experience in the community:

> I remember I was talking to _____ (an urban Appalachian male) on the street, on 13th Street, about fifteen years ago. I assumed I was a women — you know (laughter). And his little girlfriend or young wife at that time had recently had a child, and he told me in no uncertain terms that now *she* was a woman. And the implication was that because I had not yet borne a child I couldn't really say that I was a woman (laughter). I think that is tied in with the whole question of what do girls get in relationship to their schooling.[30]

As long as girls persist in the student role, by the standards of their male peers, they remain girls. To claim the status of woman means relinquishing the student role. A second aspect of urban Appalachian female cultural identity related to success in mainstream culture is tied to the extent to which girls and young women are exposed to street values. Street values are community values, and by turning one's back on these beliefs and practices, one is aligning oneself with the colonizers, those who exploit the labor and resources of rural and urban Appalachians. In Maureen Sullivan's words,

> For Appalachian individuals who in fact align themselves with the colonizers there has to be a division from community. The colonizers have learned how to work so that they'll hire this person's relative and that person's relative in order that they get that family loyalty so people don't get together and throw them . . . (i.e., the colonizers) out . . . (of the community). How would it be to be a girl who decides for herself that she's going to do something besides getting married or have the kid at fifteen or sixteen? And in a way there is some removing from the community that this involves. With Phylliss Shelton who is a prime example of a person who saw her way through the system, she says that she was insulated in a certain way from the neighborhood and community — not that she was ever really separated out from the community — and really by her mother. (With) her brothers — the expectation was never there that they would limit their traveling around the neighborhood to two blocks from home. They had the freedom to roam wherever . . . and they came home at 12:00, 1:00, or 3:00. That was fine for the boys. But Phylliss had rules and expectations that she was guided with.[31]

The girls who attended and completed high school outside their neighborhood had divided themselves from the community by abandoning friendships with girls who resided in Lower Price Hill. Their resistance to an urban Appalachian cultural identity was different from Phylliss Shelton's.

Phylliss's mother insulated her daughter from the streets by imposing restrictions on her activities. However, Phylliss did not cut herself off from her sense of place in the community and her urban Appalachian identity. She remained in school until graduation, acquired an associate's degree at a local university, had a baby, and finished her remaining two years of study for her bachelor's degree. In December 1986, Phylliss was in charge of The Identity Center Program in an urban Appalachian neighborhood in Cincinnati and at age twenty-six had determined to pursue a law degree. Her life course thus far suggests that she made important concessions to rules for success as defined by mainstream culture. At the same time, however, she had not sacrificed her cultural identity as an urban Appalachian woman. For example, although she had attained professional status as a social worker, she had remained in her local neighborhood community and, in fact, worked with local residents to enhance their identification with their urban Appalachian backgrounds.

Despite the successes of a few, it can be concluded that for most urban Appalachian youth, the neighborhood continues to be an important refuge and the public school a source of boredom and alienation. As a result, the majority (75–85 percent) in Lower Price Hill leave school to hang out in the neighborhood. Unemployment, drug trafficking, and male and female prostitution are institutionalized in the community. However, in the last fifteen years a number of social service agencies have established programs that have a strong local control component by virtue of governance structures that feature community residents occupying most seats on the directory boards governing these agencies.

One of these services, the Lower Price Hill Community School, was established in 1970 by a coalition of local community residents, an activist Methodist minister, and a locally-based social worker as a non-profit organization to assist young community dropouts and older local residents in obtaining the high school equivalency degree (the GED). During the early seventies the school became a neighborhood fixture through its policy of easy accessibility, remaining open from 9:00 to 3:00 Mondays through Thursdays, from 9:00 to 12:00 Fridays, and two evenings during the week. In addition to the flexible schedule allowing students to work at the school at odd hours, a regular flow of Youth Corps program participants whose jobs were contingent on school attendance assured a steady flow of students.

In his interviews and long-term observations of Community School students, McCarthy focused on the decision to enroll and the primary purpose for attending the school by thirty currently and previously enrolled students. All of those observed during the course of McCarthy's research had learned of the school by word of mouth. According to McCarthy, this procedure had several clear benefits:

> One benefit is that the situation had been prescreened. Students are not forced to arrive in an unknown situation; they already have an idea of what it is like, and most importantly, they know from someone they know well. Another benefit is that the decision to attend is a decision made among friends rather than a verdict which is handed down to them. In other words, they control whether or not they will go and how often. The control is perceived to be very important to the students.[32]

Thus, enrollment is voluntary; students select the times convenient to them to work on their programs and no one holds a gun to their heads forcing them to attend.

McCarthy found gender-linked patterns of motivation or purpose for enrollment and attendance in the Community School program. In analyzing interview data related to these factors, McCarthy derived four distinct patterns of orientation held by students.[33] One group of students was strongly goal-oriented and saw the GED as a way to meet work- and school-related plans; a second group, though they attended tutoring sessions regularly, was primarily interested in the school as a place to mingle with friends; a third group simply lacked the skills to pass the exam and was infrequently in attendance; and a fourth, predominantly male group, the Probationers, was required to attend school as a stipulation of their paroles from jail and was, like the third group, infrequent participants.

The largest number of young women included in McCarthy's study held the goal-oriented perspective and thus tended to view the Community School as an avenue to employment and/or attendance at one of Cincinnati's major universities with which the Community School has established formal ties. Many had been briefly married, had one or more children, and like Elaine, one of McCarthy's interviewees, had determined that, "Once I had a little girl, that's when I realized I better change."[34]

During the last eight years 60 percent of the school's 250 graduates have been women. Many have pursued work and advanced degrees in social service occupations such as teaching, nursing, and social work. Elaine's life course reflects the usual pattern of development for young women in the Lower Price Hill community. For young women, significant rites of passage include having a baby, going on welfare, and eventually acting upon goals and desires to "better themselves." The Community School provides a support system akin to the family, the metaphor McCarthy used to describe the school's social organizational milieu.

CONCLUSION

In the preceding analysis, we have focused on urban Appalachian culture and the development of social and sex-role identities in family, neighborhood, and school contexts. From the foregoing discussion, several strands emerge which when pulled together provide a backdrop for the discussion of policy to guide the construction of alternative educational structures to ease the school-to-work transition for young urban Appalachian women.

First, with respect to the impact of their culture on urban Appalachian women, their identification with place, their significant role in the family as providers of emotional strength, their capacity to perform social liaison work linking the family with the larger community, and to buffer their daughters against the deleterious effects of the street culture are aspects of women's experience that illustrate their strength and resourcefulness. The life course of low-income urban Apalachian women reflected in fictional and ethnographic narratives emphasizes these particular values and behaviors. Second, and less positively, girls and young women, although more tightly regulated and less likely than their male peers to have been damaged by drugs, alcohol, jail, and life on the streets, are inclined to follow a path that may lead them to reject the role of student in exchange for the role of woman/mother by becoming pregnant and leaving school. The life course of urban Appalachian women who reject cultural norms involves an active disassociation from street values and the adoption of middle-class values through their friendships with middle-class peers who live outside the neighborhood.

There is an alternative life course exemplified by the experience of Phylliss Shelton who, during her critical early years, was insulated by her mother from the negative influences of her neighborhood. As a result, she persisted in school but did not sacrifice her cultural identity. Not every Appalachian girl and young woman has a mother like Phylliss Shelton's to buffer her against the negative impact of street culture. An institutional structure such as the Lower Price Hill Community School is congruent with the cultural experience of young urban Appalachian women. It provides close, one-on-one tutorial instruction as opposed to whole-class instruction by an active teacher with thirty passive students. It is located in the neighborhood and managed by urban Appalachians and others who affirm an Appalachian cultural identity. Its mission as a provider of the GED and its links with college, university, and technical programs form a transitional bridge from the school to employment. Often urban Appalachian girls and young women have spent limited time outside their neighborhoods and are unfamiliar with the city, its transportation systems, resources, and the like and benefit from attending school in familiar surroundings. In considering educational policy for young urban Appalachian women, the community school concept allows partial resistance and accommodation to both urban Appalachian and mainstream cultural values.

NOTES

1. Samuel Bowles and Herbert Gintis, *Schooling In Capitalist America* (New York: Basic, 1976).

2. Paul Willis, *Learning to Labour* (Farnborough: Saxon House, 1977).

3. Arlie R. Hochschild, *The Managed Heart* (Berkeley: University of California Press, 1983).

4. Jane Gaskell, "Gender and Class in Clerical Training" (Paper presented at the Conference on Women and Education Vancouver, B.C.: University of British Columbia, June 1986).

5. Ibid., p. 3.

6. Michelle Zimbalist Rosaldo and Louise Lamphere, eds., *Woman, Culture, and Society* (Stanford: Stanford University Press, 1974).

7. Margaret Gibson, "Reputation and Respectability: How Competing Cultural Systems Affect Students' Performance in School," *Anthropology and Education Quarterly* 13: 1 (Spring 1982).

8. M. L. Kohn et al., *Work and Personality: An Inquiry into the Impact of Social Stratification* (Norwood, NJ: Ablex, 1983).

9. Hochschild, *Managed Heart.*

10. Gaskell, "Gender and Class."

11. Ibid., p. 5.

12. Ralph E. Smith, "The Movement of Women into the Labor Force," in R. E. Smith, ed., *The Subtle Revolution* (Washington, D.C.: The Urban Institute, 1979).

13. Carole Ganim, "Herself: Woman and Place in Appalachian Literature," *Appalachian Journal* 13: 3 (Spring 1986).

14. Ibid., p. 259.

15. Ibid.

16. Harriette Arnow, *The Dollmaker* (New York: Avon Books, 1954).

17. Ganim, "Herself: Women and Place," p. 273.

18. William H. Philliber, "Accounting for the Occupational Placements of Appalachian Migrants," in William Philliber, Clyde McCoy and Harry Dillingham, eds., *The Invisible Minority* (Lexington: University Press of Kentucky, 1981).

19. Kathryn M. Borman and Elaine Mueninghoff, "Lower Price Hill's Children: Family, School, and Neighborhood," in Allen Batteau, ed., *Appalachia and America* (Lexington: University Press of Kentucky, 1983), pp. 210–255; and Carol Stack, *All Our Kin* (New York: Harper and Row, 1974).

20. P. Zavella, "Abnormal Intimacy: The Varying Work Networks of Chicana Cannery Workers," *Feminist Studies* 11: 3 (Fall 1985).

21. Robert Coles and Jane H. Coles, *Women of Crisis* (New York: Delacorte Press, 1978).

22. Borman and Mueninghoff, "Lower Price Hill's Children."

23. Kathryn M. Borman, Nancy S. Lippincott, and Christopher Matey, "Family and Classroom Control in an Urban Appalachian Neighborhood," *Education and Urban Society* 11: 1 (November 1978), pp. 61–86.

24. Kathryn M. Borman, E. Mueninghoff, and Shirley Piazza, "Participation in Neighborhood Life by Urban Appalachian Children" (Paper presented at the American Anthropological Association Annual Meeting, Cincinnati, November 1979).

25. Marvin Berlowitz and Henry Durand, "Beyond Court-ordered Desegregation: School Dropouts or Student Pushouts?" in Marvin Berlowitz and Frank E. Chapman, eds., *The United States Educational System: Marxist Approaches* (Minneapolis: M.E.P. Press, 1980), pp. 37–53.

26. Thomas Wagner, "Urban Schools and Appalachian Children," *Urban Education* 11: 3 (October 1977), pp. 283–296.

27. Borman and Mueninghoff, "Lower Price Hill's Children," pp. 210–225.

28. Jean Anyon, "Elementary Schooling and Distinction of Social Class," *Interchange* 12: 2–3 (1981).

29. Elaine Mueninghoff, "A Study of Achievement Levels of the Urban Appalachian Student in a Local High School" (Unpublished manuscript, Cincinnati, 1979).

30. Maureen Sullivan, Personal Communication, 1986.

31. Ibid.

32. Timothy McCarthy, "Toward the Octopus: An Ethnographic Study of the Social Organization of the Community School" (Unpublished Ed.D. Dissertation, Cincinnati: University of Cincinnati, 1983), p. 127.

33. Ibid.

34. Ibid.

11

Black Cultural Forms in Schools: A Cross National Comparison

R. PATRICK SOLOMON

INTRODUCTION

The presence of cultural forms in schools mediated by race has been highlighted in recent years by researchers in both Britain and the United States.[1] The dynamic of race has become a significant factor in the coding of students' oppositional forms making them distinctly different from the culture white students produce in school. Weis points that "(black) student culture will automatically take a somewhat different shape and form from that of white working class."[2] The counter-school culture of Willis's white working-class lads of a British comprehensive school differs from that of black British boys of West Indian descent. Accordingly, Everhart's white working-class "kids" in an American junior high school produce cultural forms that differ from that of Afro-American students.[3] Apple has drawn attention to the similarities in the cultural forms that black youth create on both sides of the Atlantic: "This involves abstracting oneself from one's ascribed class position by a sophisticated process of distancing in dress, posture, walk and now more and more, speech. This creative cultural process provides important grounds for contesting dominant patterns of gender, class, and racial domination and exploitation."[4]

Within multi-racial societies, the lived culture of racial minorities within schools appears to be influenced by their historical and also their emerging relationships with the dominant groups. In the United States, black Americans' unequal and subordinate structural position and the creative cultural resources they utilize to extricate themselves from this

249

position has extended to black students' oppositional forms within the schools.[5] In Britain's race- and class-stratified society, a plethora of research has captured a range of black student cultural forms that have emerged from patterns of racial culture within the schools and the community.[6] Carby argues that the position of black students in British schools is an extension of the subordinacy the whole black community faces.[7] Consequently, black students' cultural forms may be contextualized partly as "students practising forms of resistance as members of the black fraction of the working class."[8]

Previous investigators have suggested that there are cross-national similarities in the way black students respond to patterns of racial culture within schools. My intent in this chapter is to focus on the lived culture of black working-class West Indian students in a Canadian urban high school, and to compare elements of their culture with those of black students in U.S. schools. Data on the West Indian group are drawn from a larger study, while information on student cultures in the U.S. is drawn from Weis, Ogbu, Gilmore, and others. Brief references will be made to the emergence of black student culture in British schools. Selected elements of culture explored in this study are students' social relations in school, their language and communication patterns, and counter-school and oppositional activities. In addition, students' contradictory attitude and behavior toward schooling will be analyzed because of their apparent commonality across black student groups in Canada, United States, and Britain. The extent to which black student cultural forms are similar or different cross-nationally will make a contribution to theories about race and schooling in multi-racial societies.

THE HUMBERVILLE STUDY[9]

This study was conducted over a two-year period (1983–1985) utilizing participant observation techniques, and an ethnographic format for recording and reporting data. Researchers investigating the cultural production process have found this methodological approach most productive in capturing the interactions and experiences of subjects in their social setting.[10] During the field study period I identified a cohesive group of black students, (whom I call the Jocks), established a working relationship with them, and recorded their day-to-day school activities in the classroom, corridors, cafeteria, gymnasium, and playground. Observation continued to a limited extent within the students' neighborhood.

Humberville Secondary is located within a working-class community of Humber Valley on the periphery of metropolitan Toronto. The most noticeable feature of the community is the diversity of its ethnoracial structure. From 1976 to 1981 residents with a mother tongue other than English and French (Canada's official language) increased by 54 percent, the largest of these groups being Italians.[11] The influx of visible minorities and immigrant groups such as Indo-Pakistanis, South Asians, and West Indians had altered significantly the racial mix of the community. For example, the high concentration of working-class West Indians in neighborhoods around Humberville Secondary has given rise to youth cultures such as the one illustrated below:

> In areas of Toronto where the West Indian community is concentrated . . . gangs of black kids can be found at any time of day, lounging about, smoking a joint, listening to reggae on somebody's radio, chatting. . . . They have dropped out of school, aren't very welcome at home. . . . They exist almost entirely outside the mainstream of society.
>
> (*Toronto Life*, March 1981)

Racial tensions between black and white, and even incidents of racial violence, have been fuelled by such social conditions as high-density population, and growing unemployment, especially among the sixteen to twenty-four age group.[12] Community organizations serving the community have identified inadequate training in school and irrelevant job skills as factors contributing to youth unemployment. Socioeconomic conditions have given rise to crime and juvenile delinquency in the Humber Valley community. Although technically a suburb, neighborhoods within Humber Valley are frequently described as inner city or "suburban ghettos." It is from this changing, working-class community that most of Humberville's students come.

Humberville Secondary, a vocational school at the bottom of a multi-level high school system, was developed to equip students with practical occupational skills. The program structure is half academics and half vocational courses chosen from such subjects as automotive servicing, custodial service, machine shop, cosmetology, sewing and tailoring, woodworking, typing, art, and food preparation. The employment patterns of past Humberville students show marked similarities with those of their parents: a high rate of unemployment, and work in low-prestige jobs for those who find employment. Harvey's study of the school and its graduates shows no intergenerational mobility in occupation; students live at a similar socioeconomic position as that of their parents.[13]

The tracking of black students to Humberville's low-level occupational program has been a source of disappointment for their West Indian immigrant parents who embrace education as the chief avenue for socioeconomic mobility for their children. As will be shown later, elements of culture black students produce at Humberville are a response to the low-level schooling they perceive as leading nowhere. It is to these lived cultural forms that we now turn.

Social Relations in School

A salient feature of the peer-group social relationships within Humberville is the limited meaningful voluntary interaction between dominant and minority group students. Outside the formal school-instituted groups for instructional purposes, racially distinct small groups are fixtures around the school site:

From Field Notes: A group of black boys engaged in a "pick-up" game of soccer on the playground. A small group of white boys sat under a tree close by conversing with each other. Inside the school building, black girls gather in small groups and engage themselves in "patois" discussions.

Racial groups operate almost entirely in separate social systems. Although there is no overt antagonism between black and white students, there are few inter-racial friendships.

Teacher: I don't see much war or fighting because of color. Not that they get along that great, but they don't get in each others' way.

Sentiments toward inter-race friendships are also expressed at home.

Jock's Mother: Most of Mitch's friends are black. He jeers his bigger brother for having all white, honkie friends all during high school, and even now at college. His twin sister also has mostly white friends.

Mitch's attitude toward his siblings' inter-racial friendships, mother explained, may be a response to their higher-level school placement, and their integration into the dominant-culture value systems.

Racial separation at Humberville is most noticeable in sports. Most school teams are dominated by black students (over 90 percent of the players on the senior basketball, soccer, and volleyball teams are black). Students comment on this domination as follows:

PS: Are there a lot of white guys trying out for the school representative team?

White student: About ten to twelve out of twenty-five guys, but the majority of those who make the team are black.

PS: Why is this so?

White student: Maybe the white guys are not as good the black guys.

The perception of black superiority over white in sports is shared by members of the Jocks.

Leroy: They (white students) don't want to come out. Some of them are not good.

The Jocks see white students as disinterested in sports except for hockey, traditionally a game dominated by whites. Because the school does not have a hockey program, white boys just "hang around and do drugs," one of the Jocks claims.

The Jocks utilize certain strategies to take over and dominate this aspect of school life. At the level of inter-house league senior students are given the opportunity to organize house teams. The Jocks capitalize on this freedom to select and thus exclude. Black cliques usually emerge from such a selection process, white students being excluded from the stronger teams or used as "fillers" for weaker teams. In game situations, team play patterns develop around black cliques, effectively isolating white players.

The Jocks' supporters on the sidelines during after-school competitions are almost entirely black; alienated white peers reject sports, even as spectators, and define it as "not theirs." So while sports bind black students at Humberville, they also serve as a vehicle to exclude white students, thus encouraging separatist cultures.

Research on inter-group social relations in U.S. schools points to similar interaction patterns between dominant and minority group students. Cusick's study of biracialism in American schools highlighted "an undercurrent of racial animosity" between black and white students. Mutual avoidance was the order of the day as students avoided each other in the corridors, lavatories, cafeterias, and in the classroom. Cusick suggests that administrators structure students' time and space in a very rigid way in order to minimize potential conflicts between the two groups.[14]

Petroni's research on the patterns of racial cleavage in a U.S. high school shows that extra-curricular activities are clearly delineated as either in the "black" or "white" domain.[15] Black students were expected to participate in and dominate athletics. The cultural stereotypes of blacks as superior athletes was further influenced by the opportunity structure, as physical education teachers and coaches pursue blacks instead of whites. On the other hand, non-athletic and academic activities such as class officers, speech and drama, majorette, and madrigals were perceived as "white" activities. Petroni observed that intra-group conflict developed when some black students, usually identified as "elites," deviate from instead of accommodating these stereotypes. Such deviations are perceived by radical blacks as "Uncle Tomism" and a threat to group solidarity. Own-group cleavages set distinct patterns along which inter-group social relationships are developed and maintained.[16]

At the community college level in the United States black-white group relations polarize in different ways than those highlighted in the elementary and secondary schools. Weis's study shows little overt antagonism between black and white students at Urban College. But existing tensions between the two groups are exacerbated because of black student's cultural pattern of chronic absenteeism and dropping in and out of school.[17] White students articulate the feeling that their academic progress is being retarded by these elements of black student culture. Weis explains that while white students may exaggerate elements of black culture because of their own prejudices, "many blacks drop in and out of class, arrive late for class, and engage in activities that otherwise serve to slow down the pace of learning."[18] In the end, Weis points out, it is this production of culture that encourages further polarization between blacks and white within the institution and hinders inter-group interaction. As one student remarks, "There wasn't any hostility; it was very casual. You're in your own little cliques."[19]

Language and Communication Patterns

> People evolve a language in order to describe and thus control their circumstances, or in order not to be submerged by a reality that they cannot articulate.[20]

A distinctive element of the Jocks' lived culture is their use of Creole. This language, also referred to as "Jamaican talk," "patois," or "pidgin English," is used extensively in classrooms, corridors, cafeteria, gymnasium, and playground. Pre-class chatter among black students is conducted exclusively in "patois." During formal instructional time these students show bi-dialectical skills by responding to the teacher in acceptable English, but communicating with their West Indian classmates in Jamaican creole.

An emerging feature of dialect use among the Jocks as well as other West Indian sub-groups at Humberville, is the inclusion of "Jamaican profanity" at all levels of discourse. While in the West Indies incorporation of "swear words" is limited to playground interactions out of earshot of teachers and other authority figures, at Humberville its use is more widespread. The following are examples:

[A Jock greeting his friend in the hallway]

"Wa-a-guan de, Missa raas claat!"
[What's going on there, Mr. (profanity)]

In an air of excitement in soccer competition, miskicks or any such "bad plays" by team members are met with disparaging hoots and shouts, such as:

Tek you raas claat ahfa de fiel' if you no know wha you a do!
[Take your (profanity) off the field if you don't know what you are doing!]

Altercations with opposition players in the heat of the competition generate profane threats in the vernacular as well. For the casual observer unaware of the origins and meanings of these cultural expressions, the verbal exchanges make little or no sense; but among the Jocks and other black students, every utterance is loaded with meaning.

Teachers often misunderstand or misinterpret "patois" phrases. In a confrontation between Weston, one of the Jocks, and a male teacher, Weston snapped at him.

"Leave me alone, no man!"
"Don't say 'no man' to me!" was the teacher's reply.

While in the Jamaican context the phrase "no man" is just a manner of speaking, the teacher may have been responding, not merely to the meaning of the term in this confrontation, but more so to the very subcultural assertation.

The Jocks' use of double-talk to show opposition to school rules is another feature of language and resistance at Humberville. The following explanation grew out of a teacher's order to lift, instead of push, a bike along the hallway.

Weston: She (teacher) said I should lift it (bike) up and I go, "You tink me crazy?" She reported to the vice principal that I called her crazy.

Conflicts between teachers and West Indian students usually generate the use of the patois, albeit offensive. Accompanying this language of resistance is a repertoire of other deviant communicative devices such as the hissing of teeth and muttering of "pshaw man" [an expression of disgust] several times.

The Jocks' chants along with reggae ("roots" or "rebel") music played on portable tape-recorders supplement their dissemination of oppositional messages in school. The inability of dominant-group Canadians to comprehend the messages communicated through reggae lyrics has given rise to its uncensored use and circulation within the school and the community at large.[21] As one Jock explains, "Most (white) people don't understand it much, only blacks."

Because the West Indian patois is spoken and understood almost exclusively by students of that culture, their dominant-group Canadian classmates, as well as teachers, are effectively 'locked out'. Carby, writing about a similar situation in Britain, comments on the teachers' dilemma:

> The ability of black students to use language as a form of resistance can be seen in the teachers' fear of being excluded from communication between pupils; this has always been regarded as an unacceptable loss of authority.[22]

There are marked similarities in the use of exclusionary language forms by black children in Canadian and American schools. Historically, the exclusionary feature of the Southern Creole (black English) of the United States and the West Indian creole or "patois," grew out of the efforts of black slaves to exclude their white owners from the communication process. Genovese points out:

> Creole was not merely a means of communication; it was a means by which black slaves retained an identity in the face of a cruel oppressive system. . . .Creole was a means by which white slavers were mocked, and through which black slaves retained their cultural integrity.[23]

In U.S. schools today, the unique language forms in use among blacks continue to be both a means of communication and a symbol of identity. Grubb sees the "black English" of Afro-Americans as a language form that "often hides the real meaning of oral communication in culturally specific semantics."[24] To illustrate his point Grubb draws on White's findings, "Black children sometimes confuse their teachers by turning undesirable labels around to indicate admirable personality traits." For example, teachers apply terms like 'clumsy lips', suggesting speech deficits, to children who persistently use black English in the classroom. On the other hand, when black children refer to somebody as having clumsy lips, they mean "a brother who can 'run it down, talk that talk and get over' with the power of words.[25]

Gilmore's study of black communicative style in a predominantly black urban elementary school in the United States brings out some interesting dimensions of resistance. He found that black students' stylized sulking (sulking facial gestures and body language) accompanied by verbal markers like "humph" were seen as resistance and a challenge to the teachers' authority.[26] Such a display of "bad attitude" by black children in grades four to six was seen by teachers as behavior that would blossom into insolence and subordination in later grades.

Gilmore sees the students' alignment with black vernacular culture as a detriment to their access to literacy. Teachers denied children full opportunity to participate in literacy programs because their "bad attitudes" were contrary to the prevailing ethos of the school. Consequently, argues Gilmore, the students' culture of resistance restricts their selection to honors programs, excludes them from special high-track classes, and limits their opportunity to become upwardly mobile in the American society. "Attitude" outweighs academic achievement.[27]

Counter-School and Oppositional Activities

The Jocks utilize the classroom, corridors, cafeteria, gymnasium, and playground to display a range of activities varying from conformism to opposition. Some of the classroom behaviors which are perceived as negative include stalling or side-tracking the teacher from lesson presentations; clock-watching and "closing their books too soon" to coerce the teacher into an early conclusion of the lesson; leaving the classroom repeatedly during seat-work, and wandering around the classroom interfering with other students.

An activity that is a major source of conflict between the Jocks and the teachers is domino playing, "Jamaican style." Weston explains:

> You know when y'u play dominoes y'u fe slam it down. Mr. Freeman came over and said, "Don't slam it down!" Leroy explained to him, 'y'u can't play dominoes without slamming it down." As Mr. Freeman walked away we slammed down the dominoes again and started laughing. Mr. Freeman came back and took me to the principal.

Domino games, played in an atmosphere of frivolity, shouting, and banging "pieces" on the table, are viewed by some teachers as subcultural and disruptive. These antics are used by cliques such as the Jocks display oppositional behaviors and openly challenge teachers' authority.

Sub-cultural, counter-school activities peak during inter-school sport competitions at Humberville. The following is an example of the nature and extent of these activities during track and field competitions:

From field notes: When not engaged in competitions the Jocks gather on sidelines around "ghetto blasters" listening, singing, or dancing to 'dub' reggae music. Among the Jocks' associates are "rasta looking" boys wearing "dread-locks" tucked under their hats. Two rolled "joints" (marijuana cigarettes) openly and proceeded to smoke them in the presence of teachers and police officers.

School dances are ideal occasions for subcultural behaviors. West Indian students demonstrate reggae dance steps as their exclusive domain. Teachers frown at the inappropriateness and vulgarity of "wall dancing" and take action to control it:

Teacher: A lot of grade nine boys lean against the wall and pull the girls unto their bodies (into an embrace) and start rubbing up against them. . . .when I make them dance in the middle (of the dance floor) some of them ask, "What is the party for?" I stopped them from doing that ("wall dance").

Some teachers at Humberville see strong linkages between the counter-school behaviors West Indian students display in school and the subculture they generate within the community. Such out-of-school delinquent behaviors as truanting, loitering around shopping centers, "smoking up," and drug pushing are seen as influencing within-school behaviors. Teachers tend to perceive these activities as behavior disorders requiring clinical intervention.[28]

The Jocks, on the other hand, articulate these behaviors as not necessarily delinquent, but as the day-to-day culture they collectively generate for sustenance and identity within the school and the community:

PS: What do you guys do for fun when on holidays?
Ike: Sometimes there are day parties from ten o'clock in the morning until nine at night; sometimes they are still going on at five next morning.
PS: What do they do at these parties?
Ike: Smoke ganga (marijuana) and things like that.
Weston: Those guys bring the genuine stuff. But when you go outside and buy, the guys (dealers) mix it with teabags.
Ike: Like Kong (a pusher); he came to school one day and was selling some marijuana. He had it rolled up, you could smell it. They mix it with teabags. I looked at him and laugh.

Another community activity of the Jocks is attending basement parties, also called "soun' sessions" by West Indians. Lately these parties have become less a gathering of acquaintances and more a commercial venture where the host hires a disc jockey, charges admission, and sells refreshments. These "soun' sessions" have become a volatile mixtures of friends and strangers with the potential for conflict ever present.

Weston: I was upstairs and I hear, "Pow, pow!" (gunfire). You want to see guys move, man! (run away).

PS: Did you hear the reason for the shooting?

Ike: Some guy wouldn't let go of the mike (disc jockey's microphone). This guy held on to the mike and said, "Ribbit, ribbit!" He got hit right in the head with a beer bottle.

Weston: I don't go to parties around here anymore.

Ike: The best time to rip off a guy is when you pull out a gun and everybody run. You come back and see the place empty. You see amplifiers and turntables. You can pick up a lot.

Within the setting of the school there are strong linkages between students' oppositional culture and the educational opportunities available to them. At Humberville, students' promotion to higher-track schools and access to work-study programs are contingent on both their academic work and behavior. Students such as the Jocks, whose lived cultural forms challenge the authority structure of the school, appear to be restricted in their access to educational opportunities.

Research on black youth and their culture of resistance in U.S. schools points to similar restrictions of access to full educational opportunities. Gilmore's research found "doing steps" (a chanted talk punctuated by a steady alternating rhythm of foot stepping and hand clapping) an activity that proved detrimental to students' access to literacy. Despite its acceptance within the community, school staff and administrators label "step dance" as "lewd," "inappropriate for school," "disrespectful," "too sexual," and as an alignment with black vernacular culture.[29] Parents within the community point out a dramatic parallel between the teachers' description of black children's cultural forms as sulking and stepping and the portrayal of black slaves in American history as either sullen or dancing. From this comparison Gilmore describes teachers' images of sulking and stepping among black school children as a brand of modern day racism. Gilmore, then, puts these behavioral events into another historical perspective. He sees sulking as showing resistance to the authority in control, while at the same time appearing to go through the routine of expected behaviors. This contradictory behavior he finds reminiscent of black slaves' relationships with their masters.[30] As will be shown later, the development of resistance and accommodation as a lived cultural pattern has become a popular feature of black students in white-controlled institutions.

DISCUSSION AND CONCLUSION

What has emerged from this cross-national comparison of black student cultural forms in school is a theme of separatism. At Humberville, the Jocks' common West Indian heritage reinforced by the group's enthusiasm for team sports provide common ground for intra-group relations. Group identity is further solidified by their unique language form, "patois" that is impenetrable by their white schoolmates and teachers. Group activities such as domino-playing "Jamaican style," singing and chanting along with pre-recorded reggae music, "wall dancing," all contribute to the elaboration of a separatist culture. These cultural forms have two "functions": they are mechanisms of solidarity for the Jocks and other black students within the school, and, at the same time, they are devices that act to intentionally exclude dominant group students.

Research studies carried out in U.S., British, and Canadian mixed-race schools have identified a high degree of own-group preferences and few inter-group social relationships.[31] The Humberville study moves beyond own-group preferences in friendship patterns and pinpoints elements of black student culture that do not merely separate, but antagonize others within the school community. This is also the case in U.S. schools.[32] First, the designation of school extra-curricular activities as either in the "black" or "white" domain lays the groundwork for the polarization of students into racial groups. These racial cleavages are quite often encouraged indirectly by school administrators to minimize potential inter-group conflicts. Cusick, for example, finds this bifurcation along race (and class) lines in keeping with patterns of the larger American social order.[33] The Jocks, in other ways, are creating a cultural form similar to that created by blacks in other multi-racial societies.

Previous studies suggest that one of the most unique features of black student lived culture in schools, for example, is their contradictory relationship with schooling and education. Studies carried out in the U.S. have highlighted this paradox: black students embrace education, the achievement ideology, and develop high educational aspirations.[34] In the meantime, however, their counter-school activities do not allow them to achieve these ends. Ogbu's study of black youth in Stockton found them:

> excessively tardy, lack serious attitude toward their school work and do not persevere in doing their schoolwork . . .as black children get older some drift into drug use and sale and pursuit of other non-academic ac-

tivities. Consequently, many do not do well in school to obtain the educational credentials they need for employment in mainstream economy.[35]

At the community college level in the U.S. Weis concludes similarly: although black students accept the process of education, "they drop in and out of school, arrive late to class, exert little effort, and engage in extensive drug use that serves to distance them from the process of schooling."[36]

The Jocks at Humberville reveal similar impulses. In discussions about career plans, individuals aspire to "go to college and study attorney," or to become a "professional hockey player." Yet they engaged in disruptive classroom behaviors, use delaying and avoidance techniques to prevent lesson presentations by teachers, and create diversions for their own entertainment and enjoyment. Truancy from school to pursue their own interests and absence from classes to participate in extra-curricular sports limit the continuity of their classroom instruction. How does one account for these contradictory behaviors in black students?

Ogbu argues that despite a conscious choice to obtain an education in order to escape from poverty, black youth become less committed to schooling as they grow older. By assessing their parents' chances of making it through education and acquiring mainstream jobs black children realize that their own chances are not very good. They gradually become disillusioned and consequently take their schoolwork less and less seriously.[37]

Weis puts black people's contradictory response to education in a historical perspective. She interprets their collective struggle for equal education as a form of opposition against dominant whites who have denied them access. On the other hand, the low-level investment of black students in Weis's study results from their perception of community college education as only "second best" and believe that "whatever blacks get is not as valuable as what whites get."[38]

The Jocks' commitment to schooling at Humberville has to be interpreted in the same light. First of all, there are serious incompatibilities between the students' career aspirations and the high school program to which they are tracked. The reputation the school has acquired within the community is reflected in its label: "Humberdump, where dummies go." Efforts of the Jocks to transfer to higher-track schools throw some light on the paradoxical situation: black students still embrace education and the achievement ideology; it is certain kinds of schooling that they reject. This complex interplay of accommodation and resistance is a marked departure from, for example, Willis's "lads" who flatly reject the achievement ideology and, therefore, find it less conflicting to engage in counter-school culture. The paradox of accommodation and resistance has become a significant feature in research findings on race and schooling. What is particularly essential here is that West Indian students in Canada are elaborating the same contradictory cultural form as that noted in the United States and Britain. This suggest the primacy of race in the creation of cultural form in a multi-racial context.

To conclude, researchers have established strong linkages between black oppositional culture in U.S. schools and the more historically rooted black-white antagonism that constitutes the racial formation in that society. Ogbu sees black students' contemporary oppositional frame of reference as continuous with the culture of resistance developed by black slaves to their subordination and exploitation.[39] While in Canadian schools black cultural form is only just emerging with recent West Indian immigrants to Canada, it nonetheless shows striking similarities to that of its black counterparts in U.S. schools. Unfortunately, by differentiating themselves from the school and falling back on their own, less-valued cultural form, black students contribute to their subordination and alienation. Inter-group antagonisms are not merely reproduced, but widened as students enter the workplace. More importantly, students' lived culture impedes their academic progress in school and therefore restricts future employment opportunities. As Apple concluded "(students') future is partly determined by the culture (they) create."[40]

NOTES

1. In Britain: Mary Fuller, "Black Girls in a London Comprehensive School" in Rosemary Deem, ed., *Schooling for Women's Work* (London: Routledge and Kegan Paul, 1980); Godfrey Driver, "Cultural Competence, Social Power and School Achievement: A Case Study of West Indian Pupils Attending a Secondary School in the West Midlands," *New Community*, 5:4 (1977), pp. 353–359; Paul Willis, *Learning to Labour: How Working Class Kids Get Working Class Jobs* (Westmead, England: Saxon House, 1977) gives samplings of an emerging West Indian youth culture. In the U.S. see John Ogbu, *The Next Generation: An Ethnography of Education in an Urban Neighborhood* (New York: Academic Press, 1974); Lois Weis, *Between Two Worlds: Black Students in an Urban Community College* (Boston: Routledge and Kegan Paul, 1985); P. Gilmore, "Gimme Room: School Resistance, Attitude and Access to Literacy," *Journal of Education* 167:1 (1985), pp. 111–128.

2. Weis, *Between Two Worlds*, p. 28.

3. See Willis, *Learning to Labour*; R. Everhart, *Reading, Writing and Resistance* (Boston: Routledge and Kegan Paul, 1983) for ethnographies on white working-class culture in schools.

4. M. Apple, *Education and Power* (Boston: Routledge & Kegan Paul, 1982), p. 114.

5. Both Weis', *Between Two Worlds*, and Ogbu's *The Next Generation* ethnographies detail black student oppositional forms.

6. In addition to the British references in Note 1 above, the following provide a good cross section of West Indian cultural forms in British schools and communities: D. Hebdige "Reggae, Rastas and Rudies" in S. Hall and T. Jefferson, eds., *Resistance through Rituals* (London: Hutchinson, 1976); K. Pryce, *Endless Pressure* (Harmondsworth Penguin, 1978); E. Cashmore, "Black Youth, Sports and Education," *New Community* 10:2 (1982), pp. 213–221; E. Cashmore, *Rastaman*, (London: Allen and Unwin, 1979).

7. H. Carby, "Schooling in Babylon," in Centre for Contemporary Cultural Studies, ed., *The Empire Strikes Back* (London: Hutchinson, 1982), pp. 183–211.

8. Ibid., p. 184.

9. All names of schools, communities and people in this study are pseudonyms.

10. John Rex's suggestions are helpful here; see "West Indian and Asian Youth," in E. Cashmore and B. Troyna, eds., *Black Youth in Crisis* (London: Allen & Unwin, 1982), pp. 53–71; also Paul Willis, *Learning to Labour*, p. 3.

11. *Census of Canada* 1976, Cat. #92–810 and 95–826; and 1981, 95–936 (3–A) & E564.

12. See M. L. Hobbs, *A Step Ahead: A Social Needs Study of the "Humber Valley" Community*, (ESPC, 1983); M. Harker, "The Nightgown Brigade," *Multiculturalism* 2:1 (1978), pp. 23–25.

13. E. G. Harvey, *Program and Organizational Review of Secondary School Occupational and Vocational Programs*, (O.I.S.E.: Toronto, 1980).

14. P. A. Cusick, *The Egalitarian Ideal and the American High School: Studies of Three Schools* (New York: Longman, 1983).

15. F. A. Petroni, "'Uncle Toms': White Stereotypes in the Black Movement," *Human Organization* 29:4 (1970), pp. 260–266.

16. Ibid., p. 263.

17. Weis, *Between Two Worlds*, p. 56.

18. Ibid.

19. Ibid.

20. James Baldwin, "If Black English Isn't a Language, Tell Me What Is?" *Roots* 1:4 (1979).

21. The more volatile socio-political conditions in Jamaica make the messages in "rebel music" potentially dangerous there. However, in Canada such lyrics, even if understood, lack political power.

22. Carby, *The Empire Strikes Back*, p. 187.

23. E. Genovese, *Roll Jordon Roll: The World the Slaves Made* (New York: Vintage Books, 1974).

24. H. J. Grubb, "The Black Prole and Whitespeak: Black English From an Orwellian Perspectice," *Race and Class* 27: 3 (1986), pp. 67–80.

25. J. L. White, *The Psychology of Blacks: An Afro-American Perspective* (Englewood Cliffs: N.J.: Prentice Hall, 1984).

26. P. Gilmore, "Gimme Room: School Resistance, Attitude and Access to Literature," *Journal of Education* 167: 1 (1985), pp. 111–129.

27. Ibid., p. 125.

28. This is a popular view with British school teachers who think that West Indian children there show marked prevalence in behavior disorders. See M. Rutter et al. "Children of West Indian Immigrants: Rates of Behavioral Deviance and of Psychiatric Disorder," *Journal of Child Psychology and Psychiatry* 15 (1974), pp. 241–262.

29. Gilmore, "Gimme Room," p. 119.

30. Ibid., p. 126. Genovese also makes a similar point in his book, *Roll, Jordon, Roll*. See chapters on the black work ethic and language.

31. For British schools see M. M. Jelinek and E. Brittan, "Multiracial Education-1. Inter-ethnic Friendship Patterns," *Educational Research* 8: 1 (1975), pp. 44–53; U. S. schools see M. H. Metz, *Classrooms and Corridors* (Berkeley: University of California Press, 1978); for Canadian schools see M. A. Ijaz, *Ethnic Attitudes of Elementary School Children Toward Blacks and East Indians and the Effect of a Cultural Program on these Attitudes* (Ph.D. Dissertation, University of Toronto, 1980).

32. See the following studies: Weis, *Between Two Worlds*; Cusick, *The Egalitarian Ideal*; Gilmore, *"Gimmee Room"*; Petroni, *"Uncle Toms."*

33. Cusick, *The Egalitarian Ideal.*

34. Weis, *Between Two Worlds*; Ogbu, *The Next Generation.*

35. J. Ogbu, "Class Stratification, Racial Stratification and Schooling," in L. Weis, ed., *Race, Class and Schooling* (Comparative Education Centre, State University of New York at Buffalo, 1986, No. 17), pp. 17–18.

36. Weis, *Between Two Worlds*, p. 134.

37. Ogbu, "Class Stratification, Racial Stratification and Schooling", p. 23.

38. Weis, *Between Two Worlds*, pp. 138–139.

39. Ogby, "Class Stratification," p. 24.

40. Apple, *Education and Power*, pp. 106–107.

12

Women's Ways of Going to School: Cultural Reproduction of Women's Identities as Workers

DOROTHY C. HOLLAND AND
MARGARET A. EISENHART*

Scholarship on the role of schools, especially institutions of higher education, in reproducing structured inequalities by gender is rare. Relatively little is known about the treatment of women in college and the reaction of women to this treatment. In this paper we contribute a case study to the literature on women's response to schooling by analyzing findings from an ethnographic study of women's ways of going to school at two universities.

Oriented by a cultural reproduction framework, but using an inductive anthropological approach, we question the ways that the women in our study take advantage of their opportunities to go to college.[2] Why does Linda, for example, work hard to complete college with good

*Acknowledgments. We would like to thank Jeff Boyer, Carole Cain, Alex Cuthbert, Valerie Fennell, Carole Hill, William Lachicotte, Judith Meece, Naomi Quinn, Karen Sacks, Judith Shrum, and Sheila Slaughter for their comments on earlier versions of this paper. We are also grateful for a grant from the National Institute of Education (NIE-G-79-0108) which funded the collection and analysis of a large part of the data. A grant from the University Research Council of the University of North Carolina made the 1983 follow-up study possible. Finally we are especially indebted to the women who participated in the study as informants and as interviewers.

grades when she intends to later drop her career as a nurse in order to raise a family? How is it that Susan, who begins her college career as someone who is good in math and science, as someone who took advanced courses in high school in these subjects, and as someone who earns a math degree, decides to earn certification in education as opposed to going on in graduate school? And what of Cylene who seemingly handicaps herself in college by deciding not to buy books?

In this chapter, we first discuss some of the reasons for combining a cultural Marxist orientation with an inductive anthropological approach in studies of women's response to schooling. We also discuss some of the methodological issues that arise when trying to mesh the two approaches. Second, we describe our own study (in which we used an inductive approach) and the cultural models of schoolwork that emerged from our data. Third, we follow the courses of individual women as they use the models and face challenges to them during college. In many of the cases, but by different routes, we find that the women have developed marginalized views of themselves as workers, and, at least in some cases, we find that having a romantic relationship with a man is more central to the women's self-definition than is working or having a career. Finally, in the conclusion, we examine the ways in which these women seem to be producing or reproducing structural inequalities by gender.

CULTURE AND THE SOCIAL REPRODUCTION OF CLASS, RACE, AND GENDER INEQUALITIES

Ten years ago it would have been peculiar to suggest that neo-Marxist studies of schooling and those of more inductive anthropologists could be conjoined. However, if we compare the work of Willis[3], a major contributor to the cultural Marxist approach, with that of Ogbu,[4] a leader in the subdiscipline of educational anthropology, we find convergencies in methods—namely, an emphasis on ethnographic techniques—and in analyses of the responses of dominated groups—working-class males in Willis's case, ethnic and racial minorities in Ogbu's studies—to schooling. Both researchers emphasize the active role that working-class and minority students take in the on-going struggle between and among subgroups in the society, and both analyze the manner in which this dynamic interaction creates and recreates the society.

In essence, they both conclude that students are likely to act in school from a collective sense of the "opportunities" afforded to people like them by society. The students' collective response comes about, to use Willis's terminology,[5] through the process of "cultural production," where subgroups in a society creatively use "discourses, meanings, materials, practices, and group processes to explore, understand, and creatively occupy particular positions in sets of general material possibilities." Their response may be oppositional and may succeed in disrupting the social status quo, but often, for various reasons and despite its oppositional character, their response results in reproducing cultural values and patterns that contribute to the reproduction of structured inequalities and of traditional class and group relationships.

A recent ethnographic study of ours provides an example of this sort of dynamic in a southern elementary school.[6] We noted that the school was not simply transmitting traditional gender roles to the fifth and sixth grades that we were observing. The students themselves were the ones who were elaborating and emphasizing gender roles and gender relations in the school.[7] The teachers were promoting asexual "good student" roles; the students, in contrast, were interested in extra-curricular gender-specific activities and in school-organized activities like the sixth-grade banquet that they could construe as a boy-takes-girl situation. We interpreted the gender emphasis of the students to be a reaction, in part, to the school-promoted age hierarchy that defined them as children. When they found opportunities to engage in more "adult" activities, such as cross-gender relationships, they did so.

Although the students' responses were oppositional to the school program, they were consistent with patterns of cross-gender relationships in adult society. Thus the school was a site in which culturally patterned gender relations were being reproduced, but the reproduction was not a case of direct socialization. The students were very active participants in the reproduction process. Willis[8] makes a similar observation about the reproduction of gender relations in his Hammertown study:

> But what we see partly on the site of the school . . . is nevertheless a larger production of cultural forms and ideology and forms of division between gender and mental and manual activity, which are more basic and virulent than anything the school could hope to mold or produce — namely, a remaking of every generation.

In this chapter, we begin from a framework similar to the one arrived at by Ogbu and Willis. But we focus on women—a category that neither Willis nor Ogbu has studied explicitly.

Why Study Women's Response to Schooling?

Studies of gender are important for developing the cultural reproduction perspective because it is not clear to what extent gender is similar to or different from race and class as a structured social division. It is also not clear in what manner gender interacts with race and class in affecting response to schooling.

Willis's opinion[9]—given in response to the criticisms of Mcrobbie and others[10] that he had neglected gender—is that gender could be analyzed from a cultural reproduction framework similar to the one he adopted in *Learning to Labor*. However, as others have pointed out, gender, as a primary social category, may possess special characteristics. After all, gender divisions are associated with biological reproduction and are elaborated in the domestic unit. Furthermore, gender bifurcates races and classes. Can we really expect to find females rebelling in school as we do males? Can we expect to find females developing the kind of alternative marginal and illegal routes to a livelihood that Ogbu[11] says some minority groups develop? Can we expect to find females opposing males in the ways that blacks oppose whites or the working-class "lads" oppose representatives of the upper classes in the schools? These questions cannot yet be answered fully.

From the research that has been done, three aspects of women's response to schooling stand out: 1) whereas the resistance of young males may be elaborated in what the British call subcultures such as the mods, the rockers, and the punks, young females tend to resist societal constraints in quieter, less flamboyant, more individualistic ways;[12] 2) while their brothers and boyfriends develop and elaborate themes from the culture of their father's workplace, girls become absorbed with the "culture of femininity" and draw upon its images of gender relations, romance, and marriage, to envision their futures;[13] 3) unlike the lads whose self-meaning is expressed in the shopfloor culture, women tend to have marginalized worker identities. They do not identify with or invest their selves in their job or occupation.[14] We will return to this third point in the discussion of our data.

Most of the previous research on women has been developed as a counterpart to studies of working-class and minority males, thus it has emphasized working-class and minority females in elementary and secondary schools. The study we report here, in contrast, took place in two universities: Bradford University and Southern University (SU), and at least at SU, involved middle-class women. Nonetheless, despite the difference in background and age, our findings bear similarities to the existing literature. For the college women in our study, we find individualistic responses to perceived oppression and we find marginalization of worker identities. In the case of worker identities particularly, we were able to observe the processes by which this cultural pattern of marginal investment in work was reproduced.

A Further Note on Our Approach

In this paper we attempt to maintain an inductive appreciation of our data yet ask questions that arise from a cultural reproduction perspective. We are aware, as Jenkins[15] among others has pointed out, that this balancing act raises some very difficult issues. One of the main issues concerns the autonomy and importance that is granted to the understandings held by the participants in the society. These "folk models" as Jenkins calls them or "cultural models" as we prefer[16] may be quite different form the analyst's model. What is to be made of these differences? There is also the problem of the locus and expression of these cultural models. Are they situated in collectives such that they are discernible only from recurrent behaviors? Are they beyond the awareness of individual participants? These issues have been and continue to be discussed at great length. Because of space limitations we must simply state our position.

Like Jenkins we propose to treat the analyst's models and the cultural models as equally important—we neither give ours nor theirs a privileged position, but consider both to be important. We agree with Jenkins at least in principle because we take the position that people act in a context that they construe. Their interpretive frameworks or cultural models do not determine the context but rather the meaning that the context has for them. This inductive anthropological interest in cultural models can be conjoined with a cultural reproduction position if we ask about, rather than define or assume, the dimensions of the group's collective meaning system.[17] (See Bullough, Gitlin and Goldstein for a discussion of analysts' confusion of their model with the group's model.)

Further, we take a cognitive approach to cultural models, meaning that we consider shared, individually grasped views of the world to be an important component of collective knowledge.[78] Similarly we consider individual processes of learning, developing, and altering cultural views in response to the vicissitudes of experience to be important components of the group processs that Willis[19] labels "cultural productions" and "cultural reproduction."

Our aim then is to try to understand the women's models of the college world, to understand their actions in relation to their models, to trace how these models develop during their experiences in college, and then to ask whether patterns leading to the recreation of traditional gender relations are being culturally reproduced.

WOMEN AT BRADFORD AND SU

The primary data on which this article is based were obtained from in-depth analyses of the experiences of eight women—four at Bradford University and four at SU—during their first three semesters of college. These accounts were gathered in 1979–1980 as part of a larger ethnographic study designed to investigate the college experiences and future plans of black and white women on the two campuses.[20]

Bradford is a historically black school; SU, a historically white school.[27] Demographic information on the two universities suggests that SU draws students of predominantly white, middle-class backgrounds while Bradford draws students of predominantly black, lower-middle-class backgrounds. In some other respects the two schools are quite similar. Both are state universities. At both schools the ratio of women to men is about the same (60:40). Also at both places 50 percent of those who apply are admitted and 60 percent of those admitted are enrolled, although Bradford is a smaller school.

To obtain participants for the larger study, advertisements asking for freshman volunteers were distributed at the two universities. Approximately 100 women volunteered. Based on screening interviews with volunteers, we chose an ethnographic sample of twelve black women from Bradford University and eleven white women from nearby SU. Because we were particularly interested in women's pursuit of careers involving math and science, we selected a sample in which women having such interests were overrepresented. We also suspect that, because we asked women to volunteer for a study of their future plans, we may have attracted women who were interested in having a career. Nonetheless the samples included women with a range of majors, interests, size of networks, and ideas about the future.

A three-semester period, from near the beginning of the informants' freshman year to the middle of their sophomore year, was chosen for intensive study in recognition of the fact that on both campuses students were required to declare a major before the beginning of their second semester as sophomores. As the study proceeded, we discovered that this period was a significant one in the college careers of the women because they were in the process of reacting to differences between high school work and college work and, at least in some cases, to the need to form new friendship groups. Our methodological strategy of choosing a range of individuals for intensive study, rather than a group as Willis did, highlighted the process of adjusting to school (only part of which was choosing a group) as it was experienced by each woman. Consequently, in contrast to Willis, we focused more on the process by which each woman responded to a new school environment than on the dynamics of school groups.

During the three-semester period, researchers conducted monthly observations of informants engaged in campus activities. Informants were also interviewed nine times over the course of the three semesters. These "talking diary" interviews were open-ended and designed to encourage respondents to discuss their experiences and concerns in their own terms. For the most part, they talked and were encouraged to talk about their college coursework, majors, activities, and friends.

A second type of interview, the "life history" interview, was conducted near the end of the study, in the middle of the women's sophomore year. This interview asked informants to think back over their lives and recount all the things they remembered about their high school experiences and about their ideas and plans for their lives as adults.

In an effort to increase the validity of the data, black researchers worked at Bradford, white researchers at SU. Also researcher-informant pairs remained together (with two exceptions) throughout the study.

In 1981 we developed a survey (based on the ethnographic data) to ascertain factors affecting women's choice of major and commitments to their majors from a broader sample (N = 362) at the two universities.[22] In 1983 when members of the ethnographic samples should have been graduating from college, an attempt was made to recontact them and learn about their current activities and plans. Most of the informants were contacted.

The in-depth analysis of the eight cases described in this paper involved reading through the approximately 200 pages per informant, searching for evidence of the ways these women think about college and what they are trying to do there. Specifically, we analyzed our data in terms of the following questions:

1. How do women understand schooling and its place in their lives?
2. What insights do they have about schooling and what actions do they take based on these insights?
3. How do these findings relate to previous research on cultural productions and the cultural reproduction of gender inequalities?

These questions, when applied to our data, directed our attention to the women's cultural models of college work — particularly the purposes of doing the work — and we have limited our discussion primarily to this topic. However, we make some reference to three other areas, related to college life, that are important to the women in our sample: romantic relationships, friendships, and family. It is necessary to bring in some information about their orientation to these other topics, especially romance, in order to understand how the women construe the context in which they do their college work. Full discussion of their understandings of these other topics must, however, take place elsewhere.[23]

SCHOOLWORK FOR WHAT?

In general, the women talk about schoolwork in terms familiar to all of us who have attended U.S. schools: grades and exams, requirements and degrees, work and study, students and teachers. They carve the academic world into similar roles and activities, and they evaluate their experience of the work of college along similar dimensions—one likes doing it or dislikes it, finds it boring or interesting; one is good at it or not good at it. All the women recognize that some people like to do schoolwork, and they all believe that some people are good at certain subjects while others cannot "do algebra" or "handle" the work in an advanced course. During their first two years of college, all the women worry, at least some, about how good their grades will be, what courses to take, and how much work they will have to do. The eight differ, however, in the point or purpose that they assign to college work. We will refer to these different views as "cultural models."[24]

We find three distinctive models of the world of college work. In all three, the purpose of doing the work is central. The models can be described as: 1) work in exchange for doing well; 2) work in exchange for finishing college; and, 3) work in exchange for learning from experts.

These models of college work affect interpretation of grades, evaluation of teachers, choice of courses and majors, and decisions to buy or not buy textbooks, purchase term papers, and allocate energy to studying. These models also affect the women's interpretation of their accomplishments, abilities, and problems in school.

During the period of study, each woman seems to hold one model as a dominant one; however, some are aware of other people's models of schoolwork and may sometimes entertain other models themselves or at least pieces of them. In only one case do a woman's experiences lead her to substantially change her model of college work.

Although all but one of the women retain their models during the period of study, most of them face some challenges to their views of school and activities at school. For all of these women the process of responding and adjusting to the challenges takes time. In confronting the challenges, some of the women experience intense struggles or develop important insights relative to the world of college work and campus life.

In the next sections, we first describe each model, relying heavily on the words and logic of the women themselves. Then we describe the struggles or insights experiences by those who hold each model. Our data reveal that for women holding the first (N = 3)—college work for doing well or for finishing—the struggles and insights of their first three semesters of college lead them to marginalized worker identities. That is, the attachment they have to a view of work as expressive of self becomes or remains weak. For those holding the third model (N = 2)—work for learning from experts—the worker identity is and remains an important part of self-definition. Significantly, romantic relationships are more important than work in the lives of the six women with marginalized worker identities, and in one of the remaining cases where commitment to work is strong, obtaining validation from men is an important aspect of worker identity. Finally, in no case do the models, struggles, or insights lead any of these women to want to organize to improve conditions for women, in either work or romance.

Work for Doing Well

Three of the women—Linda, Kelly, and Susan—view the work they do in college as a way of gaining recognition for their natural abilities and skills. All of the women talk about wanting to do well in school for their parents, but these three, all at SU, also have the goal of doing well as their own. One of these, Linda, put it this way

> I always wanted to achieve the best, to be the best that I could academically; I always wanted to make As . . . if I made a B, I felt I was a failure within; that if I had pushed a little harder, I could have made an A.

This idea of doing well is related to the idea of being good at, or having a "natural" ability for, schoolwork in general and at least one subject area in particular. Linda, for example, says,

> I'm just not a business mind [so] econ. is hard for me. My suitemate, she's a business mind, and she whizzed right through econ. I'm just more like science, natural science. It's easier for me. The whole concept seems real easy. It just comes naturally to me.

Linda, Kelly, and Susan's ideas about schoolwork and their abilities seem to have formed before coming to college. In high school, they came to believe in their own academic ability, and they learned that they did not have to work very hard to do well in school. Kelly says about her high school experience: "I really didn't have to work much to get a good grade." And Susan was able to make very good grades in high school with what she considered to be a minimum of work. Susan comments, ". . . it wasn't the amount of effort you put into it, it was more like the grade that comes out of the little bit of effort you put into it. . . ."

From the vantage point provided by this model, doing well in college should be easy for those who are naturally good at the kinds of tasks or the subject matter of school. That is, good grades should be attainable without a lot of hard work.

All three women talk about "making" grades in college. For them, good grades are made by combining ability with some, but not too much, work. Low grades are presented as the result of not doing the minimum amount of work required, of "being slack," "being lazy," or "not doing any studying at all for that test."

From the perspective of this model, courses are selected with an eye for demonstrating ability to do well as indicated by the grade one makes. Whenever possible, courses in which one is not naturally good or those that are known to be hard should be avoided. When difficult courses must be taken, the women try to stagger them across semesters and "balance them out" with easier courses, in order to maintain their grade-point averages.

In the same vein, teachers are sometimes evaluated in terms of how easy or hard they are, and this information is used by the women to balance their course selections. Teachers are also described as good or bad lecturers; some are funny, and others are hard to get along with because they want the work done in quirky ways. However, success in a class is determined primarily by one's natural ability in the subject area and by how hard one is willing to work to make a good grade.

When these women go to SU, they expect to be able to make good grades there, especially in the subject area chosen for a major. However, they find that it is not as easy as they expected. Making good grades in college means working harder in classes and taking a lot more time for studying than was necessary in high school. The increased difficulty of making good grades leads these women to question whether they do, in fact, have any natural ability for schoolwork or the subject they have chosen as a major. As will be evident later in the section on "Struggles and Insights," college is a place where difficulties such as this one are confronted.

Work for "Getting [It] Over"

The world of college is very different from the vantage point of work as a means of finishing college or getting college over with. Three of the women — Cynthia, Rosalind, and Cylene, all at Bradford — view the work they do at college as a means of finishing up a stage of their schooling, what Rosalind refers to as "getting over." From this perspective, "going to college" and getting through the work there is what matters. Going to college and getting through are important because they lead to a degree that can, in turn, be used to get a good job later. Another way to say this is that attending and completing college and receiving a degree is a means of moving up in life. Cynthia, for example, says,

> I felt like going to college would bring me a good job . . . and I wanted to become something. . . .I didn't want to just get out of high school and just set up and just wait for somebody to bring me some money.

Later, Cynthia makes it clearer that she views simply getting through college as a step toward achieveing her goals,

> If I can just pass, I'll feel all right. . . .I have to pass to get out of here.
> It's going to have to be done in order to get myself somewhere in life. It's
> just a step higher.

Associated with this view is the idea that the work and requirements
of college are somewhat arbitrary and simply tasks that must somehow
be completed. The work has no particular significance, in and of itself or
to students, except as a collection of activities that must be done or procedures that must be followed if one wants to finish. This view is reflected in the women's statements about the kinds of things that instructors require. For example, Rosalind, in talking about what her algebra
instructor is like, says,

> She's teaching a whole different way from the way I learned it. I'm used
> to taking shortcuts and in her class you cannot take a shortcut. You
> have to go from one step to the next. If you miss a step, the problem is
> wrong even if you come up with the right answer.

Later, about a history exam, Rosalind makes a similar remark,

> You have to write everything in order. You couldn't put one part here,
> at the top, and another part at the bottom.

And, finally, about a health exam, Rosalind complains,

> It was a smoking exam. Half the things we covered in class weren't even on
> the exam. You really had to know something about health to pass that exam!

When the tasks associated with getting the work done become
especially bothersome, doing them may simply not be worth the trouble.
Because tasks are perceived as arbitrary, with little future return, there is
no point in enduring a great deal of hardship to accomplish them.
Rosalind expresses this position when she says,

> I studied two weeks for that exam. . . .I forgot three things which I
> didn't care to remember because it was just too hard to keep writing.

For Cylene, buying the books she needs for classes becomes too much of
a burden. She explains that purchasing books takes a large share of the
meager financial resources she has for college, is difficult to transact
because she has problems in getting a ride to the bookstore, and is not
likely to do her much good anyway because people in the dorm "borrow"
her books right before the tests. Furthermore, buying books allows the
white man at the bookstore to get her hard-earned money. After one

semester of buying books, she sees little return on her investment and decides not to buy them again; she plans to get through without them.

These obstacles to getting finished are described for most courses and professors. The strategy adopted is simply to persist in order to get the degree. Rosalind, who is asked by the researcher on numerous occasions whether she might consider changing her major or not completing college, always answers with a resounding "no!"

> I wasn't gonna change. . . .I want my degree in biology, then I want my master's in physical therapy. . . .I wouldn't be satisfied with a bachelor's [or less].

Cynthia, who experiences considerable difficulty in the math courses required for her degree in business, is also determined to continue. She says,

> I see myself as a person that knows that if I want this fulfilled in my major, then it's [the math] going to have to be done. . . .I'm gonna have to get used to seeing it. I'm just hoping I can cope.

Cynthia, Rosalind, and Cylene all recognize that to do the work, tasks such as going to class, buying books, studying, taking tests, and writing papers—however they are defined by the school or by individual instructors—must be done. But, one can "get over" or get through without doing all these things individually. For example, some students "trade up on notes," meaning that one student will take notes for another who, for whatever reason, decides not to attend a class. Some students take turns trading up on notes with each other. Some students also share books, and some buy papers which they turn in as their own work.

These women see themselves "getting" grades, not "making" grades. Primarily grades are viewed as tokens that one must accumulate to get through courses and, eventually, college. They are important because they are necessary for finishing college and obtaining a degree. From this view, "passing" grades, as Cynthia indicated earlier, are what is needed. Cs are described as "fine" and a C+ average as "doing real good." Only Fs are a problem because they mean that one must take a course over, putting one behind and, thus, delaying one's progress toward completion of college.

Grades can also be indications of the quality of one's performance. For example, Cylene worries about how disappointed her mother will be when her grades do not measure up to her cousin's. And Rosalind talks about wanting to bring up her 2.8 average. However, getting high grades seems to be of only secondary important to the women in this group, and as Cynthia suggests in talking about getting passing grades in order to get out of college and get a good job, grades as tokens of how well one has adhered to an arbitrary set of requirements are not taken as indicating anything about one's future performance in a field of work.

Grades are "given" by teachers in exchange for work completed. Teachers are evaluated in terms of how well they make clear their requirements for grades. Earlier Rosalind was quoted as she negatively evaluated a health teacher whose test did not cover the material discussed in class. Rosalind went on to positively evaluate two other teachers as follows,

> She told us each and every thing that was gonna be on that exam. . . . She gave us an eleven-page outline. . . .She gave us a chance to pass.
>
> My English teacher is pretty nice. . . .He repeats the material two or three times to make sure everyone understands, and at the end of the class, he'll say, 'If there's anyone who does not understand, you're welcome to come to my desk." So, I like him.

Teachers are also evaluated on the fairness of their grading. Effort expended should be recognized with an appropriate grade. For Cylene, an appropriate grade is one that reflects the amount of work one has put in. In this sense, equal work should receive equal reward. Cylene criticizes one teacher because she gives higher grades to students she has had before, despite the quality of their work relative to Cylene's, and another teacher because she gives Cylene and others the same grade, despite the fact that Cylene has turned in more work. For Rosalind, an appropriate grade is one that reflects the time one has put in and not necessarily the skill one has acquired. She makes her view clear in her response to the interviewer's surprise that Rosalind has made an A in swimming but still could not swim,

> He grades you on your time in the pool, coming to class, and how hard you are trying. He grades pretty fairly.

Work for Learning from Experts

The world of college is again very different from the vantage point of work in exchange for learning from experts. Valecia, from Bradford, and Karla, from SU, see college as a place where skills can be acquired from experts. Both these women are quite explicit in their expectation that college professors be experts who can help students to learn. Valecia, an English major with hopes of becoming a broadcaster some day, organizes her view of work in college around the idea that she needs to learn good English from her instructors there,

> I love speech and English. I like writing and I like talking about what I write, but it's the proper way of [doing it] that I have trouble comprehending. I want to major in [English] and I want to get it down solid . . . .In high school, I was neglected of an English background, so English, it's a lot to learn. But since I got to college . . . the instructor now . . . he's an expert and I'm an amateur. . . .He's published five or six books and he knows every corner of a good paper. . . .I always wanted an instructor that was real strict on the way I write and he is. . . .He's been critiquing me hard. That's why if I get a good grade, I'll feel like I've accomplished something.

Correspondingly, Valecia as an amateur expects the development of good skills to be difficult and to take some time,

> I like English, but I'm having so much trouble. . . .Well, who said it would be easy? Everybody have their problems the first year. . . .I like English. Isn't that part of a major? Something you enjoy doing?. . . . Freshmen start out just like a baby . . . having to learn a whole lot of new things. I just can't get downcouraged now because I'm a freshman. I have three more years to go.

Although Valecia is aware that other students have ways of completing their work more quickly, she sounds determined to take the time to do well. She says,

> When I rush through, I do a bum job. Kids told me ways I can get it out easier, but I don't want to. I want to get the best grade and I want to put forth my best effort.

Karla, who begins college trying to decide between a major in art or physics at SU, is seeking a "broad-based education" (Valecia also mentions "wanting to have some knowledge" in other subjects, but this aspect of college is overshadowed by her concern for good English) and is interested in exploring different majors as possible careers. Karla says,

> I'm here to gain a really broad-based education and learn as much as I can. . . .I would like to look at [lots of] different fields and job opportunities. . . .I would like it if you could just take courses without having to worry about degree requirements.

Karla expects to find knowledgeable professors who can evaluate her talents in a particular field — "when it comes to college, one expects a professor to be a demi-god," but she has sometimes been disappointed. Some teachers' level of mastery of their subject is too low for them to be of much help to her. This has been a special problem in art.

I never had an art teacher I felt was really talented or good enough where their opinion would mean much as far as whether I should be an artist.

Peers likewise are not adequate sources of information or help because their skill level is no higher than Karla's. Also problematic are teachers who know their subject matter but whose testing or grading procedures do not provide Karla with accurate feedback about her growing mastery of the subject. For example, she complains about a French teacher who doesn't seem to comprehend the mathematics necessary to give partial credit, thus obscuring the extent of her progress in French. She also complains about a zoology professor whose tests in a survey course covered "picky things" rather than the "basic" or foundational knowledge that Karla had learned and believed more important to have learned in that type of course. Karla also believes that some professors, particularly those in science, must be convinced that females in their classes are to be taken seriously. Only then will these professors make an effort to teach females what they know.

Valecia also describes professors whose classes are a waste of her time because she does not learn anything new and professors whose grading and testing procedures obscure how much she has learned. The second is a problem even with the respected "strict" English teacher when he informs the class that if he feels they have improved, he will give them the grade they deserve, but if he feels that they have not improved, then he will give them an F. When Valecia gets an F after working very hard in the class and believing that she is "improving," she does not want to "accept" the grade as an indicator of her progress and complains to the dean about the grading procedure.

Grades are important to both Valecia and Karla because they are signs of learning and the development of skills. Valecia hopes desperately to get a good grade from the English professor because it would signal progress toward getting English "down solid." Correspondingly, Valecia decides to take a course that she has placed out of—but with a low score—in order to learn the material better, and later, when she discovers she is making a C in a course, she decides to drop it and take it again for a better grade, even though she will end up behind her classmates.

For Karla, grades in the fields she is considering as potential majors are particularly important. Grades in these fields indicate the level of her mastery and thus something about her chances for a successful career in that field. Grades in these fields are also important because of how they will "look" on her transcript when she applies to graduate school, where she wants to go for further, more advanced study.

STRUGGLES AND INSIGHTS

Difficulties in College

All eight women talk about their difficulties in adjusting to the work expected of them in college. For some, these difficulties are hard to overcome and involve them in protracted struggles to adjust. For others, the obstacles they perceive are fairly easily overcome. As we will show below, difficulties are associated with the models of college work described above.

The Problems of Not Doing So Well

A number of the women face the situation of having to work harder in college to get the same grades they did in high school. A number choose not to work harder and so end up with lower grades. For some this is a problem mainly because of their parents. They feel badly about disappointing their parents and develop various explanations to make their parents feel better. For Linda, Kelly, and Susan, whose major orientation to school is the idea of doing well, there is more of a problem. Not doing well is an issue that all three struggle with during the period of the study. Not being able to do well with a minimum of work is a blow to their notion of being naturally good at schoolwork. Not doing well in a particular subject area is a blow to their notion of why they are in college — to study a subject at which they are naturally good. One of their responses is to scale down their ambitions and notions of self.

Scaling down ambitions and notions of self. Kelly, after only a few weeks of college, is faced with reconciling herself to a lower rank. She "came from a background of good grades, tops in the class, never really worrying about it," and now she's "just a face in the crowd . . . just average here." She responds by dropping a goal she has had for four years to become a doctor, dropping her premed major, and switching to international studies before the end of her first semester. She hopes that in international studies, where one of her main subjects will be Spanish which she "knows" from living for several months in South America, she will be able to make "mostly As." She also decides to apply to a special school for diplomatic studies for her junior and senior years.

Even with the change in major, Kelly finds that she cannot make the kind of grades she wants and is used to. Near the end of her freshman year, she says, "It's a lot harder than I thought. . . .I wish that I could have done a lot better." Her major complaint is that she has "not learned to study" so that she can make good grades without too much work.

By the end of her freshman year, Kelly seems to have resigned her-self to a diminished commitment to doing well academically, at least at SU. She states that next year she plans to get more involved in extra-curricular activites "because I wouldn't use this time any better," i.e., she does not believe that more time spent studying is likely to help her make better grades: "It's just like [the time] would be wasted."

Consistent with her statement about using time, Kelly begins her sophomore year by accepting a job as manager of the men's hockey team. She has no particular interest in hockey: she knows nothing about the game or the players; she responds to an ad for the position because she wants to use her time "more productively" to make some money. The job requires her to spend every afternoon and to take numerous out-of-town trips for which she misses classes during the hockey season. Also during her sophomore year, Kelly finds out that she has not been ac-cepted at the special school. When we attempted to contact Kelly in the spring of 1983, we were not able to talk directly to her, but we found that she had dropped out of school.

Kelly's difficulties with schoolwork bring her view of herself as good at academic work into question. Her statements and eventual decision to allocate less time to her studies suggest a relinquishing of her identity as someone who is good at schoolwork — an identity that was important to her in high school. Concomitantly, her investment of herself in her career as a student, i.e., as a school worker, has been attenuated. In this sense, Kelly's experiences have led her to what Valli[25] refers to as marginaliza-tion of the worker identity. Like the female cleric workers in Valli's study, Kelly does not seem very attached to an identity as a full-time and serious worker.

Linda, one of the others who holds a work-for-doing-well view of college, has a similar experience and response. Like Kelly, Linda realizes that she will have to work harder in college to make the good grades she has come to expect in high school and, like Kelly, she does not step back to rethink or reconsider her view of the system. Instead she rethinks her ideas of herself in light of her model of doing well. She decides that she doesn't have what it takes. She talks about herself as lacking the mental and physical stamina, as being lazy, and as not having the intellect to do the work. Although the process is painful, she, too, adjusts her ideas of herself and "accepts" a view of herself as being average,

> I'm just very disappointed with myself. I wanted to do so much better than this. You can't be average and get into the medical field. And I don't want to be average. . . .But, right now, I guess that's just what I'll have to content myself with because I don't know if I can do any better.

One part of Linda's scaling down is to switch her major from physical therapy to nursing, because nursing requires a lower grade-point average. In May of 1983, Linda was graduating with a nursing degree and planning to begin work as a nurse.

Without a worthwhile goal, schoolwork is not worthwhile. Compared to Kelly and Linda, Susan comes up with a more novel solution. She modifies and eventually switches her view of schoolwork.

In high school Susan made good grades with little effort. She was seen as being good at math and science. It soon becomes clear to her that at SU more work is necessary to make good grades, and she encounters a chemistry course that requires more studying than she feels motivated to do. She receives a D in the course and becomes convinced that she does not want to ever take another chemistry course again. Up until the end of her first semester she had spoken of chemistry as a possible major.

Susan portrays her poor performance as stemming from disinterest. She describes herself as being "slack" and "lazy." She finds the work boring and uninteresting. She resorts to doing only the bare minimum because she doesn't know what she "wants to do." The work has no meaning for her and so doing well has lost significance for her. By the end of her third semester, she is saying such things as: ". . . right now I'm at this point in my life where I don't talk about schoolwork a lot cause I don't know what I want to do, but . . . I always have got so much work to do . . . for nothing. . . ." She dreams about taking a semester off.

Meanwhile Susan is spending a great deal of time with friends whom she describes as "mellow," who get together a lot to drink, to do drugs, and to listen to music. They are a cross between her "socialite" friends from high school who worried about their social reputation and pursued expensive activities and her friends from a male prep school who were not so reputation conscious and were more caring toward others. Her search for and her talk about friends seem to reflect an effort to sort out the kind of person she wants to be.

As Susan proceeds through school, she rejects a concern with social reputation and getting rich. She moves toward a definition of herself as a "hippie" — "a peaceful deadhead." But she still does not know what she wants to do in life. Without knowing exactly what she wants to achieve, without having a worthwhile goal for future work, the work of college does not seem compelling. She'd rather spend time with her friends, and she'd like to quit school and "go skiing out west."

Susan has trouble, however, giving up the image of herself as being good at schoolwork, her image of herself as doing well. Her sister is also in college and doing well. Susan says of her:

. . . [she's] real smart. Well, she's not real smart, she's just as smart as
me, but she's more responsible and she studies more. . . .She just got
her license to operate the [special equipment]. . . .Mom and Dad, like if
she got that, it's like . . . 'Yes, Susan, [and] what are you going to do?'
'Oh, shut up! I don't want to hear about that right now.'

In the spring of her freshman year, Susan goes to see a therapist:

I was really getting bummed out about school, cause I—I still kind of
worry about not doing anything you know. . . .I do what I have to
do . . . the bare minimum . . . my grades aren't bad, they're about . . .
a B-C average, . . . I'm just use to, well Mom and Dar are used to me
having As and Bs, and so I was, you know, just kind of bummed out
about it.

Susan does not scale down her ambitions or even her view of herself
as smart. Instead she questions the goal of working. One must know
what one wants to do or achieve; if not, the work is a waste of time. She
does not have the idea, however, that a college degree will lead to a
better-paying job than one might get otherwise. In fact, she often talks about
the "paths" that one must take to get to various jobs. Eventually she set-
tles for working for a degree in exchange for a job that will pay more
than being a waitress, but she is still searching for a more important goal.

By the end of her senior year, Susan had quit school for a semester,
not found a goal, but had come back and continued work for a math
degree because it was the easiest to finish in the least number of
semesters. She was then thinking in terms of work for getting (finishing)
a degree. She had reoriented to a "getting over" perspective. In the
follow-up interview, a few weeks before her graduation in 1983, she says:

Yeah, [I did] well enough. It doesn't take that high grades to get out of
here. You just got to stick with it for awhile.

Susan still had not found something she considered worth doing in a
larger sense, although one of her courses in her last semester—an intro-
ductory course in education—provoked her interest. The teacher happened to be very upset about the mistreatment of the lower classes in the
American educational system. Susan was impressed by his concern and
saw that perhaps she could make a difference. She was considering going
into math education.

Unless she does go into math education which at this point she feels
to be worthwhile as a goal, an outcome of Susan's struggles also seems to
be a marginalization of the worker identity. She has come to view work
instrumentally, primarily as a means of making money. Even if she does

become a teacher and invests herself in the work, she will become a case of "leakage" — a woman with abilities in math and science who majors in these subjects in college but fails to continue to graduate school or to obtain a high-paying, high-status "non-traditional" job.[26]

Struggles associated with "getting over". In general the women from Bradford encounter less of a challenge to their viewpoints than the women from SU for two reasons. First, because of their "getting over" orientation, Cynthia, Rosalind, and Cylene do not have as much meaning associated with high grades as do the SU women. When they get lower grades than they had in high school, they experience much less of a jolt to their self-definition. Second, they are more likely to have and to stick with, at least in their first year, a group of "home girls" and "home boys." They are already familiar with these peers and so are not as likely to encounter new challenges to their points of view.

"Getting over" seems to be a view of school that its holders arrive at some time before they come to college. Rosalind, in fact, specializes in "getting over." She achieved fame among her peers in secondary school when she skipped a grade. She continues to think of herself as someone who is good at getting through with a minimum of wasted effort. She is an expert in executing this point of view.

Rosalind's view, as well as Cynthia's and Cylene's, puts the lie to school as a place of experts who have something of value to teach or who have authority over one's evaluation of oneself. If schoolwork and school requirements are arbitrary, then one sensibly tries to limit the work and hassle that is imposed. And if grades — as long as they are passing grades — have no meaning with regard to assessing one's talents and abilities, then the "getting over" view of school limits the power of the teacher to affect one's evaluation of one's abilities for a job. Holding this view also means that one's identity, one's investment of self, is not in one's schoolwork.

For Rosalind and Cynthia, nothing happens to challenge or disturb the validity of their view during their first three semesters of college. During this period, both maintain a "getting over" orientation.

Getting ahead by playing up to others. For Cylene, the situation is more complex, because she realizes that some people, in particular a friend, Bea, can "get over" more easily or quickly by getting things out of others — better grades from male teachers, approval from white girls in the high school, jewelry from would-be boyfriends. People like Bea succeed by acting as though they feel more attracted to others than they do. Cylene finds such behavior a sort of going beyond what one should have to do to "get over" — a sort of going outside the job description — at school or anywhere. She finds such behavior demeaning and of questionable utility in the long run. Decent people can see through such behavior.

However, Cylene agonizes over whether she should be doing the same "in order to get ahead faster." During the study, she resists the temptation in the case of her schoolwork and strongly criticizes teachers who permit students to get ahead in this fashion. She resists even in the case of trying to get into a sorority: "I like the Thetas and I wouldn't mind pledging Theta but I just cannot go to their activities and just grin at them and smile at them all the time, just because I want to be a Theta. . . ." Finally, several very intense weeks during the time we talked with Cylene were filled with stories of her problems with and finally her rejection of Bea as a friend, a rejection stemming, in part, from Cylene's "insight" about how some people get ahead.

The view of college work as something to get over contrasts dramatically with the view of college work as a means of doing well, yet both views seem to lead women to a decreased investment in themselves as workers. For those who hold models of schoolwork for doing well, we find worker marginalization in response to not being able to do as well as expected. For those who hold the "getting over" model, we find marginalization to be implied by the model.

Perhaps the work-for-getting-over model of college could be categorized in cultural Marxist terms as an accurate insight about the nature of the system, a "penetration."[27] Perhaps the work required at Bradford truly is irrelevant and arbitrary. Perhaps anything beyond passing performance in college has little to do with later life. Perhaps the women who hold this view are better off than Linda and Kelly who have scaled down their views of their own abilities. And perhaps one could say that a view that discredits the importance of schoolwork beyond its pragmatic, instrumental value also constitutes an important insight.

However, should the "getting over" view of work be carried into the workplace, the women are not likely to invest much of themselves in their work. We were unable to contact Cylene in 1983, so we do not know whether her views had changed by the end of college, nor do we know what she was thinking then about her working life. We do have some evidence that she did not expect work identities to be central to her as an adult. She has an as yet untested identity as a business woman, but believes that her important adult activities will take place outside of work. She considers herself to be a potentially influential member of her community with a contribution to make toward helping less fortunate people such as unwanted children or older people, but she sees this identity as being realized outside of work:

> I know I want to do something . . . or [be in] some organization so I
> can help somebody, I want to help somebody — outside of a job. Other
> activities that mean a lot . . . I'd like to be in Eastern Star [a woman's
> voluntary organization associated with the Masons].

We were able to contact Cynthia and Rosalind. Cynthia expected to
graduate in May of 1984 — she still needed three courses, two that had to
be taken sequentially. She spoke of looking for a job in marketing and
waiting until she had worked for several years before having children.
She had married. Rosalind, on the other hand, had not been able to keep
going to school in the face of what to her were arbitrary courses. She had
not returned to Bradford for the 1982–1983 school year because she was
tired of "going to the same classes over and over." She was thinking of
enrolling in a technical school. When asked what was the most satisfying
aspect of her college experience, Cynthia said, "only having three courses
left." Rosalind said, "nothing."

Struggles against disadvantages. For Valecia and Karla, who hold
a view of college work as learning from experts, the struggles are quite
different. Their struggles are against barriers to learning. These barriers
are perceived as structured inequalities and personal disadvantage, and
both women have developed strategies which they believe will allow them
to overcome the barriers. In neither case is worker marginalization a
response to challenges to the model nor an entailment of it. What is
revealed clearly in the analysis of these women's struggles is the tendency
to recognize solutions more in the actions of individuals than in the actions of social groups, such as women or blacks.

Fighting disadvantages by getting around them. One way to fight
disadvantage is to try to circumvent it. For example, Karla, who recognizes that some science professors do not take female students seriously,
also believes that individual students can, and should if they want to, get
around this disadvantage. About this matter, Karla says,

> If you're a girl, you have to do very well to have people concede that you
> can do well. . . .In certain science courses . . . if you're a female, you
> have to go in there and be aggressive about answering questions and do
> a good job on your homework. . . . If you don't speak up in class the
> instructors will take the guys in the class and really try to help them
> along, but they figure if you're a girl . . . a C's good enough for you,
> and they'll spend their time on the people they think want As. If you're
> not aggressive, they will figure, and quite rightfully so, that you want to

be sort of ignored and left like a sponge in the corner to soak up the information.

Karla says she has been very successful at getting around this disadvantage at SU—her strategy being to ask at least one controversial question per class period and to make sure the professor knows her name.

Like some of the students at Bradford, Karla does not seem to encounter any serious challenges to her model while she is in college. When we contacted her in May of 1983, it seemed that she was still on the course that she had set for herself. She was about to graduate with a degree in marine biology and had been accepted at a well-respected graduate school in that field.

It should be noted that several of the other women in our sample felt disadvantaged and unfairly treated. Only in Karla's case, though, is the disadvantage considered to be connected to gender. In her case, as well as in the others, the women's insights about disadvantage bring about action to relieve the disadvantage for oneself, not for a group. The one exception, Valecia, is concerned about overcoming disadvantages for blacks as a category. However, on numerous occasions, her accounts suggest that she is more concerned about some blacks than others.

Fighting disadvantages by remediation. Like Karla, Valecia recognizes disadvantages, but in Valecia's case the disadvantaged category is black people, not women. Her ideas about how to overcome the disadvantages are also different than Karla's. In Valecia's view, disadvantages experienced by blacks derive from the obstacles that blacks face in learning and using standard English. According to Valecia, these obstacles take the form of poor preparation in elementary and secondary schools and few opportunities to be around people who "talk right." The consequences for individual blacks who fail to use "good English" are several: they "look dumb" and don't have a chance to express their points of view, demonstrate their "competence," attend college, or obtain "professional" jobs. Worse, they "make the whole race look stupid."[28]

Valecia believes that blacks should do everything they can to remediate their disadvantages, but she is not optimistic that most blacks will. One way Valecia attempts to deal with this problem is to work very hard herself at learning standard English. She believes this skill will allow her to get a good job and become a role model for other blacks, either as a news broadcaster or a high school teacher. Another way she seems to come to grips with the situation is to recognize, applaud and identify herself with other blacks whom she calls "mature" because they demonstrate the characteristics that she believes make blacks look competent. She hopes that mature blacks, especially the "girls," can be recognized for behavior that will improve the reputation of blacks as a group.

Valecia holds this view of blacks as needing to "correct" for their poor backgrounds even though she identifies many cases of "discrimination" against blacks; her sister, for example, was denied as valedictorian. A white student with lower grades was awarded the honor instead. Valecia, herself, had a white high school counselor who discouraged her from becoming a doctor. The counselor did not believe "that a black person could really succeed in this life."

During the period of the study, Valecia's understandings do not seem to be affected by the perspectives of her fellow students, some of whom are acting out very different understandings of college and the "disvantage" of being black. As indicated above, Valecia considers many of her peers at college to be immature. Instead of being seen as having a different and perhaps valid interpretation, they are seen by Valecia as being immature. One professor who does articulate an alterantive perspective manages to worry Valecia by asking her: "What's wrong with your English?" She has no answer.

It is important given our focus on gender to note that Valecia identifies structured inequalities as affecting blacks in general, not women in general. She singles out black women as a special group, but maintains black people as the primary group of reference. Even in accounts where she talks at length about doctors who try to convince women to have hysterectomies, she views this primarily as an attempt to limit the black population rather than an attempt to control women. However, it is also important to realize that Valecia's view of blacks divides them into those who are competent and incompetent, mature and immature, and males and females. Her varying attention first to blacks as a category and then to divisions within the category seem to lead her to opposing ideas about the action necessary to improve the condition of blacks as a group (see also Weis,[29] whose ethnographic study of a black community college reveals a similar type of confusion among some of the students).

When we contacted Valecia in May of 1983, we found that her plans had changed somewhat although her model seemed to be intact. She explained that during her sophomore year, she had to confront the fact that she might not be able to compete successfully for broadcasting jobs. A degree in English might not be best for her.

> I did know friends who were English majors; they had a degree but no job. So [that started me thinking that] the job market is closed in that area. That made me take some serious thought about my major. It took me about a semester and a half. I went to a lot of companies and asked them what the outlook [was] for an English major who has having a hard time pronouncing her words correctly, as the white audience recognized. . . .So that's when I decided to change my major. . . .I'm a firm believer in using my degree to the fullest. It's going to get tired of me before I get tired of it.

Valecia changes her major to public administration (with a minor in English) when she finds another expert who impresses her at college. Consistent with her model, she is undaunted by the expert's reputation for making students work hard,

> I went to this class and everybody advised me, 'Don't get into public administration. You don't just walk in and walk out. You walk in and crawl out.' So I took this man and he was as rough as everybody said . . . but you could just sit up and listen to him all day long, because of the way he articulates and gets things over.

In May of 1983, Valecia had graduated with a degree in public administration and was preparing to go to graduate school and obtain a master's degree in planning. She had been offered a scholarship at a well-known university in another state on the strength of her grades and the recommendation of her public administration professor.

Thus, Valecia's experiences during college lead her to revise her thinking about the value of an English degree for someone like herself, and, in choosing public administration, she seems to change from trying to "correct" her dialect to trying to get around the disadvantage she faces as a speaker of a black dialect. At the same time, she, like Karla, retains her view of college as a place to learn from experts, and she seems well on her way to carrying that view to graduate school.

Routes to Marginalization

In this section and the previous one we have described eight women's understandings and struggles with work-related issues at the beginning of their college careers. During this period of their lives the women are still adjusting to the differences between high school and college and to the different points of view that they are encountering while establishing a group or network of campus friends. In making the adjustments, we see them gaining some important insights and engaging in some major struggles.

The SU women, in particular, do encounter new perspectives and, in three of the cases, do have problems with grades. Before coming to college they had seen themselves as good at schoolwork because they could get good grades with little effort. In college the same amount of work brings lower grades. Although each of the three responds to this challenge to their identities of being good at schoolwork in different ways, they tend to arrive at the same point as the women from Bradford—their identities as (school) workers become less important to them.

We do not mean to imply that the women become alike in having marginalized worker identities. Their routes to de-emphasizing schoolwork as an important part of themselves are different, and their understandings of the college world different. These differences may become important in their later lives. Susan, for example, may have found a worthwhile goal in her notion of being a better math teacher for the lower classes than previous teachers have been and so may come to identify with their work. However, by the time we left them at the end of the study, we can say that six of the eight have de-empahsized "academic" pursuits as a crucial part of their own self-meaning. Performance in school has become more instrumental—more a means to an end and usually an end that has to do with making money—and less expressive of themselves as individuals.

Two of the women had arrived at college with a point of view that meant they were engaged with their work in a different way than the others. They both saw the work as relevant to acquiring knowledge and skills they wished to have and they saw the learning of this knowledge as directly important to their self-definition and who they would be in the future. Both of these maintain their orientations through the period of the study. Interestingly, both see themselves as members of disadvantaged groups. For Valecia the group is blacks; for Karla, women. In neither case, however, are their actions addressed to changing the conditions that produce the disadvantages they face.

WHAT ELSE IS IMPORTANT?

If (school)work is becoming marginalized in most of the women's lives and their struggles and insights do not lead them to collective action to try to change the system, then what is important? One other identity, that of being a female in a romantic relationship with a man, is particularly important to the women in our sample.

Susan's case is illustrative. In thinking ahead five years, Susan muses about what she will do and whether to get her teaching certificate,

> Then [if I became certified] I could just have a source of income that would be better than waiting tables. I kind of want to travel a little before I start this. Five years is enough time to goof off. I'll be twenty-six then and that's not that old. I can get married or something. Maybe and maybe not.

Susan is not unusual among the eight women in seeing marriage as an alternative to work. Others such as Linda see marriage as the main component of their future, with work as a peripheral activity. This peripheral relationship of work to marraige mirrors the importance of schoolwork relative to romantic relationships in college.

In this section we outline several features of the collective view of romantic relationships on the two campuses and comment upon the relation of romance to the academic worlds of the eight women. Here we must limit our comments to general points. However, as with their views on the point of doing schoolwork, the women have various models, struggles, and insights relative to romantic relationships.[30]

In the student cultures at both universities, the world of gender types and relationships is more often discussed and more elaborated than is the world of academics and study. The college world is populated by such types as "chicks," "wimps," "dudes," "hunks," "jerks," "cowboys," "jocks," "gays," "frattybaggers," and, for those involved closely with the fraternity scene, "Alphas," "Taus," and "Sigmas." No such proliferation of names exists for academic types.

Extensive study of the type of names at SU by Holland and Skinner[31] shows that the named types are associated with a particular cultural model of cross-gender relationships. On the female side of this model, a woman's attractiveness and prestige is validated, to a major extent, by the men who recognize her qualities, who want to go out with her, and who treat her well by showing concern and respect for her viewpoints and desires. Once established, romantic relationships are important for women because they are a sign of attractiveness, and a source of prestige, special attention, emotional support, and fun. One woman describes the situation as follows:

> All (the females) wanted a date on Saturday night. That was the most important thing 'cause now somebody else was interested in you. They found you attractive. . . .

Another describes why she cares so much and does so much for her boyfriend,

> I depend on (him) for attention. . . .He makes me feel good, he compliments me . . . he's attentive to me and sensitive to the things that I feel.

Although the romantic world at Bradford is somewhat different — romantic relationships are fraught with more difficulties and are not the important sources of attractiveness and prestige that they are at SU — they are, nevertheless, desirable and they are self-defining for women in a way that grades are not. Cylene's choice of words reveals the centrality of romantic relationships, as compared to schoolwork, to self-meaning. One can "care about grades" or not care about grades, but in the case of men, one cares or doesn't care about one's self. Of a friend who has gone through a marriage breakup and who now indiscriminately sees a variety of older men, Cylene says, "She acts like a person that doesn't care . . . about herself anymore . . . she used to care about herself and care about who she was with, and care about her name. . . ."

Thus, for all of these women, whether someone cares about schoolwork or doesn't is a personal choice of usually limited interest. But the possibility of not caring about romantic relationships is never discussed. Neither is the possibility of a lesbian relationship alluded to in the interviews. All of the women discussed here either had boyfriends or pretended that they did during most of the study period. None claimed to be disinterested in romantic relationships with males.

Correspondingly, although romantic relationships with men can be difficult, these difficulties must be faced. Men are often talked about in the interviews as trying to curtail their girlfriend's activities especially with other males and as interfering with their girlfriend's schoolwork and other interests. Romantic relationships also expose women to the risks of exploitation by bad men and to pregnancy. People — especially those that the Bradford women know — are likely to gossip, and there are the dangers of "getting hung up on a guy" or "letting a man get your mind" so that a part of one's life gets out of hand and "messes up" the other parts. But, the women talk about avoiding the problems by choosing the right men, looking for the right kind of relationship and managing the relationship. They do not talk about giving up on men altogether or scaling down their expectations for men in their lives.

As pointed out at the beginning of this section, the women differ in their views, struggles, and insights about romantic relationships. They also differ in the degree to which cross-gender attachments are more important in their self-definitions than work activities. But by and large, all but two of the eight see romantic relationships as closer to the core of their selves than they see work. Significantly, the six women who have developed marginalized worker identities make romantic relationships more central. For the remaining women, Valecia and Karla, the two areas are more equal in importance. However, in Karla's case, there is evidence that her interest in work is at least partly related to the thrill she gets at being one of the only women in her classes. She is keenly aware of the positive impression she makes with men when she is able to hold her own in science classes. Thus we think that Karla is receiving considerable prestige, attention, and support from men — things normally obtained by the other women at SU only in the context of romantic relationships — by participating with them in work activities. She also has a steady boyfriend during the period of the study. He seems important to her as a source of emotional support and as a companion for social activities. Thus Karla's relationships with men would seem to be a major component of her identity, both as a worker and outside of work.

CONCLUSIONS

This paper has followed the early college careers of eight women—four at a predominantly black university, four at a predominantly white university. It has described their developing views of college work over a three-semester period. Adhering to the open-ended, inductive approach characteristic of anthropological research we have allowed our informants to tells us not only their views of their experiences but also what experiences and thoughts they considered to be important. We first summarize our findings relative to schoolwork and then turn to some observations about the development of insights and the process of cultural reproduction.

We found three distinctive orientations to the world of college work. They can be summarized as work in exchange for doing well, work in exchange for getting [it] over, and work in exchange for learning from experts. These orientations have different entailments for a number of facets of college work. They affect interpretations of grades, evaluations of teachers, allocation of time, decisions about majors, and even decisions about buying or not buying books.

The three Bradford women with a work-for-getting-it-over view thought of their school careers in instrumental terms. The work was something that had to be done—even though it had little apparent relevance to future work and later life—in order to finish college. Their self-meanings were not expressed in their work. Three of the SU women began college with a very different orientation. They saw work as an opportunity to demonstrate their identities as talented students. As we have seen, they did not do as well as they had in high school and in response lowered their commitment to their work. By the end of the study, six of the women had marginalized (school) worker identities. The three Bradford University women brought their worker identities with them to college; we watched three of the women at SU reduce their commitment to strong worker identities.

Perhaps the waning significance of worker identities was not as much of a disruption as it might have been had the women not had alternative sources of self-meaning. The women uniformly viewed relationships with men as a world of potential involvement, achievement, and support. To varied extents, six of the women saw boyfriends as crucial to their definition of self and of more central importance to their self-definition than achievement in college. This is not to say that college was unimportant or even that all would do as Linda said she would and drop her career for her family but that the identities associated with romantic relationships, for these women, tended to be more prized than those associated with work.

The other two women, one at Bradford and one at SU, were quite distinctive in holding a view of college as a place to learn from experts. For them, the skills and information they could acquire from knowledgeable teachers were important to their view of themselves and their futures. Romantic relationships were also important to these two women but in different relation to their worker identities. In one case at least, aspects of romantic relationships are incorporated into the worker identity and are important both in and out of work.

Cultural Productions, Cultural Reproduction, and Gender

How can we assess the adaptations that the eight women in our study have made to college work? Do we have indications here that their models of work and the struggles and insights traced in their interviews are cultural productions in response to intuitions of gender-related social barriers?

At the end of their sophomore year in college, six of the eight women have little investment of themselves in their schoolwork. For them the world of schoolwork was a world of instrumental importance only. Were these responses cultural productions generated in reaction to intuited barriers to women?

The answwser appears to be "no." The marginalization of women's identities as workers was the result of a set of processes, instances of cultural reproduction, that did not involve intuition of the nature of American society for women. Recalling the processes of marginalization, we note that the women relinquished meaning from work at different points in their careers and for different reasons. None of the reasons were phrased in terms of gender.

At least two of the women at SU decreased their attachment to their work identities without altering their interpretation of the fairness of the university system; it remained for them a legitimate source of recognition for good work. They did not gain any insight about the system or its preference (or lack of preference) for women or any group for that matter. Susan, the third woman at SU, also avoided interpreting the university as problematic for women. Instead she related her problems to the lack of worthwhile goals for work.

The reaction of the Bradford women likewise cannot be attributed to their intuition of structured inequalities for women. Although it is difficult to infer the development of the views of the three Bradford University women — they brought their models of school with them to college — we can see a similarity between their "getting over" view of school and the kind of view that Ogbu[32] attributes to blacks as a result of thier intuition of an imposed job ceiling. If the "getting over" model is related to blacks as a group and not to women as a group—and we have very few indications in Cynthia, Rosalind, and Cylene's interviews that this view was associated with structural barriers faced by women—then it is difficult to describe the "getting over" view as a reaction by the Bradford University women to the structural subordination of women. In sum, the processes of marginalization of worker identities that we observed seem to be best classified as instances of cultural reproduction resulting from the dynamics of the situation. They do not seem to be cases of cultural formations or, in Willis's terms,[33] cultural productions, generated in response to the intuitions of structural barriers.

Perhaps the two remaining women—Valecia and Karla—do offer examples of the intuition of gender-specific social constraints. After all, their interpretations of their experiences do include acknowledgement of the existence of such barriers. Karla speaks in terms of barriers against women per se; for Valecia, black women are a special category.

The impact of Karla and Valecia's views on others was, however, limited. Neither they nor the other women put much energy into joining or organizing groups which oppose—either explicitly or implicitly—conventional roles for women in the workforce or in families. Instead the women adopted personal strategies and tended not to identify with women as a group.

Weis[34] notes a similar lack of identification with a collective struggle in the student culture at the black community college she studied, and she is led to ask: "Why isn't the cultural level more overtly political?" Weis's answer is to argue that the dominant ideology which blames individuals for problems and difficulties, coupled with a sense of despair about the changes that might occur through collective action, and the absence of a means of collective transformation within the black working-class culture of the students' communities, is too powerful for most students to overcome.

In our analysis, which has focused on individuals' responses, we see two of the eight women—Karla and Susan—attending meetings of political groups but not becoming personally involved with the issues or analyses presented by the groups. They attend a few events and drop out. Among the others, we see that the women simply do not register any challenge to their ideas of individual or family-centered[35] responsibility for overcoming disadvantages. Their appreciation of a "collective fate" for women was apparently not developed during their early college careers and, while the black women did not have an appreciation of a collective fate for blacks, they tended not to envision a collective solution.

In sum we have found the eight women of our study to have fairly benign interpretations of the society and a predominant emphasis upon the opportunities for, as opposed to the barriers against, individuals like themselves. Perhaps their somewhat favorable views are not surprising given their privileged position in an institution of "higher learning" and perhaps this position helps to explain why these women are unlikely at this point in their lives to be aware of structured inequalities for women.

Nonetheless, we note that even though the womens' response to college were not, for most, couched in terms of gender, there is evidence of the cultural reproduction of orientations traditionally associated with females. In response to their school experiences, six of the eight women emerged from the process with marginalized identities as workers while their involvement with romantic relationships continued to constitute a major part of their self identities. Paralleling the results that Valli[36] describes for women in training to be clerical workers, most of the college women in our study exhibited traditional female patterns of involvement in romantic relationships and disengagement from work.

Although the routes to this pattern of self-definition varied between and among the women in our study, we see a cultural reproduction of gender patterns in both studies. These gender patterns were culturally reproduced despite class and race differences. Although the varied routes to these traditional female patterns may foretell different reactions of the women to their future life experiences, at this point in their transition from school to work, we find a convergence: traditional gender orientations have been culturally reproduced.

NOTES

1. Rosemary Deem, *Women and Schooling* (London: Routledge and Kegan Paul, 1978); and Rosemary Deem, *Schooling for Women's Work* (London: Routledge and Kegan Paul, 1980); and Gail P. Kelly and Ann Nihlen, "Schooling and the Reproduction of Patriarchy: Unequal Workloads, Unequal Rewards," in Michael Apple, ed., *Cultural and Economic Reproduction in American Education. Essays in Class, Ideology and the State* (Boston: Routledge and Kegan Paul, 1982), pp. 162–180; and Angela McRobbie, "Settling Accounts with Subcultures: A Feminist Critique," *Screen Education* 34 (Spring 1980), pp. 37–49.

2. See Kelly and Nihlen, "Schooling and the Reproduction of Patriarchy", pp. 174–177.

3. Paul Willis, *Learning to Labor: How Working-Class Kids Get Working-Class Jobs* (New York: Columbia University Press, 1977); and Paul Willis, "Cultural Production is Different from Cultural Reproduction is Different from Social Reproduction is Different from Reproduction," *Interchange* 12, 2/3 (1981), pp. 48–67.

4. John U. Ogbu, *The Next Generation: An Ethnography of Education in an Urban Neighborhood* (New York: Academic Press, 1974); and John U. Ogbu, *Minority Education and Caste: The American System in Cross-Cultural Perspective* (New York: Academic Press, 1978); and John U. Ogbu, *Cross-Cultural Boundaries: A Perspective on Minority Education* (Paper prepared for symposium "Race, Class, Socialization, and the Life Cycle," University of Chicago, Chicago, Ill, October 21-22, 1983, revised May 1985).

5. Willis, "Cultural Production is Different from Cultural Reproduction", pp. 59.

6. Margaret A. Eisenhart and Dorothy C. Holland, "Learning Gender from Peers: The Role of Peer Groups in the Cultural Transmission of Gender," *Human Organization* 42, 4 (1983), pp. 321–332.

7. Gary Schwartz, "Youth Culture: An Anthropological Approach," Addison-Wesley Module in Anthropology, No. 17 (Reading, MA: Addison-Wesley Publishing, 1972).

8. Willis, "Cultural Production is Different from Cultural Reproduction", pp. 61.

9. Ibid.

10. McRobbie, "Settling Accounts with Subcultures".

11. Ogbu, "Crossing Cultural Boundaries".

12. Jean Anyon, "Intersections of Gender and Class: Accomodation and Resistance in Gender and Gender Development," in S. Walker and L. Barton, eds., *Gender, Class and Education* (Sussex: The Falmer Press, 1983), pp. 19–37; and Mary Fuller, "Black Girls in a London Comprehensive School," in R. Deem, ed., *Schooling for Women's Work* (London: Routledge and Kegan Paul, 1980), pp. 52–65; and Angela McRobbie, "Jackie: An Ideology of Adolescent Femininity," Stencilled Occasional Paper, No. 53, Women Series (Birmingham, England: Centre for Contemporary Cultural Studies, 1978).

13. McRobbie, "Jackie: An Ideology of Adolescent Femininity"; and Linda Valli, "Becoming Clerical Workers: Business Education and the Culture of Femininity," in Michael Apple and Lois Weis, eds., *Ideology and Practice in Schooling* (Philadelphia: Temple University Press, 1983), pp. 213–234.

14. Valli, "Becoming Clerical Workers".

15. Richard Jenkins, *Lads, Citizens, and Ordinary Kids: Working-Class Lifestyles in Belfast* (London: Routledge and Kegan Paul, 1983).

16. Drawing upon the work of Ladislav Holy and Milan Stucklik, "The Structure of Folk Models," in L. Holy and M. Stuchlik, eds., *The Structure of Folk Models*, ASA Monograph 20 (New York: Academic Press, 1981), pp. 1–35, Jenkins uses the term "folk models" to describe the "natives's" view of the world (Jenkins, *Lads, Citizens and Ordinary Kids*). We use the term "cultural model" rather than "folk model" in order to signal that we are using a technical term from cognitive studies for a system of shared knowledge (see Dorothy C. Holland and Naomi Quinn, eds., *Cultural Models in Language and Thought* (New York: Cambridge University Press, 1987), particularly the chapter by N. Quinn and D. C. Holland, "Culture and Cognition", pp. 3–40), and in order to avoid the connotations of "folk".

17. Robert V. Bullough Jr., Andrew D. Gitlin and Stanley L. Goldstein, "Ideology, Teacher Role, and Resistance," *Teachers College Record* 86, 2 (1984), p. 339–358.

18. See Dorothy Holland Clement, "Samoan Cultural Knowledge of Mental Disorders," in A. J. Marsella and G. M. White, eds., *Cultural Conceptions of Mental Health and Therapy* (Dordrecht, Holland: Reidel Publishing Company, 1982), pp. 193–215.

19. Willis, "Cultural Production is Different from Cultural Reproduction".

20. Dorothy C. Holland and Margaret A. Eisenhart, *Women's Peer Groups and Choice of Career* (Washington, D.C.: National Institute of Education, 1981, final report).

21. In order to protect the confidentiality of the informants in this study, pseudonyms are used for both the names of the universities and the names of the women. We have altered details of the cases and quotes so as to protect the anonymity of the informants.

22. See Holland and Eisenhart, *Women's Peer Groups*.

23. See Dorothy C. Holland and Margaret A. Eisenhart, *Women's Ways of Going to School: The Cultural Reproduction of Gender Relations in America* (n.d., manuscript in preparation).

24. It is important to consider whether these different views constitute "cultural models" of college in the technical sense of the term (see Holland and Quinn, *Cultural Models in Language*). At this point our analysis of the ethnographic and survey data, it is too early to argue that these models are shared by the members of a (sub)cultural group, although we believe they are (see also John G. Nicholls, Michael Patashnick and Susan Bobbit Nolen, "Adolescents' Theories of Educa-

tion," *Journal of Educational Psychology 77, 6 (1985), pp. 683*–692. It is also too early to argue that each view constitutes a coherent, integrated set of "proposition-schemas" and "image-schemas" (see Quinn and Holland, "Culture and Cognition", pp. 24–27), although we have some indication that they do. We are less sure about whether the models will prove to be models of college or should more properly be characterized as models of a more encompassing, cross-context activity such as "work". For discussion of the embedding of cultural models, see Quinn and Holland, "Culture and Cognition," pp. 32–35. A useful and somewhat parallel notion of embedding is also present in neo-Vygotskian "activity-theory"-for example, see James V. Wertsch, Norris Minick and Flavio J. Arns, "The Cration of Context in Joint Problem-Solving," in Rogoff B. and J. Lave, eds., *Everyday Cognition. Its Development in Social Context* (Cambridge: Harvard University Press, 1984), pp. 151–171.

25. Valli, "Becoming Clerical Workers".

26. Deem, *Women and Schooling*.

27. See for example Willis' discussion in *Learning to Labor*, pp. 119–144.

28. From our point of view, Valencia's interviews are very painful to read. She speaks from a position that we associate with white racist analysis of black dialects. In her case and in several others, we find evidence of ways that structural constraints and ideologies promoted within the society seem to be affecting the women. However, our purpose here is not to analyse these constraints but rather to describe the women's interpretations of their situations, the processes by which these interpretations develop and change over the course of the study, and the way in which these models affect what women do in school.

29. Lois Weis, *Between Two Worlds: Black Students in an Urban Community College* (Boston: Routledge and Kegan Paul, 1985).

30. See Holland and Eisenhart, *Women's Ways of Going to School*, for a detailed discussion of these topics.

31. Dorothy C. Holland and Debra Skinner, "Themes in American Cultural Models of Gender," *Social Science Newsletter* 68, 3 (1938), pp. 49–60; and Dorothy C. Holland and Debra Skinner, "Prestige and Intimacy: The Cultural Models Behind Americans' Talk About Gender Types," in D. Holland and N. Quinn, eds., *Cultural Models in Language and Thought*, pp. 78–111.

32. Ogbu, *The Next Generation*; and Obgu, "Crossing Cultural Boundaries".

33. Willis, "Cultural Production is Different from Cultural Reproduction".

34. Weis, *Between Two Worlds*, pp. 146–158.

35. Although we have not been able to discuss the women's views of family here, we believe that family figures prominently in their ideas about shared activities and responsibilities.

36. Valli, "Becoming Clerical Workers".

13

Symbolic Economy of Identity and Denial of Labor: Studies in High School Number 1

PERSPECTIVE

Three streams of work begin to flow together here. These streams of work are criticisms of new sociology of education, a description of broad changes in society and education, and the study of social interaction in school. What emerges from the fusion of these strands of work is an awareness of the inadequacy of the basic terms of critical social analysis in education, and the generation of an alternative analytic language and focus.

Each path of work — immanent critique of the new sociology, description of social change, and sociology of school life — reveals the common importance of labor in different media, particularly in symbolic interaction. Symbolic labor, the organized social production of meaning in social relations, has been ignored and denied in critical work in favor of culturalist critiques of education. At the same time, social change displays a pattern of an oscillating cycle of de-reification and commodification. Taken-for-granted meaning and patterns of action are opened up, taken apart, only then to be re-packaged and again made opaque. The opening up has en-

*NOTE: Some parts of this paper will appear in my forthcoming book, *Social Analysis and Education* (Routledge and Kegan Paul, 1987). The research reported here was in part supported by: The University of Rochester; The Spencer Foundation; The Officer of Naval Research, contract #N00014–83–K–0032.

couraged new cultural theories; even a general predisposition toward analytic textualism.

The same opening and closing dynamic that affects culture has not yet been made evident in the domain of self and identity processes. Rather, while interesting debates do occur about the changing character of self or identity,[1] identity remains a crucial reification. That means that it is a cover-up, a denial. Indeed, I think it is the most important cultural reification of our historical situation. For what the term identity accomplishes, in both popular and academic conversation, is to deny the field of social interactional symbolic labor in which it is constituted. In addition to a critical social discourse about education that already points beyond its own limitations, and a pattern of social change that opens to view processes of symbolic production, it is also our empirical work that leads to the social study of identity as symbolic labor. In our study of high schools,[2] the students directed us toward the central social production of identity; in their terms, the process of "becoming somebody."

To overcome the denial of symbolic labor in social relations and to get into the field of interaction obscured by the appearance of a solid self — an overcoming pressed upon us by historical social change — I suggest that we can understand the social process of identity-formation as the result of a symbolic economy. At a general heuristic level, the basic proposition is that social interaction displays the same structural dynamic relations as does the economy: the symbolic economy is homologous to the ordinary language meaning of "economy." Although this interactional economy may display dynamic relational features similar to the historical economy, the capitalist economy, it is different in two ways.

First, the material of this economy is not objects or things, but signs and symbols. While the same production rules as commodity production may hold, the raw materials and products of the production process are different. They are commodities, but they are symbolic commodities. Second, while there are general economic rules that apply very widely across social groups and situations, there are also specific, different symbolic economies operating among different social classes and groups. Some selections from the studies in high school illustrate this combination of general rules and class-specific differences in the workings of symbolic economies of identity.

The discursive role of "identity" itself, however, is the same in all cases. "Identity" is the denial of socially organized symbolic production. It plays the same role of obfuscating social labor in the symbolic economy that money plays in the ordinary economy of capital. Going beyond that denial to the constitutive field of social interaction entails the creation of a new language and focus for a critical social analysis of education.

AFTER THE NEW SOCIOLOGY OF EDUCATION

The denial of symbolic labor performed by the term "identity" is a general cultural accomplishment. New or radical sociology of education is part of the same prevailing general culture. It too has denied symbolic labor, in its research methods and theories. Our three year study of four metropolitan high schools led to an appreciation of how identity is produced in an organized economy of signs. But, that was because we took seriously the analyses of the participants, and not because we did what new sociology refers to as "critical ethnography." Indeed, critical ethnography is part of the culture that denies symbolic labor.

As a practice, critical ethnography is like television-watching. It denies the symbolic labor of the process of knowing. Denial of this mediating work of knowing characterizes both research objectivism and television-watching.[3] It is the hegemonic ideology of realism which persistently denies any linguistic or socially mediating apparatus of knowing. What money does for "economic" labor, and identity does for productive symbolic interaction, critical ethnography does for research. Realism is the episteme of the social relations of a labor-denying commodity society.

Denying the persistence of a mediating perceptual apparatus is the central, but not the only, quality which critical ethnographies share with television-watching. The critical ethnographers' extractive vignette use of field quotes is like the segmented, serialized television narrative. The aesthetic procedures of stripped-down images, use of close-ups to type character presentations, and talking-heads of television, are like the bare-bones classificatory operations which have disturbed detractors of fashionable critical educational ethnographies.[4] The positioning of the viewer, the spectator relation, the identification-by-denial with the apparatus, and the domestically comfortably, voyeuristically seeing of the "them" of television's world,[5] are specific perceptual practices of the prevailing cultural regime of knowledge — to which critical ethnography unwittingly belongs.

Denial of the symbolic labor of knowing practised by research in the new sociology also characterizes its theoretical understanding of society and education. The view of society as a sequence of dynamic social states[6] is backgrounded to a social analysis comprised of an antagonism between static structural social systems and dynamic individual actions.[7] Collective symbolic labor as the central social process is denied by contemporary radical social analyses of education. Structuralist approaches to cultural reproduction by positing dynamism as individual resistance, reserve the field of action to a response, to an opposition against the operation of institutional structures. Relegating collective production to cultural opposition leads to viewing the social as inert. The place of activity is ceded to individual acts of culturally-shaped "resistance." Romantic individualism is theoretically defended by dualism of structure and agency, and in studies of schools by the binary, "reproduction/resistance." Alignment of the terms of cultural/oppositional/individual against those of structure/economy/reproduction has the effect of confirming the view that social activity is reified, excepting extraordinary rupture.

This critical tradition of social analyses of education is, I think, a common-sense ideology; both in the reified form of its understanding of social life generally and in its particular representation of life in schools. Like commodity fetishism generally, it leaves out labor. Like the liberal ideology which defines "institution" outside of historic class formations, it accepts the common sense self-definition of "schools" as general, rather than class-specific social institutions. As with imaginary desire, when it sees class, it sees an externally opposed unity, rather than the internally antagonistically contradictory forms of social relation and organization of educational institutions. Like naturalized individualism which oversees such historical common sense, it displaces the specific conditions of class collective action in favor of cultural acts of resistance. The "class structure," which radical theory asserts schooling reproduces, is abstract, and distant from the concrete system of the dynamic relations of value production and exploitation that characterize class structure. It is not the method of critical ethnography or the theory of new sociology of education which overcomes the denial of labor and brings the symbolic economy of identity to the fore; rather, it is historical change in society and education and our ability to interpret it in historically appropriate terms. These changes, I think, encourage newer social analytic language of texturalism at the cultural level, and symbolic economy at the level of "individual" identity.

SOCIETY AND EDUCATION

The most evident social change of the past decade is the success of efforts of social movements to effect a cultural restoration. This restoration contains a contradictory and specifically twentieth-century dynamic.

On the one side, the language and social practices of pre-modern local attachments of integration to family, religion, and nation are valued. At the same time, there is intensified social rationalization; and instrumental and technical regulation of everyday social life, along with the marketization and privatization of social domains like schooling formerly claimed by the public sphere. The cultural "restoration" turns out to be part of a much more profound reorganization of social life; a reorganization toward a form of society which its critics call "corporatist."

Corporatism is the most general new social institutional form in the restoration. Corporatism wipes the slate clean of pre-capitalist feudal forms by realizing their integrative possibilities within the logic of commodity production. Panitch[8] defined the corporatist model as ". . . a political structure within advanced capitalism which integrates organized socioeconomic producer groups through a system of representation and cooperative mutual interaction at the leadership level and of mobilization and social control at the mass level. . . ." The important thing about corporatism is that it appears not to be state imposed, but only state coordinated. The cooperation of corporate capitalist and corporate labor bodies' representatives appears to be equal. But corporatism does not mean the end of class society.

Yet, it poses as a possibility a form of social organization that will solve the conflicts between capital and labor and also resolve the antimony between the marketizing, atomistic tendency of commodity exchange, and the organicist solidarity patterns of pre-market anti-rationalist forms of social integration. Corporatism provides for social integration according to functional realition to the commodity.

We have described the corporatist change in the institutional structure of education in some detail.[9] In broad outline, corporatism in education begins with an attack on common schooling for enabling the expression of an evil, "secular humanism." As in modern corporatism generally, while attacks are mounted on the cultural front, the social relations of schooling are systematically altered. The internal, formal culture of the school, its curriculum, is redefined. "Knowledge" comes to mean skill-learning, while the social teacher-student relation is reduced to inventories of individual basic competencies.

The corporatist reorganization serves not only the ideology of restoration, but ultimately a market, commodity society that shapes the form of all social relations. The direction of the current educational change, as part of this wider movement, is to constitute education as a commodity. Such a change requires the establishment of market practices internal to the operation of schools and then, externally, the establishment of educational markets. The final state in educational corporatism, is fiscal; private financing and ownership of what was formerly the public common school. There is evidence for the occurrence of each of these processes as a fundamental sequence of a historical institutional change in society and educaton.

Beneath the cultural restoration, and even more basic than the emergent tendency to organize social life along corporatist lines, are occurring other deep and large-scale social changes. Fundamental changes are taking place in social production, in the culture of consumption, and in the structure of persons as part of a broad societal transformation. Whether in the Marxist language of a "revolution in the forces of production," or in the post-industrial language of a change in "transforming resources,"[10] a historic change is occurring in the productive basis of society. This change is that signification has itself become a force of production to an unprecedented degree. The basic productive energy or force of production is becoming information. Information has become central in production, distribution, communication, and services.

There is a less evident, but no less important, change occurring in the cultural organization of consumption. It is no longer a question of whether advertising is important; it is, I think, the preeminent cultural form within the "sales effort" of a consumer culture.[11] The issue, rather, is that the cultural form of advertising is itself changing. The "sign," which acts as an associatively effective signal, replaces more traditionally coherent narrative and relational symbols, as the cultural means of engagement in consumption.[12] This is a shift in cultural genres, from the general realist narrative representations of television serials, to a dispersed, modernist, and non-representational use of cultural resources. Realism versus modernism is not merely a dispute among intellectuals; it is a historic conflict within the sales culture, in a new symbolic, informational, or semiotic society, and a change in mass cultural forms.

Change in the structure of persons, or, in the language of post-structuralism,[13] "subjects," occurs along with changes in production and consumption. The diffusion or "de-centering" of traditional narrative culture, corresponds to a historically different sort of subjectivity. The structure of a new type of personal functioning is better characterized by polymorphous fluidity rather than moral integration. There is already extensive debate about the existence and value of this historically "new self."[14]

Taken together as the outline of a new society, these broad changes set the stage for newer forms of institutional organizations. For example, in production, informationalism makes possible a greater degree of Taylorization, fragmentation or degradation of the labor process. Nets of techno-coordination are built upon greater dispersion of unitary work processes. In consumption, signalling that replaces symbolic representation as the cultural sales medium, facilitates a new type of symbolic incapacitation. For the power of ambiguous understanding and the mutuality of human social relations that symbolic and narrative realism possessed, even in sales culture, are now endangered by uni-directional cultural conditioning in a de-narrativized "political economy of the sign."[15] In person structure, fluidity and decenteredness are potential ego weaknesses that make new selves susceptible to the mass appeals of authoritarian unifiers. Degradation, meaninglessness, and authoritarianism are one set of intermediate resolutions to the emergent social changes.

On the other hand, informationalism promises release from surplus labor and an electronic community that will redefine and revive democratic society. The diffusion of cultural narratives can unchain the means of significance from their traditional emplacements. The attack on coherent representational realism frees signs for less burdensome use in continuously negotiated, rather than fixed, meanings. Similarly, the decentered subject may be liberated from the repressive weight of moral selfhood.

Within this contradictory new society, there occurs a general dynamic of opening and closing, of de-reification and commodification. What that means is that new areas of social life are denaturalized and demystified and readied for social use; the denaturalized becomes a social resource to be commodified. Twin pillars of contemporary culture are denaturalized and readied for commodity-use: culture-as-nature and individualism. To become a socially-useful resource, the natural has first to be de-reified, decomposed, so that it is more rationally manipulable. In this dynamic of de-reification and commodification, new analytic discourses have emerged.

The most evident new discourse created in the moment of de-reification is "literary theory," and more narrowly, textualism. Here, culture is denaturalized; signification is understood as symbolic labor. The dynamic of de-reification and commodification, of opening and closing, denaturalizes individualism as well as "natural" culture. It is this demystifying denaturalization of individualism which paves the way for a new analytic language at the individual level. I suggest that this new language is the symbolic economy of identity; a discourse that overcomes the denial of symbolic labor in the production of individual identity. Just as literary theory and textualism overcome the denial of the collective symbolic labor which is appropriated, routinized and naturalized as taken-for-granted "culture," an additional emergent language displays the interactional field in which "identity" is produced.

LANGUAGE OF ANALYSIS:
SOCIAL INTERACTION IN SCHOOL

Students work in school. Their most central activity is the work of "becoming somebody." To become somebody means to establish a credible identity in the specific context of school work conditions and exigencies. The most salient of these conditions are: organizational ideals and demands; specific cultural channels of peer-defined status; acting on the anticipation that the results of schooling will influence future social placement. The work which students do in these circumstances, the work of becoming somebody, I call identity-work. The concept of identity-work has helped make sense of a wide range of student activities, across and within the four high schools that we studied.

What I mean by identity precisely is subjective generative value: the capacity to produce culturally defined value. Identity is produced in an organized system of symbolic social relations. It is a product of collective social labor, although it is assumed by individuals and appears as the defining characteristic of the individual itself. Concepts like socialization and learning, or even the term "school" itself, have functioned to mask the process of collective labor through which the subjective capacity to generate value is produced, appropriated, and attributed to individuals. Identity-work is the production of a particular kind of value, subjective generative value or identity.

The work process through which this value is produced is organized as a social economy of interactional resources. These resources, which are culturally specific components of generalized status, are represented by a system of signs. The process of identity-work is one in which these signs of the resources of interaction are actively mobilized and used to produce identity. Identity is the most general product of an organizational economy of signs. The economy remains opaque behind the overarching denial of interactional labor which is culturally accomplished by attributing this collective production process to the sign of its appropriation: the individual. Ordinary social science concepts like subculture, and critical social analysis concepts like resistance reinforce the prevailing cultural denial of the symbolic collective process of work in which the subjective aspect of the capacity to generate social value is produced. Similarly, the concept of "school" is an ordinary language term that obscures the dynamic, productive, relational field in which this sort of collective social labor occurs.

Identity-work always occurs in specific conditions. The term "school" naturalizes and neutralizes those conditions, as if to indicate a common, universal condition. This makes sense within the contemporary narrative of "social," rather than class institutions. If we see instead of a flat narrative field of common social instituitons like school and family, a paradigmatic model, then these "schools" fall within the vertical axis of class organizations. If society becomes more organized in a corporate way, then the overriding differential class effects on social organization outweigh their shared features. In our study of high schools, the organizations made better sense vertically and paradigmatically, than in a syntagmatic narrative. Despite evident commonalities across schools

that result from state regulation, the differences are so great as to war-
rant saying that "schools" take various social forms: some are more like
welfare agencies, others like country clubs, other like securities markets,
and still others operate like paternalistic factories. "Schools" are class institutional sites where different kinds of class culturally-specific identity
work takes places.

Each class institutional site of identity work is internally torn, contradictory. Against the concept of an "organizational culture," we find
that each site of symbolic labor has a dominant cultural theme which
contains an internal contradiction or ambivalence. The internal ambivalence in the prevailing cultural theme sets the symbolic terms which
defines the students' work of becoming somebody. The message of the
official, established organization contains an implicit binary opposition
which sets the term of the participants' struggle for the attainment of
identity. Further, at each site, one element of the cultural ambivalence is
legitimated while the other is stigmatized. The internal division and stig-
matization inhibit a common collective mobilization. The appearance of
a fixed division reinforces the common-sense belief in an individual,
rather than collective production of identity. Yet, in each case, the class
cultural themes and organizationally different forms of the sites can be
reconstructed by observing and interpreting the common, though indi-
viduated, struggle to become somebody.

BECOMING SOMEBODY:
SNAPSHOT OF SYMBOLIC ECONOMIES OF IDENTITY

The class location of each school institution shapes both its organizational form and ambivalent cultural message. Each of these forms and
sets of messages sets the terms for the specific character of value and the
production of subjective value, or identity, in each economy. While there
are a variety of types of identity work, there are central activities, crucial
sorts of the symbolic labor of becoming somebody. For example, in the
inner-city school of the black underclass, controlled disengagement and
modulation of status denigration are enacted as "chillin out" and "bein
charged up." The importance of extra-curricula as the locale of identity
work is represented in a white working-class suburban school as "cranking up spirit." The status market-sensitive adjustments of competition
among children of the professional middle class are referred to as
"mellowing out," while the corporate executives' offspring mark their
identity-boundaries in doing pranks and "having fun."

In the white working-class site, the language and practices of family
and of factory comingle. In character and social routine, the patriarchal

benevolence and maternal warmth of what is called "the happy family" alternates with the police authority and semi-rationalized rejection of the discipline structure. Here, identity work is mechanically coded. It is to "crank-up" spirit, the sort of collective emotion typified by the pep rally. Yet, an overriding regulation saps the interactional generation of resources that can be worked-up into identity value by cranking up spirit, then to be traded for tangible benefit.

"Order" and "discipline" diminish talking and the "care" that is the raw material of trust. Trust is the key resource here, the fuel used in the spirit-machine. That machine makes "star" value, which is then used to buy the freedom and fantasy of bodily movement, as well as the gaze of positive recognition that enhances self-verification. The absence of the resources of care, trust, and motivation, is called "tough." "Tough" is made in hide-outs, the less-legitimate public spaces of the halls; in the alcoves. There, an alternative "counterfeit currency" of prideful macho exaggerated "tough," value is produced, with the understanding that there are no alternative resources remaining. The view that symbolic value is out of reach and finally destroyed, the sense of no usable meaning, which is the currency of productive interactional resources is expressed by the sloganized sign: "this school is beat."

Identity is divided into stars and scum. This school class divides and destroys itself by a combination of cranking and hiding. The role of the authorities is to continuously underline this division of labor, to externalize it, to project it, and finally to make it impossible to have collective independent production. The symbolic production in the alcoves by the "alcovians" cannot become legitimate value. Their productive capacity is expelled, alienated in the regular symbolic economy of school life.

The professional middle class presents a credential market. There seems to be a clear direction that identity value is the sum of accumulated grade acquisitions. But, market vagaries and pressures also require more reliable, steadier investments to insure stable and predictable identity. The tension between unlimited competitive commodity acquisition and, on the other hand, unmarketable, steady qualitative bases of identity value leads to collective efforts to control the market. Market-control occurs by introducing the non-negotiable standards of friendship and being described as "intelligence" and "cool." These resources are, however, themselves reconverted into the market terms of competition, which is thereby extended.

"Mellowing out" is the work of a conscious, rational-choice economy that withholds participation. It is the so-called "apathy," of a calculated and controlled non-caring. It bridges the market credential universalism and the immeasurable but constantly reconvertible worlds of non-negotiable, non-commodity valued attributes. But, there is a return of the repressed, and non-negotiable interpersonal resources also become negotiable.

The result is that in the middle-class professional school "becoming somebody" requires academic achievement. Everybody talks about the accomplishment level of the school. But what happens is that with the perception that in the marketplace for achievement, demand is limitless and virtually uncontrollable, youths learn to instrumentalize their performance and to withdraw their commitment to the school. After the activism comes the "apathy." They are then continuously involved in the "mellowing out," which begins in affective withdrawal from achievement, and moves to a displacement of the organizational ethos of competition into the sphere of consumption competition. Here, the economy of identity is to learn to hedge your bets to protect against over-investment. There is no hiding out, physically, but what students learn is how to withhold performance, and to simultaneously take identity credits from goal conformity and nonconformity. The threat to the organization is not the cultural rebellion of the black leathers of the "alcovians," but instead a devaluation. Identity oscillates between market commodity value and non-negotiable attributes, which are easily included in the apparently uncontrollable contest for identity accumulation. In this oscillation, the subjective generative capacity, the identity of the professional middle class is divided.

Beyond the market, in the corporate-executive suburban school, in the distance-protected open, preserved spaces of the drive-in club, teen life is also preserved as a separate category, between the family and the market. This market is less rationalized than in the professonal school, but simply presents performance as merit, although it is often postponed spatially to sports or temporarily to the image of "after-the-prom." Here, it is not the personalism and clubbiness vs. professional contradiction which first appears to characterize the internal difference of the suburban upper class. Rather, what is at issue is what might be called the space of identity value. On the one side there are incorporative, ever-caring parents. On the other, there is a world beyond the gates, the city, the "out there," the "others." Teen world is suspended delicately, but is permeably bounded.

Here, identity-work is boundary-work, That means staying in the preserve but also differentiating sufficiently within it to have a separate-from-family identity-value. Affirming 'teenness' constitutes the interactional economy of "pranks and fun" in the middle. It is bounded on one side by alcoholic mimetic rebellion, and on the other by xenophobic hatred of other "species." Scapegoating catharsis is an important element of differentiating out value, carving it out from within the enclave that already has it. Mobilization through teenness is contained in teen-center and at-home parties, chaperoned proms, and through permissive surveillance. Identity is at once closed — the clubbiness — and unbounded, ever subject to incorporation.

Inside the city, identity-value has to be fought for. Identity-value is created under conditions of an assumption of not being somebody. Identity-work means overcoming, "getting over the system," which presumes, despite its signs, that you are not somebody. Identity is made in an economy of hand-to-mouth, continuous, daily momentary self-production and affirming methods. "Drillin" means picking up, scavengering value, mini-exploitation, stealing good-naturedly from your friends and neighbors in the most invidious and ongoing set of continuous comparison processes, done in order to show, to remind that you are in fact "somebody." Nothingness is the boundary feared here, and against which the daily internal hustles of "drilling," "chillin out" enable the effort to try to get over the system and to be somebody. Fighting is a daily defense against the failure of other direct methods of self-equilibration. When that too fails, then there is the crossing-over out of the system, through the gateway of the informal solidarity of "cuz-bones," that leads to the street, community alternative economies. The school site offers small spaces for training in the performances of "poplockin," basketball fantasies, and the pimping and prostituting of the street life. Collective mobilization is contained by the inventiveness of creative value-production under a barrage of "being charged up," being derogated by the agents of the school. This inventiveness leads to factionalized groupings into "cuzbones kind" or, more likely, to very clever private hustles. The aim is either to stay in the flow, or to self-establish externally, outside "the system."

"Those who try" within the system work to equilibrate by manufacturing ephemeral value in the passing of a joke, and wise-cracks, stealing from the slower witted. Identity-value is displaced. There is the dream, the fantasy, the separate corner of existence sustained by the "big dream." Meanwhile, realistic and continuous small trading and value creatively stolen by one's interactional wits produces identity.

IMPLICATIONS

In the new society, in the society of the political economy of the sign, the sign plays the same role that the commodity once did in industrial society. It is the abstract reduction of labor, now the labor of signification. Like the commodity in the labor process, the sign is a reification of symbolic processes. The environment becomes "semanticized," and even more extensive cultural resources can be used in an interactionally ex-

ploitative producton of commodities. The moment of de-reified culture
and identity passes quickly into the expanded cycle of value production.

For social analytic work, the symbolic economy of identity means a
revision of theories of self that have abstracted the dynamic process of
de-reification and commodification into opposing theories of self, each
of which leads to a very partial politics of identity. It implies a revision of
theories of interaction towards neither extracted polarity of negotiated
order or structural embodiment. Instead, what is implied is a sequence of
collective states within a historical structure.

For the sociology of the school, symbolic economy implies a revision of the intersection of class and institutional analyses, such that the
horizontal reapresentation of "the school" is replaced into a vertical
analysis of class institutions. To the extent that corporatism is not re-
versed, schools will become social forms that are more directly linked to
other intra-class segmented institutions than they are to each other as
"common" or "public" social forms. This tendency makes it increasingly
misleading to analyze institutions outside of their vertical class integration. It is there, within the class/institutional level, that the micro-
economy of self-production will define everyday educational process.

Within the class/institutional sector this micro-production process
begins to separate from, to become disjoint, and finally contradictory to,
a mass discourse which transcends institutional production. In the contradiction between the local institutional production of identity in
school, and the societal discursive production of consumer taste orientation, a new education dynamic emerges. The contradiction between the
forces and relations of production in the semiotic society is between production and consumption. The symbolic economy of identity production
is only a moment in that historical collective dynamnic.

NOTES

1. C. Lasch, *The Minimal Self* (New York: W. W. Norton and
Company, 1984).

2. P. Wexler, *Becoming Somebody: Studies in High School*
forthcoming).

3. J. Feuer, "The Concept of Live Television: Ontology as
Ideology" in E. A. Kaplan, ed., *Regarding Television* (Frederick, Mary-
land: University Publications of America, Inc., 1983); and B. Livant,
"Working and Watching: A Reply to Shut Jhally," *Canadian Journal of
Political and Social Theory* 6, 1–2 (1982), pp. 211–215.

4. A. Hargreaves, "Resistance and Relative Autonomy Theories: Problems of Distorsion and Incoherence in Recent Marxist Analyses of Education," *British Journal of Sociology of Education* 3,2 (1982), pp. 107–126; and John V. Ogbu, "School Ethnography: A Multilevel Approach," *Anthropology and Education Quarterly* 12, 1 (1981), pp. 3–29.

5. J. Ellis, *Visible Fictions* (London: Routledge and Kegan Paul, 1982).

6. F. Alberoni, *Movement and Institution* (New York: Columbia University, 1984).

7. P. Wexler, *Social Analysis and Education: After the New Sociology* London and New York: Routledge and Kegan Paul, 1987, in press).

8. L. Panitch, "The Development of Corporatism in Liberal Democracies," *Comparative Political Studies* 10, 1 (1977), pp. 66.

9. P. Wexler and G. Grabiner, The Education Question: America During the Crisis," in Rachel Sharp, ed., *Capitalist Crisis and Schooling: Comparative Studies in the Politics of Education* (Melbourne, Australia: 1985).

10. D. Bell, "Communications Technology: For Better or for Worse," *Harvard Business Review* 1, 1 (1979), pp. 20–42.

11. S. Ewen and E. Ewen, *Channels of Desire* (New York: McGraw-Hill, 1982).

12. J. Baudrillard, *For a Critique of the Political Economy of the Sign* (Saint Louis: Telos Press, 1981).

13. R. Young, *Untying the Text: A Post-Structural Reader* (London and Boston: Routledge and Kegan Paul, 1981).

14. P. Wexler, *Critical Social Psychology* (London and Boston: Routledge and Kegan Paul, 1983), pp. 117–140; and Lasch, *The Minimal Self*.

15. Baudrillard, *For a Critique of the Political Economy*.

Contributors

MICHAEL W. APPLE is Professor of Curriculum and Instruction and Educational Policy Studies at the University of Wisconsin, Madison.

KATHRYN M. BORMAN is an Associate Professor of Foundations of Education at the University of Cincinnati.

MARGARET A. EISENHART is an Associate Professor in the College of Education at Virginia Polytechnic Institute and State University.

CARL A. GRANT is Professor of Curriculum and Instruction at the University of Wisconsin, Madison.

DOROTHY C. HOLLAND is an Associate Professor in the Department of Anthropology at the University of North Carolina, Chapel Hill.

SALLY LUBECK is an Assistant Director of the Bush Institute for Child and Family Policy, University of North Carolina, Chapel Hill.

CAMERON MCCARTHY is a doctoral candidate at the University of Wisconsin, Madison.

ELAINE MUENINGHOFF is an Assistant Professor of Education at Clermont College, University of Cincinnati.

AMAURY NORA is a Research Fellow and an Adjunct Professor, Institute for Higher Education, Law, and Governance at the University of Houston.

JEANNIE OAKES is a Social Scientist at the Rand Corporation.

JOHN U. OGBU is Professor of Anthropology at the University of California, Berkeley.

FLORA IDA ORTIZ is an Associate Professor in the Faculty of Education at the University of California, Riverside.

ALAN PESHKIN is Professor of Education at the University of Illinois, Urbana-Champaign.

SHIRLEY PIAZZA is an Evaluation Consultant at Hamilton County Community Mental Health Board, and an Assistant Adjunct Professor of Sociology at Wilmington College, Ohio.

LAURA RENDON is a Visiting Assistant Professor of Higher Education and Director of the Ford Foundation Southwest Transfer Education Research Project at the University of South Carolina.

CHRISTINE E. SLEETER is an Assistant Professor of Education at the University of Wisconsin, Parkside.

R. PATRICK SOLOMON is a teacher at Thistletown School, Toronto, Ontario, Canada.

JAMES STANLAW is a Research Associate, Bureau of Educational Research, University of Illinois, Urbana-Champaign.

LINDA VALLI is an Assistant Professor of Education at the Catholic University of America.

LOIS WEIS is an Associate Professor of Sociology of Education and Associate Dean of the Faculty of Educational Studies at the State University of New York at Buffalo.

PHILIP WEXLER is an Associate Professor of Education and Sociology and Associate Dean of the Faculty of Education at the University of Rochester.

Index

Ability, as basis for academic differentiation, 118–19
Absenteeism. *See also* Teachers, absenteeism
    of black students, 254
    of urban Appalachian students, 239, 241
    of women workers, 154
Academic integration and college attrition, 132
Academic tracking, 106, 112–13, 115, 213
    and Appalachian students, 241
    and mediocrity, 118
    as limiting opportunities to learn, 115, 119
"Act white," 177–78
Administrators, minority. *See* Minority administrators
Affirmative action, 147, 150
African-American culture, 48
African-American students. *See* Black students
Alienation of Appalachian youth, 241
American Indians, 108
    and requirements for academic success, 177
    in graduate programs, 127
Anthropology, educational. *See* Educational anthropology
Appalachian women
    and academic achievement, 241
    and mountains, 234–35

    and outmigration, 235
    and parental rules, 243
    and patriarchy, 236
    as passive, 234
    constraints on, 237, 240
    educational goals, 245
    emotional strength, 234
    family, 237–38, 243
    identification with place, 234
    mutual support, 235
    neighborhood, 238–39, 243–44
    standing tall, 236
    student role, 242
    urban, 235, 243
Appalachian values
    active engagement with life, 237
    and education, 238–45
    and middle-class success, 237, 241
    and neighborhood life, 237, 243
    and social service agencies, 238, 243
    independence, 236
    individuality, 237
    tradition, 237
Asian-American students
    and achievement, 110, 214
    in math/science/technology, 109
Assimilation into dominant cultures, 176
"At risk" students, 119
Authority
    adult, 47
    in social change, 308

319